SOVIET CRIMINOLOGISTS AND CRIMINAL POLICY

Specialists in Policy-Making

Peter H. Solomon, Jr

New York   Columbia University Press   1978

Library of Congress Cataloging in Publication Data

Solomon, Peter H
   Soviet criminologists and criminal policy.

   (Studies of the Russian Institute, Columbia
University)
   Bibliography: p.
   Includes index.
   1. Government consultants—Russia. 2. Crimi-
nologists—Russia. 3. Crime and criminals—Russia.
4. Russia—Politics and government—1953–
I. Title. II. Series: Columbia University. Russian
Institute. Studies.
JN6529.C55S66   1977   364'.947   77-3351
ISBN 0-231-04316-3

TO SUSAN

Contents

Preface

This book's aim is to assess the increase in specialist or expert participation in Soviet policy-making that occurred in the past two decades. A growth in the role of experts has characterized the politics of many industrial states. As a rule, the larger involvement of specialists reflects the professionalization of politics and increasing cooperation between generalist politicians and policy communities. The consequences of this trend for the distribution of political influence in particular countries remain an open question.

The subject of the specialist's role in *Soviet* policy-making takes on added interest because controversy has surrounded its appraisal in the West. For various reasons (to be discussed within) Sovietologists have disagreed about the extent, nature, influence, and meaning of specialist participation in policy-making in the USSR. In this book I try to grapple with these issues by studying the role of Soviet specialists in one policy realm, criminal policy. Here, criminal policy refers to policy for handling ordinary, non-political crimes.

As of the late Stalin years the only experts on crime in the USSR were criminal law scholars, engaged mainly in interpreting the law and to a lesser extent in observing judicial practice. After Stalin's death some of these scholars began conducting sociological research on crime, soon reviving much of the criminology which had prospered in Russia in the 1920s. By the mid-1960s the chief experts on crime had become criminologists, persons trained in criminal law who were doing social scientific studies. The development of regular participation by scholars in the formation of Soviet criminal policy went hand in hand with the expansion of the scholars' expertise. Hence, an analysis of the policy role of experts on crime must record how criminological research contributed to the scholars' status and how that research was used by decision-makers.

It is a pleasure to thank some persons who contributed to this book. The late Merle Fainsod introduced me to the study of Soviet politics. Under George Fischer's enthusiastic guidance I encountered the revival of sociology in the USSR. Sir Leon Radzinowicz urged me to study Soviet criminology and arranged a three-month visit at the Institute of Criminology, Cambridge, England, of which he was Director. As a graduate student I had the good fortune to study with Zbigniew Brzezinski and John Hazard, who jointly directed the doctoral thesis from which this book grew.

One person left a special mark. Jerry Hough's thoughtful reading of the thesis improved the book, and even now conversations with him provoke new questions. The book manuscript was read by Donald Barry, Walter Connor, and H. Gordon Skilling, all of whom made helpful suggestions; and Robert Sharlet read selected chapters, providing useful criticism and warm encouragement.

Over the years I have benefited from discussions with Peter Juviler, Walter Connor, Harold Berman, Leon Lipson, Janice Gross Stein, and Michael Stein. The University of Toronto with its strong cadre of specialists in Russian studies was a rich atmosphere in which to work. I would also like to thank all my colleagues in the Soviet Union whose cooperation made this study possible, and in particular N. F. Kuznetsova of Moscow University and V. N. Kudriavtsev, formerly of the Procuracy's Institute for the Study and Prevention of Crime.

Much of the research for this book was conducted in the USSR during 1968–69 under the auspices of the Inter-University Committee on Travel Grants and with the support of a Fulbright Hays Award. A short research trip to Moscow in the spring of 1974 was made possible by a grant from the Centre for Russian and East European Studies of the University of Toronto and was facilitated by the International Research and Exchanges Board. The writing of this book was supported by the Russian Institute of Columbia University, by the American Council of Learned Societies and the Social Science Research Council, and by the Office of Research Administration and the Centre for Russian and East European Studies at the University of Toronto. To all of these institutions I am grateful.

This study drew upon the resources of the library of the Institute of Criminology, Cambridge, of the Lenin Library, of the law library of Moscow University, of the Harvard Law Library and of the Robarts Library, University of Toronto. Particularly helpful were Mr Martin Wright of the Institute of Criminology Library and Mrs Mary Stevens of the Robarts Library.

Gloria Rowe and Vivienne Humphrey typed the manuscript with speed and accuracy. Beatrice Stillman of the Russian Institute helped guide it to the publishers.

Throughout my wife Susan Gross Solomon helped, supported, and demanded my best. The dedication speaks of my gratitude and affection.

Toronto, Ontario   P. H. S.
June 1977

1 Introduction

Most Western students of Soviet politics writing in the 1960s and early 1970s agreed that the post-Stalin period had witnessed a widening of the Soviet policy-making process. In contrast to the Stalin years the formation of policies in many realms had come to include new or increased participation by persons outside the top party leadership – by officials, scholars, and professionals, acting as individuals or in groups. The observers disagreed, however, about the role and significance of this participation. Some of them regarded it as unimportant, either because of its nature or because of the context in which it occurred; others regarded the participation as significant, at least in some policy realms. To illuminate the disagreement on this issue, one may locate the Western observers along a spectrum which includes four images of the Soviet policy-making process and of the role played by persons outside the political leadership.

First, on one end of the spectrum were those scholars who credited the participation of Soviet officials, specialists, and groups with minimal or no influence on policy formation. As a rule these observers believed that factional conflicts among the party leaders accounted for most policy decisions in the USSR. Participation by persons outside of the leadership seemed to occur infrequently, and when it did it was subject to manipulation by the contestants in leadership conflicts.[1]

In the second position on the spectrum were those Western scholars who conceded to the outside participants some degree of influence, but so small as to be insignificant. These observers agreed with the proponents of the first view that Soviet policies resulted mainly from leadership politics, but they regarded the participation of outsiders as more extensive than did their colleagues (although still not very wide in scope). Nevertheless, in the view of this second set of observers the influence of participation by specialists and officials remained small, because that participation itself was inferior. As a rule, the outside participants neither initiated nor took part in the discussion of policy issues, but rather joined the policy-making process at a later stage upon invitation from the leadership. For their part the leaders seemed to seek the help of the outsiders not in reaching decisions but in mobilizing support for decisions already reached.[2]

Further along the spectrum was a third group of observers who held that the outside participants did influence the formation of policies in the USSR, but stressed that their influence was subject to constraints.

Proponents of this view argued that the specialists and officials, as individuals or as groups, often presented the leaders with the options for policy from which the leaders made their choices; and that the participation of specialists and officials appeared to be both extensive and unflawed. Yet, in the opinion of these observers, the participants' influence upon policy choices was limited by the party leadership's power to ignore or overrule it. Because it was contingent upon the whims of the political leaders, the influence of specialists and officials was not as great as its scope and quality suggested.[3]

Fourthly, there were those Western scholars who agreed with the proponents of the third view about the nature of the outside participation, but did not find it necessary to emphasize the constraints upon the actors' potential for influencing policies. The proponents of the fourth view did not minimize the party leadership's capacity to make binding decisions and therefore to overrule any particular claims by specialists or officials. But these observers claimed that the leadership of the USSR did not possess unique power *vis-à-vis* specialists and officials; leaders in most Western countries as well were usually in a position to make the decisive choices.[4] Rather than suffering from peculiar disabilities, participants from outside the political leadership in the USSR seemed to be subject to constraints similar to those which affected their Western counterparts. Just as in the USA, Soviet specialists, officials and groups could usually make their claims; and policies would often result from compromises in which the political leaders served as mediators.[5]

The presence among Western observers of such widely divergent interpretations of the role and significance of outside participation in Soviet policy-making requires some explanation. How was it possible that within one decade, 1963–73, Western Sovietologists writing about Soviet policy-making could disagree so fundamentally about this question? One reason was a shortage of information about the participation and influence of Soviet specialists and officials. As of the middle 1970s Western Sovietologists had written articles on the subject and devoted sections of books to it, but they had produced few full-length, detailed empirical studies of the participation of persons outside the party leadership in individual policy realms.[6] Some of these writings did not go deeply enough into the subject to justify firm conclusions. Few of them treated the participation of a single set of persons in a series of decisions in one policy realm. And none contained much evidence about the activity of participants behind the scenes and outside of the public view, where much of the serious participation of specialists and officials occurred in Western countries.

Another possible explanation of the divergent Western interpretations of Soviet policy-making was that the observers had based their conclusions upon evidence from different policy realms, in which the role of outside participants *did* vary substantially. It was possible, for example, that in the

USSR specialists and officials participated more in the formation of education policy than in the formation of foreign policy. With this hypothesis in mind we reviewed the Western studies of Soviet policy-making, but it turned out that variations in the nature of participation in different policy realms did not explain the differences in the way Western scholars had assessed the role of outside participants in Soviet policy-making. Some of the proponents of each of the four views had considered more than one policy realm; and commentators on individual areas of policy did not divide into a coherent pattern.[7]

Although the policy area upon which an observer drew his conclusions did not correlate with his evaluation of the role of specialists and officials, another factor did, and that was the *time* when a given author wrote. Most of those who represented the first two views (minimal or small influence) wrote between 1961 and 1967; while most of the proponents of the third and fourth views (moderate or substantial influence, with or without qualifying conditions) wrote between 1968 and 1974. The pattern was not absolute; examples of the third view appeared in print as early as 1962 and 1964;[8] and an example of the second view as late as 1973.[9] Yet the central consensus among students of Soviet politics did move from the first view (1961–4) to the second view (1964–8) to the third view (1968–74). The fourth view was only beginning to find support in the middle 1970s. This gradual shift toward crediting officials, specialists, and groups with influence in policy formation could be explained in two ways. On the one hand, the shift might have reflected actual changes in the participation of outsiders in Soviet policy-making which occurred between the late 1950s and the late 1960s, which were, after all, the data bases for scholars writing between 1963 and 1973. That is, scholars writing in the early 1970s might have reached more positive conclusions than scholars writing in the middle 1960s because outside participants actually had more influence in the middle and late 1960s than they did in the late 1950s and early 1960s. Alternatively, the shift in Western scholars' interpretation might represent mainly or even entirely a change in the way they perceived participation by Soviet specialists and officials. That is, the real nature and impact of the participation might have changed less than the willingness of Western scholars to take it seriously.[10]

Despite their differences of opinion about the role of outside partici-pation in Soviet policy-making until recently most Western Sovietologists did agree about one point – that the impact on policy of Soviet officials and specialists was not comparable to that exerted by Western consultants and groups. The writers had differing reasons for advancing this contention. While the proponents of the second view stressed the inferior nature of the participation,[11] the representatives of the third view emphasized the context within which the participants attempted to influence policy, a context dominated by the 'impressive power of Party leaders to intervene' and render a decision.[12] But in the last few years the articulation of the fourth view challenged this conventional wisdom, by raising the question of the comparability of the participation of Soviet and Western officials and specialists.[13]

The purpose of this book is to address some of the questions raised by Western scholarship about Soviet policy-making by examining in detail the nature and impact of one set of specialists (criminologists) in one policy realm (criminal policy). The major emphasis is on the contemporary period, that is the middle and late 1960s; and, as shall soon become apparent, the analysis of participation in this period is carried out in such a way as to facilitate comparison with the participation of the comparable specialists in the West. It also seemed important to deal with the historical question, how the participation of the particular specialists developed since the late Stalin years. By charting how the nature and impact of the participation actually changed over the post-Stalin years, it is possible to suggest to what extent the shift of interpretation among Western scholars represented a change in reality and to what extent it stemmed from a change in perception. This study focuses around two sets of research questions:

1. In the middle and late 1960s what was the nature of specialist participation in Soviet policy-making? What effects did this participation have upon policy formulation and development? How did the participation of specialists in the USSR compare with that of specialists in the United States during the same time period?
2. How did the participation of specialists develop in the USSR from the late Stalin years through the 1960s? What changes occurred in the nature and impact of participation and just when did those changes take place? What implications did the timing of changes in the nature of participation have for understanding the disagreements in the interpretation of Western analysts?

Each of these sets of research questions requires some explanation.

THE NATURE AND EFFECTS OF PARTICIPATION

The central task of this study is to assess the nature and effects of the participation of specialists in Soviet policy-making during the middle and late 1960s. On the basis of such an assessment, we will reach a judgment about which of the four interpretations of the role of outside participation in Soviet policy-making makes the most sense; and try to determine how in one policy realm the nature and impact of specialist participation compared with that in the West. Since we do not intend to perform detailed analysis of the participation in policy-making of a set of Western specialists, it is important that we use criteria of quality and impact which have been used in the analysis of participation and influence in Western countries and therefore can be taken to represent 'Western standards'.[14]

In examining the nature of criminologists' participation in criminal policy-making during the middle and late 1960s, we use criteria suggested by Brzezinski and Huntington's comparative study of Soviet and American policy-making – *scope* (amount and level) and *quality* (timing and function). Relying on examples from the years 1956–62 and assessing Soviet participation against the standard achieved by its American counterpart, these authors reached the conclusion that 'participation from below' was both limited in scope and of low quality. The scope of participation was limited, first of all because there seemed to be so little of it; 'participation from below' was associated, Brzezinski and Huntington claimed, only with one class of policy decisions, those not associated with power struggles, and even those decisions featured only 'a certain measure of participation'.[15] The authors also implied that the scope of participation was limited in another way, namely that the participation did not usually reach the level in the political system where policy changes were initiated and ruled on. In their view, policy changes were both initiated and decided by high party officials, with whom the participants were unlikely to have direct contact.[16] In addition to being limited in scope, specialist participation was also of low quality, in the opinion of Brzezinski and Huntington. One reason, the authors claimed, was that by and large it occurred too late to have much effect on decisions, that is only after the formal proposal for policy change, which the authors regarded as tantamount to the decision itself.[17] Another reason was that the main functions of specialist participation seemed to be mobilizing support for decisions and assisting in their execution, rather than communicating information to policy-makers and advocating policy proposals.[18]

The criteria of scope (amount and level) and quality (timing and function) provide useful tools for analyzing the nature of specialist participation in the 1960s. As categories developed out of a comparison between Western and Soviet policy-making, they supply a suitable calculus for assessing how Soviet participation compared to its American counterpart. Moreover, as categories related to the potential influence of specialists on policy, amount, level, timing, and function will prove helpful in our analysis of the effects of specialists participation.

In studying the *effects* of specialist participation, we shall consider both the influence the specialist had upon the decisions in which he took part and the impact he exerted upon the development of policies over time. Each of these foci has its own utility. The decision focus has the advantage of sensitivity; it may record the influence of specialists on matters which might escape notice in the analysis of their overall policy impact. More important, as the focus most commonly used in Western studies of policy-making, the decision focus facilitates the examination of Soviet specialists participation in comparative terms.[19] Even though the indicators of influence used in Western studies are imperfect, their application to Soviet data permits one to appraise Soviet specialist participation with the same criteria used for its Western counterpart. (We will delay explicit discussion of these criteria until Chapter 9, where they are used in analysis for the first time.) The policy focus also has its advantages. One of them is that it records the cumulative impact upon policies in a given realm which specialists may have exerted over time. Besides affecting discrete decisions, a specialist may help to introduce a policy trend which emerges through a series of decisions and thus becomes apparent only through the broad examination of policy development.[20] Another benefit of the policy focus is its capacity to record whatever indirect influence specialists may have exerted upon policy. Specialists may influence policies not only through direct participation in the decision-making process, but also by such indirect means as helping to shape general attitudes of leaders and high officials or by contributing to the pool of ideas upon which policy-makers draw.[21] By considering the impact on policy separately from influence on decisions, we stand a better chance of recording cumulative and indirect influence.

THE DEVELOPMENT OF PARTICIPATION

The other major task in this study is to analyze the development of the participation of one set of specialists (criminal law scholars) during the post-Stalin years; that is to determine what changes occurred in the scope, quality, and impact of participation and just when those changes took place. The timing of changes in the nature and impact of specialist participation is interesting for two reasons. First, an understanding of the timing of changes in specialist participation can help to explain the shift in Western interpretation which we observed above. To explain this shift it is necessary to determine whether or not the nature and impact of the participation changed from the late 1950s to the late 1960s. But there is also another reason for wanting to discover *when* the putative changes in specialist participation occurred. Knowledge of the actual timing of such changes would cast light upon the relative significance of the Khrushchev and the Brezhnev regimes for the evolution of the Soviet policy-making process. If one assumes that a significant broadening of participation occurred sometime during the first two post-Stalin decades, the question arises whether it resulted from Khrushchev's de-Stalinization efforts or from later developments under Brezhnev. If the changes in participation started under Khrushchev, what impact did the Brezhnev regime have upon them? Did patterns established under Khrushchev continue? Were advances made upon them, or alternatively did a retreat away from them take place?[22]

To fully appreciate the patterns of continuity and change in the nature of specialist participation in the post-Stalin period, it is important to have a clear picture of the background against which post-Stalin changes occurred, namely the nature of specialist participation in the late Stalin years. The standard image of Stalinist policy-making credited specialists neither with much direct participation in decision-making nor with an impact upon policy. Specialists had little chance to affect decisions, because Stalin seemed to take advice from just a handful of trusted henchmen and did not regularly consult persons outside the summit of power. Lacking access to decision-making, specialists and officials alike had to rely on attempts to influence the practical effects of policy choices during the course of their implementation. Western scholars used to believe that this mechanism provided persons outside the top leadership with some opportunity to affect policies in operation, but this view seems to have lost its currency.[23] A statement summarizing recent Western thinking about Soviet specialist participation under Stalin emphasized the specialists' inability to affect policies by any means. Specialists

> were almost powerless, their ranks purged, their freedom of expression abolished, their disciplines rendered stagnant. Law and economics were more or less destroyed . . . The articulation of viewpoints was by invitation only, in the case of indispensable experts such as the military or the economists, and if it was attempted in a more spontaneous manner, fraught with the gravest danger.[24]

How accurate was this highly negative portrait of specialist participation under Stalin was hard to tell, since Western scholars had done little research on policy-making during the Stalin years.[25] To ensure that our image of specialist participation under Stalin was accurate, we decided to start our analysis of the development of participation in criminal policy-making with the late Stalin years. In this way, we hoped to provide both an empirical basis for assessing the standard image of specialist participation under Stalin and a solid background for studying the development of participation in the post-Stalin period.

In examining specialist participation in criminal policy-making during the late Stalin and early post-Stalin years, we use the same criteria as we do in our analysis of participation in the 1960s, scope (amount and level) and quality (timing and function). As the categories used in the most systematic and cogent statement of the conventional negative view of specialist participation during the late 1950s, these criteria facilitate the reassessment of that view. Moreover, by using the same criteria in all three of the periods under study – late Stalin years, the 1950s, middle to late 1960s – we make it easier to record changes in the nature of participation. We shall also pay attention to the apparent influence of specialist participation upon Soviet criminal policy during the late Stalin and early post-Stalin periods, but we shall not analyze specialist influence then as systematically as we shall for the 1960s.

THE CASE STUDY

This investigation of the participation and impact of specialists in Soviet policy-making concentrates upon one area of policy and one set of specialists – criminal policy and criminologists (criminal law scholars). In choosing a policy area for study, we were guided by two considerations: first, we tried to find a policy area which would typify a broad range of Soviet policy-making; and secondly, we sought a realm in which the relevant specialists were likely to have participated to some extent in the formation of public policy.

By criminal policy we refer to a government's policy toward all activities associated with the control and prevention of ordinary criminal behavior. These activities include the determination of the criminal law, the administration of criminal justice by police and courts, the maintenance of a penal system, and the establishment of measures of crime prevention. Thus, criminal policy as a whole is broader than any of its constituent parts, such as a judicial policy, penal policy, or policy toward crime prevention. However, we do not regard as a part of criminal policy government activities relating to the control of political dissidence or deviance; for policy in this area in most countries is usually separate from criminal policy proper and is likely to be characterized by a discrete process of policy formation.[26]

Criminal policy-making in Western countries (and one suspects in the USSR as well) has been characterized by two features, which were typical of many (if not most) policy realms: an incremental pattern of policy development; and a large role in policy-making for subsystem politics. Observing the history of criminal policies in the USA, England, and Canada, one can infer that the policies developed incrementally. Important decisions of principles, which by themselves shifted the course of policy, were rare; and changes in policy, minor and major, usually emerged gradually through a series of decisions.[27] Moreover, in these countries the process of criminal policy-making usually involved not only the top politicians but also some of the administrators, specialists and other persons concerned with the subject on a professional basis, that is those persons who formed the political subsystem of criminal policy.[28] The responsibility of members of this subsystem for the formation of criminal policy was not insubstantial. For criminal policy was not one of the few policy realms of such high political salience that the leaders took charge of it on a daily basis (like foreign policy) but one of a larger group of policy realms, in which day-to-day decision-making rested with the leading administrators, and the leaders dealt with the area only on those occasions when important decisions had to be rendered.[29]

Among policy realms characterized by a high degree of subsystem politics, criminal policy is one of the more politically sensitive. It deals with questions of central importance to any political system, questions of order and of the boundaries of socially acceptable behavior; and these questions are often emotional ones for much of public opinion. In the USSR of the post-Stalin period criminal policy took on additional significance because of its relationship to de-Stalinization, a central political question of the period.[30] Although Soviet politicians probably turned to criminal policy issues only on occasion, they were likely to have paid them close attention.

Another consideration in choosing criminal policy as the focus of this study was having criminologists as its main actors. By training and by professional position Soviet criminologists of the post-Stalin period were criminal law scholars; all had been trained in criminal law and all of them worked either in legal research institutes or on university law faculties. They differed from other criminal law scholars in that their research had a sociological cast.[31] Criminologists studied not only the criminal law itself, but also the dynamics and causes of crime, crime prevention, and the administration of justice; and criminologists stressed empirical, especially statistical, analysis.[32] In some Western countries criminal law scholars and criminologists represented two different sets of specialists; for example, most criminologists in the USA were trained and worked as sociologists rather than as legal scholars. But in the USSR, as in France and some other European countries, legal and sociological expertise about crime were combined; and the criminologists represented the undisputed crime experts.

Each of Soviet criminologists' twin credentials – as legal scholars and as social scientists – made them an interesting choice for study. The participation of *legal scholars* in Soviet policy-making had already been considered by some Western writers; but those observers had not been able to reach firm conclusions about its nature and impact. In the most thorough treatment of the problem D. D. Barry and H. D. Berman highlighted the issue of determining when legal scholars 'merely gave technical formulations of policy decisions taken by the political leaders, and when they exercised inititative in bringing the need for new policies to that attention of the political leaders.'[33] Drawing upon examples from both the criminal and the civil realms, Barry and Berman inferred that Soviet legal scholars did sometimes give policy advice both on request and on their own initiative, especially in 'matters not highly charged with politics'; but in the absence of more data, the authors were unwilling to make definite assertions about the quality or influence of the scholars' contributions.[34] Since criminologists in the USSR of the 1960s represented a sizeable part of Soviet criminal law scholars, a study of their participation might help to clarify the role of legal scholars in general in the formation of legal policies.

The study of Soviet criminologists' participation in criminal policy-making took on additional interest because of their status as *social scientists*. In recent years the questions of the role of social scientists and of the use of social science in policy-making in the USA attracted the attention of Western scholars.[35] For the Soviet context these questions were especially significant because empirical social research was a relatively new development, having revived only after Stalin's death. On the whole, Western scholars who followed the revival of social research in the USSR did not study how it was used or what role its practitioners played in policy formation. To the extent that Western analysts did worry about the political consequences of the new sociology, they focused upon the conflicts between Soviet sociologists and the philosophical establishment in the USSR.[36] Like the other branches of empirical social research, criminology revived only in the post-Stalin period. Therefore, a study of the role of criminologists would serve as one step toward an evaluation of the participation of the practitioners of the revived social research in the Soviet policy process. A study of criminologists and criminal policy-making might also show how one kind of social science research, criminological study, was used in Soviet policy-making.[37]

For the decade of the 1960s, the principal years covered in this study, *criminologists* served as the specialists whose participation in criminal policy-making came under scrutiny. But in our analysis of the development of specialist participation in criminal policy-making in the late Stalin and early post-Stalin years we were obliged to examine the activities of *criminal law scholars* of a more conventional sort. The reason was simple. After politics had forced the curtailment of criminological research in the early 1930s, there was virtually no crime study carried out in the USSR.[38] Criminology began to revive only during the late 1950s, so that one could not begin to speak of criminologists as a subgroup of criminal law scholars until the 1960s. In analyzing the participation during 1938–60 of scholars who studied substantive criminal law, we were not considering an entirely different set of specialists from the criminologists of the 1960s. The criminal law scholars of the 1940s and 1950s differed from the criminologists of the 1960s neither in their training and career pattern (as lawyers) nor in their main professional identification (as criminal law scholars). The differences lay only in the focus of research and in the methods which the scholars used in conducting it. Moreover, to a degree the criminal law scholars of the 1940s and 1950s and criminologists of the 1960s were actually the same persons. Prominent among Soviet criminal law scholars in the late Stalin and early post-Stalin years were former criminologists, men who had done sociological or statistical research in the 1920s and under pressure of political circumstances had turned to other kinds of study.[39] A number of these scholars retained an active interest in criminology, even to the point of attempting to revive criminological research while Stalin was still alive.[40] And, as we shall see, some of these former criminologists lived on to shepherd criminology's revival in the post-Stalin years. The leading criminologists of the new generation, the criminal law scholars who began their first sociological research in the late 1950s and early 1960s, were themselves the students of those same criminal law scholars who had been forced to refrain from crime study.

Since we are concerned with relating the experience of Soviet criminologists to that of other specialists in Soviet policy-making during the 1960s, it is appropriate that we consider briefly the question of the nature of their expertise. It is often assumed that the 'harder' or more solid the knowledge of a set of specialists, the more likely they were to be consulted and to be heeded by policy-makers.[41] If this proposition were valid, it would affect the typicality of Soviet criminologists' participation and influence. For criminologists in general, not just in the USSR, had relatively soft expertise. They could answer few of the questions which politicians might pose about the nature, causes, and means of preventing crime, let alone offer policy advice which was itself scientifically grounded.[42] Should this fact lead one to suspect that criminologists in the USSR would participate less in policy-making or have less influence on policies than, say, engineers or physicists?

Without denying that the nature of expertise may have some effect upon a specialist's role, we believe that this factor plays a smaller part than some observers have assumed. Recent studies of expert involvement in policy-making (in the USA) have shown that a prerequisite for specialist participation is the belief on the part of decision-makers that they need expert help – whether because of the gravity or technical complexity of the problem at hand, because of the political advantage in using experts, or because of the ready availability of expert help. Once decision-makers believe that they need experts, they usually recruit persons to fill the role. As a rule, those persons include some of the 'best available' specialists and are persons with a reputation for 'technical competence and personal integrity'. Neither of these characteristics excludes participation by specialists whose expertise is 'soft'; for in many policy realms the best available specialists possessing good reputations have nothing better to offer than 'soft' expertise.[43]

When any specialist gains access to policy-making, he becomes subject to the rules of the political game. The nature of his advice makes some difference to its chances of being accepted, but acceptance seems to depend even more upon political factors.[44] Perhaps this is as it should be, for some of the questions politicians are wont to pose to specialists involve value choices; and other questions, though scientific in form, are not open to ready answers by specialists.[45] Even the best qualified nuclear physicist is as unprepared to answer some kinds of questions posed by politicians as is the social scientist whose expertise is more limited.

Neither in gaining access to policy-making nor in influencing policy choices does the nature of a specialist's expertise appear to determine his success or failure. In recruitment into policy-making, *reputation* as an expert appears to count more than actual expertise; and although the nature of the advice which a specialist offers affects its chances of acceptance, political considerations appear to be more decisive. These hypotheses suggest that just because Soviet criminologists had softer expertise than, say, Soviet engineers the former need not have participated in policy-making any less than the latter, nor need the former have exerted less influence than the latter upon policy decisions. We are not assuming that whatever scope, quality, and impact of participation we find for Soviet criminologists would necessarily characterize the participation of most other specialists in the USSR; for the pattern of policy-making in the USSR may have varied from one area of policy to another for reasons that had nothing to do with the quality of the relevant specialists' expertise.[46] Nevertheless, we would like to emphasize that there are no grounds for assuming that because the skills of Soviet criminologists were relatively 'soft', their experience as participants in policy-making would differ from that of specialists with better expertise.

Two further points deserve mention here: why this study focused upon the policy-making role of specialists and not also of officials; and the relationship of this study to the question of interest groups in Soviet politics.

In focusing upon the participation of specialists, we were looking at only one part of the participation by persons outside of the top political leadership in the USSR (Politburo and Secretariat members, heads of Central Committee departments, and persons of ministerial rank).[47] In most policy realms the high and middle-ranking officials of the relevant ministerial and state agencies also played a part in policy formation, perhaps even a more important one than the relevant specialists. This study focused upon specialists rather than officials for two reasons. The first was a practical one; detailed information about specialist political activity in the USSR was more accessible to the Western researcher than was data about the political behavior of officials. A larger proportion of specialist participation took place in the public view, and specialists were more easily approached in person by a Western scholar than were officials. The other reason was that the question of specialist impact on policy had intrinsic interest. In recent years both Western and Soviet scholars had noticed that in industrial societies the proportion of policy issues involving specialized knowledge had increased. Extrapolating from this trend, some analysts predicted that in the future specialists deemed to possess such knowledge would come to participate in a greater proportion of political decisions.[48] The observers were uncertain, however, how such an expansion of specialist participation might affect the distribution of power and influence in such countries. Although this study is directed at the activities of scholars specializing on crime it does not ignore the role in criminal policy-making of law enforcement officials. When it was possible to determine that these officials made contributions to policy formation, such contributions will be noted; and attention will be paid to the interaction among scholars and officials in the course of the formation of Soviet criminal policy.

It should also be stressed that in this book we are studying the political behavior of Soviet criminal law scholars and criminologists *as individual specialists, not as a group*. Thus, when we use collective terms like 'the criminologists' or 'the criminal law scholars', we usually refer to those members of the profession who took part in a given decision or set of decisions rather than to the profession as a whole. Although our study falls within the interest group tradition in the sense that it deals with participation and influence in the policy-making process,[49] we do not use the term 'interest group' to depict Soviet criminologists and criminal law scholars. In the Soviet context at least this term is both ambiguous[50] and pejorative in connotation.[51] Even more important, the term's use places undue emphasis upon the question of the degree of consensus among Soviet criminologists and criminal law scholars. According to the standard definition, to constitute interest-group activity the proposals of individual scholars would have to represent views shared by a number of their colleagues. Although this might often happen in practice, it could prove difficult for the researcher to determine when it did. If one succeeded in learning which of à specialist's proposals represented views shared by his colleagues and which merely his own opinions (and also whether the specialist himself or the leaders he advised were aware of this fact), one could try to measure the effect of collegial consensus upon specialist influence. But for studying the nature and influence of specialists' participation in Soviet policy-making knowledge about collegial consensus among specialists was not essential, and it seemed pointless to exclude from consideration the activities of criminologists or criminal law scholars which did not or which might not qualify as interest-group activity.

OUTLINE OF THE BOOK

After the introductory chapter this book consists of three parts, each with three chapters. The first part studies the development of Soviet criminal law scholars' participation in criminal policy-making from the late 1930s to the 1960s. Chapter 2 analyzes the nature of criminal law scholars' participation during the last fifteen years of Stalin's rule. Chapter 3 examines the nature and impact of these scholars' participation in the first eight years after Stalin's lifetime, a period which included a major criminal law reform. Chapter 4 discusses the reasons why the participation of criminal law scholars became regularized or institutionalized in the decade of the 1960s; it includes extended analysis of the revival of criminological research in the late 1950s and early 1960s and of the structure and functions of the All-Union Institute for the Study and

Prevention of Crime (the Procuracy Institute), which was founded in 1963.

The second part of the book is devoted to the narration of three case studies of the participation of Soviet criminologists in criminal policy-making during the 1960s. The case studies concern reforms in the institutions handling juvenile offenders (1965–7), changes in the treatment of alcoholics and hooligans (1965–7), and changes in the regulations governing the application of parole and the application of special sanctions to recidivist offenders (1965–9). The studies provide a basis for the assessment of the nature and impact of criminologists' participation in criminal policy-making during 1960s.

The third part of the book makes this assessment. Chapter 8 analyzes the scope and quality of criminologists' participation, and includes separate discussion of the main types of participation of Soviet criminologists: private communications (written and oral) with political leaders and high officials; appearances in the press; membership in *ad hoc* commissions spawned by the Praesidium of the USSR Supreme Soviet. Chapter 9 evaluates the effects of criminologists' participation by scrutinizing their influence upon the decisions in which they took part and their impact upon the development of criminal policy during the middle and late 1960s. To conclude, chapter 10 reviews the participation of Soviet crime experts in historical and in comparative perspective and discusses some implications of the study as a whole.

PART ONE

THE DEVELOPMENT OF CRIMINAL LAW SCHOLARS' PARTICIPATION 1938–63

PART ONE: INTRODUCTION

When Soviet criminal law scholars took part in the formation of Soviet criminal policy in the years after Stalin's death, they were not entering the political process for the first time. Even under Stalin, as we shall see, these scholars had some opportunities to participate. The post-Stalin period did witness important changes in the role played by Soviet criminal law scholars in criminal policy-making. First, in the 1950s the scholars' participation expanded, when the criminal law reform attracted many of them to make contributions to a series of decisions. Secondly, in the 1960s the role of criminal law scholars and criminologists became regularized or institutionalized, when participation in criminal policy-making became a normal and frequent activity for some scholars. This part of the book records and analyzes the development of Soviet criminal law scholars' participation through this series of stages: from existence in the 1940s, to expansion in the 1950s, to institutionalization in the 1960s. Its purpose is to explain the changes which occurred in the nature of the scholars' participation in each of the two post-Stalin decades.

2 Criminal Law Scholars and Criminal Policy Under Stalin

During the last fifteen years of Stalin's rule Soviet criminal law scholars played a part in criminal policy-making, but their participation was neither frequent nor regular; nor did they exert much influence upon Soviet criminal policy. Most of the scholars' participation fell in two periods, 1938–40 and 1945–7, and in each of these periods the main opportunity for participation in policy-making was provided by the preparation of a new USSR criminal code. We shall begin this chapter by considering why Soviet criminal law scholars' overall participation in criminal policy-making was infrequent and irregular and by analyzing the scope of their contributions to the draft USSR criminal codes. Then, we shall take a detailed look at two examples of the scholars' participation, in order to assess its quality and its influence on policy.

Apart from helping to prepare the draft USSR criminal codes, Soviet criminal law scholars seemed to have had only occasional chances to contribute to decisions in Soviet criminal policy during the late Stalin years. The reasons lay in political factors outside of the scholars' control. Both Stalin's style of decision-making and the unusually large role of the security police in the administration of criminal justice discouraged scholarly contributions to criminal policy. Stalin's predilection for personal decision-making and his intolerance of direct criticism of his policies made specialist participation difficult in many policy realms. In making decisions Stalin usually consulted only a small circle of assistants, often overlooking both ministerial officials and specialist advice.[1] Moreover, Stalin hindered public policy debate (it did occur nevertheless) by treating most criticism other than the constructive as impermissible deviation.[2] In this atmosphere criminal law scholars tended to be cautious, both in public and in private forums. They did offer policy suggestions, but often in subtle, indirect ways.[3] Their open advocacy of policy positions came mainly after the discussion of an issue had been sanctioned, either by its initiation behind the scenes or by encouragement from a journal's editors.[4]

Participation by Soviet criminal law scholars in criminal policy-making was further restricted by the abnormal situation in the administration of criminal justice. The widespread application of terror and the power and responsibility concentrated in the organs of state security limited what jurists, scholars and officials alike, could contribute to criminal policy. Because the facts of terror and illegality contradicted official myths, scholars were allowed to study neither the crime situation nor penal practice;[5] and even judicial practice they studied only a little.[6] As a result the scholars had less information and analysis to contribute to criminal policy formation than they might have had. Fortunately, their status within the legal community remained high,[7] and some of them continued to have close ties with the leading judicial officials.[8] In normal times such ties would have provided scholars with opportunities to contribute to criminal policy-making behind the scenes, but these were not normal times. Relationships with leading judicial officials meant less when those officials themselves had restricted access to the policy process.

There was reason to suspect that judicial officials were not alone in this dilemma – that other high governmental officials under Stalin sometimes found their access to policy-making curtailed. Yet the situation of the judicial chiefs was somewhat special. The amassing of power by the NKVD SSSR had occurred partly at their expense, as the NKVD had encroached, with Stalin's backing, upon the functions of each of the judicial agencies. The Commissariat of Justice had lost to the NKVD control of the administration of penal institutions for non-political offenders;[9] the Supreme Court had lost jurisdiction over that large number of cases which sent citizens to prison after hearings of the NKVD's Special Board;[10] and the USSR Procuracy lost its capacity to oversee the legality of the administration of justice and of government operations, because the NKVD could not tolerate investigations of its patently illegal activity.[11] The loss of much of the agency leaders' capacity to execute criminal policy[12] seriously inhibited their scope for policy initiative.[13] Moreover, even in considering changes in criminal policy which were still related to the experience of the judicial chiefs, the leader often failed to take account of their opinions. During the late 1940s Stalin introduced a series of changes in the criminal law without their advice or consent. In abolishing (temporarily) the death penalty (1947) and in setting new penalties for rape (1949), Stalin reportedly did not even consult his judicial lieutenants.[14] And, as we shall see, Stalin paid no attention to Supreme Court Chairman Goliakov's suggestions for new theft penalties (1947), even though he, Stalin, had solicited them.

Despite this political context unfavorable to criminal law scholars' participation, the scholars were drawn into policy discussions by the periodic drafting of a new criminal code. Throughout most of the Stalin years a new criminal code was 'in preparation'. Between 1929 and 1936 the radical legal theorists Krylenko and Pashukanis had supervised the writing at the Institute of Soviet Construction and Law of a series of draft *RSFSR* criminal codes, which embodied their goal of a simplified criminal law in which specific crimes and punishments were omitted and judges were empowered to apply general legal principles to concrete cases.[15] When in 1936 Stalin repudiated the 'nihilism' of the legal theories of Krylenko and Pashukanis, their draft RSFSR criminal code became obsolete. Nevertheless, the preparation of a new draft criminal code started soon again. For after the Soviet Constitution of 1936 moved the criminal law from republican to all-union jurisdiction, it seemed appropriate to replace the republican criminal codes then in force (which dated from 1924) with a single all-union criminal code.[16] The first draft *USSR* criminal code was prepared in 1938, and it was followed by further draft codes in 1947, 1949, and 1952; none of these draft codes ever became law.[17]

The extent of Soviet criminal law scholars' participation in preparing the new draft USSR criminal codes was impressive. Consider, for example, their role in preparing the codes of 1938 and of 1947. Late in August 1938 the USSR Commissar of Justice, N. M. Rychkov, instructed the All-Union Institute of Juridical Sciences which was attached to his Commissariat to prepare a new draft USSR criminal code. The scholars at this institute were well qualified for the task, for as the successor to the State Institute for the Study of Crime and the Criminal and to the Institute for Criminal Policy, the All-Union Institute of Juridical Sciences housed the best and most experienced Soviet criminal law scholars.[18] Under the direction of Professors A. A. Gertsenzon and B. S. Osherovich a special commission composed of members of the Institute's criminal law sector wrote the draft code. The commission worked under great pressure of time but by the end of October managed to complete a third version of the draft code, which it circulated for comment to scholars and officials around the country.[19] Many scholars and officials had a further opportunity to make suggestions for the new draft code at a large national conference which was held at the All-Union Institute of Juridical Science in early 1939 (27 January to 4 February).[20] After the conference the commission reviewed the comments and suggestions, made its final revisions, and in the spring of 1939 submitted to the Commissar of Justice the draft criminal code and explanatory materials. Then a meeting of high officials in the Commissariat of Justice reviewed the draft in May 1939, and decided to appoint a new commission to give the draft a final revison; this commission included seven representatives of the All-Union Institute of Juridical Sciences.[21] Later that year a version of the draft USSR criminal code was published by the Institute, and throughout 1939 and the first months of 1940 scholars discussed the draft code on the pages of the law journals.[22] Early in 1940 the draft code was approved for promulgation and presented to the Supreme Soviet, but the outbreak of war intervened before the legislative organs had time to act.[23]

In 1945, as soon as the war was over, Soviet criminal law scholars resumed working on the draft USSR criminal code, and on 12 June 1946 a special edict of the USSR Council of Ministers created a governmental commission to prepare a new version.[24] A majority of this commission's members were legal scholars.[25] At the end of 1946 the commission circulated a completed draft of a USSR criminal code to the Councils of Ministers in the Union Republics, to the legal research institutes and educational institutions, and to certain scholars and practitioners of Soviet justice. Once again, the draft code was discussed in the legal press.[26] After considering the comments from these various sources, the commission reviewed the draft code once more and passed a final version on to the USSR Council of Ministers for confirmation.[27] Like its predecessor the draft criminal code of 1946 was never promulgated; but in this case the reason is unknown.

There was no cause to doubt that Soviet criminal law scholars' contributions to the preparation of the draft criminal codes of 1938 and 1947 represented participation in criminal policy-making. The preparation of the codes involved the scholars not only in the technical tasks of repackaging old law but also in the creative and politically significant job of proposing and considering changes in the law. Moreover, according to Soviet scholars with whom we have spoken, the mandates given to the drafters of the new codes facilitated substantive contributions by criminal law scholars. In writing the new codes, the scholars had to take into account existing legislation, especially that of recent vintage and of political significance; and also of any instructions which had been provided by political and ministerial leaders (usually given in an oblique form, such as 'there is an opinion that . . .' or 'the time seems ripe for . . .')'[28] But within these limits there was opportunity for the drafters to propose changes in Soviet criminal law which they and their colleagues believed to be needed. Thus, as we shall see, criminal law scholars introduced proposals for important changes in Soviet criminal law into each of the draft USSR criminal codes of the late Stalin years.

Having seen the extent of Soviet criminal law scholars' participation in the preparation of the draft criminal codes for 1938 and 1947, one was curious to learn more about it. What was the quality of Soviet criminal law scholars' participation under Stalin? How much influence did it have upon decisions in Soviet criminal policy? In order to reach tentative answers to these questions, we shall examine two examples of Soviet criminal law scholars' participation in criminal policy-making under Stalin – one of them relating entirely to their work on a draft criminal code, the other relating partly to this work. The first example concerns the issue of the retention of analogy in Soviet criminal law; and the second the severity of punishment for thieves in the USSR.

REMOVING ANALOGY

The principle of analogy, a feature of Soviet criminal law since 1922, empowered judges to convict persons whom they judged to have committed socially dangerous acts, even if those acts were not described by individual crimes in the criminal code. Using Article 16 of the RSFSR Criminal Code, the judge could 'reason by analogy' and apply that article of the code stipulating crimes most similar in kind to the offense committed. Analogy was not an invention of Soviet jurisprudence, as it was found in the codes of a number of nineteenth-century European states.[29] The principle had been introduced into Soviet law when after the Revolution legislators found it difficult to compose a list of specific offenses comprehensive enough to protect the young state 'when class enemies were abundant and when our court experience was less developed'.[30]

Analogy took on special significance in Soviet jurisprudence, when in the late 1920s the radical legal thinkers E. V. Pashukanis and N. V. Krylenko made it a cornerstone of their political program. Committed to the belief that crime would disappear, these jurists advocated the elimination of the special part of the criminal code, where specific crimes and punishments were listed, so that judges would expediently apply general principles of law to individual cases. Had the Krylenko proposals ever been effected, judges would have had to 'analogize' in almost every case which came before them.[31] During the early 1930s when Krylenko and Pashukanis gained political favor, some judges apparently adopted their ideas and applied the principle of analogy more frequently than had been the case in earlier legal practice.[32]

The political context which encouraged the use of analogy changed abruptly when in 1936 the promulgation of the Stalin Constitution placed emphasis upon the 'stability of law'. Stalin had decided to reject the idea of the weakening of law and legal institutions in preparation for their disappearance and to embrace the opposite notion that Soviet state and law must be especially strong during the period of socialist construction. Within a year of the issuing of the new constitution Pashukanis, Krylenko and associates lost their jobs (some would soon lose their lives as well), and A. Ia. Vyshinskii took over the leading position in the community of legal scholars with the mandate to restore Soviet law and justice to normalcy and stability.[33]

What did these events mean for the institution of analogy? At the Eighth Extraordinary Congress of Soviets in 1936 Stalin had decried 'the situation whereby not any one organ but a series of organs legislates'.[34] Did this statement mean that analogy was no longer appropriate for Soviet law? In his influential treatise of 1937 A. Ia. Vyshinskii answered in the negative. According to Vyshinskii analogy was still needed because the code could not forsee all possible crimes; and, if analogy were used in a careful and limited fashion, it would enhance rather than harm the stability of Soviet law.[35] Following Vyshinskii's cue, the drafters of a preliminary draft USSR criminal code (in 1937) included analogy in the code;[36] and at least two legal scholars wrote in the law journals supporting this move.[37]

But a number of Soviet criminal law scholars did not accept Vyshinskii's compromise and by the end of 1938 were arguing openly for the repudiation of the principle of analogy and for its exclusion from Soviet criminal law. The opposition to Vyshinskii on the question of analogy came from some of the criminal law scholars at the All-Union Institute of Juridical Sciences who were serving as members of the commission formed to compose a new draft USSR Criminal Code in the fall of 1938. After debating the question at length, the scholars decided by majority vote to follow the lead of its co-chairman, Professor A. A. Gertsenzon, and to eliminate analogy from the draft code.[38]

Clearly, Gertsenzon and his colleagues would not have proposed the removal of analogy unless the political context had been favorable. Stalin's new emphasis upon the 'stability of law' and his concern about a single source of law gave some legitimacy to the consideration of the removal of analogy. Apparently Gertsenzon also had the support of a strong patron in the person of I. T. Goliakov. Like Vyshinskii, who was simultaneously Procurator-General, Director of the Institute of State and Law, and editor of *Sovetskoe gosudarstvo i pravo*, Goliakov held a triad of important positions in the legal world: Chairman of the USSR Supreme Court, Director of the All-Union Institute, and editor of *Sovetskaia iustitisiia*.[39] Goliakov did not announce his support for Gertsenzon's proposal right away. The first public statement by Goliakov on the question of analogy came only at the end of November, almost a month after the commission had completed its draft code and circulated it for comments outside the Institute. And that statement was an unsigned editorial in *Sovetskaia iustitsiia*, which argued only that the removal of analogy should be seriously considered. 'If we do not eliminate analogy,' wrote the editor, 'we should in any case sharply limit its application with a series of procedural norms.'[40] Only at the Institute's conference in January 1939 did Goliakov throw unequivocal support behind Gertsenzon's bold initiative.[41]

In raising the question of the removal of analogy, Gertsenzon and his colleagues opened a controversy which was to divide the community of legal scholars for years to come. The extent of the split became obvious in the discussions at the First Scientific Conference of the All-Union Institute of Juridical Sciences (January/February 1939) where the question of analogy occupied the spotlight of much of the debate. In the opening plenary session before three hundred and fifty scholars and officials, I. T. Goliakov rehearsed some of the arguments against analogy, including the claim that 'the court often uses analogy to violate the law,' a strong statement from the Chairman of the USSR Supreme Court.[42] Then, in the session devoted to criminal law, Professor Gertsenzon presented a report on the draft criminal code in which he explained in detail the grounds for the elimination of analogy.[43] Afterwards, eleven scholars spoke to the question, five of them supporting and six of them opposing analogy's elimination from the code. The scholars appeared to be expressing their individual opinions rather than the positions of their institutes' directors;

persons from the All-Union Institute, including members of the Gertsenzon commission, spoke against the commission's decision; and scholars
from outside the Institute rose to support the commission's majority
view.[44]

Much of the argument centered around the practical question whether
or not analogy was needed. Professor Gertsenzon insisted that as of the late
1930s there was no longer any need for analogy, because the Soviet state
was no longer young and weak and infested with class enemies set on
destroying it. There was now little likelihood that new socially dangerous
acts would abound in great number before the Praesidium of the Supreme
Soviet had time to issue new edicts proscribing them. Nevertheless,
Gertsenzon proved unable to convince the proponents of analogy, who
persisted in their view that some offenders would go unpunished unless the
law remained flexible enough to account for socially dangerous actions not
stipulated in the code. Gertsenzon supported his case with another
argument – namely that in contemporary judicial practice analogy was
often abused, serving frequently as the instrument for convicting an
offender of a crime more serious than the one which he had actually
committed. To back up this contention Gertsenzon supplied evidence from
a study carried out at the Institute of more than 500 instances of the
application of the principle of analogy by Moscow courts during the year
1937. The supporters of analogy rejected this argument as well, claiming
that analogy was not used very much and that according to Vyshinskii's
exhortation further limitations would be placed upon its use.[45]

The dispute over analogy focused not only upon its practical effects but
also upon its theoretical significance. The leading opponent of analogy, A.
A. Gertsenzon, argued that, by allowing judges to legislate in individual
cases, the institution of analogy placed the judges above the law and thus
undermined the law's stability.[46] On the other hand, analogy's proponents
insisted that the carefully regulated use of the institution was consistent
with 'stability of law'. As V. M. Chkhivadze put it, analogy was
incompatible not with the stability of law but only with the slogan of the
Classical school, the 'bourgeois principle' of *nullum crimen sine lege*, which,
Chkhivadze claimed, had no place in Soviet law.[47] In other words, to
achieve 'stability of law' it was not necessary to accept the 'rule of law'.
However, P. S. Romashkin challenged Chkhivadze's assumption and
made explicit what Gertsenzon had implied – that stability of laws did
seem to require the adoption of 'rule of law.' 'It is claimed', Romashkin
said,

> that the rejection of analogy is tantamount to recognition of the
> principle *nullum crimen*. What is this? It is certainly nothing bad. We
> would be legislating a principle not of bourgeois formal democracy, but
> one of socialist legality.[48]

If analogy's opponents succeeded in interpreting Stalin's call for 'stability of law' as the acceptance of 'rule of law', they would have accomplished a major shift in Soviet legal thought. Since the Revolution Soviet jurisprudence held that the protection of the revolutionary state and society took precedence over protecting the rights of the individual. The utilitarian principle of 'social defense' had in fact held sway in Soviet legal thinking, while the classical tenet 'rule of law' had been rejected as 'bourgeois'.[49]

Romashkin's insistence that the 'rule of law' could have a place in 'socialist legality' suggested another dimension of the theoretical side of the dispute. In the Soviet context, where an expedient approach to law had predominated (recall Lenin's dictum, 'law is politics'), the embracing of the 'rule of law' signified not only a reordering of priorities, but also a qualitative change in the relationship between the legal system and the political order. For a legal system characterized by 'rule of law' would have to be *relatively* autonomous from politics (no legal system can be more than this), so that politics determined the rules of its operation through legislation, but not the details of that operation through intervention in individual cases. By supporting directly or indirectly the embracing of the principle of 'rule of law', some Soviet jurists were hinting at the desirability of further 'normalization' for the legal order as a whole.

Because it was directly related to the question of the place of 'rule of law' in Soviet jurisprudence, the principle of analogy was of important theoretical significance. Although its removal might have but a small effect on the administration of justice,[50] such a change could have affected in a major way the logic behind the Soviet criminal policy.

The effort by Gertsenzon and his colleagues to secure the removal of analogy from Soviet criminal law was almost successful. The draft code excluding the principle of analogy was approved by the conference, despite some dissenting votes, and sent to the Commissariat of Justice for examination by a revision commission.[51] Despite the appearance in the law journals during 1939 and 1940 of at least four more articles defending the retention of analogy,[52] the draft code as presented to the highest political organs still excluded the principle.[53] The draft code without analogy was approved for promulgation and sent to the Supreme Soviet in early 1940, but then the war intervened and stopped the momentum.[54]

After World War II there were a number of further attempts to produce a USSR criminal code. The draft code of 1947, which was prepared by another group of scholars, this time serving as members of a commission attached to the USSR Council of Ministers, once again removed the principle of analogy. And, in explaining the renunciation of analogy to a meeting at the Moscow Juridical Institute in 1947, A. A. Piontkovskii rehearsed all of the arguments which A. A. Gertsenzon had made eight years before – about the lack of need for analogy under contemporary conditions, about the misuse of analogy, and about its effects upon the 'stability of law'.[55] In later versions of the draft USSR criminal code (in

1949 and in 1952), the drafters continued to exclude the principle of analogy.[56] That the principle was removed from Soviet law only after Stalin's death testified to the politics of whim and caprice which characterized his rule in the later years. Had any of the four draft USSR criminal codes produced between 1938 and 1952 been promulgated, the principle of analogy would have been removed, at the initiative of a few and with the support of a majority of criminal law scholars.

PUNISHMENT FOR THIEVES

On 4 June, 1947 the Praesidium of the Supreme Soviet issued two edicts which raised drastically the punishments for theft of state, social, and personal property and which eliminated many of the distinctions between types of theft. The edicts represented the most important criminal legislation of the post-World War II period, and they constituted the most repressive legislation relating to ordinary criminals promulgated under Stalin's rule.[57] This case study of the participation of criminal law scholars in criminal policy-making concerns the attempts by some of these scholars to find ways of mitigating the effects of the new laws on theft, through further legislation and through interpretation of the edicts themselves.

The new edicts on theft were the work of the political leader, Joseph Stalin. Over the years Stalin evinced a personal interest in the prosecution of thieves, whom he had once dubbed as 'akin to traitors'. At Stalin's urging, a 1932 edict had fixed the death penalty as one option for the most serious cases of theft of state property (generally cases associated with collectivization).[58] But in May 1947 Stalin abolished (temporarily) the death penalty, and at the same time decided that it was time to intensify the repression of thieves in order to rid Soviet society once and for all of this 'pestilence'.[59]

Stalin requested I. T. Goliakov, the Chairman of the USSR Supreme Court and Director of the All-Union Institute of Juridical Sciences, to draft a new statute on the theft of state property, in which the penalties for such thefts would be raised. In complying with Stalin's request, Goliakov produced a sophisticated legal document, a draft statute of some fourteen articles, which retained and even refined distinctions currently operative in the law. Goliakov fulfilled his mandate by raising the terms of imprisonment for most categories of theft by amounts varying from 25 to 50 per cent. However, Stalin discarded Goliakov's draft entirely, and reportedly dictated in its place the simple five-article edict which was eventually promulgated. Stalin also added a second edict of three short articles which multiplied the terms of confinement for theft of personal property.[60]

In contrast to the Goliakov drafts which raised the penalties for theft in reasonable amounts, the Stalin edicts raised them in radical fashion and at the same time eliminated many distinctions between types of theft and categories of offenders. In place of a carefully differentiated set of punishments the new laws provided for the application of harsh sentences to all categories of theft. The simplest and smallest incident of theft of personal property, which under the old law drew a sentence of three months corrective work now brought a minimum sentence of five years in a prison camp. Ordinary theft of state property now earned the offender seven to ten years in confinement; and when an offender committed theft of state property for the second time, or in a large amount, or as a member of an 'organized group (gang)', he was liable to a sentence of ten to twenty-five years in a prison camp! Moreover, for any of these types of theft, the convict might be as young as fourteen years of age! Distinctions which were traditional in Russian law – between open and covert theft, between appropriation, embezzlement and other forms of theft of state property, or between theft with and without the use of a weapon – were eliminated from the law. And the one important new distinction – between ordinary theft and theft committed by an 'organized group (gang)' – was highly ambiguous, even though it could add an extra fifteen years in prison to an offender's sentence.[61]

The potential effects of the new edicts upon judicial and penal practice were devastating. For theft in all its forms (including robbery) represented close to one third of all criminal prosecutions handled by Soviet courts.[62] This meant that a sizeable proportion of criminal offenders in the USSR were now liable to receive these extra-harsh sentences, which would be allocated with little regard either to the nature of their offense or to their personal characteristics. Small wonder that most Soviet jurists were disturbed by the new legislation.

Soviet jurists were surely aware just by reading the new laws that Stalin had a hand in their origin. In any case, I. T. Goliakov made this fact obvious in his articles announcing the new legislation. Partly to fulfil his obligation to Stalin and partly to clear himself of responsibility for the new legislation, Goliakov stressed 'the serious political content of the new legislation'. He recounted in detail the history of Stalin's previous contributions to the subject of theft; and he described the purpose of the legislation in language more political than juridical in tone. The new legislation was 'to rid the Soviet Union of thieves (*vory*) and of swindlers (*zhuliki*), who were a survival of the distant [*sic*] past.'[63]

Although he was displeased with the new legislation, the Chairman of the USSR Supreme Court, I.T. Goliakov, was himself in no position to remedy the effects of the legislation, especially as he had personally composed the unsatisfactory rejected first draft.[64] In fact, to protect himself, Goliakov was obliged to make sure that the new edicts were properly implemented. Ordinary judges, however, sought right away ways to lessen the new laws' severity. A survey of court practice published six months after the edicts went into effect revealed that some judges were

using conditional sentences as a way of avoiding sending offenders away for
ten years; other judges were unwilling to apply the higher penalties for a
second offense where the first offense had not been fully prosecuted; and
some judges were avoiding higher terms for some group thefts by defining a
group as having not less than three persons. Moreover, the survey
reported, one could still hear disagreements 'about whether to apply the
laws of 4 June when a theft of socialist property had a petty character and
whether it was all right to give conditional judgments for theft of state
property, etc., even though both edicts sharply curtailed the separation
between the maximum and minimum penalties for theft.'[65]

Like their colleagues on the bench, criminal law scholars also tried to
soften the effects of the new laws. One way was through further legislative
change. As we saw above, a group of criminal law scholars served on a
government commission which drafted the 1947 version of the draft USSR
criminal code. According to A. A. Piontkovskii, who was a member of the
commission, the commission had adopted in the draft code the new higher
penalties for theft, as prescribed by the edicts of 4 June 1947.[66] However, at
the same time, the commission decided to use the draft criminal code to re-
establish 'early release from punishment' or parole. The Soviet version of
parole had been a part of Soviet criminal law until its abolition in 1938.
The commission decided to revive the institution, so Piontkovskii explained, 'because the terms of some punishments have been increased,' an
obvious reference to the new laws on theft. The actual text which the
commission included in the draft code read as follows: 'Persons sentenced
to deprivation of freedom for a period exceeding three years may, after
two-thirds of their judicial punishment, be freed from further punishment,
if it has been judged that they are no longer socially dangerous, owing to
their faultless behavior and exemplary attitude toward work.' In his
comments Piontkovskii stressed that in this form early release would
'disturb' (*kolebat*) neither the court sentence nor the stability of law; rather,
it would stimulate the re-education of prisoners.[67] Through the revival of
early release A. A. Piontkovskii and his colleagues on the commission
sought to reduce by one third the new harsh prison terms for theft, but their
attempt failed because the 1947 draft criminal code did not become law.

Another way whereby criminal law scholars in the USSR tried to
mitigate the effects of Stalin's decision on theft was through the same
means used by the judges, namely through the interpretation of the new
laws. The most important, though not the only, example of such an
attempt was an article by Professor N. D. Durmanov, which was published
in the law journal *Sotsialisticheskaia zakonnost* in the fall of 1947.[68]
Durmanov found a number of ambiguous points in the texts of the edicts,
whose interpretation might soften the edicts' overall effect. For example,
since the edicts contained no definition of theft, Durmanov attempted to
provide one. He wrote that the presence of 'theft' in an act of appropriation
of property depended in part upon the goal which the offender had in mind

in taking the property. For an action to qualify as 'theft', the object stolen had to have some material value and the person stealing it had to intend to keep or to use the object.[69] Thus, if a guilty party 'stole a snowshield and dumped it on a bonfire, 'he would not have committed a theft.[70] It is apparent that the type of offender most likely to take objects of little material value and to quickly dispose of them was the young offender; a juvenile gang out for 'kicks' might well indulge in such activities. Because Soviet criminal law had since 1935 held responsible for crimes youngsters of fourteen years and older, the application of the new edicts threatened to send these young offenders to long prison terms. By defining theft in 'subjective' as well as 'objective' terms, Durmanov was attempting to remove a portion of young offenders from the harsh effect of the new laws.

Another and more fundamental attempt to interpret the new laws in the most favorable light was Professor Durmanov's reading of the phrase 'committed by an organized group (gang)'. Just what kind of group constituted an 'organized group (gang)' mattered, for a large proportion of thefts were probably committed by groups, and the designation of these offenses as 'committed by an organized group (gang)' would more than double the prison terms to which the guilty parties might be sentenced. The edicts of 4 June left the concept of 'organized group' undefined, leaving open the possibility of a variety of interpretations. According to a broad construction, an organized group might have consisted of any two persons who planned and committed a theft together. However, Professor Durmanov chose a more narrow construction, when he asserted that an 'organized group (gang)' meant only a 'stable, organized criminal group'. Durmanov himself did not specify the exact criteria for stability or for criminal group, but the implication was that the group had to have been engaged in criminal activity prior to the offense in question. For Durmanov did state unequivocally that 'the commission of a theft by a few persons, although they shared a single criminal intent and joined in the commission of a given offense, and consequently would be considered partners in the crime,' need not indicate the presence of a 'stable, organized group'.[71]

Although legally and linguistically there was justification for Durmanov's interpretation, he was treading on dangerous political ground; for his interpretation did not fully implement the policy line expressed in the new legislation. In urging that loose criminal partnerships should not be classified as 'organized criminal groups', Durmanov was advocating the more lenient of two possible interpretations. As such, Durmanov's interpretation ran counter to the extreme repression which Stalin had sought.

Within days of its publication, the USSR Minister of Justice, the Procurator-General, and the Chairman of the USSR Supreme Court met in a special session to discuss the article. Using their collective authority, these ministerial leaders issued an unusual joint edict criticizing the 'errors' in Professor Durmanov's article and calling upon the journal's editors to show more 'political astuteness' in their editorial work and to correct the misleading impressions created by Professor Durmanov's article.[72] At the same time, I. T. Goliakov himself wrote an article devoted to 'distortion of the sense of the edicts of 4 June 1947', part of which constituted a critique of Professor Durmanov's article. Goliakov criticized Durmanov not only for his definition of an organized group, but also for his treatment of the concept of theft and for other 'mistakes'.[73]

A few months later, in March 1948, the USSR Supreme Court tried to resolve the question by issuing an authoritative definition of an 'organized group (gang)'. 'By an organized group or gang one must understand a group of two or more persons, organized in advance to commit one or more thefts . . .'[74] To the criminal law scholar Z. A. Vyshinskaia[75] the new emphasis in the Court's definition upon the element of 'advance organization' supplied the basis for one further attempt to restrict the application of the higher penalties awarded to members of 'organized groups'. In her monograph on theft of state and socialist property, published late in 1948 after the edicts had faded from political prominence, Vyshinskaia spelled out some criteria for 'advance organization'. To determine that a group had 'organized in advance to commit a theft', one had to establish that the group's members had agreed in advance 'about the composition of the group, about the object of the theft, and about the means of the theft; and also to establish the presence of some preliminary criminal activity executing the gang's idea which would unite the group for the commission of the crime, etc.'[76] No one paid much attention to Vyshinskaia's long list of criteria for advance organization. In fact, it seemed that many judges were not even observing the USSR Supreme Court's authoritative definition of 1948, for the Court found it necessary to remind judges in 1952, that 'not every theft committed by two or more persons could be considered as a theft committed by an organized group (gang) . . .' and that to qualify for this category, 'the theft must be committed after some preliminary agreement among the members of the group organized for this purpose.'[77]

Overall, the attempts by Soviet jurists, scholars and practitioners alike to mitigate the effects of the edicts of 4 June 1947, must be accounted a failure. Judges who had 'erred' on the side of lenient interpretations in the first months of the edicts' operation, soon corrected their ways. The scholars who sought to revive parole as an antidote to the long sentences failed. And those scholars who tried to interpret the new laws in a lenient vein were either criticized (Durmanov) or ignored (Vyshinskaia).

Our two examples of criminal law scholars' participation in Soviet criminal policy-making under Stalin show that even during the 1930s and 1940s scholars could participate meaningfully in the political process in the USSR. Some of the criminal law scholars' participation (e.g. the interpretation of the theft laws) represented an attempt to affect policies in the course of their implementation; this was the kind of indirect participation which Merle Fainsod associated with Stalinist policy-making.[78] But much of criminal scholars' participation in criminal policy-making was of a different kind. In attempting to secure the removal of analogy and to get parole reintroduced the scholars were personally involved in the initiation and discussion of substantive policy questions; in so doing, they used a variety of forms of communication, both private and public, including the composition of draft legislation and reports; appearances at conferences, articles in law journals, and service on revision commissions; and they succeeded in convincing leading judicial officials of the wisdom of their arguments. Overall, Soviet criminal law scholars' participation was of good quality during the Stalin years, even though it was limited in scope. The ultimate failure of the scholars to achieve the policies which they sought in the course of their participation was due to factors outside of their control, among them the chance outbreak of World War II just as the 1938 draft criminal code was ready for promulgation.

The discovery that criminal law scholars engaged in serious participation in criminal policy-making during the Stalin years has implications for Western analysis of Stalinist politics. First, it suggests that some modification was needed in the conventional image of a narrow and restricted political process under Stalin. Opportunities to communicate with political leaders during the 1930s and 1940s were limited even for some leading officials and top specialists; but Stalinist policy-making was not so narrow as to exclude direct participation by specialists in some fields at some times. Further research is needed to determine how the scope of the policy-making process varied from one policy realm to another and from time to time within any given field.[79] Secondly, the findings suggest that the Brzezinski and Huntington image of low-quality participation by persons outside the political leadership – an image purported to characterize specialist participation in general during the late 1950s – would not characterize Soviet criminal law scholars' participation in the late 1930s and the 1940s.[80] The scholars' contributions were not manipulated by the leadership to help legitimate and implement policy decisions; nor were they mainly of a technical nature. When opportunities for participation came, they were often chances to take part in the initiation and discussion of policy choices. Sometimes, scholars were in a position to try to affect a decision only during its implementation, but the function of such efforts was to modify policies in practice rather than to support or execute them. If the scholars' advice made little impact upon policy, it was not because their participation was of low quality, but for other reasons: its infrequence; the will of the dictator; and chance.

3 The Post-Stalin Expansion of Participation

During the second half of the 1950s the participation of Soviet criminal law scholars in criminal policy-making underwent a marked expansion. A larger number and a wider variety of scholars took part in policy discussions than had previously been the case. Moreover, for the first time in a generation these scholars had some impact upon decisions in criminal policy. In this chapter we shall explain how Soviet criminal law scholars' participation expanded and examine the nature and impact of their contributions. The first section outlines the development of participation from Stalin's death in 1953 to the end of the decade. The second section analyzes the nature and effects of the scholars' participation in two decisions taken in the late 1950s.

THE PATTERN OF EXPANSION

1953–6

The death of Stalin was a necessary precondition for change in the participation and influence of Soviet criminal law scholars. As long as Stalin ruled in his solitary and arbitrary way, there was no chance for frequent or regular inclusion of specialists in criminal policy-making; and as long as the security police retained its broad powers, scholars were unlikely to abandon their cautious approach to the criticism of policy and practice. Even after Stalin's death, changes in the scope of criminal law scholars' participation did not occur all at once. Between 1953 and 1955 criminal law scholars were active in the policy-making process, but their participation differed little from what it had been at certain times while Stalin was alive. Just as in 1938 and in 1946, criminal law scholars gained the opportunity for participation when a new draft USSR criminal code was prepared and discussed. As before, the drafting process enlisted Moscow scholars to serve on the drafting commission; and scholars outside the capital had chances to discuss the already completed draft. What made the scholars' participation in 1953–5 different from what it had been earlier was not its extent (which was neither more nor less than on previous occasions when codes were drafted) but rather the context in which it took place. Unlike in 1938 and in 1946, the codes on which the scholars worked in 1954 were part of a criminal justice reform which had already been initiated by the political leaders, a reform aimed at normalizing, rationalizing, and liberalizing Soviet criminal justice. This criminal justice reform was to extend throughout the decade of the 1950s; for the moment we shall be concerned with the first of its two phases, the one which went from 1953 to the end of 1955.[1]

In its first phase the post-Stalin criminal justice reform had two main components – the restoration of the functions of law enforcement agencies; and the liberalization of criminal and criminal procedure law. In 1953 Soviet political leaders decided to eliminate the Special Board and to curtail the power of the security police, thus paving the way for the strengthening of other law enforcement agencies.[2] During the next few years the USSR Supreme Court regained jurisdiction for most categories of cases previously handled administratively by the NKVD or MGB; the MVD took over from the security police the administration of the prison system; and the USSR Procuracy succeeded in reviving its role in the supervision of the administration of justice.[3] In 1953 the leaders also announced their intention to modify Soviet criminal law, in order to reduce its severity and to ensure the observance of procedural norms.[4] The changes were introduced in two ways, through a series of edicts and administrative orders issued between 1953 and 1956 and through the preparation of new USSR codes of criminal law and procedure. The edicts supplied the first steps in the liberalization of the criminal law, by removing criminal responsibility for some offenses (such as abortion), by reintroducing parole, and by reducing the penalties for petty theft and for petty hooliganism.[5] But much of the liberalization and rationalization of criminal law waited for the preparation of the new criminal code.

As far as one can tell, Soviet criminal law scholars played no role either in the fundamental decision of 1953 to reform the administration of justice in the USSR or in the series of edicts which reduced the severity of Soviet criminal law. Yet the political leaders must have been aware that in making these moves they would have the support of the legal community, scholars and officials alike. Although jurists might disagree among themselves about the proper limits of liberalization, the removal of the most harsh features of Stalinist criminal justice had wide support.[6]

Criminal law scholars' opportunity to contribute to the reform in its first phase came during the preparation and discussion of the new draft USSR Codes of Criminal Law and of Criminal Procedure. The draft USSR Code of Criminal Law (1955) continued the reform of the criminal law already started by the series of individual edicts. Its provisions included the reduction of the maximum prison term from twenty-five to fifteen years; the raising of the minimum age of criminal responsibility from twelve to fourteen; the removal from Soviet criminal law of the principle of analogy;

and the reintroduction of distinctions between grades and types of theft. As we indicated above, the pattern of scholarly participation in the preparation of the 1955 draft USSR Criminal Code was similar to that of the 1938 draft code. The preparation of the first version was the task of a group of Moscow scholars working under the supervision of the USSR Ministry of Justice. Most prominent on the team were members of the Ministry's institute, the All-Union Institute of Juridical Sciences, such as A. A. Piontkovskii, A. A. Gertsenzon, and B. S. Utevskii;[7] but scholars from the Academy of Sciences's Institute of Law were probably also included. For in the winter of 1954 the criminal law sector of that institute discussed the organization of the draft code; and two scholars from that institute published articles expressing opinions on changes which might be incorporated in the code.[8] In the summer and fall of 1954 after the first version of the draft code had been completed, the legal journals contained discussion of specific sections.[9] At the end of the year, another version of the draft USSR criminal code was circulated to law faculties and institutes outside of Moscow, to give other scholars the opportunity to comment. Shortly thereafter, a conference to discuss the draft code was convened at Leningrad University.[10]

Despite the not-insignificant role played by legal scholars in the preparation of this and other draft USSR codes, some scholars were dissatisfied with the extent of their participation.[11] Their view found forceful expression in an editorial in the leading law journal, written two months before the 20th Congress of the CPSU.[12] 'In spite of a certain degree of activization,' the editors opined, 'the participation of legal scholars in the development of Soviet legislation and in its codification is still completely insufficient and unsatisfactory.'[13] Part of the problem lay with the scholars, who, according to the editorial, did not pursue readily enough the kinds of study most useful for the improvement of legislation. But the editorial's list of the potential contributions of scholars made it clear that greater participation did not depend upon them alone. Before scholars would be willing to 'boldly reveal the mistakes' in current legislation and practice and to 'give their recommendations' for changes in the laws, they had to be convinced that politicians and high officials were ready to hear those criticisms and recommendations.[14]

Legal scholars in the USSR valued their participation in the development of legislation not only because of its tangible consequences but also because of its symbolic meaning. Many scholars believed that substantial improvement in the Soviet criminal justice system required in addition to legal reform the full transfer of the administration of criminal justice to the legal community.[15] If Soviet criminal justice were so 'normalized', its leading theoreticians, the criminal law scholars, would as a matter of course play a prominent part in the writing of a new criminal code. For this reason, the presence of substantial participation by criminal law scholars in the drafting of the new codes signified progress in the normalization of criminal justice; the absence of such participation would leave in doubt how far that process had progressed. It was not surprising, therefore, that the editors of a legal journal would seek further expansion of the scholars' role. In advocating greater contributions by criminal law scholars to codification and law reform, however, the editors could hardly have anticipated how the actions of the leader N. S. Khrushchev in the succeeding six months would encourage the expansion of specialist participation in criminal policy as well as in other policy realms.[16]

1956–9

Two political events of 1956 facilitated the expansion of criminal law scholars' participation in criminal policy-making: the de-Stalinization campaign; and the return of criminal law to republican jurisdiction.

In urging his countrymen to overcome the 'negative consequences of the cult of personality', N. S. Khrushchev called both for the restoration of 'Leninist norms' in party (and state) administration; and for the further development of 'democratic procedures' in Soviet political life.[17] Each of these tasks lent support to the idea of increased participation by specialists in the policy-making process. The 'Leninist norms' which Stalin had violated included 'collegiality' and the consultation of knowledgeable persons on policy questions. The habit of acting on his own without taking into account the views of fellow-politicians or of relevant administrators and specialists was among the clearest signs of Stalin's *hubris*. Another of Stalin's serious 'faults', according to Khrushchev, was disregarding the democratic features of Soviet politics. To strengthen 'Soviet democracy', Khrushchev called not only for the revival of local government institutions (the soviets), but also for a heightened role of the public in the formation and implementation of policy. In this case representatives of the public meant both ordinary members of society and its more interested and expert members.[18]

The implications of Khrushchev's speech for the participation of legal scholars and officials in the preparation of legislation were clear enough. But to make sure that 'Leninist norms' would be observed in the further development of the law reform, a couple of legal scholars took the trouble to remind their colleagues just how codes had been drafted in the early 1920s, while Lenin was alive.[19] Characteristic of those first Soviet codes was 'the large role played by collegiality in [their] preparation and adoption . . .' and 'the attraction to discussions of the drafts of practical workers, including local ones, from many agencies and also of members of the public; also the wide discussion of questions of codification in the specialized and sometimes in the general press.' This 'Leninist' pattern of codification, one author concluded, 'is useful to remember and to use creatively in carrying out the current codification work.'[20]

The observance of 'Leninist norms' in the codification of Soviet law might have had little meaning for the participation of *criminal* law scholars, because new USSR criminal and criminal procedure codes had already been drafted, discussed and readied for promulgation before Khrushchev spoke. Although new codes in other areas of law had yet to be prepared, the codes in the criminal area were already completed. In the summer of 1956 N. S. Khrushchev changed the situation, when he decided to return the criminal law to republican jurisdiction.[21] By returning criminal law to the republics (another 'Leninist' practice), Khrushchev provided a vehicle for reopening criminal law reform; for now the draft USSR criminal code had to be set aside and replaced with new draft legislation – a set of Fundamental Principles of Criminal Legislation of the USSR and Union Republics; and separate republican criminal codes.[22] It might have been possible to produce the required new statutes simply by dividing and editing the already prepared draft USSR criminal code. But after Khrushchev's revelations of the effects that the terror had wreaked upon the legal system and his promise of the full restoration of 'socialist legality', jurists were ready to consider changes in criminal and criminal procedure law which had not been incorporated into the 1955 draft USSR criminal code.

By encouraging more participation in policy-making and by reopening the criminal law reform, Khrushchev faciliated the expansion of criminal law scholars' participation. Yet this expansion would not have occurred without the cooperation of the scholars themselves. Even before the 20th Party Congress some criminal law scholars had indicated their desire for a wider role. Only in the relaxed political atmosphere which followed that Congress did many jurists gain the self-confidence needed to offer their criticisms of policy and to seek more opportunities to express them. The unmasking of Stalin's 'cult of personality' helped to remove obstacles to change both within legal scholarship and in legal scholars' public-related activity. During 1956 and 1957 those legal scholars who were trying to revive discarded kinds of research made great strides;[23] and scholars who wished to contribute more to criminal policy found that the new atmosphere allowed them to speak out more candidly and more publically than before. The scholars' new self-confidence contributed to the expansion of their participation in criminal policy-making during the second stage of the post-Stalin criminal law reform.

In the second stage of the post-Stalin criminal law reform Soviet criminal law scholars took part in preparing four pieces of new legislation – the Fundamental Principles of Criminal Legislation of the USSR and Union Republics, the RSFSR Criminal Code, the Fundamental Principles of Criminal Procedure of the USSR and Union Republics, and the RSFSR Criminal Procedure Code. The two sets of fundamental principles were compiled first and passed by the Supreme Soviet in December 1958; the criminal codes were completed only in 1959 and became law early in 1969. Here we shall trace the expansion of criminal law scholars' participation through the stages of the preparation of one of these pieces of legislation, the Fundamental Principles of Criminal Legislation.

The first version of the draft Fundamental Principles of Criminal Legislation was written by a commission established in the fall of 1956 under the auspices of the Juridical Commission of the USSR Council of Ministers,[24] which had come to perform some of the functions of the recently abolished USSR Ministry of Justice.[25] This drafting commission, headed by Professor B. S. Nikiforov of the All-Union Institute of Juridical Science, was composed of scholars from a variety of Moscow institutes and faculties. Whereas the 1955 draft USSR Criminal Code had been prepared by a relatively small commission of scholars who came mainly from one institute, the commission which drafted the Fundamental Principles was larger and more representative of the Moscow community of criminal law scholars. Members were chosen not because they worked at one institute charged with preparing the legislation, but because of their competence in a particular area of the law. Thus, a leading penologist Professor B. S. Utevskii, at that time head of the kafedra of corrective-labor law at the MVD Higher School, was recruited to the commission to prepare the section of the Fundamental Principles of Criminal Legislation which related to punishment.[26] The selection of the commission's membership was reportedly made at a meeting between the commission's head and Central Committee staff.[27]

The participation of Moscow criminal law scholars in writing the first version of the Fundamental Principles of Criminal Legislation was broader than it had been in the writing of the first version of the draft USSR Criminal Code of 1955. Not only did a greater number of scholars serve as members of the drafting commission, but more of them had opportunities to discuss sections of the draft legislation while it was still being composed. It was common practice for members of the commissions to consult colleagues at their places of work about the sections of the draft legislation for which they were responsible. With members of the commission hailing from a variety of Moscow institutions, a range of scholars were in a position to offer opinions about the content of the legislation. For example, when B. S. Utevskii prepared the first version of the punishment section of the Fundamental Principles of Criminal Legislation, he discussed it with his colleagues in the corrective-labor law kafedra of the MVD Higher School before submitting it to the drafting commission for its scrutiny.[28] Another way in which Moscow scholars and also some from outside the capital gained an opportunity to contribute to the new legislation at this early stage was through attendance at one of a series of conferences which were held during the period of the compilation of the first version of the Fundamental Principles of Criminal Legislation and which devoted some time to discussing plans for this legislation.[29] Although the draft USSR

Criminal Code had been the subject of one conference, that conference had been convened at a later stage in the drafting process, after the first version of the draft legislation had been completed, discussed, and revised.

Normally, the second stage of legislative drafting, that of discussion and revision of an already completed version, attracted broader participation on the part of legal scholars in the USSR than did the initial drafting stage. This was the pattern with the draft USSR Criminal Codes of 1938, 1946, and 1954; in each of these instances the discussion stage provided opportunities for comments from scholars outside the capital city as well as from law enforcement officials. It was clear that these jurists would also get their chance to comment upon the draft Fundamental Principles of Criminal Legislation during the discussion stage; but some of them believed that the discussion of this legislation and of its companion, the Fundamental Principles of Criminal Procedure, ought to be broader and more open than the discussions of earlier draft legislation. Encouraged by the new political atmosphere and the legitimacy of 'democratic' procedures, the legal journal *Sotsialisticheskaia zakonnost* lent its support to this view. The editors decided to advocate open discussion of the new legislation, after an incident at a conference in the spring of 1957.[30] One of the topics of discussion there had been the content of the companion draft law, the Fundamental Principles of Criminal Procedure, which was being prepared at about the same time as the Fundamental Principles of Criminal Legislation. The official supervising the drafting of this legislation, the Deputy Chairman of the Juridical Commission of the USSR Council of Ministers, V. N. Sukhdorev, made an appearance at the meeting, but offended the conference participants with his reluctance to discuss the content of the draft law as it then stood. Although they asked him a number of questions about the new draft and about his own views regarding it, Sukhodrev's answers were evasive. Noting the bitter feelings among the conference participants, the journal editors berated Sukhodrev and faulted the Juridical Commission itself for failing to include a broader range of scholars and practitioners in the initial preparation of the draft Fundamental Principles of Criminal Procedure. The editors charged that the Commission 'had carried out its work virtually cut off from the community of legal scholars and the army of practical workers.'[31]

It seemed that the draft Fundamental Principles of Criminal Procedure had been prepared in a more elitist and closed manner than was the draft Fundamental Principles of Criminal Legislation. For, as we have seen, the Moscow legal scholars had been deeply involved in the latter task. Nevertheless, most of their work had taken place behind the scenes, so that the bulk of practitioners and of scholars outside the capital had little knowledge of it. Up to the spring of 1957 the legal journals had published only a handful of articles relating to the draft legislation; and the popular press was only beginning to publish material on criminal policy. Therefore the editors' call for a 'business-like, comprehensive, and objective' exchange of opinion 'to be organized without the commotion of a parade', was applicable also to the Fundamental Principles of Criminal Legislation.[32]

After this incident the Juridical Commission made sure that both the draft Fundamental Principles of Criminal Legislation and the draft Fundamental Principles of Criminal Procedure were widely circulated for discussion. At first, the discussion of the draft legislation took place behind the scenes. In the summer of 1957 law faculties and institutes around the country, and also law enforcement agencies in the republics, received copies of the draft laws. After studying them, jurists at these institutions sent a large number of memoranda and letters back to the Juridical Commission. Those letters which related to the Fundamental Principles of Criminal Legislation were collected and studied by the commission which had drafted that legislation.[33] Before completing its work that commission composed a list of the changes which it recommended and sent the original draft and the proposed revisions to the Praesidium of the Supreme Soviet for consideration by the party leadership. With party approval the draft law and accompanying materials were transferred to the Commissions on Legislative Suggestions of the Supreme Soviet for further consideration.[34] As was customary, the Commissions on Legislative Suggestions appointed a subcommission of scholars and officials to edit the legislative drafts;[35] in this case, the commissions were also authorized to take the additional and unusual step of publishing the draft Fundamental Principles of Criminal Legislation (and also the draft Fundamental Principles of Criminal Procedure). The appearance in June 1958 of the draft legislation, both in the legal journals and in the journal of the local soviets, opened a second phase of discussion, this one in full public view.[36]

In the five months which followed, each issue of the legal journals carried special sections containing articles, notes and letters about the draft legislation; more than fifty criminal law scholars from all over the USSR took part in this 'public discussion'.[37] In authorizing the publication of the draft legislation and encouraging the public discussion, the political leadership sought to demonstrate the 'democratic' way in which this important legislation was being prepared.[38] Despite the fact that it was 'staged', the discussion represented a genuine exchange of opinion, as scholars responded seriously to the invitation to express their views publicly. For many of them, the public discussion provided the chance to reiterate points which they had already made in private communications to the drafting commission; for some, the public discussion provided a first chance to offer comment. Because the public discussion continued into December 1958, the month of the actual promulgation of the Fundamental Principles of Criminal Legislation, some of the contributions appeared in print too late to affect the outcome. But most of their authors followed the editors' instructions to send their comments directly to the Commissions on Legislative Suggestions as well as to the journal.[39] At the same time the journals' editors passed to the subcommission some of the correspondence received by them. Most of the suggestions made in the public discussion were available for consideration by the editorial subcommission in prepublished form.[40]

In summary, at each stage in the preparation of the Fundamental Principles of Criminal Legislation criminal law scholars' participation was broader than it had been during the preparation of the draft USSR Criminal Code of 1955. When the Fundamental Principles were drafted a larger and more diverse group of Moscow scholars played direct and indirect roles. In the discussion of the already completed draft a greater number of scholars from more parts of the country were able to offer comments. Moreover, as we have just seen, part of this broad discussion took place in public on the pages of the law journals. A public debate of this scope was a novelty in Soviet criminal policy-making; the discussions of the earlier draft codes had involved only a few persons, and access to those discussions was limited because the draft legislation was not published.

THE NATURE OF PARTICIPATION

Not surprisingly, the public debates among Soviet legal scholars which preceded the promulgation of new legislation in the late 1950s caught the attention of Western observers of the Soviet scene.[41] These debates were among the first signs of the participation of legal scholars during post-Stalin period. When some of these observers tried to assess the scholars' role on the basis of these public discussions alone,[42] they were relying upon partial evidence. As we have just seen, a significant part of criminal law scholars' contributions to the Fundamental Principles of Criminal Legislation was made behind the scenes and outside of the public eye. Fortunately, we were able to gather evidence about this 'other side' of criminal law scholars' participation, and as a result could reassess its nature and impact upon Soviet criminal policy. For this purpose we examined in detail the participation of the scholars in decisions about two issues connected with the draft Fundamental Principles of Criminal Legislation: the shape of the parole system; and the development of special sanctions for recidivists.

The parole and recidivism questions related to two core problems faced by Soviet jurists when they worked out the details of the criminal law reform – what should be the limits of liberalization; and how might Soviet criminal policy be rationalized. As a traditional instrument of a liberal or lenient policy, parole provoked disagreement among jurists of different philosophical persuasions. And whether the new leniency which already characterized Soviet criminal law should extend to dangerous and habitual criminals also divided the legal community. Philosophical considerations aside, the opportunity to reconstruct the parole system and to develop a special way for handling recidivist offenders offered a challenge to those jurists who sought a more rational penal system, and especially to the scholars who were reviving corrective-labor law and penology. In the penologists' view policies toward parole and recidivism had ought to be based upon the evidence as to what kind of parole system was more effective in reducing criminality and what kind of treatment for recidivists would best protect society and prevent future crimes.

PAROLE

As re-established in Soviet law in 1954, parole (or 'conditional early release') could be awarded to any adult prisoner for good behavior after the completion of two-thirds of the court sentence.[43] In practice, however, parole was used less often than another kind of early release, the so-called system of 'early release through labor-day counts', which had been established by administrative decree in 1953. According to this scheme a prisoner's successful performance of one full day's work in a labor camp gave him two days' credit toward his court sentence; and in some camps exceeding the norm by a certain amount merited three days' credit. Corrective-labor officials preferred early release through labor-day counts over parole, because it was easier to administer (there was no need for a court appearance) and because it seemed to encourage prisoners to do the hard work necessary for meeting the camps' production quotas. Needless to say, the labor-day system also had beneficial consequences for many prisoners, by facilitating their release after one half (or even less) of their term rather than after two-thirds as stipulated in the parole law.[44]

For the authorities the benefits of early release through labor-day counts were to some extent illusory because the system was much abused. According to penologists who conducted observations in two corrective-labor colonies in 1956, cheating, faking of documents, and concealment of defective goods were common practices. Often, some prisoners, especially experienced recidivists, would force other inmates to fulfil their work norms for them; and there were cases where a brigade of inmates would 'divide' the group's accomplishments at the end of the working day, so that at least some of its members would get credit for two or three days of their sentences. It was observed that wherever a maximum norm was set to provide prisoners with three days' credit toward their sentence, that norm was never exceeded but always fulfilled exactly. Moreover, it was established that as a rule recidivists were released earlier than first offenders![45]

These two different schemes for the early release of prisoners – parole and early release through labor-day counts – had operated side by side for three years, when in early 1957 the commission met to prepare the Fundamental Principles of Criminal Legislation. Despite opposition from corrective-labor officials, more than a few commission members, including the author of the section on parole Professor B. S. Utevskii, believed that it was time to eliminate early release through labor-day counts.

According to Utevskii, if the purpose of early release was really to encourage the rehabilitation of the offender rather than the economic performance of the labor colony, then early release through labor-day counts had to be rejected in favor of parole. With parole, Utevskii pointed out, judges would replace corrective-labor officials in deciding who would be released early; and it was at least possible that a judge would make objective decisions about early release, on the basis of each offender's criminal record and of the evidence that he had 'demonstrated his correction'. In Utevskii's opinion, the labor-day counts ought not even to be retained as a criterion for the judges' use in reaching their decisions, for the abuses in practice had shown the counts to be a poor indicator of rehabilitation.[46]

Besides dealing with the problems posed by the coexistence of two forms of early release, the commission reviewed the question of parole eligibility. Following the liberal position articulated by Utevskii, the commission decided to propose in its draft legislation that parole eligibility start after one half of the sentence for ordinary offenders, while remaining at two-thirds of the term for those guilty of more serious crimes.[47] To ensure that the labor-day counts really were discarded, the draft legislation stipulated that parole eligibility would begin only after the 'actual serving of one half [two-thirds] of the sentence'. Among those eligible for parole its award was not to be made automatically, but only when the offender had 'demonstrated his correction'.[48]

As drafted by Utevskii, the article on parole became part of the first version of the draft Fundamental Principles of Criminal Legislation, which criminal law scholars and officials discussed first behind the scenes and then in public forums during 1957 and 1958. In the course of discussion scholars made numerous suggestions for improvements in the parole provisions, some of which were reflected in the final version of the article, as it appeared in the actual Fundamental Principles of Criminal Legislation promulgated in 1958. According to members of the drafting and editorial commissions for the Fundamental Principles of Criminal Legislation, the changes which were made in the parole article stemmed directly from suggestions on the part of criminal law scholars.[49]

In discussing the proposed legislation during 1957 and 1958, Soviet criminal law scholars focused upon two questions: which offenders should become eligible for parole and what features should the parole system have. Some penologists (Liubavin, Remeson, Efimov) disagreed with Utevskii about lowering the term of parole eligibility to one half of the sentence for many offenders, arguing that the minimum term of two-thirds should be retained for all inmates. These scholars reasoned that because the criminal law reform had shortened the judicial sentences for many crimes, the offenders' rehabilitation required that they serve a minimum of two-thirds of their sentences.[50] Another controversial question relating to parole eligibility was whether recidivists should receive parole at all. Some scholars favored the elimination of parole privileges for certain categories of recidivists; whereas other scholars did not.[51] In addition, there was considerable support among the commentators for the extension of parole to offenders sentenced to corrective work, a non-custodial sanction which combined supervision with attachment of earnings. Efimov, Noi, Krakh-malnik, and even Utevskii himself came to regard as inconsistent the situation whereby an offender sent to a corrective-labor colony for one year could be released after six months, and an offender awarded the less serious penalty of one year's corrective work would have to complete the whole year's sentence.[52]

Among the features of the parole system outlined in the draft legislation which drew comments from the criminal law scholars were the status of labor-day counts and the conditions of parole. Although some scholars supported Utevskii's renunciation of labor-day counts, others were willing to have that practice continued in modified form as one criterion for court judgments about parole. The question of adding conditions to release on parole was raised repeatedly by a student of parole, the young scholar M. A. Efimov. In his various publications Efimov stressed the desirability of requiring parolees who committed new offenses during the unexpired portion of their terms to complete the original sentence in a corrective-labor institution.[53]

As promulgated in December 1958 the Fundamental Principles of Criminal Legislation reflected individual scholars' suggestions about parole in the following ways. The new law extended parole eligibility to offenders sentenced to corrective work; it added the condition that parolees who committed new crimes of the same order of seriousness as their original offenses would be returned to confinement to complete their original terms; and the new law excluded from parole privileges one category of recidivists, 'specially dangerous' ones.[54] The main alternative to parole, early release on the basis of labor day counts, was abolished in late 1958 when the Council of Ministers approved a new Statute on Corrective-Labour Colonites and Prisons of the MVD.[55] However, corrective-labor officials continued to reckon the counts for use in deciding which of the prisoners eligible for parole had 'demonstrated his correction'. Only in early 1960 did the RSFSR Ministry for the Defense of the Social Order reportedly eliminate the labor-day counts entirely.[56]

As we shall see in Chapter 7, the parole system introduced in December 1958 would not last indefinitely. In the mid-1960s challenges to it would be brought both by citizens and politicians wary of undue leniency and by scholars and officials seeking to further rationalize parole practice; and changes in parole regulations would come frequently during the 1960s. Nevertheless, these subsequent developments did not alter the fact that the parole system which went into effect in the USSR in 1959 was the product of the combined efforts of a number of Soviet criminal law scholars.

RECIDIVISTS

The idea of a special punishment for recidivists developed partly as a reaction to the criminal law reform. Not a few jurists came to the conclusion that the leniency characteristic of the reform as a whole should not benefit the serious repeat offenders. There were also some scholars and officials who believed that a special response to recidivists was part of a rational penal policy.

The initial impetus for legislation to deal with recidivists seems to have come from officials in the Ministry of Internal Affairs (MVD). But it was criminal law scholars working in that Ministry and elsewhere who did the analysis necessary to arrive at coherent proposals. Within the MVD's research section a group of scholars, including E. G. Shirvindt, I. M. Shmarov, and A. M. Iakovlev, studied more than one thousand recidivist offenders, reviewing their records and in some cases interviewing them as well.[57] The study showed that recidivists were of many types, some far more dangerous than others; on this basis the authors concluded that no single response to all recidivists was appropriate. In order to develop a differentiated approach to recidivists, the scholars proceded to construct a typology of repeat offenders, for whom different sentences and different penal institutions might be used.[58]

Outside the MVD other scholars also began to think about recidivism during 1956 and 1957. The most influential of them was B. S. Nikiforov, who as chairman of the commission which was drafting the Fundamental Principles of Criminal Legislation could introduce his proposals with ease. Like the scholars working within the MVD Nikiforov tried to categorize recidivists, but he distinguished them solely on the basis of legal criteria, rather than using psychological and sociological ones too as had the MVD group. To begin with, Nikiforov distinguished the special from the general recidivist; only persons who had committed the same offense twice, the special recidivists, deserved extra punishment, in Nikiforov's view. And of those special recidivists Nikiforov was ready to exclude from extra penalties those whose crimes were accidental or unintentional. Those offenders who deserved extra punishment constituted, in Nikiforov's words, 'only a relatively narrow group', that is 'those persons who during or after serving punishment for a crime violating or disturbing the social order . . . committed a crime of the same sort.' Persons who fell into this category Nikiforov dubbed as 'specially dangerous recidivists' and recommended that they be made eligible for an extended term of confinement, to consist of no more than half of the maximum term stipulated for the offense involved.[59]

Besides Nikiforov other scholars also suggested special punishments for recidivists. Concerned that recidivists be separated from other offenders, A. S. Shliapochnikov argued that recidivists should be removed from corrective-labor colonies and placed in prisons. Shliapochnikov also supported giving longer punishments to recidivist offenders, by treating recidivism as an aggravating circumstance. However, Shliapochnikov contended that the recidivist ought to retain his parole rights as an incentive for rehabilitation.[60] N. S. Struchkov disagreed and advocated that parole rights be denied to 'specially dangerous recidivists'.[61]

Nikiforov and his colleagues began to make suggestions about special penalties for recidivists only after the first version of the draft Fundamental Principles of Criminal Legislation had been completed (spring 1957). By the fall of 1958 when the final version of this legislation was completed it had been decided to introduce the concept of 'specially dangerous recidivist' into Soviet law and to specify sanctions for these offenders. As promulgated, the Fundamental Principles of Criminal Legislation made 'specially dangerous recidivists' liable to an extended term of imprisonment (up to fifteen years regardless of the maximum prescribed by law for the particular offense); made them subject to confinement in a prison regime; and deprived them of their parole privileges – all three of which sanctions had been suggested by one or another criminal law scholar.[62] Nevertheless, the Fundamental Principles of Criminal Legislation failed to define the criteria of eligibility for the stigma of 'specially dangerous recidivist', leaving their definition for inclusion in the republican criminal codes. The omission was due not to any subtlety in Soviet constitutional law but simply to the shortage of time available before the final version of the Fundamental Principles of Criminal Legislation was due for legislative consideration. Saving the definition of the criteria of eligibility for the republican codes did not interrupt the work of the scholars who were elaborating them; for B. S. Nikiforov himself was assigned by the chairmen of the commission drafting the RSFSR criminal code to prepare that code's article on specially dangerous recidivists.[63]

In writing the article on specially dangerous recidivists for the draft RSFSR Criminal Code, B. S. Nikiforov spelled out a more complex scheme than the one he had suggested two years earlier. The new scheme distinguished three categories of criminal offenses: those for which two occurrences in any order would qualify for the stigma; those for which three occurrences in any order would suffice; and those remaining offenses which would not count in the reckoning. For the first two of these categories Nikiforov provided detailed lists. In some ways, the new scheme was more lenient than the one which Nikiforov had originally suggested; for example, two common offenses, theft and malicious hooliganism, now required three occurrences, whereas before only two would have been enough. On the other hand, the list of offenses for which three occurrences qualified for the stigma included some offenses which Nikiforov had not even mentioned in his earlier scheme, such as speculation and swindling.[64] Taken as a whole, the changes in the scheme for selecting 'specially dangerous recidivists' were in the direction of more differentiation, and as such reflected the suggestions of Nikiforov's colleagues, most particularly of A. M. Iakovlev of the USSR Procuracy's Police Science Institute, who among the original MVD research group had continued to work on the question of recidivism.[65] Not only had Iakovlev pressed for a more differentiated scheme, but he had explicitly recommended that for such crimes as theft and malicious hooliganism three or four occurrences ought to be required before an offender became eligible for designation as a 'specially dangerous recidivist'.[66]

Even so, Iakovlev was not fully satisfied with the draft article prepared by Nikiforov for the RSFSR Criminal Code. As Iakovlev explained in a memorandum to the drafting commission and in an article, he favored moving at least three more offenses from the first category (requiring two occurrences) to the second one (requiring three occurrences) – ordinary (as opposed to aggravated) intentional murder; assault with intent to rob; and intentional infliction of bodily harm.[67] Although Iakovlev's latest suggestions were not adopted in the final version of the Code, a further change was made which met with his approval. In the RSFSR Criminal Code the second category of offenses actually required four occurrences rather than three, thus making the distinction between more and less serious offenses more striking. Moreover, to round off the scheme, an offender also qualified for the stigma when he committed one crime from the first group and two from the second.[68] Individual scholars may not have been satisfied with every detail of the recidivism regulations as adopted, but the regulations did represent a more subtle and differentiated scheme than had been originally proposed; and the law reflected the efforts of a number of scholars to distinguish dangerous recidivists from ordinary repeat offenders.

Criminal law scholars' contributions to the new Soviet legislation about recidivism in the late 1950s were significant ones. Both the original idea of distinguishing among recidivists in determining eligibility for extra punishment and the choice of criteria adopted for this purpose resulted in large part from the suggestions of criminal law scholars. Even the sanctions chosen for application to 'specially dangerous recidivists' reflected the opinions of some scholars. It was not the fault of Nikiforov, Iakovlev, or their colleagues that unlike the RSFSR some of the other union republics failed to adopt their carefully elaborated scheme for identifying and processing 'specially dangerous recidivists'. Some republics selected different criteria of eligibility for the legal stigma; while others did not even include the new institution in their codes.[69] This failure by republican officials and politicians to adopt a standard version complicated the use of the stigma in practice; and provided grounds for a later reconsideration of just which offenders deserved to be designated 'specially dangerous recidivists'.

Having examined two examples of criminal law scholars' participation in criminal policy-making in the late 1950s, we can now inquire what these examples tell us about the nature of the scholars' participation in that period. First of all, the parole and recidivism stories illustrated two general characteristics of the expanded participation – the greater diversity of scholars involved; and specialization among those who rendered policy advice. The diversity of background was expressed in the age and geographical location of the participants. Many were young men; for example, M. A. Efimov and A. M. Iakovlev were in their early thirties. Many of the scholars came from outside the capital city; the contributors to the parole discussion included M. A. Efimov (first from Leningrad then from Elabuga), A. L. Remenson and A. Liubavin from Tomsk, I. S. Noi and L. G. Krakhmalnik from Saratov, as well as the Muscovite B. S. Utevskii. Whereas the scholars involved in the 1947 and 1954 draft criminal codes had usually commented on a variety of issues raised by the intended legislation, the participants in the late 1950s tended to offer advice only on those particular issues for which they had special expertise. As a result of this specialization, a typical issue would be debated by a discrete set of scholars, varying in number from two or three to five or six. For example, the parole discussion included such specialists on parole as Efimov, Remenson and Liubavin; as well as the penologists Utevskii and Noi; and the recidivism discussion was dominated by two men, A. M. Iakovlev and B. S. Nikiforov. Soviet criminal law scholars accepted as natural this specialization of policy contribution. Members of the drafting and editorial commissions for the Fundamental Principles of Criminal Legislation claimed to have paid close attention to the arguments of those colleagues most versed in particular subjects and to have followed their advice, as long as it withstood the tests of logic and scrutiny.[70]

Secondly, the participation of Soviet criminal law scholars in the parole and recidivism decisions of the late 1950s was of good quality. As we saw, the scholars' contribution to those decisions focused upon the substance, not the form, of the new regulations. A scholar B. S. Utevskii wrote the first draft of the new parole law, and subsequent changes in that draft resulted mainly from suggestions made by his colleagues. The criteria of eligibility for the stigma of 'specially dangerous recidivist' emerged through the exchange of ideas among such scholars as B. S. Nikiforov and A. M. Iakovlev. Likewise, the timing of criminal law scholars' participation in the decisions on parole and recidivism provided no obstacle to influencing their content. The scholars did not enter the policy-making process after politicians had made the basic decisions, but were involved from the start. In each case the scholars took part in the various stages of decision-making, from initiation of ideas for change through the final review of the options.

Nor did the criminal law scholars' participation serve mainly the functions of publicizing or legitimizing legislative changes rather than those of communicating ideas or advocating policy proposals. The bulk of the scholars' participation took place behind the scenes where it could hardly serve to advertise the 'democratic nature' of the Soviet policy-making process. Even the public discussions of the Fundamental Principles of Criminal Legislation, which did serve such a publicity function, were not arranged merely for this purpose. Suggestions made during those discussions affected the final versions of both the parole and the recidivism provisions.

It also appeared that the scholars who took part in the parole and recidivism decisions influenced their results. A number of features of the parole article in the 1958 Fundamental Principles of Criminal Legislation were based upon scholars' recommendations: the rejection of labor-day counting, the extension of parole to persons sentenced to corrective work, and the revocation of parole for persons who committed new offenses. Likewise, the complex scheme for distinguishing the dangerous recidivist from the ordinary repeat offender was a product of scholars' efforts.

We have seen that the participation of Soviet criminal law scholars in the parole and recidivism decisions in the late 1950s was of wide scope, and of good quality, and probably influential as well. In assessing the quality of these scholars' *overall* participation in criminal policy-making during these years, one must determine whether their part in these two decisions typified their role in other ones. Did Soviet criminal law scholars participate in a similar way in other decisions taken in connection with the preparation of the Fundamental Principles of Criminal Legislation and of the RSFSR Criminal Code? According to a number of Soviet scholars questioned by this author, the kind of contribution made by scholars to the parole and recidivism decisions was typical of their role in the preparation and discussion of those sections of the new legislation which required policy decisions. Whenever substantive policy issues were raised, either by criminal law scholars themselves or by others, scholars contributed to their discussion and resolution.[71] It seemed safe to conclude that in the late 1950s the *quality* of criminal law scholars' participation was good. This did not mean, however, that one could make broad conclusions as well about the scholars' influence on policy. Without detailed analysis of many examples of criminal law scholars' participation, it would be misleading to generalize about their influence. For the influence of specialists, as we shall see, seemed to depend not only upon the quality of participation, but also upon other factors such as the political context and the receptivity of politicians to their proposals.[72]

Previous studies of specialist participation in Soviet policy-making would not have led one to anticipate these conclusions about the nature of Soviet criminal law scholars' participation in Soviet criminal policy-making in the late 1950s. In their overview of Soviet policy-making

Brzezinski and Huntington reached negative conclusions about the scope, quality, and impact of specialist participation in the late 1950s, including that of legal scholars. In reaching these conclusions Brzezinski and Huntington did not refer explicitly to criminal policy; they cited as examples of 'participation from below' the pension law of 1956, the industrial reorganization of 1957, the educational reform of 1958, and the abolition of the MTS also in 1958. The writers did suggest, however, that these examples were typical of specialist involvement in Soviet policy-making in this period. As in the case of the criminal law reform, each of the decisions mentioned by Brzezinski and Huntington featured extended public discussions; and in each case the authors assumed that the public discussion represented the bulk of specialists' contributions to the decision. On this basis they concluded that the participation had come too late in the decision-making process to really affect the outcome and that its main function was to publicize and legitimate the decision.[73] Donald Barry's study of the role of civil law scholars in the preparation of parts of the new civil legislation of the late 1950s did not reach such a negative appraisal of the scholars' role. But in the absence of evidence about the scholars' behind-the-scenes activity, Barry (and later Barry and Berman) offered only a tentative appraisal of the scholars' participation. Although he believed that the civil law scholars had made some substantive contributions to the new legislation, he was unable to say whether this was a regular pattern.[74] The evidence from our study suggests that the participation of Soviet criminal law scholars was of as good quality as Barry (and Berman) had suspected but could not confirm; and that the scholars' role was much more substantial than Brzezinski and Huntington's generalizations would have led one to believe.

4 The Institutionalization of Participation

The expanded participation of Soviet criminal law scholars in criminal policy-making in the USSR of the late 1950s was associated with two conditions which were no longer present in the 1960s: a connection with the preparation of new codes or their equivalent; the presence of a major law reform. By 1961 the two sets of fundamental principles and the republican criminal codes had been promulgated and the criminal law reform was over; and criminal policy-making in the USSR returned to its usual pattern of small and incremental change. The question was whether under these new circumstances scholars would continue to play a prominent part in policy development.

In the 1960s the participation of Soviet criminal law scholars was unlikely to have been as broad or extensive as it had been during the late 1950s. Some contraction in the numbers and diversity of scholars participating in policy discussions was inevitable, when the decisions taken were fewer in number and limited to specific topics. A slight narrowing of the number of scholars participating at any one time was insignificant compared to another change which occurred in criminal law scholars' policy-making role during the 1960s. It was during this decade that criminal law scholars' participation in the USSR entered a new stage, which marked an advance over its status in the late 1950s. For the first time the participation of criminal law scholars in the formation of criminal policy became institutionalized; that is, participation became a regular part of the work of the criminal law scholar and a normal rather than an unusual feature of criminal policy-making. By the middle and later years of the decade not just major legislation but most ordinary decisions in criminal policy which resulted in legislative changes involved the participation of scholars; and scholars had come to regard activities relating to new legislation as an everyday part of their jobs. The documentation for these developments follows in later chapters, where the participation of criminal law scholars (especially of criminologists) during the 1960s is examined and assessed.[1] The purpose of this chapter is to explain *how* and *why* criminal law scholars' participation became institutionalized.

It would be difficult to imagine the institutionalization of Soviet criminal law scholars' role in criminal policy-making in the 1960s without some of the prior political events of the 1950s which had facilitated its expansion. The restoration of the law enforcement agencies as executors of and contributors to criminal policy had improved the scholars' access to criminal policy-making. The more open atmosphere engendered by de-Stalinization had given the scholars the self-confidence needed for the expression of policy views and the initiation of policy changes. The scholars' role in criminal policy-making had gained legitimacy from the emphasis placed in the de-Stalinization campaign upon 'Leninist' norms of collegiality and public participation. But these political developments alone did not assure the full and immediate institutionalization of the scholars' role in policy-making in the 1960s.

Most immediately responsible for the institutionalization of scholarly participation were two developments relating directly to criminal law scholarship itself. One of these was the growing utility of criminal law scholarship, and the other was the strengthening of ties between the scholars and the law enforcement agencies. Criminal law scholarship became more useful for criminal policy-making because of the revival in the late 1950s and early 1960s of criminological (and also penological) research; and the ties between scholars and law enforcement officials were strengthened by the establishment in 1963 of new agency research institutes in the criminal law field. In the pages which follow we shall examine both of these developments in some detail. We shall also describe more briefly another factor which encouraged the continuation of regular participation by these scholars in the late 1960s and in the 1970s, namely a societal trend emphasizing 'rationalization' of decision-making both in policy and in administration.

THE REVIVAL OF CRIMINOLOGICAL RESEARCH

For nearly two decades, from the middle 1930s until the middle 1950s, virtually no criminological research was carried out in the USSR. Scholars studied systematically neither the state and dynamics of crime, nor the causes of crime and the criminal personality, nor the effectiveness of criminal justice and crime prevention. In the 1920s criminology had been a well-developed field of study in the USSR, as legal scholars and physicians had joined forces at a number of research centers to study a broad range of criminological questions. But a series of political events – first, the takeover of the field by radical legal scholars in 1929–31, and then, the gradual intertwining of the penal system with the terror – led in stages to the field's contraction and elimination by 1935. More than once criminal law scholars called for the revival of criminological study in the years which followed, and in 1945 they even gained the support of the leading law enforcement officials for such a development; but to no avail.[2]

Soon after Stalin's death in 1953 criminal law scholars began once again to call for the revival of criminological study, and in 1955 empirical research was started by scholars working inside the MVD.[3] But it was Khrushchev's public denunciation of Stalin and his cult of personality at the 20th Congress of the CPSU in 1956 which created the opportunity for a full-scale revival of criminology. That revival took place over the next seven years in three stages. First, in 1956–7, against a background of public affirmations of the need for crime study, senior criminologists who had survived the twenty-five-year break in Soviet criminology's history succeeded in establishing new research centers. These included a penological research sector, founded within the MVD by E. G. Shirvindt, the former director of the major criminology institute of the 1920s;[4] and a sector for the study and prevention of crime, founded by Professor A. A. Gertsenzon, who had been a leading specialist on criminal statistics since the late 1920s. Gertsenzon's sector started in the Procuracy's police science institute and in 1960 moved to the Academy of Science Institute of State and Law.[5] Secondly, between 1958 and 1962 criminologists old and new, at these centers and at others,[6] struggled to develop theory and methods for their field and to establish that new field's legitimacy. Gaining full acceptance for criminology was a large task, because not only criminology but virtually all empirical social research had been taboo under Stalin, and the other fields of social research were reviving parallel with criminology.[7] Finally, the revival of criminology was completed when in 1963 criminology gained sufficient acceptance from politicians and judicial officials to become the core discipline in a new Institute for the Study and Prevention of Crime, established under the auspices of the USSR Procuracy and the USSR Supreme Court.[8]

The reviving criminology of the post-Stalin period had two characteristics which made it especially significant for the institutionalization of the participation of criminal law scholars in criminal policy-making. These were the position of criminology within the discipline of criminal law, and the marked practical orientation of Soviet criminology.

The position of criminology within criminal aw was due largely to historical accident. In the USSR of the 1920s Soviet criminology had an interdisciplinary character; along with the criminal law scholars worked psychiatrists who studied the 'criminal personality'. But the rejection in 1929 of clinical study of criminals as ideologically unsound ('Lombrosian') removed Soviet doctors from crime study, leaving only the legal scholars to pursue statistical and sociological studies.[9] When Soviet criminological research petered out in the middle 1930s its only practitioners were criminal law scholars, and it was criminal law scholars who sought to revive criminological research, first unsuccessfully in the 1940s and then successfully in the 1950s. The result was that in the USSR criminology became a subfield of criminal law scholarship, just as it was in many European countries.[10] Sociology never became an alternative disciplinary base for Soviet criminology, because there was no separate discipline of sociology in the USSR until after criminology had revived in the post-Stalin period. The development of criminology within criminal law and the establishment of sociology as a separate discipline in the USSR were contemporaneous events.

As a part of criminal law, the revived criminology had the effect of strengthening the expertise of the criminal law scholars who had participated extensively in criminal policy-making during the reform of the criminal law in the 1950s. With criminological study taking place inside the field of criminal law, the criminal law scholars became collectively knowledgeable not only about the legal aspects of crime and punishment, but also about the social and psychological dimensions of crime; and they were now equipped with methods to evaluate statistically both judicial and penal institutions. The concentration of expertise in the criminal law scholars made these specialists all the more attractive to judicial officials and politicians seeking help with policy problems; and made the participation of criminal law scholars and criminologists in future policy-making all the more likely.

In spite of the beneficial effect which criminology might have upon criminal law study and through it upon penal practice, a number of Soviet scholars urged in the early 1960s that criminology in the USSR be separated from criminal law.[11] To B. S. Utevskii, for example, Soviet criminology was becoming too preoccupied with solving problems of the criminal justice system and too dependent upon legal concepts. If criminology were to become independent of criminal law scholarship, Utevskii argued, the criminologists would be more likely to view crime in its broadest social context and to perform significant critical analyses.[12] But Utevskii and the other proponents of an independent criminology did not win broad support among criminal law scholars or law enforcement officials; for the arguments against splitting criminology off from criminal law were more opportune. As Professor Gertsenzon put it, Soviet criminology had a mission, to help prevent crime and to improve the criminal justice system; and this mission could be best accomplished within the framework of criminal law study. In this way a broad range of scholars and practitioners could be made conversant with the facts about crime and responsive to suggestions for improved penal practice.[13]

The second characteristic of the reviving criminology which encouraged the participation of criminal law scholars and criminologists in criminal policy-making was the practical orientation of Soviet criminology. In many countries, criminology was predominantly an applied social science; but in the USSR the focus upon practical results placed Soviet criminology further than most along the spectrum from pure to applied research. Soviet criminological research usually had practical implications, and the results were almost invariably reported directly to interested government agencies. Typical themes included studies of crime and its causes in particular districts; the effectiveness of penal measures and institutions; the organization of juvenile crime prevention and of theft prevention measures in theft-prone industries; and the effects of migration upon crime. Moreover, criminologists also performed extra-research tasks. They assisted the law enforcement agencies by organizing their criminal statistics, by preparing manuals of operation, by helping to educate law enforcement personnel, and by advising agency chiefs.

The marked practical orientation of Soviet criminology was due in part to its position within the field of criminal law (which we have discussed) and in part to the interests and inclinations of the criminologists. More important, we believe, than either of these factors was the need for Soviet criminologists to secure the legitimacy of their reviving field of study. As a victim of Stalinism, criminology had every chance to benefit from the 'undoing of the cult of personality'. But the criminologists themselves realized that they had to convince the authorities that criminology would be a worthwhile and not a dangerous enterprise.[14] For there were opponents of criminology (as of empirical social research in general): some who feared its ideological implications; some who questioned its practical payoff; and others who 'were simply afraid of innovations'.[15]

During the first half-dozen years of criminology's revival (1957–63), a dialogue took place between criminologists who were seeking to demonstrate their field's utility and authorities, political and law enforcement, who were attempting to discern in what ways criminology could be most useful. The partners in the dialogue took their cues from one another. For example, the majority of the earliest criminological research studies (1957–60) focused upon the dynamics and causes of crime in individual districts; their main practical benefits were the suggestions offered by the researchers to local law enforcement officials.[16] Recognizing the utility of these 'local studies', the head of the CPSU Secretariat's Department of Administrative Organs, N. R. Mironov, wrote in 1961, 'the most important practical significance of crime study in the USSR falls within the limits of particular localities, where the results of study can be used to correctly determine the means which state and social agencies will exploit in the struggle against law violations.'[17] During the late 1950s, criminologists also undertook some studies of significance to current policy issues (recall Iakovlev's research on recidivism), but for the meantime the political leadership did not acknowledge this dimension of criminology's potential utility.

In 1962, however, a major shift occurred in the Soviet leadership's attitude toward empirical social research as a whole which affected the definition of criminology's practical role and the future of criminological research. The proponents of empirical social research outside of criminology had been fighting an up-hill battle to secure the acceptance of sociology since 1956.[18] Finally, after the 22nd Party Congress had given tentative approval to sociological study in 1961, a special meeting on the future of social science was held in 1962 at the USSR Academy of Sciences.

There, for the first time, Khrushchev's ideological deputy L. Ilichev announced that the party leadership had decided to end its ambivalent approach to empirical social research and replace it with unequivocal support for the expansion of a *practically-oriented* sociological enterprise.[19] In another speech the philosopher and party spokesman for the social sciences, P. N. Fedoseev, underscored the kind of social science the party leaders were accepting; the 'social assignment' (*sotsialnyi zakaz*) of researchers, he asserted, would be 'to produce results from which they would make practical suggestions, which would then be realized.[20] Since the realization of practical suggestions would often require political decisions, Fedoseev and Ilichev were now including in their notion of social scientists' practical role a contribution to policy formation.

Just six months after the Academy of Sciences meeting on the social sciences, the party journal *Kommunist* transmitted editorially the leadership's desire that legal research, especially of an empirical variety, also be utilized in policy-making. The journal seemed to echo Fedoseev's words, when it explained, '*It must be arranged that the conclusions and generalizations of scholars will not lie on the shelves of archives but will find the shortest route to those agencies which are occupied with law-making and with the application of legal norms*' [italics in original].[21] Just as social researchers in general were to contribute to decision-making by providing suggestions 'which would then be realized', so legal researchers were expected to make a similar contribution by dispatching their conclusions to 'organs occupied with law-making'. *Kommunist*'s editors emphasized that these contributions to 'law-making' by legal scholars needed to be regularized. The scholars' participation in the preparation of the Fundamental Principles of Criminal Legislation and the Criminal Code had been exemplary, but the infrequency of such engagements was to be deplored.[22] Moreover, *Kommunist* continued, it was especially important that those legal scholars who performed sociological research (like criminologists) participate fully in 'law-making'.

> Concrete sociological research must play an important role not only in evaluating existing legal norms but also in the process of preparing new legal acts. . . . In issuing a law, the legislator [sic] is obliged to predict its social effect, in what direction it will guide the given social process. . . . To answer these questions we are calling upon the legal research institutes and upon legal science.[23]

The acceptance of criminological research and the definition of its practical role as contributing to the development of criminal policy had obvious consequences for the participation of criminal law scholars. If criminology was being accepted and supported because of its utility and the practitioners of criminology were being urged to direct their conclusions to the 'agencies occupied with law-making and the application of legal norms', then the criminal law scholars who performed criminological research would surely be drawn into the policy-making process. They would be required at the minimum to supply written memoranda on their research which related to policy questions and they might well be asked to give oral advice and to make suggestions for policy changes as well. In fact, the reference to the participation of criminal law scholars in the making of the 1958 Fundamental Principles of Criminal Legislation suggested that it was just these kinds of activities which were being encouraged.

Soviet political leaders did not merely acknowledge their appreciation of the utility of criminological and criminal law scholarship for criminal policy-making; they also took steps to ensure that the results of research and the conclusions of the researchers would actually be utilized. The same *Kommunist* article announced a fundamental reorganization of the legal research institutes in Moscow, which produced three new institutes, each attached to one or more government agencies.[24] Just two years before, in a reform of natural science, the leaders had affirmed the principle that applied research institutes should be joined to the ministries which most benefited from their work.[25] Adopting this principle for legal science, the political leaders decided to affiliate legal research institutes with the USSR Procuracy, the USSR Supreme Court, the RSFSR Ministry for the Defense of the Social Order, and the Juridical Commission of the USSR Council of Ministers. Such affiliation, they believed, would improve the communication of research results, and also give the law enforcement agencies the opportunity to use the institutes to perform research and staff work for them.[26]

The most important of these institutes for criminology and criminal law scholarship was the All-Union Institute for the Study and Prevention of Crime. Formed in 1963 and placed under the auspices of the USSR Procuracy and the USSR Supreme Court, the 'Procuracy Institute' (as it was called) drew together most of the scholars from other research institutes who were studying criminal law and procedure, criminology, and police science. In the course of the decade which followed, the Institute almost doubled in size with the addition of new young criminologists and criminal law scholars.[27] The other two institutes which resulted from the reorganization were the All-Union Institute of Soviet Legislation, under the Juridical Commission of the USSR Council of Ministers, and the All-Union Research Institute for the Defense of the Social Order, attached to the ministry of that name.[28]

The revival of criminology which we have just described encouraged the continuation and the regularization of criminal law scholars' participation in criminal policy-making by setting off a chain of related developments. As a part of criminal law scholarship criminology enhanced the expertise of Soviet criminal law scholars, adding to their previous competence new knowledge and new skills. When criminologists used their research techniques to study a series of practical problems of criminal justice, the leadership was quick to recognize the utility of such study and to solicit its further development. While encouraging criminological study, the leaders also called for the continuation of the participation in 'law-making' which criminal law scholars had performed during the late 1950s. To achieve the development and application of criminological research and the participation of criminologists in criminal policy-making, the leaders concentrated criminological scholarship in research institutes attached to law enforcement agencies.

AN AGENCY INSTITUTE FOR CRIME STUDY

The concentration of a large part of Soviet criminal law and criminological studies in the All-Union Institute for the Study and Prevention of Crime further encouraged the institutionalization of criminal law scholars' role in criminal policy-making. The new institute was attached to the USSR Procuracy and to the USSR Supreme Court, and as a result its scholars developed a close and structured relationship with leading officials of those agencies.[29] This relationship was of no small importance, for the chiefs of the Procuracy and of the Supreme Court, along with those of MOOP, had become fully responsible for administrative decision-making in the realm of criminal policy; and they were taking an increasingly large role in the initiation of changes in criminal policy as well. In examining the relationship between criminal law scholars (criminologists) and the leading officials of the USSR Supreme Court and the USSR Procuracy we shall consider both the involvement of these officials in the work of the Institute and the scholars' involvement in the work of those law enforcement agencies. Then, we shall discuss what consequences this relationship had for criminologists' role in criminal policy-making.

The basis for involvement by Procuracy and Supreme Court chiefs in the work of the Institute was defined by the Institute's statute. These officials held three formal powers in relation to the Procuracy Institute – the power to appoint its officers and senior staff, the power to approve the composition of the Institute's Academic Council (*Uchenyi sovet*), and the power to approve the Institute's annual plans and reports.[30] Through their *nomenklatury* the Procurator-General and the Chairman of the USSR Supreme Court controlled the appointments of the Institute's director, of its two deputy directors, of the heads of ten research sectors,[31] and of all senior research workers who had previously been on the *nomenklatury* of one of those agencies.[32] These positions included all of the posts in the Institute which carried administrative responsibilities except those of heads of the Institute's party and trade-union organizations.[33] The Academic Council, whose composition the Procurator-General and Chairman of the USSR Supreme Court approved, was the highest body guiding the Institute's work. As in most academic institutions, its membership included both leading scholars and administrators from the Institute and outsiders whose own positions made them competent to judge the Institute's work. The Academic Council of the Procuracy Institute was assigned the tasks of 'discussing the Institute's plans, defining the tasks of its sectors, discussing the themes of the Institute's work and other important questions relating to its scientific work', and also of hearing defenses of *kandidat* and doctoral dissertations.[34] The annual plans and reports which the Procuracy and Supreme Court chiefs approved played a special part in the work cycle of the Procuracy Institute. Before each research year began, the Institute prepared a detailed plan of its work; and at the end of the year, the Institute prepared an annual report, describing what had been accomplished and indicating which of the planned tasks remained to be completed during the following year.[35]

The way in which the leaders of the Procuracy and the Supreme Court chose to use their powers vis-à-vis the Institute gave them strong informal ties with the Institute's staff and a direct involvement in the Institute's work. To begin with, the persons chosen for the Institute's top administrative posts came themselves from the law enforcement agencies. The Director of the Institute (1963–9), I. I. Karpets, had served in the Criminal Investigation Department of the RSFSR Ministry for the Defense of the Social Order; he did, however, have scholarly inclinations and was celebrated as the first person 'from the rank and file of the police' to have achieved a doctoral degree.[36] V. N. Kudriavtsev, the deputy director for academic affairs, was a legal scholar who prior to joining the Institute had headed a sector in the apparat of the USSR Supreme Court. Kudriavtsev became a leading scholar at the Institute and later (in 1970) its second director.[37] G. I. Kocharov, the deputy director for administration, came to the Institute from the USSR Procuracy's Department of Criminal Investigation.[38] Thus, each of the three principal law enforcement agencies supplied one of the three officers of the new Institute.

Another informal tie between the Institute and the leaders of the judicial agencies was established when representatives of the agencies joined the Institute's Academic Council. These persons included N. V. Zhogin, Deputy Procurator-General, V. M. Terebilov, Deputy Chairman of the Supreme Court, B. M. Blinov, RSFSR Procurator, and A. I. Kudriavtsev, Deputy Minister for the Defense of the Social Order of the RSFSR.[39] Participation in the work of the Institute's Academic Council brought these ministerial leaders into direct involvement with the Institute's work. During 1965 and 1966, the Council met thirty-six times, during which it approved some two dozen dissertations, discussed substantive, technical, and methodological aspects of the Institute's work, and considered in detail the Institute's plans and reports.[40]

Approval of the annual research plans of the Institute gave the heads of the USSR Procuracy and USSR Supreme Court a way to shape the direction of the Institute's work. But in practice the officials exercised little control, choosing rather to make initial suggestions and to comment at various stages in the planning process itself. The procedure for composing the Institute's annual plan illustrates a cooperative style of relations between the Institute and its sponsors.[41] Usually, in November of each year, the Institute's directorate (director, assistant directors, heads of sectors, and representatives from the Institute's social organizations, the party and the trade union) met to establish guidelines for the next year's plans. The guidelines had to take into account the Institute's immediate responsibilities to its sponsors, special tasks assigned from the outside, and any all-Institute projects to which individual sectors would contribute staff. Then, the sectors met individually to compose their own draft plans. In so doing, they began with items which remained incomplete from the previous year's plan, added to these any obligations which the guidelines suggested, and then considered other projects which sectors as a whole or their members individually desired to carry out. Then, on the basis of sector plans, the Directorate compiled a composite draft plan and passed it along for comments to interested practical organs, including the Institute's sponsors, and other research institutions. Finally, the Institute's Academic Council met to discuss the draft plan and to introduce any changes required to gain the approval of the Institute's sponsors or of the Council itself. The changes made at this last stage were usually minor ones.[42] The earlier phases had given ample opportunities for interested parties to contribute directly to the plan's development. Moreover, in anticipation of the review by the Procuracy and the Supreme Court officials, criminologists were obliged to cast their proposals within the framework of these officials' expectations.[43]

An important component of the USSR Supreme Court and USSR Procuracy's involvement in the work of the Procuracy Institute which was not mentioned in the Institute's statute was the receiving of private reports on the various research projects in progress or completed at the Institute. Upon completing a research project or a phase of a project, scholars often prepared internal reports on their findings for interested government agencies. As a rule, only after dispatching the internal reports did scholars write articles for publication, either in open or closed format.[44] Who received the reports and what form they took varied with the nature of the research. When a study related either to the work of the USSR Procuracy or the USSR Supreme Court, the researcher would send these agencies a *spravka* (note) or a *dokladnaia zapiska* (report) or a *dokladnoe pismo* (report letter). When a study related to a current policy issue, not only those agencies but also the Praesidium of the Supreme Soviet might receive one of these communications.[45] And, should a study prove relevant to government agencies other than the legal ones, they also would be informed of its results, usually by means of a *predstavlenie* (representation).[46] The main advantage of these special reports was that they facilitated rapid and direct communication of the results of research to their principal users.

But it was also possible for the authors to be more frank about the problems they discussed than they might be in openly published communications, and to cite criminal statistics which otherwise could be given only in percentage form.[47]

Just as the heads of the USSR Supreme Court and the USSR Procuracy were involved in the work of the Procuracy Institute, so the scholars from the Institute contributed regularly to the work of these agencies. The scholars' contributions to the agencies' work had two purposes: improving the operations of those agencies; and advising their chiefs about administrative decisions.

Scholars from the Procuracy Institute helped agency operations by developing and explaining to officials at various levels new and improved methods of work; and by taking part in educational programs designed 'to raise the qualifications' of law enforcement officials. Methodological aid included the preparation of manuals of operation, some of which described usual procedures of the agencies,[48] others of which instructed the officials in the analysis of criminal statistics and in the performance of simple research.[49] Another kind of methodological aid was the 'methodological letter', which informed officials about new and improved methods of work. One such letter, prepared jointly by the Procuracy Institute's juvenile delinquency sector and the USSR Procuracy's juvenile affairs department, described the exemplary experience of the Leningrad city procuracy in organizing juvenile delinquency prevention.[50] Occasionally, Institute scholars helped officials on an individual basis; for example, a team of criminologists showed a group of officials and volunteers in the city of Vladimir how to mount a local crime study.[51] Educational programs for officials included special seminars and lectures ('study measures' and 'inter-*oblast* seminars') attended by court and procuracy workers. In 1966, according to the annual report, Institute scholars gave 266 lectures and seminars, and in the process fifty-two of them travelled to sixty-seven different cities![52] Scholars also spoke to groups of officials at conferences arranged by the law enforcement agencies, which included a number of regional conferences which did not receive notice in the legal periodicals.[53] In addition, the Procuracy Institute accepted as graduate students a substantial number of 'practical workers', many of whom remained at their jobs to study part-time or by correspondence. Most of them then continued their careers as procurators and as judges after receiving their advanced training from the Institute.[54]

A second way in which scholars from the Procuracy Institute took part in the work of the USSR Procuracy and USSR Supreme Court was through advising the heads of these agencies in administrative decision-making. The main instruments for offering this advice were the USSR Supreme Court's Advisory Council (founded in 1963) and the USSR Procuracy's Methodological Council (founded in 1960), both of which consisted mainly of scholars. These councils were founded in the early

1960s as a result of the same impulse which encouraged the establishment of the Procuracy Institute – the desire among politicians and ministerial leaders to see the expertise of legal scholars brought to bear in decisions about policy and operations in the administration of justice.

The USSR Supreme Court Advisory Council's responsibilities included: (1) helping the court examine juridical questions arising from court practice, including requests for 'authoratative interpretations' (*rukovodiashchie raziasnenii*) for the application of laws by the courts and for edicts (*postanovleniia*); and (2) discussing the preparation by the Supreme Court of methodological aids and collections of legislation. The council met four times a year and was composed of the leading legal scholars from Moscow and of some members of the USSR Supreme Court and of lower courts.[55] In 1968 the criminal section of the Supreme Court Advisory Council (there was also a civil section) included thirteen scholars, seven of whom came from the Procuracy Institute.[56]

In practice, members of the Supreme Court Advisory Council had considerable opportunity to contribute to administrative decision-making. Not only were many of the Court's administrative orders (or 'sublegislation') discussed at advisory Council sessions, but sometimes criminologists were called upon to prepare suggestions for or drafts of future Court edicts.[57] Moreover, individual members of the Council were sometimes invited to attend sessions of the Supreme Court plenums and meetings of its Collegium.[58]

The work of the Methodological Council of the USSR Procuracy (established in 1960) paralleled that of the Supreme Court Advisory Council. Headed by a Deputy Procurator-General and staffed in part with scholars from the Procuracy Institute, the Methodological Council met four times a year to consider legal questions arising from the practice of procuracy offices and to discuss plans for publishing methodological aids for Procuracy officials. As members, Institute scholars took part in discussions of the Procuracy's sublegislation (*prikazy* and *ukazaniia*). Also, members of the Methodological Council were invited to attend sessions of the Collegium of the USSR Procuracy and meetings with senior Procuracy officials.[59]

The considerable involvement of Institute scholars in the work of the USSR Procuracy and the USSR Supreme Court and the equally substantial involvement of the agency chiefs in the work of the Procuracy Institute encouraged the institutionalization of criminal law scholars' role in criminal policy-making. First, through their contributions to the operations of the agencies, the scholars came to take part both in decision-making at the administrative level and in the implementation of policies. Secondly, the scholars' relationship with the leading law enforcement officials gave the former a regular line of communication with key actors in the formation of criminal policy. Whether through research reports or through private conversations, the scholars could easily pass on to the officials their suggestions regarding policy or practice, as we shall see, the scholars did so regularly. For their part the law enforcement officials could easily turn to the scholars for solutions to policy problems, when the scholars were prepared for policy work. The evidence suggests that the officials did this frequently; according to the Institute's reckoning, its scholars took part in the preparation of more than twenty different legislative projects in 1965 and the same number again in 1966.[60] Apparently, the officials did not hesitate to turn to the Institute at a moment's notice; for the scholars complained repeatedly in their annual reports about the 'supplementary assignments' which prevented them from fulfilling all of their planned ones.[61]

Let us summarize how the revival of criminological research and the placement of criminological and criminal law studies in an agency institute encouraged the institutionalization of participation by scholars in criminal policy-making. The revival of criminological research enhanced the expertise of the criminal law scholars, giving them both new and useful information about the operation of judicial and penal institutions and methods for obtaining such information and for assessing the likely effects of proposed solutions to policy problems. As a result, the criminal law scholar-criminologists had by far the best available expertise about crime and the operation of the criminal justice system. The concentration of criminological studies in an agency institute helped to establish regular ties between these scholars and the leading law enforcement officials, thus improving communications between the two parties and an awareness of each other's needs.

In addition to these changes in the nature and position of criminal law scholarship, external factors also encouraged the institutionalization of scholars' participation in criminal policy-making during the 1960s. Just as the Khrushchevian emphasis upon democratization and open policy discussion had helped the expansion of participation in the late 1960s, so in the middle and late 1960s a new political theme gave support to the institutionalization of criminal law scholars' participation. That theme was rationalization. Gradually, during the course of the 1960s, the introduction of 'rational' or 'scientific' methods or approaches into administration and policy-making gained the approval and support of officials, scholars, and politicians alike. Their combined efforts, which derived from a variety of motivations, produced the thrust of the 'movement'.

Briefly, this rationalization movement consisted of three interrelated trends – the growth in Soviet government of a scientistic ethos; the widespread effort in economy and government to rationalize administration; and the discussion by prominent philosophers and their protégés of the rationalization of the policy-making process itself. The scientistic ethos consisted of a belief in science, both the entity and the idea, as the source of progress and as a method for dealing with immediate problems. The growing importance of science and technology for military and economic development in the 1960s had prompted the Soviet leadership to raise science's status to improve its application to technological goals.[62] At the same time, the leaders also supported the use of 'scientific methods' in the management of Soviet institutions as a way of improving their efficiency. The effort to rationalize administration began with the revival of Taylorism (scientific organization of labor) in the early 1960s.[63] This led in the late 1960s to the dramatic expansion of management studies.[64] Since the rationalization both of operations and of management decisions required improved use of information and expertise, the emphasis upon rationalization gave considerable stimulus to the use of specialists in administration, including applied social scientists.[65] Rationalizing decision-making on the policy level (the 'scientific management of society') also became a subject of discussion, if not of actual practice. Leading philosophers sought to explain and improve decision-making at this high level by suggesting how a systems approach and other ways of using information and expertise could make decisions more rational.[66]

The rationalization movement and each of its components soon became visible in the late 1960s and early 1970s in the administration of the legal system. The scientistic ethos was particularly prominent in the speeches of the Minister of Internal Affairs, N. A. Shchelokov.[67] For their part, Procuracy Institute scholars soon became engaged not only in methodological aid for law enforcement agencies but also in bringing the 'scientific organization of labor' to them and in studying how scientific proposals were best implemented into procuracy work.[68] The new value attached to 'scientific decision-making' at the policy level may be illustrated by the way criminal law scholars' participation in decision-making was portrayed to the Soviet public. In 1958 when the Fundamental Principles of Criminal Legislation were first promulgated, scholarly participation was touted as an example of the 'democratic features' of the Soviet political process; but in 1969, when those same Fundamental Principles were revised, the participation by scholars was praised as giving the legislation 'a scientific basis'.[69]

The rationalization movement in Soviet society during the mid and late 1960s and the early 1970s probably encouraged the participation of specialists in a number of policy realms. The movement may even have had a major impact in facilitating participation by scholars and professionals in policy realms where such participation had not yet developed fully. In the case of criminal policy, where the role of criminal law scholars and criminologists was already substantial before the rationalization movement got under way, the effect of the movement was to encourage the continuation of that participation, and thus to reinforce the institutionalization of the scholars' role.

PART TWO

CRIMINOLOGISTS'
PARTICIPATION IN THE 1960s:
CASE STUDIES

PART TWO: INTRODUCTION

Until the middle 1960s, when Soviet criminal law scholars' participation in criminal policy-making became institutionalized, these scholars were not regular participants in the ordinary decisions through which Soviet criminal policy usually developed. In the late 1950s and before, their policy-related activities had been associated with the preparation of new codes, and in the most recent case with a major criminal law reform as well. Yet the middle and late years of the 1960s were a time when Soviet criminal policy-making was characterized by a series of individual decisions, each of which affected particular aspects of that policy. In indicating that the scholars' participation became institutionalized during these years, we suggested that they became involved with a large number of these decisions. The purpose of this part of the book is to examine their role in three sets of decisions and to provide material for assessing the scope, quality, and impact of the scholars' participation in succeeding chapters. Since by the 1960s criminological research had revived in the USSR, it was now possible for us to focus upon those criminal law scholars who were also criminologists. In the course of our discussions of participation during the 1960s we will generally refer to these scholars as 'criminologists', and reserve the term 'criminal law scholars' for references to the whole community of criminal law specialists, including those working on substantive law and procedure.

In choosing decisions for study, we had in mind two criteria. First, we sought decisions which related to the expertise of criminologists, that is decisions concerning the administration of justice or crime prevention. These were the decisions most likely to have attracted *criminologists'* participation, far more so than changes in criminal procedure[1] and most changes in the substantive criminal law.[2] Secondly, we sought decisions which had resulted in legislation rather than in administrative decrees. We reasoned that legislation was more likely to have involved public debate as well as private communication and discussion; thus the politics of legislative change would provide a fuller spectrum of the types of participation which criminologists might perform.[3] Between 1965 and 1969 there were introduced into Soviet criminal law nine different legislative changes relating to the administration of justice or crime prevention, and it appeared that criminologists played a part in all of them. This legislation centered around four subject areas—juvenile delinquency, alcoholism and crime, recidivism and parole, and the penal system.[4] Here we consider the legislation from the first three of these four areas; we excluded the fourth area (the penal system) for lack of sufficient data.[5]

The decisions which we have selected for study shared one characteristic of all criminal policy decisions of the middle and late 1960s: each of them accounted for small rather than fundamental changes in Soviet criminal policy. By itself, none of the decisions taken on juvenile delinquency, alcoholism and crime, or recidivism and parole had much effect upon the direction or course of Soviet criminal policy as a whole.[6] The decisions did differ, however, in the degree of conflict or controversy associated with them, a characteristic sometimes thought to affect specialist participation. Some Western authors suggested that the presence of disputes among decision-makers enhances the participation of specialists; while other authors argued just the reverse.[7] Our three sets of decisions represented a wide spectrum of decision-making types – some made cooperatively, in settings virtually free from political conflict, and others resulting directly from disputes.[8] This was fortunate, for it allowed us to determine how criminologists' participation varied with the degree of political conflict in the decisions; and thereby to take into account any effects which the style of decision-making may have had upon the quality and impact of criminologists' participation.

Before we proceed to the stories of these decisions, it is well to describe briefly the highlights of Soviet criminal policy in the years immediately preceding them, 1961 to early 1963. Paradoxically, these first years of the implementation of the new codes also brought with them a conservative policy trend, namely a new emphasis upon 'law and order'. Symptomatic of this temporary shift away from the liberalization of criminal policy were some increases in the severity of punishment and the circumvention of legal procedure in the prosecution of one category of offenders, the so-called social parasites.

Among the increases in the severity of punishment were the following changes: the establishment of exile as a form of supplementary punishment; and the revival of the death penalty as an optional sentence for those guilty of rape, serious economic crimes, attempts on the life of a policeman, and actions seriously disrupting corrective-labor institutions. In addition, persons guilty of some serious offenses lost their parole rights, and all parolees became subject to the revocation of parole when they committed a new crime as serious as their original one; and the commission of any crime in a corrective-labor colony became grounds for designation as a 'specially dangerous recidivist'.[9] The decisions to introduce these changes were reportedly taken by a narrow group of politicians, largely in response to recommendations from MVD officials.[10] Yet although scholars played little direct part in the decisions, they welcomed some of them. As we saw above, some scholars had urged further restrictions in the parole system a few years before, and some of them also believed that the criminal law reform had made Soviet law excessively lenient for certain categories of crime.[11]

Another example of the conservative swing in Soviet criminal policy of the early 1960s was the anti-parasitism statute of 1961. This new law empowered public bodies such as Comrades Courts to convict and punish persons who refused to work and led 'an anti-social parasitic way of life'. Not only was the law's wording vague, but it also delegated to popular justice functions which the Fundamental Principles of Criminal Procedure had reserved for the courts. On both of these grounds a draft of the statute had elicited strong criticism from legal scholars and from law enforcement officials, such as G. Z. Anashkin of the USSR Supreme Court; but as a pet project of N. S. Khrushchev the law was promulgated all the same. Subsequently the USSR Supreme Court managed to restrict the statute's application, until new 1965 legislation limited its enforcement to the courts. Nevertheless, the anti-parasite law left Soviet jurists with the bad memory of the promulgation of legislation which violated the procedural guarantees stipulated in the reform legislation and of which leading jurists had openly disapproved.[12]

As an expression of a conservative penal philosophy, a 'law and order approach' to crime control is rarely without its proponents; and from time to time this approach may dominate criminal policy-making in any country. But such periods tend to be short-lived and are usually succeeded by periods in which criminal policy represents a more balanced set of concerns. The USSR of the 1960s was no exception to this pattern; for, as we shall see, 'law and order' considerations lost their pre-eminence during the course of the decade. In the middle years some officials and politicians still presented this viewpoint in policy discussions, and one of the important decisions of the period derived partly from this kind of logic. But by the middle 1960s Soviet criminal policy came to represent an eclectic mixture of tendencies, no longer qualifying for designation either as conservative or as liberal. More characteristic of the period was the emergence of a pragmatic and flexible approach to criminal policy, which transcended the liberal/conservative dichotomy.

5 Delinquency Prevention

In the 1960s the most important institutions dealing with juvenile delinquency in the USSR were the commissions of juvenile affairs attached to city and regional soviets.[1] At the time of their establishment in 1961 the commissions were entrusted with a broad range of duties, but they did not have the resources needed to fulfil them. This case study deals with the decisions taken in 1966 to strengthen both the commissions and the network of voluntary patrons who assisted them.

The juvenile affairs commissions were the latest in a series of community institutions designed to handle difficult children and young offenders.[2] The commissions differed from their predecessors in the range of duties assigned to them. While the earlier commissions on the placement of children and adolescents had dealt only with placing young persons in homes and special schools, the juvenile affairs commissions had other major responsibilities. One of these was quasi-judicial in nature; the commissions heard and disposed of a large proportion of cases of juvenile wrongdoing, thus acting as a kind of juvenile court. After the age of criminal responsibility had been raised in 1958, some agency had been needed to adjudicate cases involving under-age offenders; the juvenile affairs commissions took over this job in 1961.[3] Besides the quasi-judicial function, the commissions also had administrative duties, including the coordination of community juvenile delinquency prevention and the supervision of state and social institutions which dealt with difficult children, such as special schools and police-operated 'children's homes'.[4]

Despite the range and importance of the juvenile affairs commissions' responsibilities, they were designed to be 'public' (*obshchestvennye*) organizations rather than governmental bodies. As such, the commissions' membership was composed entirely of volunteers, who devoted an evening or two a week to the commission after completing their regular jobs. Moreover, with the exception of a few particularly important commissions (for example in the cities of Moscow and Leningrad), juvenile affairs commissions lacked any full-time staff![5] The assignment of serious operational responsibilities to a 'public' organization without staff assistance was characteristic of N. S. Khrushchev's attempt to increase the role of the community in the maintenance of public order. Beginning in 1959, Khrushchev had encouraged the establishment of a number of 'public' institutions, including the well-known Comrades Courts and the public patrols (*druzhiny*). Like these other institutions the juvenile affairs commissions were intended to start the process of removing from governmental bodies their *raison d'être*.[6]

When the idea of the new commissions was first raised in 1958, legal scholars specializing in the juvenile field warned how lack of staff could hinder the commissions' work. The struggles of many commissions on the placement of children and adolescents to operate without staff was enough argument for V. S. Pronina and for V. G. Tadevosian.[7] 'Experience has shown', wrote Tadevosian, 'that the absence of qualified full-time staff has seriously hampered the commissions' work. This mistake must not be repeated now.' Tadevosian believed that each of the new juvenile affairs commissions needed at least three or four staff persons, including a full-time secretary and at least one inspector.[8] Tadevosian had ample opportunity to make his views heard, since he served as a member of the commission which drafted the model statute for the juvenile affairs commissions.[9] One might have expected Tadevosian's opinion to have carried considerable weight, since this scholar at the Institute of State and Law had served for many years as Head of the Juvenile Affairs Department in the USSR Procuracy; and he was also one of the initiators of the move to establish the commissions.[10] In fact, when he first supported the formation of juvenile affairs commissions in early 1958, Tadevosian had assumed that they would be well-staffed. Evidently, his image of the commissions had to be modified to accord with N. S. Khrushchev's emphasis on the public's role.

Lack of qualified staff turned out to be only one of a number of operational difficulties encountered by the commissions almost immediately after their formation. Recognizing the chaotic situation in the work of many commissions, the Praesidium of the RSFSR Supreme Soviet convened a meeting of one hundred and fifty chairmen and members of local commissions in June 1962. At this 'exchange of experience' it came out that by and large the commission chairmen were not even aware of the scope of the commissions' responsibilities.[11] Not long after this meeting a criminologist named E. V. Boldyrev undertook a detailed study of the commissions' operations, which both documented and analyzed their shortcomings.[12]

Boldyrev discovered that the commissions spent virtually all of their time performing their judicial functions. Consequently, they neglected their other tasks, such as the coordination and encouragement of juvenile crime prevention activity. Moreover, even in their judicial role, the commissions' performance had its shortcomings. Commissions rarely gathered even the basic information about the young offenders on whom they were required to pass judgment – on family background, parents' occupations and income, living conditions, and performance at school or at work. Nor did the commissions keep records of their work beyond minutes of their meetings; they did not maintain any statistics nor did they analyze their own work or the state of juvenile crime in their jurisdictions.

In general their work showed little forethought or planning.[13]

Boldyrev isolated three factors which seemed to contribute to this inadequate performance. The first was the membership of the commissions. Although members were usually drawn from party *aktiv*, often they were not qualified specialists, such as teachers, doctors, lawyers, or psychologists. Lacking training, some of the members proved to be incapable of coping with the complexity of their assignments; and some of them also shirked their responsibilities, by not attending the meetings regularly. A second factor was that even well-qualified members often did not understand their rights and duties. One reason was that the 1961 statute on the juvenile affairs commissions was short and general; and it had not been sufficiently augmented by commentaries.[14] A third problem which plagued the more active commissions was a lack of authority necessary to take initiatives – for example, in committing children for adoption, in intervening on behalf of working young in disputes at work, or in dealing with schools which expelled students. Boldyrev suggested that measures should be taken to correct each of the shortcomings which he had identified. In particular, he proposed that the statutes of the commissions on juvenile affairs be amended to clarify the nature of the commissions' obligations and to establish for the commissions the powers which they required.[15]

Boldyrev's recommendations to strengthen the juvenile affairs commissions came at a time when Soviet political leaders became particularly concerned about juvenile crime. Not without cause were they anxious; for current statistical data showed increases both in the number of offenses committed by minors and in the proportion of total crime represented by such minors' actions.[16] In late 1963 party leaders issued a secret party edict on juvenile crime prevention, which led to new efforts to mobilize and organize crime prevention resources.[17] These efforts included special delinquency prevention campaigns in Leningrad, Riga, and Vladimir;[18] and the establishment of juvenile affairs sections or groups in procuracy offices throughout the USSR down to the city and regional levels.[19] The edict also legitimated initiatives by law enforcement officials to improve other laws and institutions relating to young troublemakers.[20]

Aware of the shortcomings of the juvenile affairs commissions both from Boldyrév's account and from their own, spot checks (*proverki*), officials of the juvenile affairs departments of the RSFSR and USSR Procuracies decided to seek corrective legislation. In the summer of 1964 the USSR Procuracy made proposals to the Praesidium of the Supreme Soviet; and the Praesidium established in the fall of 1964 an *ad hoc* commission to study 'problems in the struggle against juvenile crime' and to prepare legislation to deal with these problems.[21] The membership of the *ad hoc* commission included both judicial officials and scholars, from legal research institutes and from centers for educational or psychological research. The commission's assigned tasks were to evaluate various suggestions on ways of improving juvenile crime prevention; and afterwards to prepare drafts for legislative changes which the commission had approved.[22]

When the Praesidium's *ad hoc* commission first met, it decided to delegate responsibility for analyzing the proposals for the juvenile affairs commissions to one of its most capable members, the criminologist G. M. Minkovskii. A man of unusual acumen and tenacity, Minkovskii headed the Procuracy Institute's sector for the study and prevention of juvenile crime; moreover, he also was the director of the coordination group for research on juvenile crime in the USSR. Minkovskii was helped in his studies of the juvenile affairs commissions by his colleague V. S. Pronina, now a senior research worker at the Institute. Trained in administrative rather than in criminal law, Pronina was well qualified to study the commissions.[23]

During late 1964 and the first half of 1965 Minkovskii and Pronina studied the work of the juvenile affairs commissions and considered the various suggestions which had been submitted to the Praesidium's *ad hoc* commission. On the basis of their analysis, the criminologists then brought forward their own set of proposals for discussion by the *ad hoc* commission.[24] These proposals drew heavily upon previous analysis and suggestions by scholars and officials. In arguing that the commissions needed more extended powers and that their statutes ought to spell out their duties more clearly, the criminologists echoed their colleague Boldyrev's suggestions. Minkovskii and Pronina also supported measures to rationalize the commissions' work, including record-keeping, analysis of the state of juvenile crime on the district level, planning, and checking on the fulfilment of commission orders.[25]

Minkovskii and Pronina laid particular stress upon one proposal which was not found in Boldyrev's writing – namely, that the juvenile affairs commissions now be provided with full-time staff.[26] According to Minkovskii, the idea of reviving the proposal for full-time staff, which Tadevosian and Pronina herself had made in 1958–9, originated among Procuracy officials;[27] but the adoption of this idea became Minkovskii and Pronina's special concern. The proposal had become politically feasible in late 1964 largely because of changes in the USSR's political leadership. During the last few years of Khrushchev's rule, when Boldyrev wrote his suggestions, the idea of adding full-time staff to a public organization might have been interpreted as tampering with one of the leader's pet projects. But Khrushchev left the seat of power in September 1964; and his successors seemed to care less about the replacement of governmental bodies by public organizations.[28]

In developing their proposal, Minkovskii and Pronina attempted to show both the need for full-time staff and its legitimacy. They argued, first of all, that the increase in case loads and in the commissions' supervisory and coordination functions made full-time staff a *sine qua non*. One could not draw up a long list of functions, requiring planning and record-keeping, and then entrust all this work to volunteers alone. Minkovskii and Pronina bolstered their argument with evidence suggesting that full-time staff made a difference; their data showed that the commissions of Moscow and Leningrad which had been served by full-time secretaries since 1961, had performed better than the commissions in other cities.[29] Furthermore, Minkovskii and Pronina supplied an answer to any theoretical or ideological objections which might be raised against the addition of full-time staff to the commissions. Minkovskii and Pronina claimed that the commissions on juvenile affairs were not 'purely public institutuons', but 'organs of a new type, which combined simultaneously features of governmental agencies and public organizations.' Although they were 'public' in their makeup (most of the commission members participated on a voluntary basis), the commissions performed governmental functions, especially in their judicial role.[30]

Shortly before Minkovskii and Pronina submitted this set of proposals to the Praesidium *ad hoc* commission, they had the opportunity to discuss them with a large group of their professional colleagues. The occasion was the first annual coordination conference on juvenile crime, convened in the spring of 1965 and held at the Procuracy Institute in joint session with the Procuracy Institute's Academic Council.[31] Especially helpful suggestions for the reforms of the commissions came from the Riga criminologists; L. N. Kliuchinskaia reported how under her guidance the juvenile affairs commissions in Latvia had already begun experimenting with record-keeping and planning.[32]

Minkovskii used the forum provided by the conference to initiate discussion of an idea of his own – the improvement of the wardship system.[33] The Soviet Union did not have professional social workers to offer guidance to difficult children; but in the post-Stalin years there had emerged an informal system of wardship (*shefstvo*), whereby individual volunteers became *shefy*, or patrons, for young troublemakers. The informal system had its shortcomings. The *shefy* found it difficult to perform their duties because they lacked legal authority to intervene in the lives of their charges. Sometimes, the parents of young offenders resented the intrusion of an outsider into the home and refused him admission. In addition, the persons attracted to the positions of *shefy* were often not well qualified for the post.

Still Minkovskii believed that *shefy* could play an important role in delinquency prevention. Many young offenders clearly needed additional adult supervision and support. Studies had shown that more than half of the delinquents came from families with only one parent, usually because of a divorce.[34] Moreover, there was evidence that where the wardship system was well organized it could affect the recurrence of violations. Research in Leningrad by N. N. Grabovskiia demonstrated that young offenders who had *shefy* were less likely to commit new offenses than their counterparts who did not have *shefy*.[35]

A radical step toward improving the *shefy*, one requiring a large financial investment, would have been the professionalization of the position. In fact, Minkovskii did admire the more professional system of 'curators' used in Poland (the curators attended special schools and received a regular stipend for their contribution). But at the coordination conference (and later on) Minkovskii limited his proposals to measures which could be accomplished within the framework of existing budgetary arrangements. He suggested first that in a new statute the rights and duties of *shefy* and of parents be clearly delineated and that *shefy* be given powers to intervene in family affairs; secondly, that the attempt be made to attract *shefy* of better quality by raising their status to that of 'public guardians' and by establishing 'some material incentives'; thirdly, that the work of public guardians be organized and supervised by the juvenile affairs commissions.

The audience at the conference which heard Minkovskii's presentation responded positively to the suggestions for improving the *shefy*. A number of them, including the senior Leningrad criminologist M. D. Shargorodskii, spoke in support of the upgrading of *shefy* into public guardians.[36] Not long after the conference, Minkovskii proposed this idea to the Praesidium *ad hoc* commission, which was considering reforms in delinquency prevention.

The main discussions at the *ad hoc* commission during the spring of 1965 were not of the public guardians but of the set of proposals presented by Minkovskii and Pronina for the reform of the juvenile affairs commissions. After some debate the *ad hoc* commission approved the proposals in principle and appointed a team of scholars and officials (from the Procuracy Institute and from the USSR Procuracy's department on juvenile affairs) to prepare a draft model statute for the juvenile affairs commissions.

All summer Minkovskii and his colleagues were engaged in the preparation of a new and detailed statute for the commissions and of a series of special reports explaining the main innovations in the statute.[37] But Minkovskii and Pronina also found time to extend their advocacy of commission reforms into a public forum, by submitting an article to the government newspaper *Izvestiia*. The authors took special care to justify the addition of permanent staff to the commissions. They noted that the case load of the juvenile affairs commissions now included one half of all criminal cases involving juveniles, as well as all non-criminal cases involving children's misdeeds, which were referred by the police or the children's rooms. According to the criminologists, the commissions which dealt with juvenile delinquency before 1935 did have permanent staff. Besides arguing for the full-time staff, Minkovskii and Pronina also outlined the claims which they had previously advocated to the Praesidium *ad hoc* commission – the need for well-qualified members, for rationalizing the commissions' work, and for supplying commissions with new powers.[38]

In the early fall the *ad hoc* commission discussed the proposed 'public guardians'. On deciding in favor of Minkovskii's basic scheme, the commission ordered the preparation of a statute, specifying the rights and duties of the guardians, providing for their supervision by the juvenile affairs commissions, and supplying some incentives for the guardians. In choosing the particular incentives to be listed in the statute, the commission modified somewhat the criminologist's original proposal. Whereas Minkovskii had suggested offering 'some material rewards' to guardians who performed well, the commission decided that moral as well as material incentives should be used to encourage the volunteer guardians. Thus, the statute was to stipulate that better guardians would receive either honors or prizes and paid vacations.[39]

During the fall of 1965 the team of scholars and officials who had worked on the model statute for the juvenile affairs commissions also undertook the drafting of the model statute for public guardians. At the same time as they were preparing the draft, Minkovskii and his colleague Melnikova wrote an article on the guardians for a legal journal. In the article the criminologists reviewed the case for the reforms and discussed the various measures which had been included in the draft law.[40]

In December or January the Praesidium's *ad hoc* commission completed its work on the two model statutes and sent the drafts to the Praesidium of the Supreme Soviet for its consideration. It is not certain just when the Praesidium of the Supreme Soviet, or the party leadership, gave its final assent to the draft laws, but it appeared that these decisions occurred during the spring of 1966. At a conference at the party Academy of Social Sciences in June 1966 Minkovskii spoke about the new public guardians as if that institution were already a *fait accompli*.[41] In July 1966 a party-state edict on criminal policy stated that 'the institution of public guardians *will be introduced*', and that 'improvements in the juvenile affairs commissions *are mapped out*' [Italics added].[42]

The decisions taken by political leaders on the reforms of the juvenile affairs commissions and the establishment of public guardians for juveniles required legislative action by republican level soviets or their praesidia. For the draft statutes which the USSR Praesidium of the Supreme Soviet approved were only 'models', which the republican praesidia could then adapt somewhat to local conditions. At times such 'adaptations' produced significant differences in the law of the various republican constituencies.[43] However, in the case of the new statutes on the juvenile affairs commissions, it seemed that republican level promulgation did not introduce significant changes into the statutes. Comparison of the RSFSR and Latvian SSR statutes on the commissions revealed no differences of note, and both of them seemed to match the content of the model statute submitted by the *ad hoc* commission.[44] In this case, the republican legislative activity seemed to belong to the output phase of the decision-making process.

The content of the RSFSR statute on juvenile affairs commission, issued in June 1967, offered no surprises to persons who had followed the work of Boldyrev, Minkovskii, and Pronina. In forty articles the new statute spelled out the composition, responsibilities, and powers of the commissions. Membership on commissions was to vary from six to twelve persons, all of them qualified specialists; and full-time secretaries, and for some commissions full-time inspectors too, were provided. Among the responsibilities of the commissions, the organization and coordination of the juvenile crime prevention effort was listed first, ahead of their judicial functions. The duties of the commission included planning and checking their own operations, studying the local crime situation, and keeping records. Moreover, the commissions did obtain new powers, including the right to issue orders obliging other governmental organs and social organizations to report on their fulfilment within two weeks; and the right to intervene in factories which employed young persons to check on the implementation of the quotas, to verify work conditions, and to ensure that no young persons were fired without prior consultation with the commission.[45]

The RSFSR statute on public guardians, promulgated in December 1967, also reflected closely the draft model statute submitted by the *ad hoc* commission. It specified the obligations and the powers of guardians and it provided both moral and material incentives for good performance of the assigned tasks. Another provision, which was new to this writer, was the order that methodological direction of the public guardians was to be provided by the regional departments of education. These departments were 'to familiarize the public guardians with the fundamentals of pedagogy, psychology, and legal knowledge' – no small task.[46] Whether this provision was a part of the draft submitted by the *ad hoc* commission or was added to it at a later stage, we do not know.

The implementation of the new laws reforming the juvenile affairs commissions and introducing the public guardians also involved some participation by criminologists. Appropriately two legal scholars whose work was closely associated with the commissions, V. S. Pronina and L. G. Kliuchinskaia, wrote book-length commentaries on the new statutes.[47] Far more extensive than the usual exegesis on legal texts, these commentaries provided considerable guidance to commission members on the handling of specific questions not covered in the law itself. Another dimension of the implementation of these reforms was checking the progress of their execution, but for this matter Procuracy officials rather than scholars took the responsibility.[48]

A study of the reform of the juvenile affairs commissions and the introduction of public guardians shows decision-making with a minimum of conflict. To our knowledge, no serious disagreements arose among the decision-makers or between decision-makers and specialists about the purpose or outlines of the reforms. Questions of substance were left almost entirely to the discretion of criminologists and officials and controversies over details, like the question of incentives for public guardians, were resolved through quiet bargaining within the confines of the *ad hoc* commission. The fact that the decisions on delinquency prevention were taken cooperatively did not mean that they were of little political significance. In issuing the secret party edict of 1963, the party leadership had displayed special concern for delinquency prevention. We suggest that the smooth and seemingly conflict-free introduction of needed reforms might have stemmed from the political consensus about the urgency of this question.

6 Alcoholism and Hooliganism

The middle 1960s were far from the first time a Russian government had grappled with the problem of alcohol and crime; both the Tsarist regime and Soviet leaders of earlier generations had sought palliatives for this problem. In the search for remedies two alternative, though not mutually exclusive, approaches to the problem of alcohol and crime had developed. One approach attacked the root of the problem, excessive drinking. Variations of this strategy included the prosecution or the treatment of alcoholics and restrictions on the sale or use of liquor. The Tsarist government carried the latter to its logical extreme in 1914 by legislating total sobriety.[1] The other approach focused upon the criminal consequences of intoxication, especially upon the brawls and public disturbances which drunken persons often created. In 1922 the young Soviet state ruled all such activity illegal, by introducing a new crime, 'hooliganism', which has remained in Soviet criminal codes to this day.[2]

The relative prominence of these two approaches varied during the years of Soviet power. In the 1920s both approaches to alcohol and crime coexisted, as renewed efforts were made to study and prevent alcoholism, while at the same time hooligans were brought to the courts.[3] But in the 1930s punishing the hooligan became the dominant means of handling the problems of crime and drink, as Stalin introduced a series of measures increasing the severity of sanctions applied to hooligans. The minimum sentence for a hooliganism conviction became one year's deprivation of freedom.[4] In the decade immediately after Stalin's death the pendulum swung back again. By a special edict in 1956 establishing a new category 'petty hooliganism', post-Stalin liberalizers substantially reduced the penalties applied to many hooligans.[5] Moreover, in an attempt to renew the struggle against alcoholism and its effects, Soviet leaders introduced in the late 1950s a variety of restrictions on the sale, production, and consumption of alcoholic beverages.[6] But the implementation of many of these restrictions was half-hearted and thus prevented the regime from assessing the effect of the measures upon the incidence of public disturbances caused by drunkards.[7]

Much to the chagrin of politicians the brawls and drunkenness continued during the 1960s; indeed, hooliganism remained one of the most widespread of all crimes in the USSR.[8] Furthermore, as an especially conspicuous offense hooliganism easily aroused public ire. Soviet journalists and officials reported receiving numerous letters from 'enraged citizens' calling for action against the miscreants.[9] But Soviet politicians in the 1960s had more telling indicators of the seriousness of the alcohol and crime problem. Statistical data interpreted by criminologists revealed that not only were drunkards and hooligans a nuisance, they were also potentially dangerous. Intoxicated persons committed two-thirds of all murders, three-fifths of all rapes, and one half of all thefts recorded in Soviet courts; and a large proportion of juvenile offenders were also drunk at the time of their criminal acts.[10] Most of the offenders appeared to be chronic alcoholics, not casual drinkers;[11] and there was a significant correlation between alcoholism and recidivist crime.[12] Data on the relationship between hooliganism and serious crime was no more encouraging; previous incidents of hooliganism dotted the criminal records of murderers, assailants, and thieves.[13]

During the middle 1960s Soviet political leaders decided once again to tackle the alcohol and crime problem. At first, they considered introducing a complex of measures to reduce alcoholism; later, they decided instead to apply harsher sanctions to hooligans and to other criminals who offended while intoxicated. The decisions of the Soviet leadership about alcoholism and hooliganism during the 1960s form the subject of our second study of criminologists in decision-making.

The story of the alcoholism and hooliganism measures of 1966–7 began in the winter of 1965, when the Supreme Court, at the urging of the head of its criminal division, G. Z. Anashkin, proposed to the Praesidium of the Supreme Soviet the introduction in the RSFSR of compulsory treatment for non-criminal chronic alcoholics.[14] According to article 62 of the RSFSR criminal code, compulsory treatment could be applied to chronic alcoholics only when they had already committed crimes.[15] The idea of a broader application of compulsory treatment was *not* a novelty; in a meeting of Gertsenzon's sector at the Institute of State and Law in 1961 A. M. Iakovlev had presented a thorough report on the extension of compulsory treatment to non-criminal chronic alcoholics whose behavior was anti-social.[16] During the early 1960s varieties of compulsory treatment for non-criminal alcoholics had been introduced in ten of the fourteen other republics.[17]

Apparently, Anashkin regarded compulsory treatment of alcoholics as a means of attacking hooliganism as well as alcoholism. In an *Izvestiia* article answering an angry citizen's letter about hooliganism, Anashkin explained: 'practice had shown' that educational work rather than repression was the most effective means of reducing crime. To perform educational work, he continued, one needed to study and eradicate the conditions which facilitated crime; and the principal condition provoking hooliganism was alcoholism. An effective way of combating alcoholism, Anashkin claimed, would be the establishment of compulsory treatment.

Together compulsory treatment of alcoholics and the existing punishment of hooligans would constitute 'the right combination of educational and repressive measures'.[18]

The Praesidium of the Supreme Soviet reacted favorably to the Supreme Court's proposal to extend compulsory treatment of alcoholics; but it decided that it was time for a full consideration of the measures which might be introduced to combat alcoholism. Therefore, the Praesidium established an *ad hoc* working commission to study the struggle against drunkenness and alcoholism.[19] The 'alcoholism commission', as we shall call it, included among its members representatives of government agencies (judicial agencies, ministry of trade, ministry of education, ministry of health) and of scholarly institutions (lawyers, sociologists, psychiatrists, and others). Its chairman was Professor A. A. Gertsenzon from the Procuracy Institute, whose interest in the problem of alcoholism and crime dated from the late 1920s, when his monograph on that subject was published.[20]

During the spring and summer of 1965 the commission collected submissions both from interested ministries and from academic institutions. But the brunt of the staff work for the commission was performed by the Procuracy Institute's general criminology sector, headed by Gertsenzon. The criminologists who worked under Gertsenzon summarized the submissions, prepared a series of detailed reports on special themes, and submitted a series of recommendations.[21]

During the summer of 1965, while the Gertsenzon sector was preparing reports and recommendations, a major public discussion of alcoholism and crime took place. The government newspaper *Izvestiia*, perhaps in response to cues from its sponsor the Praesidium of the Supreme Soviet, initiated the discussion by printing for five days in late June stories, commentaries, and letters from the public about drunkenness. Afterwards, the editors invited scholars and officials to submit their views in a 'round-table discussion', which continued at intervals throughout the summer.[22] In leading off the discussion A. A. Gertsenzon suggested one extension of compulsory treatment for alcoholics in the RSFSR and various restrictions on the sale of alcoholic beverages, especially vodka. Gertsenzon also placed special emphasis upon effective anti-alcoholic propaganda.

As the discussion in the press continued, the two points which received the most attention were compulsory treatment and the advisability of further restrictions upon sales. There was near unanimity on the appropriateness of some form of compulsory treatment for chronic alcoholics, but the discussants disagreed about the functions of the proposed treatment centers (*profilaktori*). The criminologist Gertsenzon, a psychiatrist, N. Troyan, and a member of the USSR Procuracy, A. Kholiavchenko, emphasized the educational goals of the *profilaktori*, but police colonel Kosogovskii construed compulsory treatment as punitive sanction.[23] In the discussion on restricting the sale of liquor, a Komsomol

Central Committee member, Volodin, and the specialist on juvenile crime, G. M. Minkovskii, indicated strong support for restrictions which would keep young workers away from drink – curtailment of sales of alcoholic beverages in the morning and anywhere in the vicinity of a factory. But G. Rozantsev, head of the administration for the organization of trade in the RSFSR Ministry of Trade, doubted whether any restrictions on sale would prove effective.

Early in the fall of 1965 Gertsenzon and his colleagues at the Procuracy Institute completed their studies of alcoholism and crime and delivered to the commission a series of reports and recommendations. Despite the objections of Rozantsev, Gertsenzon did propose a series of measures to limit the sale of hard liquor and to change the balance of production from vodka to weaker beverages like wine and beer. To gain acceptance of these proposals from trade and financial officials, Gertsenzon suggested that the tax structure of the USSR be reformed to replace revenue supplied by liquor sales with new sources of income. Such modification was in order, for the sale of vodka and hard liquor alone had provided more than one tenth of the total state income derived from the turnover tax.[24]

Another of Gertsenzon's recommendations to the commissions focused upon improving anti-alcoholic propaganda. According to Gertsenzon, the effectiveness of specific measures like compulsory treatment or restrictions on sale would be enhanced by the creation among the public of 'an atmosphere of intolerance to alcohol'. To stimulate and maintain such an atmosphere, a permanent anti-alcoholism campaign had to be introduced; and to manage such an effort a public institution was required, an All-Union society for the fight with alcoholism. Gertsenzon envisaged a large voluntary organization operating on national, provincial, and local levels. In addition to its propaganda effort, the society would be responsible for checking the implementation of other anti-alcoholism measures.[25]

Gertsenzon contended that the implementation of both concrete measures and of a propaganda campaign against alcoholism would benefit from presentation in a comprehensive anti-alcoholism law.[26] After discussion, the Praesidium's alcoholism commission accepted this contention and entrusted Gertsenzon's sector with the task of drafting a project law 'on the fight with alcoholism'. During the fall of 1965 the criminologists drafted the law and presented it to the commission; and by the end of the year the commission had approved a draft and forwarded it to the Praesidium of the Supreme Soviet, along with detailed explanations (in the form of an *obstoiatelanaia zapiska*) and reports on specific themes (*spravki*).[27]

According to Professor Gertsenzon, the draft regulation included the introduction of compulsory treatment for non-criminal alcoholics and the expansion of the network of special institutions for compulsory and general treatment; new measures to limit the sale of hard liquor and to change the balance of production between vodka and weaker beverages like beer and wine; the systematic replacement of income in the state budget derived from sale of alcoholic beverages; the establishment of an All-union society for the fight with alcoholism; and the introduction of 'systematic daily anti-alcoholism propaganda and educational work' beginning in secondary schools.[28]

During the first weeks of 1966 the draft law received considerable support in the press. One Nikolai Atarov led off a discussion in *Literaturnaia Gazeta*, with an article entitled 'A law against alcoholism is needed', and he argued persuasively that similar laws in Poland and in Czechoslovakia had proven helpful.[29] A specialist in public health propaganda claimed in another presentation that anti-alcoholic propaganda had a good future, if its message became more sophisticated than urging a complete break with drink.[30] Even the Ministry of Trade's spokesman Rozantsev seemed to have modified his previous position on the sales restrictions.[31] On 3 February the editors of *Literaturnaia Gazeta* concluded the discussion, by reporting on the letters which they had received from the public.

> Not most, but absolutely all . . . fully shared the opinion expressed in N. Atarov's article and developed by the other authors. . . . *Literaturnaia Gazeta* thanks all of the participants in the discussion, and as the opinion turned out to be unanimous, we consider the discussion closed![32]

The draft alcoholism law could hardly have received a better press.

Three days later, on 6 February 1966 A. A. Gertsenzon appeared once again in *Izvestiia*, to argue for a unified system of anti-alcoholic measures and calling for further discussion of the new draft.[33] Gertsenzon's new appeal was not unusual; authors of legislative drafts often wrote in their support while the drafts were under consideration; one need only recall the article by Minkovskii and Pronina in *Izvestiia* describing their proposed reforms in the juvenile affairs commissions. But the further discussion of the new draft sought by Gertsenzon did not take place; for two months there were no further articles on alcoholism and crime in the government newspaper.[34]

Only after a hiatus of the two months did the reasons for the curtailment of public discussion of alcoholism prevention measures become apparent. With no prior warning, on 21 April 1966 *Izvestiia* published an article by the Minister for the Defense of the Social Order (MOOP) V. S. Tikunov, calling for intensified repression of hooligans.[35] The chief of MOOP had decided that a new attack on the criminal consequences of drink was the most effective approach to the problem of alcoholics and hooligans, and apparently he had already gained the assent of other politicians.

It seemed that Tikunov did not reach this conclusion all at once. His proposed repression of hooligans had a history, just as the measures to prevent alcoholism did. During the middle 1960s Soviet law enforcement officials became increasingly aware of irregularities in the enforcement of hooliganism laws. The Supreme Court took action by issuing an edict, exhorting judges to distinguish more carefully among the different grades of hooliganism and between hooliganism and other crimes.[36] But as Justice Anashkin pointed out, the judges were not the whole problem; difficulties in hooliganism enforcement stemmed at least as much from police practice.[37]

The police minister Tikunov was well aware of the discretion exercised by militiamen in handling concrete incidents of hooliganism. According to him, some police officers, on encountering public fights, failed either to make arrests or to report the events. Frequently, when an officer did arrest the participants, he reported it as 'petty' hooliganism even though it deserved to be deemed 'ordinary' or 'malicious'; naturally, the officer would also adjust his description of the events to match the offense he had chosen. Furthermore, when cases of hooliganism or malicious hooliganism were 'booked', local police departments gave them such low priority that often the cases had to be dropped when the statutory time limitations for investigations had expired. Tikunov blamed these difficulties upon the laziness of policemen, who did not bother to report or investigate hooliganism cases.[38]

By themselves such irregularities would probably have provoked MOOP to take the usual corrective measures – issuing administrative orders calling for the elimination of the shortcomings.[39] But further information suggested to the ministry's leaders that the poor hooliganism enforcement had serious consequences, which deserved more than ritual expressions of concern. To begin with, a routine check (*proverka*) of two hundred serious crimes committed during 1964 revealed that forty-two offenders (21 per cent) had records of previously uninvestigated and unprosecuted hooliganism offenses.[40] Curious about the apparent relationship between poor hooliganism enforcement and the incidence of serious crime, MOOP officials instructed their staff to examine the statistical records for further evidence about the relationship between hooliganism and more serious crime.[41] The resulting study of selected provinces (1962–5) revealed that wherever a significant increase in hooliganism convictions was observed, there was a corresponding decrease in convictions for serious crime.[42]

Continuing the investigation, Tikunov and his colleagues turned for assistance to the Leningrad chief of police Iu. Lukianov.[43] With the ministry's help, the Leningrad city police instituted an experimental crackdown on hooliganism during the first two months of 1966. Once again the results showed that along with a 54 per cent rise in convictions for hooliganism went a 20 per cent drop in convictions for serious crime, as compared with the first two months of 1965.[44]

Although it was tempting to conclude from such data that hooliganism was 'the breeding ground for serious crime' or 'the primary school for hardened criminals', one could not, as Tikunov probably realized, infer than an attack on hooliganism would necessarily lower the *incidence* of serious crime. For it was more than likely that the observed changes in the conviction rates for serious crimes represented changes in police practice which resulted from the hooliganism campaign.[45] However, for a person who was already inclined on philosophical grounds to favor the repression of hooligans, the possibility that this repression might lower the incidence of murder, rape, or violent assault was sufficient grounds for action.[46]

When, at a conference of senior police officials in mid-March 1966, Minister Tikunov first proposed taking measures to intensify the repression of hooligans, he probably explained his reasoning.[47] But in the *Izvestiia* article in April Tikunov mentioned neither the research nor the experiments which his ministry had carried out. He simply stated that policemen had 'underestimated the seriousness of hooliganism' without telling why he thought that hooliganism was a serious offense.[48]

In none of a series of public appearances which followed the *Izvestiia* article did Tikunov actually propose legislative changes. Rather he repeated that his main concern was improving the enforcement of existing law.[49] Evidently, Tikunov did believe that any improvements in enforcement would require dramatic action. To rouse the police and the public to new heights of vigilance, he promised 'to start a campaign against hooligans'.[50]

The decision to issue new hooliganism legislation and to include in it increased sanctions both for hooligans and for persons who committed crimes while intoxicated was a private one; there were no discussions in the press among scholars or officials about the appropriateness of these measures. This was somewhat surprising, since *Izvestiia* had called for discussion of Tikunov's article;[51] but during the four weeks which followed it, there appeared but one article on hooligansim in the government newspaper.[52] These facts seemed to suggest that the question of hooliganism legislation was raised shortly after Tikunov's article and that it was decided quickly.

Two further facts suggest that Soviet leaders reached their decision to legislate against hooligansim at least by the middle of May. The first was the beginning in late May of an extensive press campaign against hooliganism; and the second was the establishment at the end of that month of an editorial commission to refine the rough draft of a hooliganism law which MOOP officials had prepared during that month. Starting in late May and continuing through June, *Izvestiia* printed a series of letters, commentaries, articles, and personal statements concerning the dangers of hooliganism and the need for public vigilance in repressing it. The authors included journalists, officials, and 'representatives of the public', but scholars (not a criminologist) accounted for only one of the many items.[53]

Around the beginning of June, the Praesidium of the Supreme Soviet appointed a small editorial group to prepare a finished legal draft for the hooliganism legislation. Formally a subcommission of the Commissions on

Legislative Suggestions of the Supreme Soviet, the group worked closely with the Praesidium's juridical sector. Within a few weeks' time the group had executed the decision in good legal language; its effect upon the final product was apparently no more than that.[54] The editorial group which prepared the hooliganism legislation did include a few criminologists, but both they and their colleagues were extremely reluctant to discuss their participation with me. Their reluctance seemed to stem from personal distaste for the new hooliganism law.[55]

In choosing to promulgate a law against hooliganism, Soviet political leaders also decided to disregard and lay aside the draft alcoholism prevention law which Gertsenzon and his team had prepared for the Praesidium of the Supreme Soviet. Of the provisions included in the anti-alcoholism law, only the extension of compulsory treatment for non-criminal alcoholics in the RSFSR was approved. This widely supported measure, which had originated with the USSR Supreme Court, became law in 1967 after republican authorities took the opportunity to shape the legal instrument which they desired. Each of the other three provisions in the anti-alcoholism law – to establish a society for combating alcoholism, to introduce new restrictions on the sale of alcohol, and to improve anti-alcoholic propaganda – was rejected out of hand.[56]

The politicians had chosen, in Anashkin's words, 'a combination of repressive and educational measures', but the combination was not the one favored either by Anashkin or by the criminologists who had worked on the problem.[57] Why did Tikunov succeed in gaining acceptance for a 'war against hooliganism' and the criminologists fail to gain assent for a 'war against alcoholism'? In addition to any 'rational' considerations, at least three factors may have weighed in the balance. The first was the personal stature of Tikunov, apparently high at that time; the second was the political strength of the MOOP relative to other judicial agencies and institutions; the third was a possible continuation of the conservative backlash against the post-Stalin liberalization of the law. In any or all of these ways external political considerations may have intervened in favor of hooliganism rather than alcoholism measures.

As for the legislation itself, the new hooliganism law introduced changes both in procedural and in substantive law. To encourage policemen to prosecute hooligans, various aspects of procedure were simplified. For the first time the chief of police or his deputy could apply a fine to a petty hooliganism offender without a court hearing. Moreover, new provisions also were designed to speed up trials for hooliganism and malicious hooliganism.[58] On the substantive side, the penalties for petty hooliganism were increased and new minimum terms established for hooliganism and malicious hooliganism.[59] But these new minimum terms were hardly as significant as a new provision that for offenses other than hooliganism intoxication at the time of the crime might now serve as an aggravating circumstance. From the summer of 1966 on, drunken offenders would be liable to harsher penalties than sober ones; or to give an example, an unpremeditated murder committed 'out of hooliganistic motives' might draw a longer sentence than a planned killing for mercenary reasons.[60]

Since a public campaign was meant to accompany the new hooliganism legislation, its announcement on 26 July 1966 was not without considerable fanfare. We have already described how the press had 'prepared the public' during June with letters and stories about hooliganism. On 23 July, three days before the passage of the hooliganism law in the Supreme Soviet, Soviet authorities arranged for the transmission over national television of a hooliganism trial direct from the provincial city Riazan. The effect turned out as calculated, when 'hundreds of incensed viewers' wrote to the television station and to MOOP calling for repression of hooligans.[61] The party leadership spoke the truth, when it announced on July 26 that 'the public' had demanded a new hooliganism law![62]

An effective campaign against hooliganism required public participation as well as outrage; so the press and media continued the attempt to rouse citizenry to action. Feature pages in the national press described party, trade union and factory meetings which had been called to discuss hooliganism.[63] The party-state edict which accompanied the hooliganism law also entrusted local party activists with the task of agitation on hooliganism.[64] Moreover, a television press conference with leading officials of the Procuracy, Supreme Court, and MOOP was also staged to help explain the law and the campaign to the masses.[65]

The extensive publicity effort to mobilize support for the new measures and to mount a campaign did not attract the participation of criminologists or legal scholars. Journalists, party officials, and officials from the judicial agencies bore the full responsibility for the popular aspects of implementing the hooliganism decisions. Where criminologists did participate was in the intellectual side of implementation. The Procuracy Institute prepared a collection of articles on the hooliganism law for a restricted audience of other scholars and of the judicial officials who had to implement the reforms.[66] Later another group of scholars produced a collection on the difficulties in the law's implementation.[67]

The problems in implementing the new legislation were severe. Even during the first 'campaign year' policemen and judges 'did not apply the full severity of the law' against hooligans;[68] and many of these officials failed to do so just because of the temporary quality of the crackdown.[69] The compulsory treatment of chronic alcoholics also proved difficult to introduce in the RSFSR, because of a shortage of facilities in which to place the alcoholics. The new network of *profilaktori* intended for this purpose did not materialize during the late 1960s.[70]

With such poor implementation, it was not surprising that these measures did not alleviate the problems of alcoholism and hooliganism. Within a few years of the promulgation of the hooliganism law debate over the remedies for alcoholism and its criminal consequences returned to the

Soviet press. As in 1965 the discussion raised the question of restrictions on the production and sale of alcoholic beverages, and the very proposals included by Professor Gertsenzon in the draft anti-alcoholism law were reiterated.[71] However, this time the Soviet leadership decided to introduce the restrictions, in a 1972 edict on alcoholism prevention.[72] The irony was that Professor Gertsenzon did not witness this particular swing of the pendulum; for in 1970 A. A. Gertsenzon had passed away.[73]

Under Brezhnev just as in earlier periods the Soviet leadership vacillated between two approaches to the problem of alcoholism and crime; sometimes it emphasized the repression of hooligans; and other times, the prevention and treatment of alcoholics. The decisions of 1966 were the result of the leadership's change of mind in midstream. For a period of more than a year, scholars and officials did the leaders' bidding, by working together to prepare a series of alcoholism prevention measures. But when the Minister for the Defense of the Social Order Tikunov intervened with a new call for the repression of hooligans, the leadership decided to favor his approach.

Thus, the decisions resulted from a conflict of views between those persons who favored emphasizing alcoholism prevention and those who sought to punish hooligans. As far as we know, the adherents of these two approaches did not argue their differences in public or private forums; neither of them even addressed the other's arguments. However, the simultaneous acceptance of the proposals for action against hooliganism and rejection of most of the anti-alcoholism draft law made it clear to all concerned that the leadership had chosen one set of measures over the other.

7 Parole and Recidivism Reforms

In the middle and late 1960s Soviet politicians and law enforcement officials showed as much concern for the deterrence and correction of criminal offenders as they did for the treatment of alcoholic offenders and juvenile delinquents. Their concern provoked careful scrutiny of a number of legal sanctions – of the parole system; of special measures applied to the habitual criminal; and of the relative merits of applying short prison terms or community sanctions to the less serious offender. Although some of these issues became controversial, the authorities refrained from rendering even preliminary decisions until they had received results from specially commissioned criminological research. Only then was the machinery set in motion which led to the decisions to introduce certain changes in parole regulations and in the definition of 'specially dangerous recidivist' and to take no legislative actions concerning short-term sentences or 'corrective work'.

As we saw in Chapter 2, parole (conditional early release) was reintroduced into Soviet criminal law in 1954 after a fifteen-year absence and then consolidated and expanded in the 1958 Fundamental Principles of Criminal Legislation. The scheme set in 1958 provided a differentiated system of parole eligibility. Generally, ordinary offenders became eligible after one half of their term and more serious offenders after two-thirds; 'specially dangerous recidivists' were excluded entirely from parole privileges. The only condition attached to the parole was that the commission of a new crime of the same seriousness as the original one would send the parolee back to confinement to complete his original term as well as his new sentence.[1]

Not surprisingly the parole scheme established in 1958 underwent some modifications during the early 1960s. As an instrument of a liberal penal policy, parole was open to attack during the 'law and order' mood of 1961–2. Moreover, jurists striving to develop a rational parole scheme themselves supported some changes after observing parole practice for a few years. The result was that during 1961 and 1962 two further categories of offenders were excluded from parole eligibility – persons who violated the parole condition (by committing a new crime while on parole); and persons guilty of a short list of the most serious crimes, generally those which carried an optional death penalty.[2] Although these changes did make the parole scheme tougher, they also had a rational basis. Persons who committed new crimes while on parole were surely poor risks for another parole; and persons guilty of the most serious crimes might well be denied parole on grounds of social defense.

The main problem with the Soviet parole system after 1958 was not its legal framework but the way it was implemented in practice. As in most countries, early release in the USSR was intended not as a right but as a privilege, granted only to prisoners 'whose exemplary behavior and honest attitude toward work' had demonstrated their correction.[3] The responsibility for evaluating offenders was shared by officials of corrective-labor colonies and by the courts. The officials were expected to screen the eligible prisoners; and judges were then to examine each individual case on its merits before awarding the parole decree. But in practice, officials of corrective-labor colonies paid little attention to the selection of parolees and tended to recommend every eligible offender who had not egregiously misbehaved. Likewise the courts usually rubber-stamped the release of persons whom the custodians referred to them; judges rarely bothered to scrutinize individual cases.[4]

Leading judicial officials were well aware of these practical deficiencies in the awarding of parole. The Supreme Court issued a series of decrees in 1961, in 1963, and in 1965, exhorting judges to correct the shortcomings.[5] Procuracy leaders also took officials and judges to task for shirking their responsibility in awarding parole. Deputy Procurator-General A. Mishutin complained that the 'formal attitudes of many officials and judges toward their duties' had led even to cases where non-eligible offenders had been paroled; and he noted that few parolees were referred after release to the supervision of 'collectives', as provided in the law.[6]

As we saw in Chapter 2, the legal stigma of 'specially dangerous recidivist' was introduced into Soviet criminal law in 1958 as a way of increasing the punishments for offenders deemed to pose a great social danger. When an offender's combination of crimes met the criteria established in the republican criminal codes of 1960–1, he became eligible for this legal stigma, which led automatically to the loss of parole privileges and made him liable at the judge's discretion to receive an additional term in custody beyond the statutory limit for the offense under consideration.[7]

The conservative swing of the early 1960s affected the criteria for this stigma, just as it had affected parole eligibility. In 1957 the drafting commission for the Fundamental Principles of Criminal Legislation had flatly rejected an MVD request to provide corrective-labor officials with the authority to prolong the terms of inmates who committed new crimes while in confinement.[8] But when the proposal came up again in 1962, its MVD sponsors met with more success. Although the Praesidium of the Supreme Soviet did not grant corrective-labor officials personally the right to extend sentences, it did empower judges to do so by designating such offenders as 'specially dangerous recidivists'.[9] Thus, any person who committed a crime while serving a term for another crime could henceforth be designated a 'specially dangerous recidivist' regardless of the seriousness of the new offenses or of the original one. This change represented a notable departure from the previous RSFSR law which required that when just two crimes served as grounds for the stigma they had to be very serious ones. The practical effect of the new law was that an offender sent to a corrective-labor colony for ordinary robbery or for malicious hooliganism became eligible for designation as a 'specially dangerous recidivist' after a single escape attempt.

The first few years of using the stigma of 'specially dangerous recidivist' brought to light serious flaws in its legislative construction. Particularly vexing for judges was the inadequate and inconsistent definition of the grounds for the stigma's application in the various republican criminal codes. Usually an offender's eligibility for the stigma depended upon the combination of offenses he had committed, but the particular combinations varied from republic to republic, thus creating complex jurisdictional tangles when the offenders' crimes were committed in more than one republic. (There were even a couple of republics where the code failed to contain the stigma entirely.)[10] Moreover, as the studies of the criminologist A. M. Iakovlev demonstrated, even the common core of the legal definitions of 'specially dangerous recidivist' in the various republics did not effectively isolate those hardened criminal elements for which the concept was designed.[11]

At the beginning of 1965 the USSR Supreme Court took the initiative and recommended that the Praesidium of the Supreme Soviet consider further changes in parole regulations and in the definition of 'specially dangerous recidivists'.[12] Agreeing with the court's proposals, the Praesidium decided in consultation with court leaders to go a step further and commission studies of the effectiveness of the existing parole system and of the effects of the definition of specially dangerous recidivist in practice.[13] At the same time, the Praesidium decided that it would be useful to have studies of two other measures of short-term confinement sentences and or 'corrective work'. Prison sentences of less than a year had drawn criticism from prison officials and other jurists for not allowing time sufficient for rehabilitation. In turn this criticism suggested the need to probe the utility of non-custodial sanctions like corrective work, which, for less serious offenders, might supply an alternative to the short-term prison sentence.[14]

The Praesidium of the Supreme Soviet selected the criminal law sector of the Procuracy Institute to perform studies of these four institutions of the penal system. Under the direction of the able and experienced B. S. Nikiforov members of this sector, with some help from MOOP institute scholars, spent the research year 1965 engaged in study of the effectiveness of parole, recidivism regulations, short-term sentences, and corrective works.[15]

The tasks of Nikiforov's researchers who were studying parole might have been simpler, had not parole become a controversial issue during the course of 1965. Ordinary citizens and high judicial officials openly expressed contempt for the 'softness' shown in releasing offenders early. For example, two participants in a philosophical discussion of criminal responsibility sponsored by the newspaper *Literaturnaia Gazeta*, a police sergeant and a philosophy instructor at the Moscow Aviation Institute, attacked parole; as the policeman put it, 'if you get fifteen years, you should sit fifteen!'[16] Other participants took a more liberal position, but G. V. Anashkin of the Supreme Court felt the need to comment on the dispute.[17] 'True,' Anashkin wrote,

> the parole procedures do require further improvement . . . [But] the complete abolition of parole, it seems to me, would not foster the educative aims of punishment, as is required. . . . It would be unfair if Petrov who behaves badly and Ivanov who has long since repented his act and has embarked firmly on a course of reform, were both required to serve their full sentences. The problem is one of not making mistakes when judging whether or not granting of parole (to an individual) will result in new crimes.[18]

Persons hostile to parole included high judicial officials as well as representatives of the public. In a discussion about parole reported in a law journal during the summer of 1965, the exchanges became so intense that the moderator, the chief of the prison system, had to remind the participants that the question at hand was not whether to abolish parole, but how to apply it properly! In spite of this admonition, first deputy chairman of the USSR Supreme Court, V. Kulikov, was not miffed. Summarizing the discussion, Kulikov claimed that there were just two positions on parole – either you extend its operation or you contract it. How, he asked, could one expand parole 'when about one-third of parolees committed new crimes?'[19] Kulikov's statistics differed sharply from those cited by criminological studies.[20]

The hostility to and rejection of parole by some citizens and officials appeared to be a manifestation of backlash against the post-Stalin liberalization of the criminal law. The reformers had assumed that mild sentences and early release upon demonstration of good behavior would serve the process of re-educating the criminal. But the persons who rejected parole subscribed to a different penal philosophy, which ranked rehabilitation behind deterrence and retribution as a purpose for punishment. If one regarded the alleged deterrence of offenders through harsh sentences as the principal goal of penal sanctions, then parole would appear to weaken the impact of the court's sentence by shortening it.

When, in the fall of 1965, the Supreme Court met to discuss parole, the opponents of that measure were more restrained. Kulikov and his sympathizers did not enter the deliberations actively, but merely listened as most of their colleagues stipulated that parole should be retained, but with improvements in law and in practice. G. Z. Anashkin, L. Smirnov, Chairman of the RSFSR Supreme Court, A. F. Gorkin, Chairman of the USSR Supreme Court, and N. V. Zhogin, Deputy Procurator-General, discussed what the particular improvements should be.[21]

Listening to the lengthy discussion at the Supreme Court plenum, V. N. Kudriavtsev, deputy director of the Procuracy Institute, could not contain himself. Rising to speak, Kudriavtsev admonished the judges, saying that instead of exchanging opinions, they should have been looking to the results of research and the testimony of specialists. If they were to scrutinize the results of the ongoing scientific study of the effectiveness of parole, they would discover that parole was a successful institution worthy of retention, and they would find indications of how parole could be improved in practice.[22]

Kudriavstev was anxious to reduce the emotion and controversy which had surrounded the question of parole throughout 1965 and to shift the consideration of parole reform to a more temperate and rational plane. Just a few weeks later he found another opportunity to underscore his advocacy of the 'scientific approach'. A judicial official named Andreev wrote yet another attack on parole, in which he decried the weakening of the courts' authority, when 'hardly any criminal served the whole term to which he was sentenced', and in which he observed that 'there were no incentives to good behavior in real life'.[23] Responding to Andreev in *Izvestiia*, Kudriavtsev posed the question, 'On what grounds were Andreev's assertions based? On emotions? On personal observations? On guesses and suppositions?' Only scientifically based conclusions, Kudriavtsev insisted, were 'admissible in our time'. Research on parole had already demonstrated that at the minimum parole did not make the situation worse; it was not necessary to return to the sad experience of the 1940s when there was no parole at all.[24]

It was in the context of controversy about the utility of parole and about the manner in which parole should be evaluated that Z. A. Vyshinskaia and S. A. Shlykov of the Procuracy Institute sat down to write out their conclusions about the parole research. Not surprisingly they took a defensive stance. They believed that their first task was to demonstrate that parole had justified its continued existence; only then could they consider what improvements could be made in the existing parole scheme. Vyshinskaia and Shlykov assumed that the crucial test of the parole's utility lay in recidivism rates. They discovered that during the years 1962−5 almost half of all offenders in confinement had been released on parole.[25] How had the parolees among this group performed in comparison with those who had finished their sentences? A sample study comparing parolees and non-parolees released during 1962 indicated that within the first three years after release, parolees committed new offenses almost two times less frequently than offenders who had served out their full terms.[26] Without carefully matched samples, according to age, social background, and number and type of offenses committed, Vyshinskaia and Shlykov could not conclude that parole had actually improved the chances of correction; for they recognized that offenders chosen for parole were intended to constitute a better risk group than those who remained in confinement. But the authors did argue that their results were *prima facie* evidence that parole had not backfired; parolees did no worse than might have been expected. The results of the study were sufficient, in the authors' opinion, to shift the burden of proof to those persons who rejected the utility of parole and its right to exist.[27]

When Vyshinskaia and Shlykov turned to examine how parole actually operated, they uncovered many shortcomings, the correction of which might strengthen the institution and improve its performance. In parole selection, for example, the authors found that the behavior of prison officials and of judges was as inadequate as had been previously believed. Prison officials did not carefully determine the success of reformation and the parole risk of each eligible inmate; often before recommending a person for parole, they simply checked that he had not committed a new offense while in prison.[28] The officials also failed to prepare detailed records of prisoners for the courts. For their part, the courts would process parole petitions *en masse*, sometimes devoting a single session of half a day or a day to stacks of requests.[29]

The execution of the early release also had weaknesses. In theory, the offender selected for parole was meant to benefit from help in job placement and from subsequent public supervision. But Vyshinskaia and Shlykov discovered that jobs were often not provided and that when they did materialize it was only after the court hearing so that judges had little opportunity to assign parolees to public supervision. Nor did judges pay much attention to this question; for only 5 per cent of parolees were assigned to 'collectives'.[30] The researchers regarded this omission as serious because their data showed that most parolees who failed committed their new crimes during the first nine months after release.[31] The authors also noted that young criminals, aged eighteen to twenty-four, persons who they assumed would benefit from supervision, formed a disproportionately high part of the repeaters.[32]

On the basis of these findings, Vyshinskaia and Shlykov made a series of recommendations – first, that the text of Fundamental Principles of Criminal Legislation be amended to include a statement of the criteria to be used by courts in parole selection and an indication that judges might assign parolees for supervision; secondly, that judges be restricted to hearing no more than fifteen parole petitions per session, and that special public organizations be formed to help parolees; and thirdly, that the terms of parole be changed.[33] In this last suggestion Vyshinskaia and Shlykov proposed that the existing terms of parole be made stricter to allow the return of parolees to confinement as parole failures not only for the commission of a new crime of seriousness equal to their original offense, but also for the commission of any new crime or administrative violation![34]

Public controversy and strong emotions did not affect the research carried out by the Procuracy Institute criminal law sector on specially dangerous recidivists, short-term sentences, and corrective works. None of these questions received any attention in either the popular or the legal press during the year of research, 1965. The problem of 'specially dangerous recidivists' was assigned to a senior research worker at the Institute, I. M. Galperin. Galperin's task was to study the actual use of the legal stigma and on the basis of the evidence to prepare a new definition of 'specially dangerous recidivist' which would become the uniform definition for the USSR and be included in the emendations to the Fundamental Principles of Criminal Legislation.

As of 1964 the RSFSR criminal code listed four ways an offender might qualify for designation as a 'specially dangerous recidivist': first, by committing two offenses from a list of most serious crimes; secondly, by committing one offense from this list and two offenses from a second list of somewhat less serious offenses; thirdly, by committing four offenses from the second list; and fourthly, by committing an intentional crime of any sort while serving a sentence for another crime in a corrective-labor institution.[35] One practical problem was posed by the fact that the second list of offenses, crimes for which four occurrences were needed to qualify an offender for the stigma, included ordinary degrees of theft, robbery, and swindling. This meant that the habitual petty thief was likely to draw an extended sentence, as a dangerous offender guilty of a series of murders and rapes. In his monograph on recidivism, in 1964, A. M. Iakovelev had recognized this problem and recommended that these offenses (and also malicious hooliganism) be removed from the list of crimes which made offenders liable for the stigma; for, as far as he was concerned, petty thieves were not 'especially dangerous'.[36]

Galperin approached the same problem with additional data at his disposal. His study of a sample of court records showed that judges actually named as 'specially dangerous recidivist' only 16 per cent of those whose eligibility was based upon group three offenses. In practice most judges did not treat the habitual petty offender as 'specially dangerous' and did not assign him extended sentences. In their discretion judges had for the most part mitigated the effects of bad law.[37] But this finding did not please Galperin, for he personally believed that the habitual petty offender *did* require some extra deterrent beyond the ordinary sanctions which his offenses provoked. Galperin's solution to the dilemma of the under-application of overly harsh law was to reduce that law's severity just to the extent necessary to eliminate the discrepancy between law and practice. Instead of removing the habitual petty offender from the ranks of legally defined recidivists, Galperin suggested the establishment of a new category, 'dangerous recidivist'. Dangerous recidivists would be liable for special sanctions which were not as harsh as those applied to the 'specially dangerous recidivist'.[38]

Both Galperin and Iakovlev recognized that the stigma of 'specially dangerous recidivist' should not be applicable to habitual petty offenders, but their solutions for the problem differed. Galperin sought a new category of recidivists for the petty offenders, while Iakovlev preferred to drop the petty offender entirely from the ranks of legally defined recidivists, leaving judges to apply the remedies called for by the offenders' specific offenses.

Galperin also argued that the stigma of 'specially dangerous recidivist' should not apply to the bulk of inmates who committed a second crime while in confinement, as it had since 1962. For it turned out that persons guilty of crimes in confinement were often not hardened criminals, but ordinary offenders who had erred a second time. Citing data from a study of 250 cases, Galperin showed that as a rule the offenses which had made these men eligible for the designation were not serious; most of the offenses consisted of escape attempts, disturbances of prison order, and a variety of common offenses. Moreover, in assigning the stigma, judges were not expected to pay attention to the seriousness of the original crime which had deprived these men of their freedom. This situation led Galperin to ask rhetorically, 'should an attempted escape in and of itself stand as the sole criterion for labelling an offender a specially dangerous recidivist with attention paid neither to the circumstances of the crime nor to his past record?' The right answer, Galperin opined, was surely 'no'. What was required, he suggested, was placing conditions upon the designation of 'specially dangerous recidivists' on the basis of crimes committed in confinement. The designation ought to be restricted, he claimed, to cases of serious disruptions of prison order or of attempted escapes where the circumstances were aggravated *and* where the original crimes were also serious.[39]

The non-custodial sanction of 'corrective work' was studied by a team of researchers from the Procuracy and MOOP Institutes, headed by A. S. Mikhlin. Although it was introduced in the 1920s, this peculiarly Soviet sanction became widespread only in the 1960s. It imposed upon the offender certain conditions: he was required to continue working at a regular job where he would be supervised by the 'collective', and where he would contribute up to 20 per cent of his salary as a fine. A relatively mild penalty, corrective work was generally applied to first offenders and to persons who had committed less serious offenses; as such it represented a substitute for short-term imprisonment.[40]

Mikhlin's research showed that *prima facie* corrective work was a successful measure. The recidivism rate among offenders who had served a term of corrective work, albeit a low-risk group, was only 9 per cent, compared with a rate of 20 to 30 per cent for offenders who had served short-term sentences in labor colonies.[41] Moreover, Mikhlin found that small improvements would make the sanction even more effective. The failure rate for corrective work was much higher among second-time offenders than among first offenders; therefore, Mikhlin advised, the sanction ought not to be used for the second-timers.[42] In addition, corrective work was more successful when the offender continued at his former place of employment than when he was assigned a new job; therefore, judges should be encouraged to keep the convict at his old job (if he had one).[43]

T. L. Sergeeva and L. F. Pomchalov, the criminologists who studied short-term imprisonment, presented a far different story. Short-term sentences had a high failure rate; many of the convicts returned to prison only months after their release.[44]. The researchers deduced that the terms spent in confinement were just too short. Although the sentences were usually set at six months to a year, the actual time which the offender spent in the colony turned out to be much less, for it has generally been cut in half as a result of the parole and reduced further by the subtraction of any time which the convict had spent in custody while awaiting trial. On the average, the person sentenced to a year or less in a corrective-labor colony spent four months there.[45] It seemed to Sergeeva and Pomchalov that this was hardly enough for the establishment of an educational or a work program to develop the convicts' habits and skills. Therefore, they recommended that short-term sentences be used less frequently; that the minimum term for any custodial sentence be set at one year; and that special institutions be provided for short-term offenders.[46]

All of the research which we have just described, on parole, on specially dangerous recidivists, on corrective work, and on short-term sentences was completed by the end of 1965. During the winter of 1965/66 the research teams under the guidance of Professor Nikiforov prepared for the authorities a series of special reports—of *spravki* and of *dokladnye pisma*—which contained the results of their research, their analysis, and their recommendations. The Procuracy Institute then forwarded the reports directly to the Praesidium of the Supreme Soviet, which had commissioned the research and as well to the Supreme Court, the Procuracy and the MOOP.[47] Versions of the reports were published a few months later for a restricted audience of officials and scholars; openly available articles describing the research and recommendations followed during the course of the subsequent year and a half.[48]

In the spring of 1966 the Praesidium of the Supreme Soviet reviewed the reports from the criminologists and submissions which the Supreme Court and other judicial agencies had prepared, and reached a preliminary decision about the advisability of legislative changes. In June the Praesidium formed a special *ad hoc* working commission of officials and scholars (including B. S. Nikiforov and A. M. Iakovlev), for the purpose of preparing legislation on parole and considering other changes which might be introduced in the Fundamental Principles on Criminal Legislation.[49]

In establishing the commission, the political leadership had apparently already decided to introduce changes in parole regulations. The party-state edict of 23 July described the leaders' intentions regarding parole in a highly specific manner. The leadership 'intended' (*imeetsia v vidu*) to introduce changes in the Fundamental Principles of Criminal Legislation 'to establish supplementary limitations on the application of early release . . . to persons who had already been convicted of serious crimes . . . and to raise the responsibility of persons . . . released early . . . for the commission of new crimes.' While 'intended' did not mean a final decision, the specificity of the changes outlined suggested that the leaders already knew their minds on the parole question.[50] It appeared that the question of changes in the other sanctions – short-term sentences, corrective work, and the concept of specially dangerous recidivist – had not been resolved, but remained open questions for the new commission and the judicial agencies to resolve.

The question of short-term sentences became the object of debate at a large conference which the Supreme Court Advisory Council sponsored in August of 1966.[51] More than three hundred judicial officials and scholars, including most of the leading personnel of the court system, attended the gathering, whose purpose was to discuss a wide range of possible improvements in the court system and in crime prevention.[52] Short-term sentences had been emphasized in the preparatory materials published a few months before the conference; I. I. Karpets, director of the Procuracy, devoted an article to the theme and a survey of opinions on that sanction was also published.[53]

When the short-term sentences were discussed at the conference, there was little exchange of opinion; the issue at hand was the probable effects of the introduction of a one year minimum sentence. In his report to the conference, I. I. Karpets outlined what he thought would be the beneficial effects, and in so doing he cited the research carried out by the criminologists. G. Z. Anashkin of the Supreme Court spelled out the other side of the argument. Anashkin pointed out that from the middle 1930s until 1959 there had been such a minimum sentence, but that it had produced no beneficiary effects; recidivism rates then were no lower than in the 1960s. Moreover, Anashkin ventured that many judges would be reluctant to use non-custodial sanctions like corrective work for offenders whom they currently awarded short prison terms; instead the judges would assign the one year minimum term in corrective labor colonies. Thus, the establishment of a one-year minimum sentence would increase the repressiveness of the law without introducing beneficial results. Anashkin's argument drew support from G. M. Minkovskii of the Procuracy Institute and from some other judges; only the Chairman of the Uzbek Supreme Court spoke in favor of Karpet's proposal.[54]

The discussion at the Supreme Court conference apparently ended the advocacy of a minimum short-term sentence. When the *ad hoc* commission on changes in the Fundamental Principles of Criminal Legislation reconvened, it did not give further attention to this question. Also, the commission decided that changes in the application of the non-custodial sanction 'corrective work' would not require legislative change; administrative orders could be used to direct judges to make improvements in their application.[55]

The *ad hoc* commission of scholars and officials did have to resolve the remaining question of a standard definition of 'specially dangerous recidivist'. It took some time to hammer out the most appropriate definition, especially since the changes in parole regulations had to be worked out simultaneously. It was only in the fall of 1967 that the commission reached a final consensus on the package of changes in the Fundamental Principles of Criminal Legislation, which included both new parole regulations and a new standard definition of specially dangerous recidivist.[56]

Although the draft law was ready for final consideration by political leaders in 1967, the actual legislation was issued only in the summer of 1969, because for practical reasons the judicial leadership wanted these changes promulgated simultaneously with the new Fundamental Principles of Corrective-labor Law, on which the preparatory work was progressing more slowly.[57]

The Amendments to the Fundamental Principles of Criminal Legislation introduced three principal changes in the regulations for adult parole.[58] First, it established a new and standard means for distinguishing those offenders whose parole eligibility began after two-thirds rather than one half of their term. According to the new system, all persons sentenced for any premeditated crime for more than three years deprivation of freedom and persons who were serving their second confinement sentence would have to wait out two-thirds of their time; previously, the republican codes had defined this group according to a list of serious offenses. The net impact was a small increase in the number of offenders who would sit out two-thirds of their sentence and a much simpler system for determining their eligibility. Although Vyshinskaia and Shlykov had not recommended this change, it was inconsistent neither with their thinking nor with that of other legal scholars. The institution of parole had been retained intact, and the shift of some categories of offenders to eligibility after two-thirds of their terms echoed the suggestions of a number of scholars in the late 1950s that two-thirds serve as the benchmark for most or all offenders.

The second change in the parole regulations might be regarded as a weakened version of the Vyshinskaia and Shlykov recommendations. While the original law sanctioned the revocation of parole only when the parolee had committed a new crime of the same degree of seriousness as his first one, the new regulations stipulated that any new criminal offense would be grounds for revocation. Vyshinskaia and Shlykov would have gone a step further and made the commission of administrative offenses grounds for terminating the parole.

Thirdly, the new regulations did include an effort to improve the parole selection procedure. It was not, however, the recommendation of Vyshinskaia and Shlykov which was used, namely to include in the Fundamentals a list of general criteria by which judges would render decision. Rather, the new regulations stipulated that henceforth representatives of the observation commissions would have to countersign the parole petitions submitted by prison authorities. This measure was intended to encourage prison officials to make their selections more responsibly.

Just as Iakovlev and Galperin had suggested, the new definition of 'specially dangerous recidivist' no longer included four or more occurrences of ordinary theft, robbery, swindling, or speculation among the criminal records which might warrant that designation.[59] Basically, it was Iakovlev's rather than Galperin's plan which was accepted; the habitual petty offender was removed from the purview of legal recidivism altogether; and no special category of 'dangerous recidivist' was provided. However, the new parole regulations might in practice have discriminated against this group of offenders, since, as persons who had most likely spent more than one term in confinement, their parole privileges would begin after two-thirds rather than after one-half of their terms.[60]

The new legislation also reflected Galperin's proposal for restrictions in the application of the stigma of 'specially dangerous recidivist' to offenders who committed a crime while in confinement. According to the new regulations, the stigma could be applied to these persons only when the original offense placing them in confinement was fairly serious (at least group three as redefined) *and* the crime committed in confinement was serious enough to draw a five-year penalty. The modified regulations effectively excluded from liability offenders who attempted escapes, except when they had used force in the process.[61]

Criminologists did not play a large role in the execution of the parole and recidivism reforms. The scholars did write short commentaries to help judicial officials, explaining the meaning of the new regulations and speculating on their application to certain types of case.[62] But scholars played no part either in publicizing the changes or in mobilizing support for them.

When political leaders explained the changes to the public, they pointed proudly to the careful study which lay behind them. In a speech to the Supreme Soviet later reprinted in the national press, Supreme Soviet deputy R. Nishanov, also a Secretary of the Uzbek Communist Party,[63] announced

This draft law was originally drawn up by a commission formed by the Praesidium of the USSR Supreme Soviet. On the commission's instructions, sociological and criminological research was conducted with the participation of the central departments and scientific institutions . . . the purpose of the research was to establish the categories of individuals to which the provisions contained in the draft law would be applied in the future.[64]

In explaining how the parole and recidivism decisions were reached, Nishanov was correct to point to criminologists' contributions; but he did not do them full justice. As we have seen, reforming parole was not the central question in the parole discussions which took place among Supreme Court justices and in the press during 1965; at that early stage, the issue was the philosophical justification for parole's very existence. The most important contribution which criminologists made with their research was in proving that parole was worthy of retention and thereby shifting the focus of discussion from parole's existence to its reform. Only after this had been accomplished could criminologists' concrete suggestions on improving parole be seriously considered.

Moreover, with the shift in the focus of the parole discussions went a change in the style of decision-making. Although the parole reform began in an atmosphere of controversy, by the time the decisions were taken the conflicts had been superseded by a cooperative effort to shape a more effective parole system.

In telling the stories of three sets of decisions in Soviet criminal policy during the 1960s, we have not been concerned with analyzing criminologists' participation. The task of evaluating the nature of that participation and its impact on criminal policy remains for the following two chapters. However, it is appropriate to make one observation here, because it affects the organization of our analysis of criminologists' participation.

As we pointed out at the beginning of this part, the three sets of decisions are marked by varied styles of decision-making. Conflict and controversy characterized the alcoholism and hooliganism decisions, while the juvenile delinquency decisions told the story of a smooth, cooperative effort. The scenario of the parole and recidivism decisions provided an interesting variation, where initial controversies faded during the course of the decision-making process.

As different as these three sets of decisions were in the degree of controversy associated with them, and perhaps in other respects too, *criminologists' participation differed little from one set of decisions to another.* For example, in none of the decisions was criminologists' participation episodic; for each it spanned a number of phases of decision-making. Moreover, in each case criminologists did attempt through their participation to contribute to the main substantive questions involved in the decisions.

This observation suggests that for the evaluation of the quality of criminologists' participation the better strategy is to treat the three case studies as a single source of generalizations, rather than to attempt to generate insights through the comparison of the different studies. We have adopted this strategy in Chapter 8 where we evaluate the scope and quality of criminologists' participation; and for almost every generalization therein, all three case studies provided supporting evidence.

Although the degree of conflict or controversy associated with the decisions did not seem to affect the quality of criminologists' participation, it may have affected the nature of their impact on decisions. When in Chapter 9 we assess criminologists' influence on the decisions in which they participated, we will consider this question.

PART THREE

THE SIGNIFICANCE OF SCHOLARLY PARTICIPATION

8 The Nature of Participation

The middle and late 1960s represented a special time in the development of the participation of Soviet criminal law scholars. These were the first years since the 1920s in which criminologists, as opposed to ordinary criminal law scholars, could take part in the formation of Soviet criminal policy; and they were also the years when the participation of Soviet crime experts became a regular feature of criminal policy-making in the USSR. The purpose of this chapter is to analyze the scope and quality of Soviet criminologists' participation during these years. It has already been shown (in Chapter 3) that in the late 1950s the scope and quality of criminal law scholars' participation reached good levels, but there was no guarantee that these levels would be maintained in the 1960s. The part played by scholars in the preparation of major legislation during a criminal law reform might have differed considerably from their role in the formation of policies through the usual pattern of slow and incremental development.

The previous three chapters presented the stories of three sets of decisions in Soviet criminal policy of the middle and late 1960s, in which Soviet criminologists played a prominent part. This chapter uses those decisions as a basis for analyzing the scope and quality of the scholars' participation. In the course of this chapter, we rely again upon the criteria suggested by Brzezinski and Huntington's study – amount and level (scope); and timing and function (quality).

AMOUNT OF PARTICIPATION

In arguing that the participation of Soviet criminal law scholars (including criminologists) became institutionalized during the 1960s, we have already implied what would be the extent and regularity of criminologists' participation. Once scholarly participation became a normal feature of criminal policy-making and of the criminologists' own professional roles, it followed almost by definition that they would take part regularly and in large amounts. The evidence clinches the argument. To begin with, one or another criminologist took part in most of the decisions which related to their expertise. They contributed not only to the decisions described in the case studies just presented, but also to other decisions mentioned at the beginning of Part Two, including those relating to the reform of penal institutions.[1] Administrative orders also required help from criminologists at times. And various criminologists made contributions to the 1966 party-state edict on criminal policy, either through helping to develop legislation mentioned in the edict or through indirect influence on its main themes.[2] Secondly, at least for scholars at agency institutes like the Procuracy Institute, policy-related work became a component part of the scholars' own professional activity. As we saw above, criminologists reported their research findings to government agencies on a regular basis, not just when they were solicited. And the scholars often helped to prepare draft legislation and to advise about administrative orders.[3] Thirdly, it should also be noted that the involvement of individual scholars in particular decisions tended to be long-term rather than episodic in nature; it usually spanned the various stages of the decision-making process. For example, certain criminologists took part in suggesting, in elaborating, and in drafting the reform of the juvenile affairs commissions. The role of other criminologists in the controversy over alcoholism and crime spanned a year and a half, during which time they studied the problem, prepared draft legislation, and discussed the issues in the press. The parole and recidivism reforms called for criminologists knowledgeable on those questions to perform special research before any decisions were taken and also to sit on the *ad hoc* commission which wrote the new legislation.

When we say that in the middle and late 1960s Soviet criminologists participated a great deal in criminal policy-making – in relation to the range of decisions taken in criminal policy, in relation to their own work loads, and in relation to the decision-making process in individual cases – we are speaking about the sum of the activities of individual scholars. Naturally, *all* criminologists did not take part in policy-making to an equal extent; more senior, distinguished, or outspoken scholars played a more prominent part than other ones, in the USSR just as in other countries. Nor was there reason to expect that as many scholars would be involved in criminal policy-making at any one time as during the late 1950s; for in the middle and late 1960s, instead of the reconsideration of many facets of Soviet criminal policy which the law reform of the 1950s had entailed, there were a series of discussions about particular issues. Even under these conditions a sizeable number and respectable range of criminal law scholars and criminologists took part in the making of one decision or another. For any given decision in which scholars played a part, two categories were almost invariably represented: the directors and deputy directors of Moscow research institutes; and the well-established Moscow scholars whose specialty related to the issue at hand. The directors and deputy directors of the institutes became involved in policy discussions whether or not the issues related to their particular expertise. As the representatives of their institutes best known to high law enforcement officials, the directors and deputy directors were often asked to provide the 'view of science' on a given question. Thus, when parole came under attack in 1965 V. N. Kudriavtsev, the Procuracy Institute's deputy director, presented to a USSR Supreme Court debate some research findings and recommendations which followed from the work of B. S. Nikiforov and his sector at that institute.[4] Likewise, the institute's director, I. I. Karpets, offered his views on short-term sentences in another Supreme Court meeting, even though he had played no part in the research which he cited. Moreover, in 'clearing' the reports prepared by members of their institutes for use of high law enforcement officials, the heads of the institute sometimes added their names to the recommendations.[5]

Apart from scholars who headed the institutes, those criminologists most likely to take part in the discussion of a particular policy issue or to serve on a given commission were those with special competence or interest in the issue at hand. Among these scholars those with a good reputation and physically present in the capital city had the best chance for extended participation. In each of the decisions we examined the leading Moscow specialists on the issues involved were the most active consultants: Boldyrev and Minkovskii for juvenile delinquency; Gertsenzon for alcoholism; Nikiforov and Iakovlev for recidivism. This was not to say that other scholars in or outside of Moscow had no opportunities to present their views. Other Moscow scholars, as members of research teams or sectors headed by leading participants, made important contributions to the decisions. Thus, members of Minkovskii's sector like V. S. Pronina; Vyshinskaia and Galperin from Nikiforov's sector; and the whole of Gertsenzon's sector at the Procuracy Institute did research and analysis of the issues ripe for decision. Likewise, scholars in other cities played some part in the decisions. Specialists on juvenile delinquency from around the USSR attended a conference where they heard and commented upon Minkovskii's plans for reforming the juvenile affairs' commissions and for instituting public guardians; and the issue of measures to combat alcoholism and its effects upon crime became an issue of public debate during and after Gertsenzon's team prepared its draft legislation.

LEVEL OF PARTICIPATION

When Soviet criminologists took part in criminal policy decisions during the 1960s, their communication often reached *high levels* of the political-administrative structure. A substantial part of their activity in decision-making brought them into direct contact with top law enforcement officials, and the scholars also had some contact with the Praesidium of the Supreme Soviet.

Leading criminologists regularly communicated with the chiefs of the USSR Procuracy and the USSR Supreme Court. These interchanges took both written and oral forms. The written correspondence included memoranda and reports from research projects and studies, legislative drafts and explanatory materials, and annual research plans and reports from the Procuracy Institute. Oral communication included both formal speeches at sessions of Supreme Court plenums, of legislative commissions, or of the Institute's Academic Council, and informal conversations, during or around these meetings.[6] Each of these types of communication with the law enforcement leaders often concerned matters of policy. Many reports, such as those from the alcoholism study or from the parole research, related directly to current issues. Likewise, the drafts of legislation which ministers had to scrutinize were preparations for decisions. Direct oral exchanges between criminologists and Procuracy or Supreme Court chiefs could also deal with questions of criminal policy. Recall the Supreme Court plenum on the parole reforms; or the discussion of juvenile affairs commissions at the expanded meeting of the Institute's Academic Council, which was attended by some high officials; or the *ad hoc* legislative commissions for each of the decisions, which included leading judicial officials as the representatives of their agencies. In each of these instances, the formal discussions, if not the informal exchanges as well, dealt with current policy questions.

The chiefs of the law enforcement agencies with whom criminologists had such regular contact were among the highest politicians who dealt with criminal policy on a regular or day-to-day basis. Above these politicians stood only the members of the party Politburo and Secretariat, most of whom were generalists responsible for more than one policy area.[7] On roughly the same level of the political structure as top law enforcement officials stood party leaders below the Politburo and the Secretariat, that is the Central Committee *apparatchiki* who ran the Department of Administrative Organs and its sector for legal affairs.[8] But it appeared that the Central Committee staff did not play as large a role in the formation of Soviet criminal policy in the 1960s as did their ministerial counterparts.

In each of the decisions studied here, the chiefs of the USSR Procuracy, the USSR Supreme Court and the MOOP served as the principal initiators and as major arbiters of change. Even when lower officials and scholars supplied the ideas, as in the case of the new measures in juvenile delinquency prevention, the law enforcement chiefs made the formal proposals of change to the Praesidium of the Supreme Soviet. After making the proposals, these ministerial leaders kept in touch with the proceedings by receiving the research reports, special studies, and legislative drafts prepared by the *ad hoc* commissions. In addition, as regular attendants of sessions of the Praesidium of the Supreme Soviet, the Chairman of the USSR Supreme Court, the Procurator-General and the Minister for the Defense of the Social Order had ample opportunity to continue voicing their opinions even at the time of the final decision.[9]

In contrast, the party *apparatchiki* with responsibilities in the legal realm seemed to have played a relatively passive role in the decision-making process for our three sets of decisions. They did not initiate the proposals leading to the decisions; nor did they perform the basic staff work related to them.[10] As the initiators of changes in policies, the law enforcement agencies supplied the documentation for the proposals; and the materials used by the Praesidium of the Supreme Soviet in its eventual deliberations were reportedly compiled by the Praesidium's legal affairs department.[11] It appeared that the role of the leading *apparatchiki* working in law enforcement (the Deputy Chief of the Department of Administrative Organs and the Head of that Department's Legal Affairs Section) in the policy-making process was consultative in nature.[12] In the course of the initiation and advocacy of policy changes, the ministerial leaders normally informed the party officials about their plans and sounded out the latter's opinions. At the same time it was probable that party leaders as well, such as the Secretary, with responsibilities in the legal realms, also solicited the views of the leading members of the Department of Administrative Organs.

The discovery that in the decisions studied the top law enforcement officials played a more active part than the relevant Central Committee staff is somewhat unexpected. A number of Western scholars believed that the opposite pattern usually prevailed. Brzezinski and Huntington, and also A. Avtorkhanov, wrote that Central Committee *apparatchiki* were the principal source in Soviet policy-making both for policy proposals and for argumentation, thus implying that ministerial officials played a secondary role in the policy process.[13] In contrast, my Soviet informants insisted that in criminal policy-making the party *apparatichik*'s role was rarely such a large one. The duties of the legal affairs section of the Department of Administrative Organs were mainly supervisory and concerned with questions of cadres and of policy execution. In the course of supervision, department instructors collected information about the operation of the legal system, so that their superiors the Department chiefs might keep informed about the legal realm. But neither the instructors themselves nor their departmental superiors played a large part in the initiation or advocacy of policy proposals.[14] Consistent with this picture of the work of the Department of Administrative Organs was the nature of criminologists' contacts with it. Evidently, when criminologists were called to 'the TsK', it was more often to help with supervisory work, such as a *proverka*, than to consult on policy matters.[15]

In addition to their contacts with those politicians and high officials who specialized in criminal policy, Soviet criminologists also had occasional contact with the Praesidium of the Supreme Soviet and through it with the top political leaders. One way Soviet criminologists came in touch with the Praesidium was through sending it research reports in which its members had shown interest; for example, the reports from the research on parole and other sanctions which the Praesidium had actually commissioned. Another mechanism which brought criminologists into contact with the Praesidium was their participation on the Praesidium's *ad hoc* commissions. Normally, the Praesidium's staff appointed the commissions, directed their work, and collected the reports and legislative drafts for perusal by the Praesidium's membership.[16] Soviet criminologists' communications to the Praesidium of the Supreme Soviet linked them with the highest governmental body passing on criminal legislation. Any criminal legislation of national significance was considered by the Praesidium of the Supreme Soviet whether the Supreme Soviet, the Praesidium itself, or a republican praesidium or soviet would actually promulgate it. In all three of our case studies the Praesidium of the Supreme Soviet was the formal decision-making body.

Furthermore, in communicating to the Praesidium of the Supreme Soviet, criminologists reached members of the Party Politburo. Two Praesidium members, N. A. Podgornyi and L. I. Brezhnev, were themselves members of the Politburo; and as party leaders in the Praesidium, they were responsible that Praesidium decisions reflected the intentions of the party leadership as a whole.[17] Therefore, they were likely to discuss some of the questions awaiting Praesidium decisions in the Politburo *before* recommending outcomes to the Praesidium. In so doing, they might well relay to their colleagues some of the criminologists' suggestions or argumentation. In the cases studied here, the Politburo must have considered many of the questions at least in principle, for some of the decisions were mentioned in the party-state edict of 1966; but we know nothing about the content of the Politburo discussions.[18]

In addition to contact with politicians and top law enforcement officials, criminologists also kept in close touch with middle-level officials, such as Procuracy and Supreme Court staff below the top ranks. Not only did many criminologists work jointly with these officials on legislation (for example, on the alcoholism law or the juvenile affairs commissions statute), but criminologists also conferred with the officials on a variety of practical tasks.[19] The middle-level law enforcement officials represented an important group of actors in criminal policy-making, since like criminologists they too took part in many aspects of decisions, from suggesting changes through to drafting and execution. Close touch with this group, as well as with high-level officials and politicians, might have helped criminologists affect the attitudes and thinking about crime among other policy actors and thus to influence policy development indirectly, as well as directly through their participation in decision-making.

TIMING OF PARTICIPATION

One criterion of the quality of criminologists' participation suggested by Brzezinski and Huntington's study was the timing of participation. Brzezinski and Huntington argued that most specialist participation occurred after decisions had been taken and too late to have much impact upon the content of decisions. They were able to reach this conclusion, by placing the 'decision' early in the decision-making process. They assumed that the public initiation of a change by a party leader was tantamount to a decision in favor of the question; for 'by generating a policy proposal, the party leadership also approves and legitimizes it'.[20]

The analysis thus far has suggested that the initiation of new measures did not always follow this pattern; in criminal policy of the 1960s law enforcement chiefs, not party leaders, initiated the changes. Nevertheless, this discrepancy need not harm Brzezinski and Huntington's argument. Extending their case, one might suppose that, when the party leadership accepted ministerial proposals for further consideration, it was taking a preliminary decision on the issues at hand; and further that these preliminary decisions might often be the decisive moments, after which further developments would prove inconsequential. According to this line of argument, only participation before the initial acceptance of the ministerial proposal would be reckoned as occurring before the decision, that is during the input phase.

To answer this extended version of the Brzezinski and Huntington argument and to demonstrate that criminologists' participation did occur primarily during the input phase of decision-making, requires us to make one of two possible counterclaims. Either we must establish that criminologists' part in decisions took place largely before the preliminary acceptance of proposals by the party leaders; or we must show that the preliminary decision did not constitute such a decisive moment that subsequent participation was of little consequence for the decision itself. These arguments are important, because it is clear that most of criminologists' participation did occur *before the final decision*, that is before the legislative drafts had been approved for promulgation. In each of our three sets of decisions criminologists' research, special reports, press appearances and service on *ad hoc* commissions took place before the final decision. Only their commentaries on the ensuing legislation and their part in editorial commissions (recall the hooliganism case) occurred after the final decisions had been taken.

Of criminologists' activity which took place before the final decisions, only a portion occurred also before the ministerial proposals for change. Sometimes criminologists did make contributions to those proposals; for example, the proposals for reforms of the juvenile affairs commissions derived in part from research results and from scholars' discussions with Procuracy officials. Likewise, the idea of changing the definition of 'specially dangerous recidivist' had been raised at meetings of legal scholars and in the professional literature. Moreover, criminological research on alcoholism and crime may have been partly responsible for the Praesidium of the Supreme Soviet's interest in a broad package of anti-alcoholism measures.

The larger part of criminologists' involvement with these decisions took place after the proposals by the Procuracy and the Supreme Court and after the preliminary decisions taken by the Praesidium of the Supreme Soviet (or its party group) to give the questions further attention (see Figure 1). It was only after the Praesidium had accepted the principle of new alcoholism legislation that an *ad hoc* commission was established to

Initiation	Preliminary Decision	Mapping the Decision	Final Decision	Output
Research results Proposals		Commissioned research		Editorial work
		Studies for *ad hoc* commissions		Commentaries
		Other research reports		
		Private discussions		
		Public debate		
		Legislative drafts		

Figure 1   Criminologists' Participation by Stages of Decision-making

carry out further study and prepare suggestions for legislation. Only after the Praesidium approval was a commission formed to investigate changes in juvenile delinquency legislation, which in turn entrusted Minkovskii and colleagues to draft a new statute for the juvenile affairs commissions. And the Praesidium of the Supreme Soviet commissioned research on parole, recidivism, short-term sentences, and corrective work, only after it had decided that these questions were ripe for legislative consideration. Articles and debates in the press were also focused during the period between the proposal of change and the final decision. Both Minkovskii articles relating to juvenile crime prevention and also the *Izvestiia* alcoholism debate appeared while criminologists were completing their studies of the questions for the *ad hoc* commissions.[21]

Since the larger part of criminologists' participation took place during the long middle stage, between the preliminary decision and the final decision disposing of the question, it becomes of cardinal importance to assess the nature of the preliminary decision. We must answer the following question: in our three case studies, did the party leaders of the Praesidium of the Supreme Soviet decide the questions when they accepted the ministerial proposals for further consideration?

In none of the three sets of decisions did the preliminary decision actually prefigure the outcome. The preliminary decision on the alcoholism/hooliganism question bore almost no relationship to the

eventual result, for, although the leadership had authorized the preparation of an anti-alcoholism law, it set aside the draft which emerged from
the *ad hoc* commission in favor of new measures against hooliganism. There
were no such dramatic changes in the development of the juvenile affairs
commissions statutes and of the parole/recidivism reforms, but the
preliminary decisions on those questions still were not the decisive
moments. In both of these cases, the preliminary decisions marked the
party leadership's acceptance of the possibility of reforms and its
sanctioning of their *raison d'être*. The leadership could not rule on their
content until scholars and officials had elaborated the details of the
legislation.

The juvenile affairs commission reforms began when the Procuracy
proposed changes in the status and responsibilities of the commissions in
1964. But the elaboration of concrete measures and their incorporation
into a new statute was carried out by scholars and officials during 1965,
after the Praesidium had accepted the Procuracy's proposals for further
consideration. It was during this time that the suggestion to transform the
shefy into public guardians emerged. The actual content of the changes
introduced in the 1967 legislation was determined only in early 1966,
shortly before the final decision was rendered.

The idea of parole reforms had been suggested by the Supreme Court
early in 1965, but the leadership did not decide what changes, if any, it
would introduce until after a year of research and discussion had passed.
The research was commissioned by the Praesidium of the Supreme Soviet;
and the discussion includes Supreme Court justices as well as criminologists and legal scholars. Only after this research and discussions were
completed in early 1966 was a decision reached on the parole changes. The
content of the new definition of 'specially dangerous recidivist' was
determined even later by the *ad hoc* commission appointed in the summer of
1966 to draft changes in the Fundamental Principles of Criminal
Legislation. More than a year passed before the *ad hoc* commission reached
a consensus about which combinations of crimes should warrant the
designation of 'specially dangerous recidivist'.

We see, then, that for the measures introduced in criminal policy during
the 1960s, the preliminary decision was not the decisive moment, but only
a step in the development of the decisions. In most of the decisions we have
studied, the shape of the outcomes was determined not at any one moment
of decision but by a gradual development over the course of the
decision-making process.[22] Since that development ended only with the
final decision, it has to be the final decision, not the preliminary one, which
marked the end of the input phase of the decision-making process for those
decisions. There is, then, no doubt that Soviet criminologists' participation
in these decisions occurred mainly during the input phase.

FUNCTIONS OF PARTICIPATION

Brzezinski and Huntington also claimed that specialist participation related more to output than to input; according to them, mobilization of support for decisions, legitimating them, and helping to refine their details were the principal functions served by specialists. The authors had assumed that output functions were of less import for decision-making than input ones; for although specialists could affect a decision by affecting its implementation, their direct impact would be exerted through contributing information and arguments to decision-makers. Hence, Brzezinski and Huntington reasoned that their assessment of the functions of specialist participation indicated low-quality participation.[23]

Our analysis of the timing of criminologists' participation suggests that Brzezinski and Huntington's reading of the functions of specialists' participation might not apply to criminologists in the 1960s. For since most of criminologists' participation took place before the decision, it was likely that a good portion of it would serve input functions. Still, it is well to examine the evidence. The task here is to determine whether criminologists' participation was directed primarily at the formulation of decisions or at the process of executing them. Did the scholars' contribution serve mainly the input functions of communication and advocacy or the output functions of execution and publicity? To organize the discussion we shall consider separately the functions performed by each of the principal types of participation—private communication (written and oral); commission work; and publications (professional and popular).

PRIVATE COMMUNICATIONS

Private communications between specialists and decision-makers did not enter into Brzezinski and Huntington's analysis, nor for that matter into most studies of Soviet policy-making, because of the difficulty in obtaining information about them. But in this instance, field research did provide the author with evidence about this dimension of specialist participation. By definition, the function of publicity does not apply to private communication; for it would be logically impossible to mobilize popular or professional support for a decision or to legitimate it in the public eye through communications which were either secret or the property of a handful of persons. Therefore, this first part of the analysis of the functions of criminologists' participation focuses only upon the three remaining functions which private communications might serve—communication, advocacy, and execution.

Criminologists communicated with ministerial leaders and with other actors in the political process in four different ways, two of them written and two of them oral.

One type of written communication was the research reports which criminologists sent to ministerial leaders and to other politicians and officials. The primary function of research reports was the communication of information to decision-makers. Reports of unpublished research, like the analyses of weapons used in murders or of patterns of theft in the construction industry or of trends in crime rates were meant to keep decision-makers informed.[24] Likewise, reports of the parole and recidivism research commissioned by the Praesidium of the Supreme Soviet also provided leaders with information upon which to base decisions; most of this research was made public only two years after the private reports were dispatched. The parole and recidivism reports were good examples of how internal reports could become vehicles for advocacy as well. Although the basic purpose of the reports was providing information, the authors did not hesitate to make recommendations; they went beyond mere reporting and took stands on the issues. It was also possible that research reports could serve the execution of decisions. One could imagine follow-up research on the application of measures which would help decision-makers in taking corrective actions. Both the hooliganism law and the law establishing public guardians were subjects for such investigations, but this research was carried out mainly by officials, not by scholars.[25] The research of criminologists during the 1960s had little relationship with the execution of recent decisions.

Another type of written communication by criminologists during the 1960s was the special studies, which resulted from their work in legislative preparation. The alcoholism commission entrusted to Gertsenzon and his colleagues the preparation of a series of special studies on alcoholism and crime, most of which were included as explanatory material which accompanied the legislative drafts. Likewise, the Minkovskii team prepared lengthy explanations of each of the proposed features of the new statutes for the juvenile affairs commissions. Just like the research reports, these special studies were vehicles for passing information to decision-makers and for rendering pleas about specific features of pending decisions. Perhaps, these studies also contributed to the execution of decisions, when they touched upon small technicalities relating to the choice of language or the form of legislation. Still, it would appear that the two input functions, communication and advocacy, were far more important than the output one.

The leading Moscow criminologists also had frequent opportunities to communicate *orally* with ministerial leaders.[26] To begin with, the director, deputy directors, and sector heads of the Procuracy Institute regularly participated in meetings with Procuracy and Supreme Court chiefs. These meetings included sessions of Supreme Court plenums and the Supreme Court advisory council, of the Procuracy Collegium and the Procuracy Methodological Council, of the Academic Council of the Procuracy

Institute, and of the *ad hoc* commissions of the Praesidium of the Supreme Soviet. There were also occasional conferences organized either by scholarly institutions or by the judicial agencies.[27]

Any of these various meetings could serve as a forum for policy discussions, and the criminologists present were likely to take part. We saw how V. N. Kudriavtsev spoke at a Supreme Court plenum on parole reform; and how I. I. Karpets and G. M. Minkovskii took part in discussions about short-term sentences at the conference held by the Supreme Court Advisory Council. An expanded session of the Procuracy Institute's Academic Council heard discussion of juvenile delinquency reforms, in which Minkovskii gave the principal report. Moreover, in the discussion of policy questions in the *ad hoc* commissions, criminologists like Gertsenzon, Nikiforov, and Minkovskii played leading roles.[28]

From our case studies it appeared that the principal function of scholars' presentations at formal gatherings attended by ministerial leaders was the advocacy of position on policy issues. In each case – Kudriavtsev's appeal for more attention to parole research, Karpets' submission in favor of one year minimum sentences and Minkovskii's hesitation about them, and Minkovskii's speech on the juvenile delinquency reforms – the criminologist defended a point of view. When in their presentations they cited the results from research studies, they performed the communication function as well as that of advocacy.

Through their participation in meetings with ministerial officials and leaders, criminologists may also have helped the execution of legislative decisions. Some sessions of the Supreme Court plenums and Procuracy collegium produced administrative orders, to which criminologists sometimes did make contributions.[29] But it appeared that criminologists played no part in any administrative orders relating to the implementation of the sets of decisions which we have studied. For example, even though the implementation of the hooliganism law required a number of administrative orders, criminologists did not take part in their formation.[30]

In addition to oral communication during the course of meetings, criminologists could also speak privately with their ministerial colleagues. It was likely that private conversations occurred frequently, because some criminologists were personal friends of leading judicial officials.[31] The director and deputy directors of the Procuracy Institute had come to know judicial officials when they had worked in the judicial agencies. V. N. Kudriavtsev was friendly with certain Supreme Court justices; and Kudriavtsev wrote articles jointly with deputy Procurator-General N.V. Zhogin.[32] G. I. Kocharov was a favorite among his former Procuracy colleagues because of his pleasing temperament.[33] I. I. Karpets was so well regarded by his former MVD colleagues that he was invited to leave the Procuracy Institute's directorship in 1969 for a high post in the MVD.[34] Institute sector heads, like Gertsenzon and Nikiforov, also had had opportunities to form acquaintanceships with leading judicial officials.

Both Nikiforov and Gertsenzon were major actors in the criminal law reform of the 1950s; Gertsenzon was actually the head of the commission which drafted the RSFSR criminal code.[35]

The various formal meetings which we have described above provided ample opportunities for Institute scholars to maintain and develop the friendships and acquaintanceships which they had formed earlier in their careers. Behind the scenes at such meetings scholars and officials often engaged in private, informal conversations.[36] Although the topics of discussion were diverse, one can assume that they sometimes touched upon current policy questions awaiting decision, especially when those questions were being discussed at the formal meetings. When this happened, criminologists had the opportunity to engage in communication of information and advocacy of their viewpoints.

Taken as a whole, the four different types of private communication — research reports, special studies, formal meetings, and personal conversations — represented a sizeable portion of criminologists' participation in the decision-making process. The functions served by this private communication was almost entirely in the input functions, communication and advocacy.

SERVICE ON COMMISSIONS

Western scholars have found it difficult to determine the nature and functions of Soviet legislative commissions. Even recently, when Barry and Berman wrote about the commissions, they were unsure about the commissions' work and the role of legal scholars on them. Although Barry and Berman realized that *ad hoc* commissions did perform technical work of drafting and editing legislation, they did not know to what extent those commissions were also engaged in determining the substance of legislation; and whether legal scholars on the commissions were involved in such substantive deliberations.[37]

Not only Western scholars but Soviet commentators as well found it difficult to explain the work of the *ad hoc* commissions.[38] The institution of *ad hoc* commissions had not been carefully planned, but had emerged gradually in response to 'the demands of life itself'. As improvised bodies, the *ad hoc* commissions varied both in function and in institutional affiliation. Furthermore, in the 1960s, other types of 'commissions' were also involved in legislative work. To understand the work of Soviet criminologists on the *ad hoc* commissions attached to the Praesidium of the Supreme Soviet, it is well to begin by distinguishing these commissions from two different kinds of commissions — the Juridical Commission of the USSR Council of Ministers and the Standing Commissions on Legislative Proposals of the Supreme Soviet.

The Juridical Commission of the USSR Council of Ministers was a legal agency founded in 1956 to perform those functions of the recently abolished USSR Ministry of Justice which related to the systematization and improvement of all-union legislation.[39] The commission's responsibilities included two kinds of work – the review of draft legislation to be issued by the USSR Council of Ministers, usually relating to economic questions; and the drafting of new codes in various fields of law (recall that the Commission served as the responsible agency for the drafting of the Fundamental Principles of Criminal Legislation of the USSR and Union Republics, issued in December 1958). In the 1960s this Commission had little to do with criminal legislation.[40]

The Standing Commissions on Legislative Proposals were committees of the Supreme Soviet. Comprised solely of deputies, who lived and worked throughout the USSR, these commissions met just for a week prior to the biennial sessions of the Soviet. At that time they reviewed legislation to be presented at the forthcoming session and considered proposals for future legislation. The Standing Commissions themselves played no role in the preparation or drafting of legislation; although sometimes this work was done by their *ad hoc* 'subcommissions', whose membership consisted of Moscow-based scholars and officials.[41]

It is also important to distinguish the various types of *ad hoc* commission. The official nomenclature singled out two types of commission on the basis of their institutional affiliation. Thus, a given *ad hoc* commission might be either a 'subcommission to the Standing Commissions on Legislative Proposals' or a 'special temporary commission' attached to the Praesidium of the Supreme Soviet.[42] These two types of *ad hoc* commission did not differ either in membership or in administration. Both consisted of scholars and officials; and both were appointed and supervised by the juridical section of the apparat of the Praesidium of the Supreme Soviet.[43] The chief differences lay in the functions performed by the commissions.

Informally Soviet jurists were wont to call some commissions 'working' and others 'editorial' commissions. Working commissions were those which prepared the first drafts of legislation (*pervonachalnyi proiekt*) and often preliminary studies as well. Editorial commissions engaged only in the revision of already prepared drafts.[44] From the description of a Soviet official, it appeared Praesidium commissions were always working commissions; they 'engaged in the preliminary consideration of questions awaiting decision by the Praesidium', or 'prepared suggestions for legislation'.[45] The subcommissions to the Standing commissions on legislative proposals could be either working or editorial commissions.

The Praesidium Commissions and the subcommissions to the Standing commissions on legislative proposals also seemed to differ in the policy areas which they covered. Whereas the subcommissions dealt with a variety of areas, the Praesidium commissions dealt mainly with legal policy.[46] A possible explanation is that the preparatory study and drafting carried out by Praesidium commissions in legal policy was a ministerial responsibility in many economic fields; in economic policy, *ad hoc* commissions may have been used only at a later stage in the decision-making process.[47]

To complete the survey one should also mention the 'consultative groups', formed by the juridical section of the apparat of the Praesidium of the Supreme Soviet. Like the editorial commissions, consultative groups of scholars and officials were invited to comment upon already existing legislative drafts. Apparently, the consultative groups were formed earlier in the decision-making process, thus providing a mechanism whereby the Praesidium could obtain specialists' commentary on legislative drafts well before it presented them to the Standing Commission of the Supreme Soviet. Consultative groups appeared especially useful for screening legislative proposals and drafts which had been prepared inside particular ministries, as was often the case with legislation in economic policy.[48]

Most of the commissions in which Soviet criminologists participated during the 1960s were 'special temporary commissions' of the Praesidium of the Supreme Soviet. The *ad hoc* commissions on alcoholism and crime, juvenile delinquency, and parole and recidivism were all of this type. This meant that, if our characterization of Praesidium commissions was correct, criminologists' work on them should not have been limited to technical work like drafting or editing legislation, but should have embraced the study of issues, discussion of tactics, and elaboration of suggestions for action.

Our three case studies fully supported this inference. Long before legislative drafting began, the alcoholism commission deputized Professor Gertsenzon and colleagues to study alcoholism and crime and the remedies previously used for it. Criminologists then prepared recommendations for legislation, which were discussed by the commission, and only then was the draft alcoholism law prepared. The scholars on the juvenile delinquency *ad hoc* commission did similar work. Minkovskii and his colleagues analyzed the suggestions for reform, presented their own proposals, and took part in discussions, all before legislative drafting began. Likewise, criminologists on the commission for parole and recidivism reforms discussed and determined which combination of crimes would warrant the stigma of 'specially dangerous recidivist'.

Through their work on the *ad hoc* commissions of the Praesidium of the Supreme Soviet, criminologists lobbied for their views and supplied information, as much as they helped shape the legal form of the eventual reforms. Thus, they performed the input functions of communication and advocacy, as well as the output function of execution. In addition, criminologists occasionally served on editorial commissions, such as the commision which revised the hooliganism law of 1966. In this effort, however, criminologists' role was clearly limited to the technical jobs of making the legislation legally sound, a task of execution.

Although for Soviet criminologists service on *ad hoc* commissions during the 1960s provided a vehicle for communication and advocacy, this need not have been the case for other specialists serving on other *ad hoc* commissions. The variety of commissions, and particularly the range of functions which the subcommissions of the Standing Commissions on Legislative Suggestions seemed to serve, makes it difficult to predict the significance of a commission's work without knowledge of the particular commission.

PUBLICATIONS

During the 1950s and 1960s the most visible form of specialist participation in Soviet policy-making consisted of articles on policy questions in newspapers and journals. The publishing activity of specialists served as the principal source for Brzezinski and Huntington's analysis of outside participation in policy-making, as it did for that of most Western scholars. Specifically, Brzezinski and Huntington based their argument that specialists executed and mobilized support for decisions upon their interpretation of public debates in *Pravda* and *Izvestiia*, such as those related to the industrial reorganization of 1957 or the 1958 educational reforms.[49] Consequently, consideration of the functions of criminologists' publishing activity in the 1960s might provide the most sensitive test of the authors' thesis about the functions of outsiders in policy-making.

The publications of Soviet criminologists may be divided into two groups, according to the audience at which they were directed: professional literature – journals, monographs, collections of articles, textbooks; and mass circulation literature – articles in the press and popular legal literature.[50]

Naturally legal scholars wrote in the professional journals about matters other than policy. But when they did turn to questions of legal policy, their articles could take a variety of forms, which corresponded roughly to the different functions which they might perform in policy-making. The scholars might analyze problems in the legal system, suggesting the need for reforms; they might discuss already ripe policy questions which awaited politicians' decisions; they might report or explain decisions already taken; or they might solicit professional support for such decisions.

The professional publications associated with our three case studies included the first three of these types of expression. Prior to the emergence as issues of the questions of alcoholism and crime, juvenile affairs commissions, and parole/recidivism, criminologists contributed analyses calling attention to these questions. For example, Boldryev wrote about the operations of juvenile affairs commissions, and Stepichev and Iakovlev probed the shortcomings of the concept 'specially dangerous recidivist' as it was then defined.[51] Once these questions attracted political attention, the criminologists published versions of the special research and studies

which they had performed. These included both the specially commissioned research on parole and recidivism, and the studies of alcoholism
and on the juvenile affairs commissions prepared for the *ad hoc* commission
on which criminologists served.[52] After the decisions had been taken, the
criminologists also wrote commentaries on the new laws, exploring their
meaning for the legal profession.[53]

This list suggests that the bulk of criminologists' professional writing
served input functions. When criminologists published their research or
called attention to needed reforms they engaged in communication and
advocacy. This advocacy probably did attract the support of colleagues for
the proposals, but since the proposals had not yet been accepted by
politicians, the writing could hardly mobilize support for *decisions*. If
politicians did decide in favor of criminologists' proposals, their writings of
months before could serve to legitimate the decisions in the eyes of fellow-
scholars; but this could happen only after the fact, if advocacy were
successful.[54]

None of criminologists' professional writing was designed to mobilize
support for decisions. In fact, the main effort to rouse the legal profession's
backing for the hooliganism law was a hortatory article written not by a
criminologist but by a party *apparatchik*, the head of the legal affairs section
of the CPSU Department of Administrative Organs.[55] Among criminologists' professional writing their main contribution to the output side of
decisions was the commentaries which they wrote on new legislation. Their
function was facilitating the implementation of new legislation.

The basic purpose of scholars' appearances in the mass press differed
from that of their professional writing. As part of their civic obligation,
scholars wrote in the press to inform the public about the law, both its
philosophical dimensions and its practical consequences. The editors of
national newspapers, especially *Izvestiia* and *Literaturnaia Gazeta*, not only
cooperated by making space available to legal scholars, but even solicited
some of their contributions.[56] Current policy questions and recent
legislation were one subject about which legal scholars wrote in the
national press, but there were a variety of forms which the scholars' articles
on this subject could take. As legal reporters, scholars could describe issues
of legal policy; as moral tutors, they could explain the law and encourage
obedience and support for it; or as informed specialists, they could use this
public forum to express their views on policy questions.

An examination of criminologists' appearance in the national press
during the middle 1960s revealed that the latter form was the most
common. Criminologists' articles were neither neutral descriptions of
current problems nor exhortations for citizens to support the law; rather
they were systematic, sometimes impassioned defenses of positions in policy
debates.[57] Consider the reforms of the juvenile affairs commissions and of
parole. In Minkovskii and Pronina's article on the juvenile affairs
commissions, they defended the proposals which had been placed before

the Praesidium commission and which they were incorporating into the draft statute.[58] The point of V. N. Kudriavtsev's article on parole was his argument that the public not prejudge parole before the research on its effectiveness had been completed.[59]

In the alcoholism and hooliganism decisions as well criminologists' press appearances were vehicles for arguing a case. When Gertsenzon and Minkovskii joined in the debate of summer 1965, they offered their opinions on some of the proposals which criminologists were considering for the anti-alcoholism law.[60] After Gertsenzon delivered the completed draft law to the Praesidium of the Supreme Soviet, he wrote another article for *Izvestiia*, supporting the package which his group had prepared.[61] Just after the hooliganism decision, a legal scholar (not a criminologist) wrote an article proposing improvements in the forthcoming legislation.[62] But in the fanfare in the media which announced the new hooliganism law and created the campaign atmosphere, criminologists played no part! In June and July of 1966 correspondents and officials wrote most of the articles on hooliganism; and the same persons penned the announcements of the decisions and the justifications for them. The law enforcement agencies arranged the television publicity for the hooliganism measures; and even the pamphlet literature was written mainly by officials.

Soviet criminologists themselves agreed that their press appearances on policy questions served as a mechanism for the advocacy of positions; but about the effectiveness of these appearances the criminologists disagreed. Some of them minimized the importance of articles in the press, claiming that what appeared in this form was 'only a reflection' of previously articulated arguments. Others, however, regarded the press as one arena for the airing of policy disputes. It was claimed that a well-timed newspaper article ensured that decision-makers heard the arguments more than once; and their appearance in published form as well as in internal reports seemed to make decision-makers less loath to disregard the communications.[63]

In summary, the analysis of the functions of criminologists' participation showed that for all types of participation – private communication, commission work, and publication – the input functions of communication and advocacy predominated. In helping to edit legislation and in commenting on it after promulgation, criminologists did also help to execute decisions, but they did little, if anything, to help publicize the decisions. Criminologists did not take part in the mobilization of support for the decisions, either among the public or among fellow-professionals. To summarize these findings visually, Table 1 is presented.

This examination of Soviet criminologists' participation in Soviet criminal policy-making in the middle and late 1960s has shown it to have been of broad scope and of good quality. The amount of the scholars' involvement in the policy-making process was large, and this activity brought them into

TABLE I   Types and Functions of Participation*

| Types | Functions | | | |
| | Input | | Output | |
	Communication	Advocacy	Execution	Publicity
Private	+ +	+		
Commission	+	+	+	
Publication	+	+ +	+	

* Each + signifies a positive relationship between the type of participation and the function listed. A double + + indicates an especially strong relationship.

contact with high levels of the political-administrative hierarchy. Their efforts took place almost exclusively before final decisions were taken, and the functions served by their participation were mainly communication and advocacy rather than publicity and execution. As a whole, Soviet Criminologists' participation in criminal policy-making turned out to have been serious and potentially influential. In the realm of criminal policy at least, there seemed to be no grounds for suspicion that the scope or quality of specialist participation in the USSR made it less significant than specialist participation in the West.

9 The Effects of Participation

Now that it has been shown that the participation of Soviet criminologists in criminal policy-making in the middle and late 1960s was of broad scope and of good quality, it remains to discover what were the effects of this participation. We shall examine the effects of criminologists' participation in two ways: by scrutinizing their influence upon the decisions in which they took part and by assessing their overall impact upon the evolution of criminal policy. It was only natural that we should assess how criminologists influenced the results of the decisions studied in Part Two; such a focus on individual decisions was typical of comparable studies of political influence in the United States.[1] By itself, however, the study of these individual decisions might record only part of criminologists' effects on Soviet criminal policy in the 1960s. Though in this period any particular decision produced only an incremental change in Soviet criminal policy, a series of those decisions might have introduced a new trend into Soviet criminal policy, which criminologists might have affected. We were led, therefore, to consider the impact of criminologists upon the development of Soviet criminal policy during the 1960s, as well as their influence on specific policy decisions.

INFLUENCING DECISIONS

In this analysis of Soviet criminologists' influence on decisions in Soviet criminal policy, we borrow a definition of influence and two methods for assessing it from the work of students of decision-making in the United States.[2] One of the methods for assessing influence is indirect and the other only approximate; partly for this reason, both can be used with the information available about Soviet criminologists' role in decision-making. Naturally, the results generated by these methods have a tentative character; but no more so than the results of prominent studies of influence in American policy-making. At least, these methods do enable one to discern readily whether Soviet criminologists exercised the same apparent influence over policy decisions as did some Western political actors.

Western scholars have been far from unanimous about the proper meaning of 'influence'. Some have treated the concept so broadly as to denote any expression of a preference by a political participant which later came to fruition.[3] Others proposed a very narrow construction, such as 'making a decision-maker choose other than he would have in the absence of the act of influence'.[4] In its broad definition the concept of influence loses much of its meaning, since influence may be ascribed to actors even when decisions coincide with their preferences only by accident. On the other hand, the narrow definition also has its drawbacks, among them that its use makes it seem as if the exercise of influence in government is an infrequent occurrence. Using this definition, Wilson discovered that interest group leaders in the USA rarely influenced politicians making decisions;[5] nor, one might add, would Soviet specialists. Part of the problem with the narrow definition of 'influence' is that it assumes that the decision-maker and the influencer start with different if not conflicting points of view. Yet, as we have already suggested, many important decisions are made in settings marked more by cooperation than by conflict; and often the influencer does not change the decision-maker's mind as much as reinforce his interest in a particular option or suggest variations in approach which make that option viable. The notion of influence which we prefer is a third variant, one which falls between the first two in the tautness of its criteria. The notion is that of William Gamson, who, relying upon Robert Dahl's insights on the subject, defined an act of influence as 'changing the probability of a given outcome'.[6] According to this formulation the mark of an actor's influence is the fact that, whatever the actual outcome, he has managed to make his preference more likely than it previously was. The mere fact that an outcome coincides with his preference is not a mark of influence; and in some cases where the decision goes against an actor's preference, he may still have exerted some influence. However, an actor need not change a decision-maker's mind in order to have influenced a decision; the actor has merely to have improved the chances that his preferred option be adopted.

This definition has become widely accepted because it captures what many political scientists mean by influence. But the special strength of the definition, which is not always recognized, is that it encompasses a variety of mechanisms of influence and a variety of decision situations. An actor can 'change the probability of outcome' not only by changing the decision-maker's mind, but also by such means as: suggesting ideas to decision-makers who had no preferences on a subject; providing decision-makers with data or argumentation which seemed to support or explain their predispositions; or taking part in discussions which hammered out solutions to problems through the exchange of information, analysis, and opinion. Largely because this definition encompasses these various mechanisms of influence, it is applicable to both of two major classes of decision – those which resulted from conflict situations and those reached primarily through cooperative efforts.[7]

To include influence which may occur in a cooperative decision is important, first because many decisions result from cooperation rather than from conflict (including those in Soviet criminal policy of the 1960s);[8] and secondly, because the study of cooperative decisions may actually reveal more about the influence of specialists than that of decisions wrought in conflict. This supposition reverses the conventional wisdom that conflict decisions make the best case studies of influence. Conflict decisions are useful when the researcher's goal is to compare the influence of different actors;[9] for example, one can infer from the hooliganism decision of 1966 that in that instance the Minister for the Defense of the Social Order carried more weight than a senior scholar.[10] However, this case tells one little about the influence of the scholar, who for his part may also have changed the probability of outcome to some degree. Only through studying other decisions, where specialists did not conflict with more powerful opponents, may one learn about the effects of specialist political activity.

Although the definition of influence used here is properly comprehensive, it does not solve a basic difficulty confronting the student of influence. As Dahl wrote,

> One of the most serious problems in the study of influence arises from the fact that, no matter how precisely one defines influence and no matter how elegant the measures and methods one proposes, the data within reach even of the most assiduous researcher require the use of operational measures that are at best somewhat unsatisfactory.[11]

Even with a plethora of data about the changing predispositions of decision-makers and about the interaction among actors in decision-making, it would be difficult to assess how the behavior of individual participants changed the probability of outcome, when decisions were reached in a cooperative way. The distinctions between the contributions of one actor and another can be difficult for even the actors themselves to recognize.

The way Dahl and Gamson 'compensated for the unsatisfactory character of all existing operational measures of influence' was to employ a combination of them.[12] Unlike Dahl, however, in choosing two indirect methods of assessing the influence of Soviet criminologists upon decisions in criminal policy, we did not strive to be 'eclectic'.[13] The two methods for measuring influence which we employ complement one another; one examines the input side and the other the output side of the decision-making process. Because they focus upon different aspects of decisions, the two methods provide a check on each other's results. While by itself neither method would constitute a sufficient test of influence, the two together provide a convincing calculus.

The first indirect method for assessing criminologists' influence in decision-making is to use 'secondary criteria'. According to this procedure, the analyst who lacks hard data about the variable under consideration selects other variables, secondary criteria, which are clearly correlated with the variable under study. Thus, in studying influence, one gathers data about factors which would tend to enhance influence or which might be considered consequences or corollaries of influence.[14]

Among the variables which are correlated with influence are the criteria of scope and quality of criminologists' participation which were studied in the previous chapter. Here are some illustrations of how level, timing, and functions of participation can serve as indicators of influence.

One of the aspects of scope which we studied was the level in the political hierarchy at which participation took place. Western studies have demonstrated that level is related to influence in at least two ways. According to Wilensky, the higher the level in the hierarchy an actor reaches, the greater his impact upon decision-makers, as stages of summarization are thus obviated.[15] Smith found that the more levels in the political-administrative hierarchy reached by specialists the more influence they were likely to have.[16] Since the empirical analysis in Chapter 8 has shown that Soviet criminologists communicated with persons at a multiplicity of levels, including high ones, the secondary criterion 'level of contact' suggests a high degree of influence, *ceteris paribus*.

Timing of participation in decision-making may also be treated as a secondary indicator of influence. We have already explored (in Chapter 8) the reasons why contacts between specialists and decision-makers should be focused fairly early in the decision-making process for specialists to have maximum impact upon decisions; and we have also demonstrated that Soviet criminologists did participate primarily during the crucial input state.

A further dimension of timing also seemed to affect the quality of scholars' communication. Smith discovered that the earlier in the research process contacts between scholars and decision-makers began, the more influence the scholars were likely to have. His explanation was that decision-makers who were aware of research in progress often developed a stake in it and were thus more receptive to studies once completed.[17] As we have seen, ministerial leaders who were actively involved in the criminal policy decisions were all apprised of the ongoing research relevant to these decisions, since they had approved the planning of the research and followed its progress at meetings of the Institute's Academic Council and through its annual reports.

The relationship between the functions of participation and the degree of influence was a cardinal point in Brzezinski and Huntington's analysis; as we have seen, the authors treated involvement in input functions as more conducive to influence on decisions than involvement in output ones. Chapter 8 demonstrated that criminologists performed primarily the input functions of communication and advocacy rather than the output ones of publicity and execution.

Level, timing and functions of participation were not the only criteria which could serve as secondary indicators of influence. In addition to these, one can suggest other characteristics of criminologists' participation or of the environment in which it took place which were related to the degree of probable influence on decisions. Let us consider five further propositions which are supported by Western writing.[18]

(i) *The Lower the Specificity of Decision-Makers' Demands upon the Specialist, the Greater the Latter's Scope for Influencing the Outcome.*
In exploring the role of intellectuals in public bureaucracies, Robert Merton contrasted the different ways a decision-maker might frame demands to a scholar. On the one hand, he might ask the scholar 'to assemble pertinent facts upon the basis of which later decisions might be "intelligently" made', thus giving the scholar 'broad scope . . . for defining problems, deciding what are pertinent data, and recommending alternative policies'.[19] On the other hand, the decision-maker might just as easily call upon the specialist at a later stage in the decision-making process to answer more specific questions, about the relative merits of two alternative strategies under consideration or about means for implementing a chosen action. That the scholar or specialists had more scope for influence in the first of these alternative cases was almost common sense.

When Soviet criminologists became involved in decisions, they often had a broad mandate. As we saw, the alcoholism commission and the scholars who performed studies for it were asked to explore the full range of anti-alcoholism measures which had been previously attempted in Russia and in the West. They had the opportunity not just to comment upon leadership proposals but to put together a package of recommended measures. In a like manner the Praesidium commission investigating juvenile crime was not limited to reforming the juvenile affairs commissions, but was encouraged to undertake a full examination of preventive measures applied to juveniles. In the course of this examination, the scholars on the commission developed the idea of 'social helpers', a notion which itself led to further legislation. The mandate of the parole researchers may have been narrower, since their task was to justify the continuation of the parole system through study of its operations, rather than to invent alternatives or suggest major changes. Still, taken as a whole, the four research projects associated with the changes in the Fundamental Principles of Criminal Legislation (parole, recidivism, short-term sentences, and corrective work) did represent a full investigation of some penal sanctions prior to any political commitments to take action upon them. In short, the phrase 'assemble pertinent facts upon the basis of which later decisions might be made', accurately described the contributions of Soviet criminologists to these decisions.

(ii) *The Richer the Quality of Information Provided by Specialists Relative to the Information Provided by Others, the More Effect it will have upon Decision-Makers.* Both Karl Deutsch and Robert Merton have commented upon the importance of the quality of information supplied by specialists. In discussions of cybernetic models of information flow, Duetsch suggested that, all things being equal, the effect of information 'beamed' at a receiver depended upon the richness of the information so sent.[20] Reasoning along similar lines Merton hypothesized that decision-makers showed ambivalence towards specialists on social policy because the knowledge which they provided was less sound or 'determinate' than that which an adviser on a technological question might offer.[21] More recent research has shown that, practically speaking, the relative quality of the information provided to the decision-makers should be substituted in the equation for absolute quality. According to Lazarsfeld and Reitz, decision-makers who perceive the need to make decisions often rely upon advisers regardless of the scientific soundness of their advice. Such decision-makers are forced by the logic of their situation to seek the 'best available advice' rather than some theoretical optimum.[22]

More often than not, Soviet criminologists did provide the best available information on criminal policy questions. The only thorough, statistically-based, studies of parole and recidivism and of the juvenile affairs commissions were those prepared by the criminologists. Since the scholars consulted with judicial officials, there was usually no reason for the officials to add further documentation. However, when the MOOP proposed the new measures against hooliganism in 1966, it provided its own statistics on the relationship of hooliganism to other crimes. Although the inferences which MOOP officials drew from that data may have been unsound, they presented them so convincingly that there was no noticeable difference between the quality of their communications and those of the criminologists on alcoholism prevention.[23]

(iii) *The More Personal Contact a Specialist has with Decision-Makers, the more Influence he is Likely to Exert.*
Western analysts agree about the importance of personal relations in the process of influencing decisions. In his research on the RAND Corporation, Bruce Smith discovered that personal relations made a considerable difference in the effectiveness of specialists' attempts to secure decisions.[24] Moreover, Lazarsfeld and Reitz also determined from an inventory of studies that the personal relationship between the social analyst and the decision-maker had a bearing upon the use of the social scientist's advice.[25] Robert Merton hypothesized that the indeterminacy of social knowledge increased the importance of the personal dimension in the adviser-client relationship. 'The more indefinite the objective standards of appraisal, the greater the possibility of interpersonal relations, sentiments, and other non-objective factors determining the clients' confidence in the expert.'[26]

The previous chapter illustrated in detail the nature of Soviet criminologists' personal relationships with leading judicial officials. Contacts between criminologists and ministerial officials were regular and frequent, and some criminologists were even the personal friends of ministerial colleagues.

(iv) *The More Special Means of Communication Specialists Use, the More Influence They are Likely to Have.*

Smith has pointed out that officials (decision-makers) rarely have the time or the inclination to read lengthy reports or research monographs. To communicate effectively, therefore, specialists normally 'resort to a number of supplements to (and sometimes substitutes for) the practice of open publication and scholarly exchanges . . .' These substitutes might include special or summary reports of research and various forms of oral briefing.[27] Moreover, Wilensky found that decision-makers preferred special or secret materials to openly available ones, even though the qualitative differences might be nil.[28] As we have seen, Soviet criminologists invariably reported their research results in special reports, *dokladnye pisma* and *spravki*, which were both short enough for decision-makers to read and secret enough for them to value.

(v) *The Less Radical or Innovative Specialists' Suggestions, the More Likely That They Will be Heeded.*

Robert K. Merton stressed that specialists could not expect to be successful if they made proposals which ran counter to a decision-maker's values or expectations.[29] Likewise, Charles Lindblom has described the art of political communication as making one's own points in ways which appeal to the decision-makers' values or perceptions; such tactics would not usually be possible, if radical changes are contemplated.[30] As it turned out, the decisions in criminal policy during the 1960s in which criminologists participated were all ordinary decisions, and on the whole criminologists' suggestions were also ordinary, in that they called neither for radical changes nor for fundamental decisions.

We have just seen that each of five secondary criteria discussed here, as well as scope, timing, and function, which were discussed in Chapter 4, correlated positively with probable influence of criminologists upon the decisions in which they participated. The cumulative effect of positive results from all of these secondary indicators suggests that criminologists did exert considerable influence upon those decisions. This inference becomes even stronger when it is reinforced by the results of another indirect method of assessing criminologists' influence, a method based upon the results of the decisions.

The second method of appraising criminologists' influence is what Gamson called the 'relative frequency approach'.[31] The analyst isolates the decisions in which specialists took part, compares the number of decisions which turned out favorable to the specialists' views with those which went against them, and constructs an index of the relative frequency of success. The principal difficulty with such an index rests with the assumptions which underlie it. For example, in using this index, one assumes that at the time of specialists' entry into decision-making process the chances of any particular outcome are fifty-fifty, when the actual odds may be very different. Gamson has suggested that the normal bias is against parties which attempt to introduce changes, but this suggestion does not eliminate the required assumption.[32] Another difficulty with this method is that it does not differentiate the effects of various actors who argue along similar lines. One is forced to assume that the effect upon the decision of actors arguing along similar lines is equally apportioned.

Our three case studies provided seven different issues upon which decisions were taken involving criminologists' participation: reform of the juvenile affairs commissions, introduction of public guardians, extension of compulsory treatment of alcoholics to the RSFSR, the establishment of other alcoholism prevention measures, parole reforms, reforms in the treatment of recidivists, and changes in the application of short-term sentences.[33] These seven decisions serve as the building blocks for an index of the relative frequency of criminologists' success.

In constructing our index of relative frequency, we were concerned only with the preferences of those criminologists who were actively involved in the political process for the particular decisions concerned. To appraise how well decisions matched their preferences we distinguished between five different types of outcome – decisions which (1) fully reflect criminologists' preferences; (2) reflect criminologists' preferences in the main or in significant part; (3) run somewhat against criminologists' preferences; (4) run counter to criminolgists' preferences; (5) have outcomes which are neutral in relationship to criminologists' preferences, or about which criminologists had no clear preference.

Of the seven decisions considered for this index, only one ran counter to criminologists' preferences, and that was the rejection of alcoholism prevention measures in favor of legislation combating hooliganism. On one decision criminologists' preferences were too divided for us to draw any conclusions: the decision not to restrict short-term sentences to a one-year minimum agreed with Minkovskii's thinking but not with that of Karpets. Two decisions matched the preferences of the criminologists who had worked on them down to the smallest details: the reforms of the juvenile affairs commissions (Minkovskii) and the establishment of compulsory treatment of alcoholics (Gertsenzon). Three decisions matched criminologists' preferences in the main: the parole decision included some of Vyshinskaia and Shlykov's suggestions and did not contradict any of them; the recidivism decision affected the thrust of Iavkolev and Galperin's concerns and in its details matched concrete suggestions from each of them; the establishment of public guardians represented the realization of Minkovskii's idea in all but one detail – the inclusion of moral as well as material incentives for the guardians.

In tabular form the results appear as follows:

TABLE 2 Decision Outcomes and Criminologist's Preferences

How Decisions relate to Criminologists' Preferences	Number of Decisions
Fully accord	2
Accord in the main	3
Run somewhat against	0
Run counter	1
No clear relationship	1

Taking only the six decisions where the criminologists involved displayed clear preferences, one discovers that, in five out of six decisions the outcomes accorded either fully or in the main with criminologists' preferences. This result was fully as good as that reported by Gamson in his study of the relative frequency of positive outcomes achieved by 'influentials' in community politics.[34] The small number of cases from which our index is constructed naturally limits the inferences one can draw from it, but the results may be taken as one indicator of the probable influence of criminologists on the decisions.

If we use decision outcomes as an indicator of criminologists' influence, we may reach some tentative conclusions about the effects which the degree of political conflict or controversy had upon criminologists' influence. In all of the decisions where the level of political conflict was low (juvenile affairs commissions, compulsory treatment of alcoholics, recidivism, public guardians), decision outcomes tended to match criminologists' desires; but in the decisions where the level of political conflict was high (hooliganism, parole, short-term sentence), there was no pattern to be found. Although the hooliganism decision went against criminologists' desires, the parole decision for the most part reflected their wishes; and the decision on short-term sentences bore no relationship to criminologists' views. It appears, therefore, that the absence of political conflict or controversy enhances the probability of specialist influence; but that the presence of disputes by itself has little effect.[35]

We have seen that two different indirect methods of assessing criminologists' influence on decisions in criminal policy strongly suggest that criminologists were influential in those decisions. By itself, either one of these assessments might stand only as a basis for hypothesizing influence, but together they call for a stronger assertion. Not only do the results reinforce each other, but the two assessments measured complementary phenomena. One assessed the nature of criminologists' input to the decisions, the other considered how the output, that is, the decisions themselves, reflected the criminologists' concerns. To ascertain that criminologists' participation was of good quality, took place under propitious circumstances, and led to positive outcomes, we would suggest, was to supply the basis for a *prima facie* case of influence and for a case as good as that found in most Western studies of political influence.[36] It is fair to conclude that Soviet criminologists exerted considerable influence upon some of the decisions in which they took part.

IMPACT ON POLICY

In influencing the results of a number of criminal policy decisions in the middle and late 1960s, Soviet criminologists were likely to have exerted some impact as well upon the development of that policy. At the minimum the scholars affected the details of Soviet criminal policy which were involved in the decisions in which they took part. The question remains whether the criminologists also contributed to some strand of criminal policy, new or old, which was not chosen in a single decision, but evolved through the course of a series of decisions. To find the answer, one must identify trends or tendencies in Soviet criminal policy of the middle and late 1960s and relate them to the participation of criminologists. The policy trends of a given period may represent either the continuation of policy from a previous period or new policy; thus, in principle, the contribution of Soviet criminologists might have been associated with old or with new strands of policy. Although it would be desirable to describe the scholars' contributions both to continuity and to change in policy, as a practical matter it is easier to study their association with policy change. Although one can identify policy changes and the activities of scholars which related to them, it is usually hard to distinguish the effects of scholars' support for the *status quo* from the natural bias in stable systems which favors the continuation of previous policies. Only in cases where a policy change was proposed and subsequently rejected would opposition to change on the part of scholars even be noticeable. In this discussion of criminologists' policy impact in the 1960s, we deal mainly with their contribution to the emergence of a new trend in Soviet criminal policy.

Our procedure in analyzing the impact of Soviet criminologists upon criminal policy in the middle and late 1960s consists of the following steps. First, we try to identify seemingly new policy trends during this period and to confirm their novelty through comparison with the previous period in Soviet criminal policy, the late 1950s and early 1960s. Then, we examine in what ways these new trends were related to the participation of Soviet criminologists, both to their direct involvement in decision-making and to indirect ways they might have affected policy development. Lastly, we assess briefly the importance of the new trends for Soviet criminal policy as a whole.

In looking for trends in criminal policy it is customary to identify the policy in a given period with a certain penal philosophy. A criminal policy is said to be liberal or conservative, or in the process of liberalizing or tightening up. Not surprisingly, some (a minority) of the actual participants in Soviet criminal policy-making viewed the issues in terms of this familiar dichotomy,[37] as did some Western observers as well. However, when taken as a group, the decisions in Soviet criminal policy during the middle and late 1960s did not reflect a consistent penal philosophy. Although the hooliganism decision constituted a step in a repressive or conservative direction, the juvenile affairs commissions reforms and the establishment of public guardians were liberalizing measures; and the extension of the compulsory treatment of alcoholics and the modification of the classification of recidivists belonged to neither category. Soviet criminal policy during the 1960s was neither liberal nor conservative.

Nevertheless, there was a trend in Soviet criminal policy of the 1960s, which all of these decisions embodied to a greater or lesser degree, and that was *an increased emphasis upon crime prevention* as a dimension of criminal policy. The novelty of this change lay not in the rhetoric about preventing or eliminating crime, but in the *de facto* treatment of crime prevention as an operative goal used for assessing the merits of proposed measures and the effectiveness of existing institutions.

As a stated aim, crime prevention had been associated with Soviet criminal policy since 1917.[38] Marxist-Leninist theory proposed that the construction of socialism would bring the gradual disappearance of crime, and Soviet criminal policy was meant to encourage this inevitable process. Under the influence of progressive (mostly Positivist) ideas, Soviet jurists of the 1920s encouraged prophylactic as well as repressive measures as means of achieving this end. But during the Stalinist years, when repression increased in scope and intensity, the emphasis upon crime prevention receded into the background. Stalinist repression did not seem to be serving the aim of reducing crime, but instead other goals, such as the maintenance of order and the definition of conformist behavior. After Stalin's death the scope and intensity of repression was reduced, and crime prevention gradually regained its place as a goal in Soviet criminal policy. Although the reduction of repression took immediate effect, the re-emergence of crime prevention as a purpose of Soviet criminal policy occurred more gradually.

During the middle and late 1960s there were two new developments which indicated that crime prevention finally was becoming an *operative* goal in Soviet criminal policy. These were (1) the increasing use of prophylactic and educational measures in dealing with offenders and in counteracting criminogenic situations; (2) the increasing availability and reliance upon statistical and social scientific analyses evaluating criminal policy and operations. Both of these developments could be observed in the decisions studied here and in other decisions of the 1960s.

The use of prophylactic and educational measures in dealing with offenders, real or potential, is a good indicator of a genuine interest in crime prevention. Unlike various types of control measures or of criminal repression which, although justifiable in terms of the goal of crime prevention, could easily serve other purposes, measures to re-educate offenders or to counteract criminogenic conditions unambiguously serve the goal of crime prevention. Both the extension of treatment for alcoholics and the juvenile delinquency reforms represented new prophylactic and educational measures established during the 1960s. As we saw, the juvenile affairs commissions received new full-time staff largely to assure that they would fulfil their assigned duties of supervising and coordinating juvenile delinquency prevention in their districts. The public guardians were introduced to improve the resources of volunteers who came forward to assist young troublemakers and their families. Likewise, the establishment of compulsory treatment of alcoholics in the RSFSR was intended to serve as a means of preventing hooliganism and dangerous crime, by attacking a criminogenic problem (alcoholism) through educational measures. Other decisions in criminal policy during the 1960s also extended or improved the system of prophylactic measures. These included the extension of the responsibilities of the observation commissions to include helping offenders returning from confinement; and the application of administrative (police) supervision to more serious offenders when they returned to freedom.[39] Moreover, as a consequence of the 1963 party edict on juvenile delinquency and the 1966 party-state edict on crime, the middle and late 1960s saw an increasing number of crime prevention campaigns on the city or town level.[40]

The expansion of statistical and social scientific analysis for use in the evaluation of policy and operations also suggested the increasing significance of crime prevention. As we saw in Chapter 4, the post-Stalin revival of crime study was integrally related to renewed concern with crime prevention; and criminologists encouraged the link by justifying the study in terms of its contributions to crime prevention. Naturally, most crime studies treated crime prevention as their orienting purpose. Each of the decisions treated in our studies drew upon statistical and social scientific analysis, and in each case this analysis was related to the goal of crime prevention. The juvenile commissions reforms were based upon studies demonstrating their inadequate performance of prophylactic duties. The parole decisions followed the commission research on the effects of parole upon recidivism rates; and the modification in the definition of 'specially dangerous recidivist' were introduced to account for the finding that the category was sometimes applied to offenders for whom its prophylactic significance would be minimal. Even more striking was the use of statistical data by MOOP officials, when they defended their proposal for increased repression of hooligans. Through the analysis of statistics the officials tried to demonstrate how the repression of hooliganism would prevent more serious crime. Local officials also had available statistical analyses upon which to base operational decisions, partly because they themselves were performing more research. The movement to encourage operational research in the administration of justice on the local level gained momentum, when in 1965 the Procuracy 'suggested' that its staff undertake critical inquiries into local crime rates and crime prevention efforts.[41] Then, in 1966 the party leadership solicited 'the systematic and deep analysis of the crime situation in every republic, krai, city and region'.[42] By the late 1960s procurators in a number of regions engaged in statistical studies of one sort or another; and, although their scientific quality was uneven, these studies were usually aimed at improving crime prevention.[43]

Both features of the trend toward treating crime prevention as an operative goal in Soviet criminal policy turned out to have developed fully only in the years 1964–70, when criminologists became regular participants in the political process. The previous seven years, 1957–63, had seen only the beginning of the application of prophylactic and educational measures and of the empirical assessment of the effectivenss of policy measures. Under Khrushchev politicians indulged in much rhetoric about crime prevention, but the programs they encouraged related more to Khrushchev's campaign to enlist public involvement in the crime struggle than to the actual prevention of crime.[44] Some of the measures were prophylactic only in an indirect way; for example, the Comrades Courts, informal bodies which resolved disputes and punished petty infractions, were prophylactic only to the extent that by punishing small offenses they succeeded in averting crimes in the future. Nor did the 'crime prevention' programs of this period receive adequate financial support; as we saw, the absence of appropriations made it impossible for the juvenile affairs commissions to employ the staff necessary for coordinating delinquency prevention on the community level, while at the same time hearing many cases involving young offenders. Not only were crime prevention measures often indirect or poorly supported before the middle 1960s, but they also played a very small part in criminal policy as a whole. This was especially so in 1961–2, when the conservative turn in Soviet criminal policy made repression of criminals the first priority.

Likewise, empirical analysis of the effectiveness of existing or proposed measures in criminal policy was the exception more than the rule in the late 1950s and early 1960s. The new provisions regarding 'specially dangerous recidivists' established in 1958 and 1959 were unusual in owing their origins partly to criminological analysis; in fact, the study of recidivists performed by the Shirvindt team was among the first policy-related crime studies of the post-Stalin period. More typically, the decisions in Soviet criminal policy during these years were based upon opinions – opinions about which legal norms were the fairest; and opinions about which norms would prove most effective. For example, the question of parole caused much disagreement about what the 'best' parole scheme would be; for jurists differed both in the degree of leniency they deemed appropriate and in their assessments of the likely effects of various parole schemes. As a consequence, there was much groping in the attempt to set up a fair and effective parole system, and the liberal policy envisaged by the draft Fundamental Principles of Criminal Legislation in 1957 was modified in 1958, 1961, and 1962 by changes which tightened its application, as well as making it more differentiated. In contrast, during 1964–70, the continuing search for the optimal parole system utilized findings of empirical study about what effects particular features of parole policy had on the criminal careers of offenders released early.

This new tendency to treat crime prevention as an operative goal in Soviet criminal policy was closely related to the presence of criminologists in the political process. As we have seen, the very revival of criminology and the entry of criminologists into decision-making was premised upon the contribution which these specialists would make through their analysis to crime prevention. In addition to this, criminologists appeared to have encouraged this trend, both through their influence upon individual decisions and through more indirect means. During the 1960s criminologists were influential in a number of decisions which introduced new prophylactic measures – the juvenile affairs commissions reform, the introduction of 'social helpers', the expansion of the compulsory treatment of alcoholics. For the reforms which concerned juvenile offenders criminologists supplied many of the proposals which constituted the reforms. In addition, for virtually all of the decisions studied in Part two criminologists supplied statistical or scientific data which related the issues to the goal of crime prevention. Through their participation in decisions criminologists directly encouraged the increased emphasis upon crime prevention.

Also important for the emergence of crime prevention as an operative goal in Soviet criminal policy were certain indirect mechanisms of scholarly influence on policy – influence upon leadership attitudes toward crime control and contributions to the general pool of ideas about the subject. By helping to shape the way politicians and law enforcement officials viewed crime and criminals, the criminologists might have influenced the way these men approached specific policy issues or problems. For example, if through their communications decision-makers came to value the goal of crime prevention more highly, this fact might be reflected in the evolution of criminal policy. As it was, from the beginning of criminology's revival in the late 1950s criminologists had been propagating the goal of crime prevention and the utility of crime study for that purpose; and during the 1960s scholars came to have closer contact with law enforcement officials and leaders than before. The assumption is, therefore, that if these law enforcement officials did come to value crime prevention highly, they were reflecting in part their contact with criminologists.

Two types of evidence suggested that during the 1960s law enforcement officials in the USSR were becoming increasingly concerned with crime prevention: the observations of Soviet criminologists; and the public statements of officials. Three different senior criminologists, each of them cautious by nature, reported to the author that criminologists seemed to have made law enforcement officials more aware and concerned about crime prevention and study. In fact, two of these scholars suggested that criminologists' effect upon the attitudes of law enforcement officials was the most important form of criminologists' impact upon criminal policy.[45] Public statements by leading officials seemed to confirm the observations of the criminologists. Of course, one must remember that only a minority of ministerial leaders in the legal field wrote in the press or scholarly journals. But in the middle and late 1960s the active publicists among law enforcement leaders did express considerable enthusiasm for the use of prophylactic measures and for the role of statistics and social science in criminal policy. As illustrations, consider the comments of Deputy Chairman of the Supreme Court G. Z. Anashkin, Deputy Procurator-General N. V. Zhogin, and Minister for the Defense of the Social Order, N. A. Shchelokov.

Zhogin, who had some background in scholarship, had been a strong supporter of criminology from its incipient moments; thus it was not surprising that later on he supported crime prevention and called for 'constant and deep study of practice to yield scientifically-founded recommendations for legislation'.[46] Anashkin, a leading liberal in criminal policy, also supported the goal of crime prevention. He wrote in 1965 that practice had demonstrated that educational and prophylactic measures were more useful than repression and that the best way to strengthen the effectiveness of such measures was through careful study of the causes and conditions facilitating crime.[47] Perhaps more indicative of a change in attitudes of law enforcement officials presumably effected by criminologists was the strong support for crime study and prevention from a figure not previously associated with the liberal group among officials, the Minister for the Defense of the Social Order, N. A. Shchelokov. Both in *Pravda* in 1967 and later that year at a conference, Shchelokov took a stand.[48] To improve crime prevention, he claimed, much more scientific study was required; as it was, there were 'too few criminologists', and the problems of crime and delinquency had been understudied; an insufficiency of useful recommendations 'was one of the reasons why practical measures in the fight with this evil [crime] were not always effective'. Moreover, Shchelokov continued, 'scholars have the right to demand that we [the officials] perform research and that we study and apply their recommendations.[49] These attitudes did not characterize all law enforcement leaders during the middle 1960s; indeed, in analyzing the parole decision, we saw that some leading officials resisted the new reliance upon 'scientific standards' for the evaluation of how effectively parole reduced crime. The criminologist V. N. Kudriavtsev was forced to admonish some of the judges to rely upon analysis which related facts to the goals of criminal policy rather than upon uninformed opinion or bias.[50] However, as a consequence of criminologists' participation in policy work, it appeared that some of the leading law enforcement officials had become more concerned with crime prevention and had come to respect the contributions which social science could make toward that goal.

Another, even more indirect, way in which scholars could affect policy was by contributing to the general pool of ideas which related to the policy realm in question. Not infrequently have scholars in the West developed and publicized lines of thought or concrete policy suggestions which policy-makers at first either rejected or failed to consider. Yet later, after seven, ten or even twenty years, the same policy-makers or new ones embraced those very ideas or policies, often without recognizing their earlier proponents. In this way Soviet criminologists' ideas about the primacy of crime prevention and about the use of scientific methods might well turn out to have made their gratest impact not in the 1960s when the ideas were first propagated, but in the 1970s or 1980s, after they became more familiar to officials and politicians.[51] Obviously, this study cannot fully evaluate this kind of indirect influence by Soviet criminologists. However, there was some evidence that suggestions made by criminologists in the middle 1960s but rejected at the time finally came to fruition in the early 1970s. One has only to recall what happened to the suggestions made by Professor Gertsenzon and his colleagues for the control of the alcohol and crime problem. In order to prevent some of the many criminal acts committed by persons in an intoxicated state, Gertsenzon proposed in 1965 that a variety of measures be taken to reduce the incidence of drunkenness, measures which included restrictions on the production and sale of alcoholic beverages. In 1966 Soviet leaders decided to reject Gertsenzon's program in favor of another approach to drunken offenders, namely increasing the severity of the sanctions applied to them. But six years after the rejection of Gertsenzon's proposals and three years after his death Soviet leaders decided to adopt measures to reduce drunkenness which included most of Gertsenzon's proposals. Thus, after a time lag Soviet leaders finally embraced the suggestions of a criminologist which they had previously rejected.

We have seen, then, that both through their participation in decision-making and through indirect means criminologists encouraged the new emphasis upon crime prevention which appeared in Soviet criminal policy during the 1960s. Naturally, the scholars were not wholly responsible for this trend; the death of Stalin and the process of de-Stalinization were necessary preconditions for this change. Yet, without criminologists' efforts crime prevention might have come into prominence more slowly, if at all, during that decade.

To gain more perspective upon the impact of criminologists upon Soviet criminal policy in the 1960s, one ought to consider as well how the new trend in policy, emphasis upon crime prevention, related to Soviet criminal policy as a whole. The answer was unambiguous. The emphasis upon crime prevention proved wholly compatible with the continuing primacy of repression and stigmatization as the main functions of the criminal justice system.[52] The addition of new prophylactic measures during the late 1960s did not interfere with the usual work of the administration of justice in maintaining law and order and in processing deviants. Nor did the new scientific analysis of the criminal justice system lead to challenges of either the severity or existence of repressive sanctions. Criminological studies tended to improve the efficiency of criminal justice more than to change its character.

Further evidence that the emphasis on crime prevention was just a new strand in Soviet criminal policy and not a departure from previous norms is found in the principal criminal policy statement of the 1960s, the party-state edict of 1966.[53] This edict was a comprehensive summary of criminal policy, which stated goals and general principles and noted recent and anticipated decisions on concrete questions. According to Professor Gertsenzon, the edict 'determined the basic lines of Soviet criminal policy for contemporary conditions.[54] The edict placed the party's support behind the broad use of crime study to improve the administration of justice and crime prevention; and it mentioned various prophylactic measures decided or under consideration – the juvenile commissions reforms, public guardians, compulsory treatment for alcoholics. But at the same time the edict also emphasized law and order and the stigmatization of troublemakers. The hooliganism measures, which the announcement of the edict accompanied, increased the repression of drunken rowdies, and in the process marked them as the deviants of the hour, wretches 'who crudely flouted the legal order.' Furthermore, other decisions mentioned in the edict were aimed at improving the maintenance of law and order; for example, the creation of motorized police patrol units for large cities and new measures to improve the investigation of persons hiding from pursuit. On balance, the edict portrayed Soviet criminal policy as a mixture of different approaches to the problem of controlling criminal behavior, of which crime prevention was certainly the newest but not necessarily the principal one.[55]

By helping to develop and to make more prominent a new strand in Soviet criminal policy, Soviet criminologists of the 1960s contributed to an important, but not fundamental, policy change. That the change was not fundamental, however, need not detract from our assessment of their policy impact. For innovations or major shifts seemed to occur infrequently in the criminal policies of most nations; and the decade of the

1960s was poorly suited for innovations in criminal policy, coming as it did on the heels of an important and popular criminal law reform. With but a few exceptions, politicians, officials, and scholars alike seemed more intent on adjusting the law to make it work better than on seeking wholly new approachs to crime control. In this context the criminologists' achievement was substantial. The emphasis upon crime prevention constituted the principal new trend in Soviet criminal policy during the middle and late 1960s; and criminologists' part in promoting it demonstrated that they had succeeded in exerting a moderate impact upon the criminal policy of the time.

10 Specialist Participation Reconsidered

This study has charted the development of Soviet criminal law scholars' participation in criminal policy-making from the late 1930s through the 1960s and has assessed the nature and effects of criminologists' participation in Soviet criminal policy-making during the middle and late 1960s. In the final chapter we aim not to summarize this analysis but to go beyond it, first by drawing together the main findings for each of these lines of inquiry and examining their implications; and then by exploring the significance of the study as a whole.

CRIMINAL LAW SCHOLARS' ROLE IN HISTORICAL PERSPECTIVE

The history of criminal law scholars' role in the formation of Soviet criminal policy suggested four findings which deserved further attention and explanation:

> that under Stalin Soviet criminal law scholars did take part in criminal policy-making and that their participation in those years was generally of good quality;
> that the principal changes in the scope and influence of criminal law scholars' participation in Soviet criminal policy-making occurred in 1956;
> that from 1957 to 1970 there were no major and lasting changes in the scope and quality of Soviet criminal law scholars' participation;
> that during the 1960s the participation of Soviet criminal law scholars became institutionalized.

Let us consider the implications of each of these findings.

The first finding concerned Soviet criminal law scholars' participation during the later Stalin years (1938–53). Contrary to expectation, it turned out that during those years the scholars played a part in criminal policy-making and that their participation was of good quality. On each occasion when a new draft USSR Criminal Code was prepared Moscow scholars took an active role in its drafting and in the course of this work introduced policy proposals, such as the removal of analogy and the revival of parole. Later on, some of their colleagues from outside the capital city also joined the discussion of these and other policy issues. The quality of Soviet criminal law scholars' participation while they worked on the draft codes was good on a number of counts. They dealt with the substance as well as the form of the draft legislation. Much of their participation occurred well before any final decisions about the legislation had been taken. And the main function served by their presence in the political process was the advocacy of policy views, not the mobilization of support for new policies. (Even when the scholars' participation occurred during the implementation of decisions, as in the case of the 1947 laws on theft, its purpose was to modify the decisions' effects, not to develop support for them.)

Indeed, the quality of Soviet criminal law scholars' participation during the later Stalin years appeared to have been no worse than it would be in the 1950s and the 1960s, when the scholars came to participate more often and with more effect. *The main differences between criminal law scholars' participation in the three periods studied here lay not in its quality but in its scope and impact.* During the Stalin years the scope of the scholars' participation was limited in a number of ways. Through their part in the preparation of the draft criminal codes, the scholars came to participate in only some of the decisions taken or contemplated in criminal policy. A number of decisions unrelated to the draft codes resulted in important new criminal legislation, but as a rule the scholars did not contribute to them. Nor in the course of their policy-related activities did the scholars have a direct line of access to the center of decision-making. The leading law enforcement officials with whom the scholars communicated were themselves excluded from many of Stalin's decisions. Not only the scope but also the impact of criminal law scholars' participation in criminal policy-making was limited. The scholars succeeded in influencing the leading law enforcement officials and as a result getting some of their suggestions incorporated in the draft criminal codes. But since none of those draft codes ever became law, the scholars' actual influence upon Soviet criminal policy was close to nil.

From previous Western literature on Soviet politics one would have anticipated neither the presence of serious participation by criminal law scholars in criminal policy-making under Stalin nor the good quality of that participation. The memoirs of former Soviet scientists and engineers showed that Stalin occasionally summoned individual scholars for consultation;[1] and some Western observers acknowledged that more or less veiled policy discussions occurred from time to time in the professional journals.[2] But there were no indications in the Sovietological literature that even under Stalin Soviet scholars openly proposed and debated policy recommendations;[3] and, as we have seen, Soviet criminal law scholars did just that. The role of these scholars in criminal policy-making, however, did not suggest a need for wholesale revision of the conventional image of Stalinist policy-making as a narrow and closed process; indeed, the virtual exclusion of criminal law scholars from decision-making which occurred outside of the preparation of new draft criminal codes supported that image. The presence of some participation by Soviet criminal law scholars and its good quality did imply that the reality of Stalinist policy-making was more complex than the traditional Western image had it; and that in some policy realms at some times even the Stalinist political process included specialist participation.

We have joined the discussions of the second and the third findings about the development of Soviet criminal law scholars' participation because the implications of these two findings were closely related. The second finding concerned the timing of the post-Stalin improvements in the scope and influence of participation. It appeared that the key dividing line in the history of those scholars' participation in criminal policy-making came near the beginning of 1956. Before then, during the years 1953 to 1955, the scholars took part in criminal policy-making, but the scope and influence of their participation differed little from what they had been during the Stalinist years. In 1953–5, just as in 1938–53, a number of Moscow scholars helped prepare a draft USSR Criminal Code (1955) which was not passed into law, and the scholars had little bearing upon the new laws which actually were promulgated, such as the laws which launched the post-Stalin reform of the criminal law. In contrast, during 1956–8 – after Khrushchev's Secret Speech had encouraged more specialist participation through its emphasis upon collegiality and public participation in policy formation – both the scope and the impact of criminal law scholars' participation improved. More scholars of more diverse backgrounds took part in criminal policy-making. The preparation of the draft Fundamental Principles of Criminal Legislation of the USSR and the Union Republics used a larger commission of scholars than had the preparation of the earlier draft codes; and the scholarly discussions of the completed draft legislation were broader and more public than before. Moreover, in contrast with earlier periods when criminal law scholars had virtually no impact upon Soviet criminal policy, in the late 1950s the scholars did exert influence on some decisions. We cannot speak with certitude about the extent of their influence in this period because we did not examine enough of the decisions in criminal policy taken during the late 1950s; but it was clear that at this time the scholars began to have some effect upon the formation of Soviet criminal policy. This was not surprising, since the improvement in the status of the leading law enforcement officials improved the scholars' access to the centers of decision-making and greatly increased their potential for influencing policy.

In retrospect, the shift in the scope and influence of criminal law scholars' participation in 1956 was of lasting importance; for it marked the beginning of a new post-Stalin pattern of participation by criminal law scholars, a pattern characterized not only by good quality, but also by wide scope and by moderate influence. Our third finding about the development of criminal law scholars' participation concerned the persistence of this pattern – namely, that during the years 1956 to 1970 there were no major and lasting changes in the scope or quality of criminal law scholars' participation. In the middle and later years of the decade of the 1960s, criminal law scholars' (criminologists) participation was of broad scope and good quality just as it had been in the late 1950s. Now that it was institutionalized, the scholars' participation involved them in a number of individual decisions on different issues in criminal policy, and in each case their contributions were serious, timely, and related to the substance of the issue. It also appeared that the scholars had influenced some of the decisions in which they took part in the 1960s, just as they had in the late 1950s. Their overall policy impact probably grew in the 1960s because of the cumulative effect of their ideas about crime prevention. The one interruption in the contributions of criminal law scholars to criminal policy formation in the USSR came in 1961–2, when during a 'law and order' swing the leadership took most of its decisions in criminal policy without consulting criminal law scholars. This phase was short-lived, and by 1963 many issues in criminal policy-making again involved the help of criminal law scholars and criminologists.

The findings that the nature of criminal law scholars' participation improved in 1956 and then, with the exception of two years, stayed at roughly the same levels of scope, quality, and impact throughout the 1960s, bore on an issue in the study of Soviet policy-making: that was the problem of accounting for the shift in the way Western Sovietologists assessed Soviet specialist participation in the post-Stalin period. As we explained in Chapter 1, those scholars who wrote in the early or middle 1960s and relied upon data from the late 1950s and early 1960s generally reached a low assessment of the nature and impact of specialist participation; whereas those scholars who wrote in the late 1960s or early 1970s and relied upon data from the middle or late 1960s usually evaluated participation more highly. The problem of interpreting this shift in assessment reduced to a single question – to what extent did the shift represent a change in reality, that is an actual improvement in specialists' participation, and to what extent did it represent instead a change in the way the observers perceived participation and its impact? The answer suggested by this study was unequivocal. The findings that criminal law scholars' participation was of wide scope and good quality as of the late 1950s and by and large remained so throughout the 1960s indicated that, for one policy realm at least, there was little change in reality; and only a change in observers' perceptions would explain the shift in interpretation. Of course, the development of specialist participation in criminal policy-making may not have typified the development of specialist participation in other policy realms. There was no reason to assume that the emergence of participation of good quality and wide scope took place at the same time and place in other policy realms; in fact there was evidence to suggest that in some other policy areas specialist participation reached its full development only in the late 1960s.[4] Nevertheless we suspect that criminal policy was not a unique field and that, in some other fields as well, by the late 1950s specialist participation was already serious and influential. If this were so, the shift in the Western interpretation of the role of specialists in Soviet policy-making would reflect, at least in part, a change in perception.

This conclusion raises the question of why some Western scholars came to perceive the role of specialists in Soviet policy-making differently in the late 1960s than their colleagues had earlier on. One possible reason was the availability of new studies, which provided more data upon generalizations could be based. New studies there were, but few of those written in the late 1960s and early 1970s supplied evidence of behind-the-scenes participation, which had been notably missing from the data available to scholars writing in the early and middle 1960s.[5] Yet even without this kind of evidence in the late 1960s some Western scholars were willing to draw inferences about such behind-the-scenes activity and to offer bold hypotheses about the participation and impact of specialists. This willingness suggested that the new perception of the specialists' role had roots in another source, namely, the growing detachment of Sovietologists, especially of the younger generation, from the totalitarian image of Soviet policy-making. By the early 1970s the new perception of the specialist's role gained further support from the emergence of a new paradigm of Soviet policy-making, one which incorporated aspects of the pluralist model.[6]

The possibility that the negative evaluation of the role of specialists in Soviet policy-making in the late 1950s reflected analysts' perceptions as much as reality makes it incumbent upon Western Sovietologists to reopen the question of the nature of the Soviet policy-making process during those years. If criminal law scholars participated in a serious and meaningful way, so might have some other scholars and professionals. Yet without fresh and solid studies of the scope and quality of specialist participation in other policy realms, it would be difficult to characterize specialist participation in the first post-Stalin decade; and it would be even more difficult to draw any firm conclusions about the timing and the patterns in the emergence of specialist participation in the various policy realms.

The fourth finding about the development of Soviet criminal law scholars' participation was that during the 1960s it became institutionalized; that is, that participation by scholars became a regular feature both of criminal policy-making and of the scholars' own work roles. As we saw, the process of institutionalization was facilitated by the revival of criminology and by the founding of new agency institutes for research on crime and the administration of justice; and this process was reinforced by the rationalization movement which developed in the USSR after 1965. The immediate significance of the institutionalization of criminal law scholars' and criminologists' role in criminal policy-making lay in its encouragement of the participation of scholars in individual decisions in criminal policy which were unrelated to major legislation. But the institutionalization of participation also had the long-range effect of making it more likely that the participation would continue on a regular basis. Because regular patterns have more staying power than isolated precedents, the institutionalization of criminal law scholars' participation in criminal policy-making helped to assure its continuation in the future.

This did not mean that over the years the scope and influence of criminal law scholars' participation could not vary. For one thing, there could be times when criminal policy developed very little and few decisions were taken. For another, politicians might at times prefer not to hear from experts whose views they already knew. In other words, despite institutionalization there could still be periods of slack in criminal law scholars' participation, like the years 1961–2. At that time the scholars had not stopped commenting on policy questions, but the leadership had stopped listening and had failed to seek scholarly advice for most decisions. During the 'law and order' swing the decision-makers had presumed that repression had its utility and they did not want to hear how scholars appraised this tactic. From 1963 to 1973 there were no comparable slack periods in criminal law scholars' participation, but this did not mean that they would not appear in the future. At any time leaders could abandon temporarily their 'rational' approach to some aspects of criminal policy, fall back on old myths and stereotypes, and disregard the potential contributions of scholars. With the participation of criminal law scholars institutionalized, however, such slack periods in their participation were likely to be short-lived and isolated in particular subfields of criminal policy.

Having reviewed the developement of Soviet criminal law scholars' participation in criminal policy-making in the post-Stalin years, one can now examine the effects of the Khrushchev and Brezhnev regimes upon the broadening of political process in the USSR. The greatest advance in Soviet criminal law scholars' policy role occurred during the Khrushchev period; these years saw the scope of scholars' participation widen and their participation become influential for the first time. Under Brezhnev, the achievements of the Khrushchev period were consolidated, as criminal law scholars' role in policy-making became institutionalized. One should note, however, that the pattern obtained in criminal policy-making was not repeated in all realms of policy; there were some policy realms in which the expansion of participation by specialists occurred only during the Brezhnev years.[7] It is fair to conclude that the initial broadening of the policy-making process in the USSR to include extensive and influential participation by specialists occurred under Khrushchev, while under Brezhnev the trend was continued and consolidated.

Each of the two leaders should be given some credit for the expansion and consolidation of specialist participation which occurred under his rule. Khrushchev's attempts to make Soviet policy-making more collegial and to some extent more democratic encouraged the expansion of the role of specialists. Brezhnev's support for the effort to make policy-making more 'rational' and to improve the changes of finding effective solutions to policy problems facilitated the continuation of the expansion of specialist activity in policy-making. Yet, it would be a mistake to assign either leader full responsibility for these developments. Once the conditions hindering specialist participation had been removed in the middle 1950s, a marked increase in specialist involvement in Soviet policy-making may have been inevitable. Moreover, the expansion of participation by specialists may have reflected the influence of social trends such as increasing division of labor and changes in the structure of knowledge, as some observers East and West suggested.[8] The argument that the growth of specialist participation in the USSR owed more to social trends than to leadership choices gains support from the observation that this tendency occurred independently of developments in the substance of policies. Under Khrushchev there was a general correspondence between the reformist character of policies and the changes in the policy-making process; but under Brezhnev policies in many realms took on a more conservative cast (e.g. of economic policies and policies toward culture and dissent), while the broadening of the policy-making process continued all the same. Although the Brezhnev regime accepted specialist input as a component of 'rational' policy-making, it was not clear that it could have prevented its continued expansion and consolidation.[9]

CRIMINOLOGISTS' ROLE IN COMPARATIVE PERSPECTIVE

Chapter 9 showed that in the 1960s Soviet criminologists had considerable influence upon some decisions in Soviet criminal policy and exerted a moderate degree of impact upon the development of criminal policy as a whole. In decisions relating to delinquency prevention and to parole and recidivism regulations, and to a lesser degree the control of drunken rowdies, the scholars left their mark upon the policies and programs adopted. Moreover, through their policy-making activity the criminologists encouraged a new trend or tendency in Soviet criminal policy as a whole, an increased emphasis on crime prevention. In relation to the past history of criminal law scholars'.impact upon Soviet criminal policy, the criminologists' achievements were impressive; clearly, the impact of crime specialists had increased markedly since the Stalin years, when their suggestions had been regularly ignored. The question remained what meaning Soviet criminologists' influence on policy in the 1960s had in comparative terms. Because we used criteria and methods for assessing influence which derived from studies of policy-making in the U.S.A., we felt confident that our terms of assessment had relative meaning. At least when we concluded that criminologists in the USSR 'had considerable influence upon some decisions', we meant approximately the same thing as if we had made the same statement about American criminologists. Nevertheless, it was difficult to reach a full appreciation of the influence achieved by Soviet criminologists without referring to the impact exerted upon criminal policy by criminologists in Western countries.

Since we had not conducted extensive primary research on the influence of criminologists in the USA and England, it was impossible to rigorously compare their influence with that of Soviet criminologists. But there were enough secondary sources available to make *tentative* generalizations about the influence of criminologists in those Western countries. And we were able to supplement those secondary sources with data resulting from some primary research which we had conducted in England in 1968.

Before comparing the impact of American and British criminologists upon criminal policies in their countries with that of their Soviet colleagues, it is well to take note of two potential difficulties. First, the criminologists in those two Western countries did not have the same profile as did their Soviet counterparts. By and large, American and British criminologists were not criminal lawyers, but hailed from a variety of disciplines, especially from sociology. As sociologists these criminologists might have lacked the access to policy-makers which criminal law scholars in the USSR had.[10] Secondly, the use of the middle and late 1960s as the time period for comparison could make the comparison unreliable. Those years might have represented a time of unusually great or unusually little influence on the part of the American or British scholars, or for that matter on the part of the Soviet ones. Yet, it is our belief that neither of these potential difficulties was a real one. During the 1960s leading criminologists in the USA and England who worked in sociology departments seemed to have had considerable access to criminal policy-making; and there seemed to be no basis for inferring that their influence on criminal policy during this period was unusual in any respect.

On the basis of the limited evidence about American and British experience the influence of criminologists upon criminal policies in the USA and England in the middle and late 1960s appeared to have been no greater than that of Soviet criminologists upon criminal policy in the USSR. Or, to put it the other way around, *Soviet criminologists seemed to have had about as much influence on criminal policy as did their counterparts in at least two major Western states*. Let us review, briefly, the evidence on the influence of criminologists on the formation of criminal policy in each of those Western countries.

During the middle and late 1960s American criminologists played a part in a number of decisions in criminal policy, with varying results. On some issues they had considerable influence, but on others almost none. Two important changes in government policies toward the control of juvenile delinquency reflected the influence of criminologists. The idea for the first of these changes – the shift in juvenile court procedure from an informal paternalistic to a formal adversarial process – had its origins in the writings of criminologist Paul Tappan.[11] In California, the first state where legal reform produced this shift, two members of the five-man commission which proposed and drafted the legislation were criminologists.[12] The second of the changes in policies toward controlling juvenile delinquency, the youth and community action programs of the 1964 'War on Poverty', was grounded in assumptions deriving from the popular theory of delinquency expounded by two criminologists, Richard Cloward and Lloyd Ohlin. These scholars also helped to develop the model for these programs, the Mobilization for Youth experiment, and one of them (Ohlin) served on the President's Commission on Juvenile Delinquency which gave the idea of community action programs crucial support.[13] In contrast to the apparent influence of criminologists in decisions relating to controlling juvenile delinquency was their near failure to affect policies relating to violent crime and riots. Criminologists played an active part in the work of several federal commissions assigned to find remedies for the outbreak of crime, violence, and riots which afflicted America during the course of the 1960s.[14] Despite thorough and sometimes inspired contributions to staff studies and to commission reports, the criminologists' work on most of these commissions had little impact on federal policies.[15] Criminologists also participated indirectly in another aspect of American criminal policy-making during the middle and late 1960s, the revision and rewriting of the criminal codes in a number of states. Some of the new state codes reflected recommendations set out in the Model Penal Code, whose preparation included some participation by criminologists.[16] It appeared, then, that although in the 1960s criminologists in the USA made some contributions to criminal policy, some of their political activity went for naught and a part of criminal policy-making went on without their help.

In England during the 1960s the pattern of criminologists' participation in criminal policy-making resembled the pattern in the USSR more than the one in the USA. Scholars at two research centers, both founded at government initiative in the late 1950s – the Institute of Criminology in Cambridge and the Home Office Research Unit in London – regularly supplied the government with research reports and memoranda.[17] Moreover, a number of scholars served on commissions established to study proposals for changes in criminal policy.[18] Although during the 1960s British criminologists made proposals on many issues in criminal policy, they influenced only some of the decisions taken. For illustration of this point consider the 1967 Criminal Justice Act, an omnibus law which resembled the Soviet party-state edict of 1966 in the scope and variety of issues which it covered. The 1967 Criminal Justice Act included five changes directly related to criminologists' expertise: the introduction of suspended sentences; the introduction of parole; changes in regulations governing fines; the elimination of preventive detention; and the establishment of extended sentences for habitual offenders who had previously been among those eligible for preventive detention.[19] Criminologists may be said to have influenced only the latter two of these provisions.[20] First, in the early 1960s, criminologists inside and outside the government had been prominent among those who urged the abolition of preventive detention. A number of them had also conducted research supporting this step,[21] research which was cited both by the Advisory Council on the Treatment of Offenders in its 1963 report and by the Labor Government in its White Paper which promised an end to preventive detention.[22] Secondly, criminologists helped to define the content of the new legislation on extended sentences for habitual offenders. After the Home Office's Criminal Division had drafted the provisions in 1966, the Home Office Research Unit had the opportunity to review those provisions, along with the rest of the draft legislation planned for 1967. The Unit's deputy director, W. H. Hammond, recommended some changes in the criteria of eligibility for the extended sentences, changes which were subsequently adopted.[23] By coincidence the purpose of Hammond's recommendations was the same as some of A. M. Iakovlev's proposals for Soviet legislation on recidivism, namely, the elimination of habitual petty offenders from the pool of persons eligible to receive additional sentences.[24] In 1972 the British Parliament passed another major criminal justice act, and once again criminologists seemed to have contributed to some, but not all of the provisions. The introduction of a new penal sanction, 'community service', reflected the ideas and arguments of certain scholars, particularly of those serving on the Wootton subcommittee of the Advisory Council on the Penal System, but other changes, such as the new day training centures and the expansion of probation hostels, resulted from the recommendations of Home Office officials.[25] In England, just as in the United States, it appeared that criminologists had influenced some of the decisions taken in criminal policy during the middle and late 1960s, but had failed to make an impact on many others.

Against the background of the apparent influence of criminologists in the USA and in England upon the criminal policies of those countries, the impact of Soviet criminologists on Soviet criminal policy during the middle and late 1960s was a solid achievement. It seemed that Soviet criminologists, representatives of a newly revived branch of scholarship, had attained a roughly similar degree of influence upon policy decisions taken in their country as had their counterparts in two Western countries. This conclusion probably surprises some readers as much as it did the author of this study. There were at least two reasons why one might not have expected that Soviet criminologists would appear to have been as influential as American or British ones: first, because the Soviet scholars' participation seemed to have peculiar characteristics presumably not shared by the participation of their Western colleagues; and second, because of the presence of constraints upon the influence of Soviet criminologists which were presumed not to apply to their American and British counterparts.

The characteristics of Soviet criminologists' participation which did not seem optimally conducive to influence on policy were the level of their contacts in government and the weak grounding of their policy recommendations in social science research. Soviet criminologists' main contacts were not with the very top generalist politicians, the Party leaders, but rather with high-ranking specialist politicians and administrators, represented by the heads of the USSR Procuracy, the USSR Supreme Court, and the MOOP. In addition, the advice proffered by Soviet criminologists on policy issues, though often influenced by and supported with statistical data, was not itself based upon social science. In none of the decisions (with the possible exception of the revision of the criteria for specially dangerous recidivists) could the scholars have predicted the success of the remedies they proposed, or explained why the remedies they supported would work better than other possible approachs.

Either direct contact with Politboro members or policy proposals grounded in social science might have improved Soviet criminologists' potential for influencing criminal policy. However, the absence of these characteristics was hardly reason for questioning the performance of Soviet criminologists relative to their American and British counterparts. For both of these same characteristics, or shortcomings, pertained also to the participation of criminologists in the United States and England. Just as in the USSR criminologists in those Western countries influenced decisions more through communication with leading government officials rather than through contact with the very top politicians. For example, Cloward and Ohlin's proposals affected the youth and community action programs associated with the 'War on Poverty' largely because officials in the Department of Health, Education and Welfare adopted their ideas; and those officials adopted the ideas after serving jointly with Ohlin and other scholars as members of the President's Commission on Juvenile Delinquency.[26] Likewise, W. H. Hammond of the Home Office Research Unit succeeded in promoting changes in the draft legislation on habitual offenders when he convinced officials in the Home Office's Criminal Division, who went on to justify the changes to the politicians.[27]

Nor were the proposals for policy change made by the British and American criminologists any more grounded in social scientific research than were those offered by Soviet criminologists. This shortcoming was an object of criticism by scholars in each of those Western countries. Writing about American criminologists' habit of offering advice without a scientific basis, Daniel Moynihan blamed the scholars, who, he claimed, had no business making policy proposals when their skills prepared them only for evaluating of existing programs.[28] In contrast, an observer of the criminologist's role in policy-making in England, Roger Hood, attributed the shortcomings in criminologists' advice to difficulties inherent in the advisory process. Once policy-makers identified a policy problem, Hood claimed, they usually wanted advice right away, and the resulting pressure of time precluded the elaborate research required to assess the likely effects of alternative lines of action.[29] Because of time constraints politicians sought and scholars provided the 'best available advice', even though it was not as a rule scientifically based.[30]

The other reason why one might not have expected that Soviet criminologists would appear to have been as influential in criminal policy-making as their American and British colleagues was the common belief that any Soviet scholar's capacity for influencing policies was constrained either by the large amount of political power held by the Soviet political leadership or by some other 'peculiar' feature of the Soviet political environment. As we saw in Chapter 1, Western observers had often stressed the presence of limitations upon the Soviet specialist's capacity to affect policy; and the observers usually implied, if they did not state in so many words, that the constraints faced by Soviet specialists were much greater than those faced by Western specialists and hence different in kind. In pointing to constraints upon the capacity of Soviet specialists to influence policy, Western observers were not on the wrong track. Soviet criminologists surely were subject to some limitations upon their capacity to influence policy; and it was likely that the limitations faced by Soviet criminologists were somewhat greater than those faced by their American counterparts. We would contend, however, that the differences between the constraints faced by Soviet and by American specialists were of degree rather than of kind; for *many, if not most of the factors which constrained the Soviet specialist's capacity to affect policy were the same ones which affected specialists in the United States.*

To begin with, the influence in policy-making both of Soviet and of Western specialists, including criminologists, was contingent upon the way political leaders reacted to their advice. In both countries the power of political leaders normally exceeded that of specialists sufficiently to permit the leaders to overrule, ignore, or misuse specialist advice.[31] This fact was not hard to explain. While specialists had to rely upon just a few political resources – chiefly their status as experts – politicians in office had at their disposal a variety of resources including control of organizations, commitments of followers, money, and legal authority. Neither in the USA nor in the USSR did political leaders exercise their potential for rejecting specialist advice most of the time; for a variety of reasons leaders did accept the advice of specialists some of the time (because they were persuaded by the arguments; because their disagreements with specialist advice were too minor to warrant intervention; or because they wanted to respond to specialist demands). Yet, because the leaders usually *could* overrule the specialists, the latter's influence was never certain.[32] The not small number of examples of American and of Soviet leaders' overruling, ignoring or misusing the advice of natural and of social scientists made those specialists aware of their weakness vis-à-vis the politicians.[33] Conscious of their situation, some specialists were wont to moderate their advice in anticipation of the reactions of their clients.[34]

It was still possible that the capacity of Soviet criminologists to influence policy was more constrained by leadership power than was that of Western criminologists. Soviet leaders did not appear to have held so much more power than American ones as to make a difference to specialists in the political process;[35] but the rules of the political game in the USSR did seem to place the Soviet specialist at a somewhat greater disadvantage vis-à-vis his clients. In the United States a specialist could fight back *after* political leaders in the various branches of government rejected his advice. He could take his case to the public, either through individual effort or by forming a political organization to lobby for his point of view. During the last few decades there were a number of instances when scientists or social scientists who failed to win their cases through their roles as advisors donned the hats of 'citizen' to continue the political fight.[36] In the USSR, however, the formation of political organizations was illegal, and access to the press was not always available for the reopening of a policy debate after it had been resolved.[37] The very idea of resisting a political decision was illegitimate in the USSR.[38] While the American specialist could in principle fight back after a decision went against him, the Soviet specialist could not. In practice, the advantage held by the American specialist over his Soviet counterpart seemed to lie less in the actual use of the potential to fight back than in the threat that he might do so. Although American specialists usually could take their case to the public (unless security regulations intervened), such action was fraught with difficulties. For one, it involved an investment of time and of money which could detract from the specialist's other work; for another it ran the risk of offending political leaders and government officials. In going around the decision-makers who had rejected his advice, a specialist might sacrifice his future access to decision-making circles (at least within the current administration). As a result, only on occasion did American specialists take the trouble to fight back against unfavorable decisions.[39] In the USA just as in the USSR the primary channel for specialist influence on public policy was expert consulting, not public politics.

Besides dependence upon leadership actions, specialists' capacity to influence policies seemed to be constrained by another factor, namely its association with small or moderate changes in policy. In both the USA and the USSR specialist influence tended to be associated with incremental changes in policy rather than with innovations. One reason was that in many policy realms, including criminal policy, small or moderate changes were the usual kind. If major policy shifts were relatively rare in criminal policy, it was not surprising that criminologists' influence would be associated mainly with small changes.[40] Another reason why specialist influence in general and criminologists' influence in particular tended to be associated with smaller changes rather than with innovations was that the opportunities to promote innovations came infrequently. Any chance of successful promotion of an innovation in policy depended upon the presence of a condition over which the scholars had little control, namely a demand in society for innovation. Demand for innovation seemed to develop only when preceded either by a crisis or by a major social change.[41] In the absence of a demand for innovations, attempts to promote them would usually fail, at least in the short run; and such attempts could result in negative reactions on the part of professional colleagues, which might weaken a specialist's reputation as a policy expert.[42]

It was possible that certain features of the Soviet criminologist's work environment made him more constrained from promoting innovations in policy than was his Western counterpart. One of these features was institutional position. Merton contrasted the situation of the 'unattached intellectual', who could easily criticize established policies and hence easily propose innovations in them, with that of the 'bureaucratic intellectual', who because of his position inside government was 'largely limited to developing more effective modes of implementing decisions and of introducing alternative possibilities for action which do not violate the values of the bureaucracy'.[43] Analyzed according to Merton's scheme, the position of Soviet criminologists was ambiguous. Although most of them worked in research institutes rather than directly in a bureaucracy, those institutes were attached to bureaucratic agencies and the scholars did perform staff functions for them. In our judgement, these Soviet criminologists' scope for criticizing criminal policy was neither as a narrow as that of the prototypical 'bureaucratic intellectual' nor as broad as that of the 'unattached intellectual'. Yet it was far from clear that Soviet criminologists' potential either for criticizing policy or for promoting innovations in it depended upon their institutional position. As a rule, other Soviet criminologists who worked in universities were no more critical than were their colleagues at the institutes.[44]

Another feature of the Soviet criminologist's work environment which may well have affected his willingness to criticize current policy and hence his capacity for promoting innovations in policy was his official role definition. As defined by the Party, the Soviet criminologist's functions were constructive rather than critical in nature.[45] His job was to help develop and implement policies, rather than to criticize and evaluate the assumptions behind them.[46] Obviously, the distinction was one of emphasis which in practice could not be clear-cut; and it would be incorrect to suggest that Soviet criminologists never criticized or evaluated both government policies and the assumptions which lay behind them. By and large, however, Soviet criminologists did conform to the official role model; and hardly any of them engaged, even on occasion, in thorough-going or radical critique of Soviet criminal policy, as did some American criminologists of the criminal policies in their country.[47] In all probability many Soviet criminologists willingly avoided such a task, for they tended to share the prevailing notion in Soviet elite circles that loyalty precluded the most trenchant kinds of policy criticism.[48] By refraining from such criticism of regime policies, Soviet criminologists tended to promote moderate changes in policy rather than innovations.

Because of their official role definition Soviet criminologists appeared to have been somewhat more inhibited from promoting innovations in criminal policy than were their American or British counterparts. This may have lessened the long-term impact of criminological thought upon the future development of criminal policy in the USSR. However, constraints on the initiation of major policy changes were not likely to reduce the scholars' influence upon current policy choices. If anything, one might argue, a stress upon small and feasible changes in policy would enhance their role.

In summary, then, there was little reason why Soviet criminologists should not have been as influential in criminal policy-making during the 1960s as were American or British criminologists. The recommendations of the Soviet scholars were no less grounded in social science research than were those of their Western counterparts, nor was the level of the former's contacts in government lower than that of the latter. Likewise, the Soviet scholars' capacity to influence policy was constrained for the most part by factors which also affected American and British criminologists, among them the natural disadvantages of the expert in dealing with a powerful client and the normally slow and incremental manner in which criminal policies change. As we have indicated, there were some small differences in the ways these constraints affected Soviet and Western criminologists. But these differences were not, in our view, great enough as to militate against similar achievements on the part of the scholars in affecting the course of criminal policy in their respective countries.

SPECIALIST PARTICIPATION AND SOVIET POLITICS

In the beginning of this book we outlined four images of the role of specialists in Soviet policy-making which were prevalent among Western Sovietologists writing in the 1960s and 1970s. These images ranged from minimal or no influence (first image), to small but insignificant influence (second image), to some influence limited by a number of constraints peculiar to the Soviet political process (third image), to influence no significantly limited by constraints found only in the USSR (fourth image). It should come as no surprise that the fourth of these images was the one which came closest to characterizing the participation of Soviet criminologists in the formulation of criminal policy in the USSR during the middle and late 1960s. In Chapter 9 we learned that these scholars had exerted considerable influence upon some of the decisions in which they had taken part and that they had in addition made a moderate impact upon the face of Soviet criminal policy as a whole. And in the analysis just presented we discovered that although Soviet criminologists were subject to definite constraints upon their capacity to influence criminal policy, most of these constraints were not peculiar to the Soviet setting; similar limitations also affected criminologists and other specialists who took part in policy-making in the USA.

Before exploring the implications of this conclusion, it was important to determine how typical Soviet criminologists' role in criminal policy-making was of the role of other Soviet specialists in policy-making in other areas. If the participation and influence of criminologists was typical, one could generalize from their experience about the role of specialists in Soviet policy-making as a whole. If the participation and influence of criminologists differed substantially from that of most other specialists, one would be led instead to inquire why this was so.

Earlier writings on policy-making in the USA and in the USSR suggested that the scope and influence of specialist participation varied from one policy realm to another.[49] One such study added, however, that the influence of criminologists in criminal policy-making – at least in the USA – was probably close to the average for specialists in other policy realms. Surveying the available literature relating to specialist influence in American policy-making, Dean Schooler, Jr., found that the influence of scientists and social scientists was high in policy realms like economic, security, and science policies; moderate in realms like trade, conservation, and other 'regulative' policy areas; and low in foreign and social policies.[50] The author classified criminal policy as regulative, and although he did not discuss the influence of crime specialists on American criminal policies, he suggested that the level of their influence would be moderate.[51]

There were a number of reasons for believing that in the USSR of the 1960s specialists participated widely not only in criminal policy-making but also in a variety of other policy realms. First, factors which had encouraged the expansion and institutionalization of criminal law scholars and criminologists' participation were likely to have affected the participation of specialists in other areas of policy. The new demand on the part of the Soviet leadership for expert advice which had stimulated the revival of criminology and its use in policy-making must have affected other specialists, especially those who performed social research.[52] Likewise, the rationalization movement which had reinforced the institutionalization of criminologists' role in policy-making should have encouraged the participation of specialists in other policy realms.[53] Secondly, recent (by and large unpublished) studies of specialists participation in the USSR have shown that by the late 1960s specialists had come to play a regular part both in aspects of foreign policy-making[54] and in the formation of policies for science and technology.[55] It also appeared that specialists played a similar role in economic and in educational policy-making.[56] (The timing and the pattern of development of specialist participation in these policy realms sometimes differed from that of criminologists' participation; but by the end of the 1960s the participation of the relevant specialists was broad and regular in each of these areas of policy).[57] This evidence suggested that specialists probably participated in the formation of policies in still other realms as well. For the policy areas in which specialists were known to have actively participated included a variety of policy types; and the expertise of the specialists involved was often soft.

The studies of specialist participation in policy realms other than criminal did not indicate how much influence the relevant specialists had exerted on policies, but they did help us to estimate the probable levels of influence. In each of the policy areas studied the quality of specialist participation during the 1960s was good, just as it had been for criminologists; the specialists' contributions to policy formation had occurred before the decisions were taken and had served the functions of communication and advocacy. Although good-quality participation on the part of a specialist did no guarantee him influence on decisions, it did enhance his potential for influence. One could not predict whether in any particular instance that potential was realized, but one could infer that this potential for influence was realized *part* of the time and that specialists in policy realms other than the criminal sometimes attained the same (or even a greater) degree of influence on policies as had the criminologists.[58]

One can safely conclude that between 1956 and 1970 the participation of specialists broadened in a good number of areas of Soviet policy-making and that specialist influence probably grew in most of these as well. What, then, were the implications of the changes in the nature and influence of specialist participation in Soviet policy-making for the development of Soviet politics and for its study in the West?

The growth of specialist participation and influence in Soviet policy-making might have been accompanied by a change in the structure of power within the Soviet political system. In gaining access to policy-making and in coming to influence decisions more frequently, specialists might have obtained a greater share of the resources available for influencing policies, and as a result become more powerful than they had before. To be sure, the specialists' prime political resource, their status as experts, was more highly valued than before, thus increasing their potential for influencing policies; indeed, it was this change which had led to the expansion of their participation and influence in the post-Stalin years. In comparison with the political leaders, however, the specialists' share of political power did not change a great deal. For the status of expert remained but one of a number of political resources, of which the leaders retained a large amount, including a virtual monopoly of decision-making authority. The increased scope and influence of specialists' participation in Soviet policy-making had in the post-Stalin years only a small effect upon the structure of political power in the USSR.

The growth of specialist participation and influence in Soviet policy-making during the post-Stalin years might also have affected the nature of the resulting policies. The effects of specialist influence on the nature of policies depended in part upon the kind of advice which the specialists gave. Naturally that advice could vary in quality, but if one assumed that on the average specialist advice was of somewhat better quality than advice available to Soviet leaders from other sources, the growth of specialist influence would tend to increase the effectiveness of Soviet politics.[59] Just how much more effective Soviet policies became due to the growth in specialist influence depended not only upon the quality of advice offered by the specialists, but also upon the attitudes of the Soviet leadership toward policy change. When and where the leaders were flexible and open to innovations, a rise in specialist involvement could lead to dramatic changes in policies.[60] When the leadership took a conservative stance and discouraged specialist advice not premised on the main lines of current policy, a rise in specialist participation would produce only marginal improvements in policies. The record of the Brezhnev regime on openness to policy change was at best uneven. Although in such policy realms as science policy and relations with the West the Brezhnev regime accepted new ideas, in many aspects of social and economic policy it took conservative stands. For this reason the rise in specialist participation and influence in Soviet policy-making under Brezhnev resulted mainly in marginal improvements in programs in most policy realms. Of course, if this pattern changed in the future and the Soviet leadership opted more often for radical change, it could use specialist advice to this end. But the prospects for this happening in the near future were not good.

Our conclusion that during the 1960s specialist participation in Soviet policy-making was both broad and moderately influential had implications not only for the development of Soviet politics but also for the way it was perceived and studied in the West. The conclusion suggested that a model of Soviet policy-making developed by Jerry F. Hough and termed by him 'institutional pluralism' might be appropriate for assessing, if not also for characterizing, Soviet policy-making in the 1970s.[61] Hough's model depicted Soviet policy-making as marked by regular debates among such elite figures as officials and specialists in the various policy realms. As a rule the debates were resolved when political leaders selected the policies to be followed. In making their choices the leaders often responded to proposals offered by specialists or officials; and as a result the leaders sometimes served as brokers, resolving the differences of opinion among the other participants in the policy-making process. We believe that as of the beginning of the 1970s the policy-making process in the USSR resembled this model of institutional pluralism.[62] But in using the word 'pluralism' one must be careful not to impute to Soviet policy-making all of the characteristics of *democratic* pluralism, the model often used to describe American policy-making. Hough used the word 'pluralism' in order to stress that such central features of democratic pluralism as broad-ranging policy debates and leaders' serving as mediators or brokers were present in Soviet policy-making. But as Hough was aware, there were other features of democratic pluralism which institutional pluralism did not share. First, a cardinal institution of democratic pluralism, the organized interest group, had no place in institutional pluralism; political actors kept their debates within the framework of party and state institutions and did not form separate organizations for lobbying. Secondly, the model of institutional pluralism did not assume that the press and publishing institutions were largely free from political control as did democratic pluralism. Thirdly, institutional pluralism did not require such wide boundaries of political discourse as did democratic pluralism; it did not include for example the right to criticize political leaders by name. Fourthly, institutional pluralism could exist in a setting where political power was concentrated, whereas democratic pluralism assumed more dispersal of power and authority.

Although the Soviet policy-making process of the late 1960s and early 1970s fell far short of the model of democratic pluralism, its resemblence to the model of institutional pluralism showed how far it had evolved away from the narrow policy-making process of the Stalin years. It might be asked whether the trend toward a broader and more pluralistic policy-making process which developed during the first two post-Stalin decades might go on, so that the third and fourth decades since Stalin would witness the development in the USSR of democratic pluralism. I find this possibility unlikely. Unlike institutional pluralism, democratic pluralism was and remains incompatible with some basic features of the Soviet political order, such as the concentration of political power in the hands of the party leaders, the absence of autonomous political organizations, and the control of press and publications. Further development of Soviet policy-making in the direction of democratic pluralism would require changes in these features of Soviet politics, but changes in any of them would represent fundamental transformation of the Soviet political system. For this reason Soviet policy-making was unlikely to evolve from institutional to democratic pluralism. Only a series of crises could force Soviet leaders to allow the policy-making process in the USSR to cross that great divide.

Notes

1. INTRODUCTION

1. Robert Conquest, *Power and Policy in the USSR: A Study in Soviet Dynastics* (London, 1961); T. H. Rigby, 'Policy-making in the U.S.S.R., 1953–61, *Policy-making in the U.S.S.R.: Two Views* (Melbourne, 1962), pp. 3–4; Sidney Ploss, *Conflict and Decision-making in Soviet Russia: A Case Study of Agricultural Policy, 1953–1963* (Princeton, N.J., 1965); Carl Linden, *Khrushchev and the Soviet Leadership, 1957–1964* (Baltimore, 1968); Michel Tatu, *Power in the Kremlin From Khrushchev to Kosygin* (N.Y., 1968); Sidney Ploss, 'Interest Groups', *Prospects for Soviet Society* (ed. Allen Kassof; N.Y., etc., 1968), pp. 76–103.

2. Zbigniew Brzezinski and Samuel Huntington, *Political Power USA/USSR* (N.Y., 1964), especially pp. 191–234; Alfred Meyer, *The Soviet Political System An Interpretation* (N.Y., 1965), pp. 233–7; Frederick C. Barghoorn, *Politics in the USSR* (First edition; Boston and Toronto, 1966), pp. 216–37; Henry Morton, 'The Structure of Decision-making in the USSR: A Comparative Introduction', *Soviet Policy-making* (ed. Peter H. Juviler and Joel J. Schwartz); and William R. Keech, 'Soviet Interest Groups and the Policy Process: The Repeal of Production Education', *American Political Science Review*, LXII, No. 3 (September 1968), pp. 840–951. Sidney Ploss, 'New Politics in Russia?' *Survey*, XIX, No. 4 (autumn, 1973), pp. 23–35.

3. L. G. Churchward, 'Comment on Dr. Rigby's Paper', *Policy-making in the U.S.S.R.*, loc. cit., p. 30; L. G. Churchward, 'Policy-making in the U.S.S.R., 1953–1961', ibid., pp. 36–42; Donald Barry, 'The Specialist in Soviet Policy-Making: The Adoption of a Law', *Soviet Studies*, XIV (1964), pp. 152–65; H. Gordon Skilling, 'Interest Groups and Communist Politics', *World Politics*, XVIII, No. 3 (April 1966), pp. 435–51; Peter H. Juviler, 'Family Reforms on the Road to Communism', *Soviet Policy-making*, loc. cit., p. 54; Loren Graham, 'Reorganization of the USSR Academy of Sciences', ibid., pp. 155–6; Philip D. Stewart, 'Soviet Interest Groups and the Policy Process: The Repeal of Production Education', *World Politics*, XXII, No. 1 (October 1969), p. 50; Robert J. Osborn, *Soviet Social Policies: Welfare, Equality and Community* (Homewood, Ill., 1970), pp. 13–16; Franklyn Griffiths, 'A Tendency Analysis of Soviet Policy-Making', *Interest Groups in Soviet Politics* (ed. H. G. Skilling and F. Griffiths; Princeton, 1971), pp. 335–78; Richard Judy, 'The Economists', ibid., pp. 209–52; Donald Barry and Harold Berman, 'The Jurists', ibid., pp. 291–334; Joel Schwartz and William Keech, 'Public Influence and Educational Policy in the Soviet Union', *The Behavioral Revolution and Communist Studies* (ed. Roger Kanet; N.Y., 1971), pp. 151–86; Frederick Barghoorn, *Politics in the USSR* (second edition; Boston, 1972), pp. 206–8.

4. We are speaking here of the leadership as a whole. To make decisive choices political leaders in the USSR and in the West often had first to reach agreement

among themselves.

5. David Lane, *Politics and Society in the USSR* (N.Y., 1971), p. 257; Jerry F. Hough, 'The Soviet System: Petrification or Pluralism', *Problems of Communism* (March-April 1972), pp. 25–45.

6. As of 1976 there were only two book-length empirical studies of outside participation in Soviet policy-making: Franklyn Griffiths, 'Images, Politics and Learning in Soviet Behavior toward the United States', Ph.D. thesis (Columbia University, 1972); and Richard B. Remnek, *Soviet Scholars and Soviet Foreign Policy: A Case Study in Soviet Policy towards India* (Durham, N. C., 1975). Neither of the studies used interviews with Soviet scholars as a major source, and neither of them described the activity of specialists behind the scenes.

7. This does not mean, of course, that there might not actually be significant differences in the nature of Soviet specialists' role in various policy realms; only that such differences as emerged in the Western studies of these years did not match or explain the authors' assessments of that role. For citations to the studies, see notes 1–4.

8. Churchward, loc. cit.; Barry, loc. cit.

9. Ploss, 'New Politics in Russia?', loc. cit.

10. A possible obstacle to Sovietologists' acceptance of outside participation as a serious and influential factor in Soviet policy-making was their attachment to the totalitarian model as a means of explaining Soviet politics. As elaborated by Friedrich and Brzezinski in the early 1950s, the totalitarian model placed primary emphasis upon the centralization of power in the hands of the dictator and upon his use of controls to get decisions implemented. Neither the policy-making process nor participation in it were topics of central interest. See Carl Friedrich and Zbigniew Brzezinski, *Totalitarian Dictatorship and Autocracy* (Cambridge, Mass., 1956).

The writings of the leading Sovietologist of the elder generation, Merle Fainsod, also de-emphasized the policy-making process. In the 1953 edition of his book Fainsod did comment in passing that bureaucratic interests found expression in the policy process in the USSR, but the main emphasis in his writings was upon the way persons outside the leadership could affect policy in the course of its execution. See Merle Fainsod, *How Russia is Ruled* (Cambridge, Mass., 1953), especially pp. 350–3.

11. Brzezinski and Huntington, op. cit., pp. 191–234; Morton, loc. cit., p. 12; Barghoorn, op. cit. (1966), p. 231.

12. Juviler, loc. cit., p. 55; Graham, loc. cit., p. 159; Stewart, loc. cit., p. 47; H. Gordon Skilling, 'Group Conflict in Soviet Politics', *Interest Groups in Soviet Politics*, loc. cit., p. 391.

13. Hough, loc. cit.; Jerry F. Hough, 'Political Participation in the USSR', *Soviet Studies*, xxviii, No. 1 (January 1976), pp. 3–20.

14. Of course, the 'Western standards' might not always be optimal and might themselves be responsible for the way Western scholars evaluated the role of specialists in policy-making. James Q. Wilson suggested that the view that pressure groups were highly influential in American policy-making would not be supported by the evidence, if 'influence' were defined in a narrow way. See James Q. Wilson, *Political Organizations* (N.Y., 1973), p. 316.

15. Brzezinski and Huntington, op. cit., pp. 202–12.

16. Ibid.

17. Ibid., pp. 204–5; 212–16.

18. Ibid., p. 212; pp. 221-3.
19. See for example, Robert Dahl, *Who Governs?* (New Haven, Conn., 1961); and William Gamson, *Power and Discontent* (Homewood, Ill., 1968).
20. Yehezkel Dror, Charles Lindblom, and others have observed that in the real world policies are often not chosen according to an approximation of rational method, but rather evolve as political actors grapple with concrete policy questions one by one. Because policies can develop incrementally through a series of decisions, Dror suggested that one should not equate policy-making with decision-making and instead treat policy-making as an 'aggregate form of decision-making' (p. 13). Dror's suggestion was well taken, for in treating policy-making in this way one can avoid prejudging whether a given policy was set by a principled decision or evolved incrementally. Whatever relationship obtained among the various decisions in a series becomes apparent in the course of examining the policy-making process over time. The individual decisions might turn out to have produced a policy trend step by step; or one of the decisions might turn out to have set a line of policy which succeeding decisions merely implemented; or the decisions might represent a mixture of the two patterns, at one and the same time implementing broad principles of action determined by politicians and developing those principles through concrete decisions.

Thorough discussions of the rational and incremental models of policy-making are found in Yehezkel Dror, *Public Policy-making Reexamined* (San Francisco, 1968), pp. 12-13 and 129-53, and in Amitai Etzioni, *The Active Society* (N. Y., 1968), p. 12. See also, Charles Lindblom, *The Policy-making Process* (Engelwood Cliffs, New Jersey, 1968), p. 4; Raymond Bauer, 'The Study of Policy Formation: An Introduction', *The Study of Policy Formation* (ed. Raymond Bauer and Kenneth Gergen; N.Y. and London, 1968), p. 18; Enid Curtis Bok Schoettle, 'The State of the Art in Policy Studies', loc. cit., p. 179; Robert Salisbury, 'The Analysis of Public Policy: A Search for Theories and Roles', *Political Science and Public Policy* (ed. Austin Ranney; Chicago, 1968), p. 155.
21. John Maynard Keynes argued that the 'power of ideas' which had been in the air for a while was far greater than usually acknowledged, more powerful, he believed, than the power of vested interests. For his statement, see Osborn, op. cit., pp. 15-16.
22. For a discussion of the question of continuity and change in *public*, as opposed to specialist, participation see Jerry F. Hough, 'Political Participation in the Khrushchev and Brezhnev Periods', loc. cit.
23. See Fainsod, op. cit.
24. Skilling, 'Group Conflict in Soviet Politics', loc. cit., p. 400. For a similar view, see Schwartz and Keech, 'Public Influence and Educational Policy', loc. cit., p. 178.
25. Recent analysis has suggested that the negative portrait of the role of specialists in Soviet policy-making under Stalin may have been overdrawn. Using bits of information culled from secondary sources, Jerry F. Hough demonstrated that policy debates were carried on in many policy realms during the years 1949 to 1953; and he argued convincingly that many demands for policy changes reached Stalin's ears, only later to be rejected. See Merle Fainsod and Jerry F. Hough, *How Russia is Ruled* (third edition, forthcoming), ch. 5.
26. In most countries most of the time policies for the handling of ordinary criminals and for the operation of the system of law enforcement have been

separate from policies for the control of persons and groups whom politicians perceive as threatening to the political order. A discrete set of legal norms customarily implements policies regarding political deviants; and there are often special organizations for policing such offenders. See Austin T. Turk, 'Political Criminality and Political Policing', unpublished article (Toronto, 1974). Of course, in times of stress for a political regime the two categories of criminality may merge, and ordinary crimes like theft take on political significance (consider the significance of stealing grain during the famine conditions of the Russian Civil War). Moreover, though policies in the two realms are usually formulated separately, their implementation may be closely related. The same government officials may be responsible for *some* decisions relating to each area; and at times dissidents and authorities alike may try to manipulate the categories of political act and of crime – the dissidents claiming that acts like robbery are justifiable as politics and the authorities claiming that demonstrations are criminal disorders. On the manipulation of these categories, see I. L. Horowitz, 'Social Deviance and Political Marginality', *Social Problems*, xv, No. 3 (winter 1968), pp. 280–96.

27. Edwin Lemert, *Social Action and Legal Change: Revolution within the Juvenile Court* (Chicago, 1970), pp. 1–30. See also R. S. E. Hinde, *The British Penal System, 1797–1950* (London, 1951); David Rothman, *The Discovery of the Asylum* (Boston, 1971); and Georg Rusche and Otto Kirchheimer, *Punishment and Social Structure* (N.Y., 1939).

28. The notion of political subsystem was set out by J. Leiper Freeman in *The Political Process: Executive-Bureau-Legislative Committee Relations* (Garden City, New Jersey, 1955) and further developed in Emmette S. Redford, *Democracy in the Administrative State* (N.Y., etc., 1969), pp. 96–106.

29. As Bauer puts it, 'busy men do not have the resources to treat many issues as salient and . . . their strategies for handling salient and nonsalient issues are probably quite different.' See Bauer, loc. cit., p. 17.

30. For the effects of de-Stalinization on Soviet criminal policy, see Chapter 3.

31. Soviet criminologists were considered both by themselves and by other Soviet scholars to be social scientists as well as legal ones. Interviews with Soviet criminologists served as a good source of their self-perception; see also the official definition of Soviet criminology in the textbook *Kriminologiia* (second ed., rev. and enl.; M., 1968), pp. 7–24. The Soviet Sociological Association accorded leading criminologists recognition as social scientists by placing them upon their committees and including them in association symposia and conferences.

32. For citations to many examples of this work, see Peter H. Solomon, Jr., 'A Selected Bibliography of Soviet Criminology', *Journal of Criminal Law, Criminology and Police Science*, Vol. 61, No. 3 (1970), pp. 393–432. Referred to hereafter as Solomon, 'Bibliography'.

33. Barry and Berman, loc. cit., p. 322.

34. Ibid., p. 321. On the basis of observation more than of detailed study, Peter Juviler recently claimed that Soviet criminologists had some effects on criminal policy formation, but he emphasized that Soviet politicians often failed to follow the scholars' advice. According to Juviler, divisions of opinion among criminologists reduced their potential effect. Peter Juviler, 'Crime and its Study', *Soviet Politics and Society in the 1970s* (ed. Henry Morton and Rudolph Tokes; N.Y., 1974), pp. 204–5.

35. The rapidly expanding literature on the uses of social science and on the

political activity of its practitioners testified to the topicality of these questions. For an exhaustive catalogue of research on these questions, see Paul Lazarsfeld and Jeffrey Reitz, 'Toward a Theory of Applied Sociology (A Progress Report)', (Bureau of Applied Social Research, Colombia University; N.Y., 1970); and Gene M. Lyons, *The Uneasy Partnership. Social Science and the Federal Government in the Twentieth Century* (N.Y., 1969).

36. See Susan Gross Solomon, 'Theory and Research in Soviet Social Inquiry', thesis for M.A. and Certificate of the Russian Institute (Columbia University, 1967); René Ahlberg, *Entwicklungsprobleme der Empirischen Sozialforschung in der UdSSR, 1917 - 1966* (Berlin, 1968), *Science and Ideology in the Soviet Union* (ed. George Fischer; N.Y., 1968); Zev Katz, 'Sociology in the Soviet Union', *Problems of Communism*, Vol. xx, No. 3 (May-June, 1971), pp. 22–40; Elizabeth Ann Weinberg, *The Development of Sociology in the Soviet Union* (London, 1974).

37. Although the use of social science in policy-making was not a central focus of this study, the case studies about Soviet criminologists' participation in criminal policy-making contain much information relating to this question. See Chapters 5, 6 and 7.

38. On the demise of Soviet criminology in the 1930s, see Peter H. Solomon, Jr., 'Soviet Criminology: its Demise and Rebirth', in *Crime, Criminology and Public Policy Essays in Honour of Leon Radzinowicz (* London, *1974), pp. 571 –93;* and also in *Soviet Union,* 1, No. 2 (1974), pp. 122–40.

39. A number of these scholars began writing about the history of criminal law and criminal justice. M. N. Gernet undertook a multi-volume study of the history of Tsarist prisons; A. A. Gertsenzon explored the contributions of Jean Paul Marat to criminal law theory; and B. S. Utevskii wrote a history of the principle *nullum crimen sine lege, nulla poena sine lege.* For references to these and other historical writings by criminal law scholars, see *Sovetskoe ugolovnoe pravo. Bibliografiia 1917–1960* (compiled by F. M. Asknazii and N. V. Marshalova; M., 1961), pp. 162–90.

40. Solomon, 'Soviet Criminology', *loc. cit.*, p. 582.

41. This proposition was usually defended by those who defined an 'expert' according to actual expertise rather than according to reputation for competence. For criticism of this 'empiricist tradition' in the study of experts and politics, see Ben L. Martin, 'Experts in Policy Processes: A Contemporary Perspective', *Polity*, VI, No. 2 (winter 1973), pp. 449–57.

42. Daniel P. Moynihan, *Maximum Feasible Misunderstanding: Community Action in the War on Poverty* (N. Y., 1969), pp. 167–206; James Q. Wilson, 'Crime and the Criminologists', *Commentary*, LVIII, No. 1 (July, 1974), pp. 47–53.

43. See David Donnison, 'Research for Policy', *Minerva*, x, No. 4 (October 1972), pp. 519–36.

44. Such factors may include the leaders' opinions and ideological preconceptions, the risk and costs associated with a proposal, the pressure of time, symbolic needs, and others. For examples of how political factors may affect the fate of specialist advice, see Joel Primack and Frank von Hippel, *Advice and Dissent: Scientists in the Political Arena* (N.Y., 1974). See also Harvey Brooks, 'The Scientific Advisor', *Scientists and National Policy-making* (ed. R. Gilpin and C. Wright; N.Y., 1964), pp. 73–96; and Robert Gilpin, *American Scientists and Nuclear Weapons Policy* (Princeton, N.J., 1962).

45. Weinberg has dubbed such questions 'transscientific'. See Alvin Weinberg, 'Science and Transscience', *Minerva*, x, No. 2 (April 1972), pp. 209–22.

46. See William Zimmerman, 'Issue Area and Foreign Policy Process', *American Political Science Review*, LXVII, No. 4 (December 1973), pp. 1204–12.

47. In the USSR persons of ministerial rank included the heads of USSR ministries, of USSR State Committees, of the USSR Procuracy, USSR Supreme Court, the State Bank, Gosplan, and other national agencies.

48. Daniel Bell, 'The Post-Industrial Society: Technocracy and Politics', paper prepared for the Seventh World Congress of Sociology, Varna, Bulgaria, 1970; Sanford Lakoff, 'The Political Theory of Scientific Society', paper presented to the Symposium on Science and Democracy at the Annual Meeting of the American Association for the Advancement of Science, Chicago, 27 December 1970 (revised draft, August 1971); Zbigniew Brzezinski, *Between Two Ages: America's Role in the Technetronic Era* (N.Y., 1970); V. G. Afanasev, *Nauchnoe upravlenie obshchestvom* (M., 1965); P. A. Rachkov, *Rol nauki v stroitelstve kommunizma* (M., 1969); N. V. Markov, *Nauchno-tekhnicheskaia revoliutsiia: Analiz, perspektivy, posledstviia* (M., 1971).

49. See for example the studies in *Soviet Policy-making*, loc. cit., and in *Interest Groups in Soviet Politics*, loc. cit.

50. Political scientists who elaborated the theory of 'interest groups' defined the concept in an abstract and broad way. To David Truman, for example, interest groups consisted of collections of persons who both shared a viewpoint on an issue and interacted to some degree. David B. Truman, *The Governmental Process* (N.Y., 1951), pp. 33–8. However, the descriptive literature about interest groups in the USA, including writings of Truman himself, usually identified interest groups with professional associations or lobbying organizations; the interest groups were thus characterized, definition notwithstanding, by an organized and stable existence over time and by some identification with a profession or an institution. The inconsistency between the theoretical definition and the actual use of the term becomes particularly misleading when the term is transferred from the study of Western politics to that of the USSR. The behavior of Soviet scholars and professionals may often meet the criteria for the abstract or theoretical definition of an interest group, but it rarely matches what is commonly understood by the term. As most readers are aware, permanent organized lobbies or pressure groups have long been proscribed in the USSR and regarded as illegitimate by Soviet authorities. Moreover, already available data indicate that on many issues Soviet specialists in a given field do not share the same view and that divisions of opinion among the specialists in a field may vary from issue to issue and often cut across institutional lines. Judy, loc. cit.; Griffiths, 'A Tendency Analysis', loc. cit.; Griffiths, 'Images, Politics and Learning', loc. cit.

51. Another disadvantage of the term 'interest group' is its pejorative connotation for Western and especially for Soviet readers. Even for the Western reader 'interest group' activity may connote the selfish defense of personal, material interest, often exercised through 'pressure'; whereas much specialist participation in the USA represents merely the communication and advocacy of professional opinion. To the Soviet reader, however, 'interest group' usually suggests a politics of conflict based upon *material* interest, a notion which contrasts sharply with the official conception of Soviet politics. Significantly, H. Gordon Skilling discovered in his interviews with Soviet scholars that they regarded themselves as specialists engaged in consultation rather than as members of interest groups pressuring the leadership. My interviews with Soviet legal scholars, sociologists, and science policy specialists confirmed Prof. Skilling's finding. *Interest Groups in Soviet Politics*, loc. cit., p. 6.

2. CRIMINAL LAW SCHOLARS AND CRIMINAL POLICY UNDER STALIN

1. Khrushchev's Secret Speech of 1956 provides ample evidence of Stalin's leadership style. See N. S. Khrushchev, 'Secret Speech Concerning the Cult of the Individual', delivered at the Twentieth Congress of the CPSU, 25 February 1956, as printed in *The Anti-Stalin Campaign and International Communism* (ed. the Russian Institute of Columbia University; N.Y., 1956), pp. 1-90.

2. See Merle Fainsod, *How Russia is Ruled* (first edition), op. cit., p. 182.

3. Jerry F. Hough has rightly stressed that within the realm of 'constructive criticism' it was possible to make suggestions for policy changes. But usually these suggestions had to be made carefully, without blaming policy problems upon 'objective factors' and without giving detailed argumentation for one's viewpoint. Hough's observations were based upon a reading of *Pravda* and *Izvestiia* for December 1951. See Hough, 'Communication and Persuasion in The Analysis of Inputs,' in Hough, *The Soviet Union and Social Science Theory* (Cambridge, Mass., 1977), pp. 191-6.

4. This observation was based upon my reading of the three main legal journals: *Sotsialisticheskaia zakonnost* (1937-53); *Sovetskaia iustitsiia* (1937-41), and *Sovetskoe gosudarstvo i pravo* (1937-53).

5. See Solomon, 'Soviet Criminology', loc. cit., pp. 578-82.

6. V. V. Kulikov and Kh. B. Sheinin, 'Verkhovnyi sud SSSR i iuridicheskaia nauka', *SGiP* (1974, No. 3), p. 7.

7. One mark of the criminal law scholars' status was the appointment of three of them to the USSR Supreme Court. I. T. Goliakov served as the court's chairman from 1938 to 1948, and M. M. Isaev and A. A. Piontkovskii sat on the bench from 1946 to 1951. Scholars were not seated on the high court during the Khrushchev or Brezhnev years. Ibid.

8. The leading center for criminal law study during the later Stalin years, the All-Union Institute of Juridical Sciences, had close ties both with the Commissariat (later Ministry) of Justice to which it was attached and with the USSR Supreme Court, with which it shared its director in the person of I. T. Goliakov (1938-48). Founded in 1937, the All-Union Institute represented a continuation of the former State Institute for the Study of Crime and the Criminal (1925-31) and of the Institute of Criminal Policy (1931-7). On the history of this institute, see B. S. Utevskii and B. S. Osherovich, *Dvadtsat let vsesoiuznogo instituta iuridicheskikh nauk* (M., 1945) and Solomon, 'Soviet Criminology', loc. cit.

9. When the NKVD SSSR was formed in 1934, it drew together the penal institutions which had been administered by the OGPU and by Narkomiust.

10. See John N. Hazard, *Law and Social Change in the USSR* (London, 1953), p. 88.

11. Procuracy officials steered away from checking on NKVD activities after complaints by some of them led in 1937 to a mass purge of Procuracy staff. See N. V. Zhogin, 'Ob izvrashcheniiakh Vyshinskogo v teorii sovetskogo prava i praktike', *SGiP* (1965, No. 3), pp. 26-7. See also V. Z. Samsonov and A. P. Safonov, 'Prokurorskii nadzor za tochnym ispolneniem zakonov ob ispravlenii i perevospitanii osuzhdennykh', *Na strazhe sovetskikh zakonov* (M., 1972), pp. 344-55; and *Organizatsiia suda i prokuratura* (M., 1967), p. 173.

12. By no means is this meant to imply that the judicial chiefs did not retain control over the implementation of policy in the area of criminal policy remaining in their

hands—the administration of the court system and the application through the courts of the criminal law. In our view, Harold Berman was correct in arguing that in operational terms the systems of terror and of justice were more or less separate from one another. See Harold Berman, *Justice in the USSR: An Interpretation of Soviet Law* (rev. ed. ENl.; N.Y., 1963), pp. 7–9.

13. In a recent article the Deputy Chairman of the USSR Supreme Court, S. G. Bannikov, emphasized just how circumscribed the Supreme Court's role as an initiator of legislative changes became in the 1930s and 1940s. He cited only three examples of suggestions made by the court and did not indicate that any of these were actually accepted. Moreover, Bannikov observed with some amazement that the 1938 Law on Court Organization had removed legislative initiative from the list of the Supreme Court's official functions; this formal right was returned to the court only in 1957. S. G. Bannikov, 'Zakonodatelnaia initsiativa Verkhovnogo suda SSSR', *SGiP* (1974, No. 3), p. 14 (also interviews).

14. The 1949 edict raising the responsibility for rape was reportedly Stalin's response to a complaint from a fellow-politician following the rape of his daughter. For the text of this edict and of the edicts on the death penalty and on theft, see *Sbornik dokumentov po istorii ugolovnogo zakonodatelstva SSSR i RSRSR, 1917–1952 gg.* (ed. I. T. Goliakov; M., 1953), pp. 426–35.

15. I. T. Goliakov, 'Osnovnye problemy nauki sovetskogo sotsialisticheskogo prava', *Trudy pervoi nauchnoi sessii Vsesoiuznogo instituta iuridicheskikh nauk, 27 ianvariia-3 fevralia 1939* (ed. I. T. Goliakov; M., 1940), p. 26.

16. At the time of the new constitution's promulgation and of the reaffirmation of the stability of law, a commission was in the process of drafting the latest in the series of RSFSR codes of the Krylenko type. The commission hastily reoriented its efforts in 1936, but its final product was rejected anyhow. See G. Volkov, 'O proekte novogo Ugolovnogo kodeksa', *SZ* (1937, No. 3), p. 12.

17. Besides the criminal code, draft USSR codes of criminal procedure, civil, and civil procedure law were also prepared during these years. For information on the criminal codes, see V. I. Ivanov, 'Razvitie kodifikatsii ugolovnogo zakonodatelstva', *Razvitie kodifikatsii sovetskogo zakonodatelstva* (M., 1968), pp. 205–6.

18. See Utevskii and Osherovich, op. cit.; and Solomon, 'Soviet Criminology', loc. cit.

The other major legal research institute in Moscow during the 1930s was the Academy of Sciences's Institute of Law (earlier the Institute of Soviet Construction and Law). Until 1937 this institute was the center of radical legal scholarship as represented by the 'legal nihilists' Pashukanis and Krylenko. Since most of traditional criminal law scholarship was irrelevant to the concerns of this group, the institute failed to attract established scholars, and tended to recruit younger researchers of a Marxian perspective, some of whom did not always observe the distinction between scholarship and ideology. After Pashukanis, Krylenko and many of their supporters were purged in 1937, the institute's criminal law section had to be rebuilt, and it was not until after World War II that the Institute of Law became once again an important center for Soviet criminal law scholarship. For analysis of the writings of Pashukanis, see Robert Sharlet, 'Pashukanis and the Rise of Soviet Marxist Jurisprudence, 1924–1930', *Soviet Union*, 1, No. 2 (1974), pp. 103–21.

19. 'Vo Vsesoiuznom institute iuridicheskikh nauk: Rabota sektsii ugolovnogo prava', *SIu* (1938, No. 23–4), p. 61. 'Pervaia nauchnaia sessiia vsesoiuznogo

instituta iuridicheskikh nauk', *Trudy pervoi nauchnoi sessii,* loc. cit., p. 2.
20. The conference at the All-Union Institute of Juridical Sciences was the largest in legal science for many years. It included representatives from all the republics, from legal research institutes and educational institutions, institutes of forensic science, etc., 'without exception'. There were 357 persons in attendance (194 from out of town and 223 from Moscow), including 63 practical workers from the Commissariats of Justice of the USSR and RSFSR, the USSR and RSFSR Supreme Courts, the Procuracies of the USSR and RSFSR, and the College of Advocates. 'Pervaia nauchnaia sessiia', loc. cit., p. 1.

For a summary of the conference, see 'Vo vsesoiuznom institute iuridicheskikh nauk, nauchnaia sessiia', in three parts: *SIu* (1939, No. 8), pp. 21–31; *SIu* (1939, No. 9), pp. 26–30; *SIu* (1939, No. 10), pp. 22–9; and for the complete stenographic report, see *Trudy pervoi nauchnoi sessii,* op. cit.
21. *Informatsionnyi Biulleten VIIuN* (1939, No. 5), p. 6; B. Khlebnikov, 'Nauchno-issledovatelskaia rabota v oblasti ugolovnogo prava v 1939 g. (Svodnyi plan institutov NKIu SSSR)', ibid. (1939, No. 6), pp. 12–16.
22. *Ugolovnyi kodeks SSSR. Proekt* (M.: Vsesoiuznyi institut iuridicheskikh nauk, 1939). For discussions, see *SIu* and *SZ* for 1939 and 1940.
23. A. A. Gertsenzon, 'Puti razvitiia sovetskoi nauki ugolovnogo prava', *SGiP* (1947, No. 11), p. 81.
24. A. A. Piontkovskii, *Stalinskaia konstitutsiia i proekt ugolovnogo kodeksa SSSR* (M., 1947), pp. 3–4.
25. Interviews.
26. See *SZ*, 1946–7.
27. Piontkovskii, op. cit.
28. Interviews.
29. A. A. Gertsenzon, 'Osnovnye printsipy i polozheniia proekta ugolovnogo kodeksa SSSR', *Trudy pervoi nauchnoi sessii,* loc. cit., p. 147.
30. Piontkovskii, op. cit.
31. This would have resulted had any of the draft RSFSR criminal codes of the early 1930s been passed and promulgated.
32. Berman, op. cit., p. 45.
33. See ibid., pp. 52–7.
34. M. D. Shargorodskii, 'Analogiia v istorii ugolovnogo prava i v sovetskom ugolovnom prave', *SZ* (1938, No. 7), p. 59.
35. A. Ia. Vyshinskii, *K polozheniiu na fronte pravovoi teorii* (M., 1937), p. 32.
36. Volkov, loc. cit., pp. 11–22.
37. Ibid.; Shargorodskii, loc. cit., pp. 50–60.
38. 'Vo vsesoiuznom institute', loc. cit.; interview with A. A. Gertsenzon. Professor Gertsenzon indicated to me that of all his activities in criminal policy-making during the course of forty-five years as a criminal law scholar, it was his initiative of the struggle against the principle of analogy of which he was most proud.

The text of Article 2 of the draft code which effectively removed the principle of analogy ('The Exact Observance of the Criminal Law of the USSR') read as follows: 'No one may be convicted or punished other than according to the exact grounds of the USSR Criminal Code.'
39. On Goliakov's various positions, see Donald Barry, 'Leaders of the Soviet Legal Profession: An Analysis of Biographical Data and Career Patterns', *Canadian-American Slavic Studies,* VI, No. 1 (spring 1972).

40. 'K razrabotke proekta obshchei chasti ugolovnogo kodeksa Soiuza SSR', Part One, *SIu* (1938, No. 20–1), p. 18.

41. Goliakov, 'Osnovnye problemy', pp. 26–30.

42. Goliakov gave as an example the case of a man who 'for performing a few cuttings according to the Muslim tradition' was convicted of abortion by analogy! Ibid., pp. 29–30.

43. Gertsenzon, 'Osnovnye printsipy', loc. cit., pp. 146–9.

44. 'Preniia po dokladu A. A. Gertsenzona i sodokladi B. S. Utevskogo i V. S. Trakhtereva', *Trudy pervoi nauchnoi sessii*, loc. cit., pp. 170–94. the speakers included V. M. Chikhvadze, B. S. Mankovskii, M. D. Shargorodskii, M. M. Isaev, A. V. Laptev, P. S. Romashkin, A. A. Piontkovskii, A. N. Trainin, V. D. Menshagin, S. Potravnov, and V. Levshin.

45. Gertsenzon, 'Osnovnye zadachi', loc. cit.; 'Preniia po dokladu A. A. Gertseznona', loc. cit.

46. Gertsenzon, 'Osnovnye zadachi', loc. cit., pp. 148–9.

47. 'Preniia po dokladu A. A. Gertsenzon', loc. cit., p. 171.

48. Ibid., pp. 180–241.

49. In the 1920s even the rhetoric of the Positivist 'social defense' school was adopted, when the 1924 RSFSR Criminal Code provided for 'measures of social defense' in place of punishments. After such euphemisms were discarded in the 1930s, the principles of social defense still commanded much allegiance.

50. How much the removal of analogy from Soviet criminal law in the late 1930s would have improved the administration of criminal justice in the USSR is debatable. Gertsenzon was probably right when he pointed out that, if analogy were removed, some judges and prosecutors 'who have been accustomed to the presence of analogy for a long time will find it difficult . . . for they will have to study the crime situation carefully and follow the latest instructions from the appropriate agencies up to the Supreme Soviet about new forms, of crime, changes in the criminal law, etc.' Gertsenzon, 'Osnovnye zadachi', loc. cit., p. 148. It is likely that those prosecutors and judges who lacked higher legal education (a sizeable percentage at that time) would be especially vulnerable to these new burdens. However, there would always be room for analogizing by prosecutors and by judges wherever the definitions of criminal offenses (*corpora delicti*) were broad; and the removal of analogy would not have affected administrative proceedings at all. The Special Boards of the NKVD would still be empowered to send to prison for five years 'persons recognized as socially dangerous'. See Hazard, *Law and Social Change*, op. cit.

51. *Informatsionnyi Biulleten VIIuN* (1939, No. 5), p. 6.

52. P. V., 'Poniatie analogii v sovetskom ugolovnom prave i praktika ee primeneniia', *SIu* (1939, No. 3), pp. 8–13; G. Nadzharov [aspirant, All-Union Legal Academy], 'O primenenii analogii v sovetskom ugolovnom prave', *SZ* (1939, No. 6), pp. 64–6; R. Stepanova, 'Za sokhranenie instituta analogii v sovetskom ugolovnom prave', *SZ* (1939, No. 12), pp. 59–63; M. D. Sharagorodskii, 'Problemy proekta Ugolovnogo Kodeksa SSSR', Part One, *SIu* (1940, No. 5), pp. 10–15.

53. Interviews.

54. Gertsenzon, 'Puti razvitiia', loc. cit. I have found no evidence to support Barry and Berman's suggestion that the draft code failed to meet Stalin's approval. See Barry and Berman, loc. cit., p. 318.

55. Piontkovskii, op. cit., pp. 10–12. Analogy was removed by Article Three of the 1947 draft USSR criminal code, which stated: 'No one can be punished for an act or omission for which criminal responsibility has not been established by the laws of the USSR.' Ibid., p. 10.

56. Interviews.

57. For the texts of these edicts, see 'Ob ugolovnoi otvetsvennosti za khishchenie gosudarstvennogo i obshchestvennogo imushchestva', Ukaz Prezidiuma Verkhovnogo Soveta SSSR ot 4 iiunia 1947 g.; and 'Ob usilenii okhrany lichnoi sobstvennosti grazhdan', Ukaz Prezidiuma Verkhovnogo Soveta SSSR ot 4 iuniia 1947 g.–both in *Sbornik dokumentov po istorii ugolovnogo zakonodatelstva*, loc. cit., pp. 430–1, or in *Vedomosti Verhovnogo Soveta SSSR* (1947, no. 19).

58. I. T. Goliakov, 'Usilenie okhrany gosudarstvennoi, obshchestvennoi i lichnoi sobstvennosti', *SZ* (1947, No. 9), p. 4.

59. See 'Ob otmene smertnoi kazni', Ukaz Prezidiuma Verkhovnogo Soveta SSSR ot 26 maia 1947, *Sbornik dokumentov po istorii ugolovnogo zakonodatelstva, loc. cit.*, p. 429; and 'O primenenii smertnoi kazni k izmennikam Rodiny, shpionam, podryvnikam-diversantam', Ukaz Prezidiuma Verkhovnogo Soveta SSSR ot 12 ianvaria 1950, ibid., p. 435.

60. Interviews.

61. Goliakov, 'Usilenenieokhrany', loc. cit., pp. 4–7.

62. My estimate of the share the various forms of theft must have played in Soviet criminality during the late 1940s is based upon an extrapolation backwards from 1960s data. In the 1960s, theft of all kinds represented about 30 per cent of the crimes brought to trial and a larger percentage of undetected offenses. In the later 1940s, when there were greater shortages of goods and when juvenile offenders (a theft-prone group) were brought to the courts (rather than siphoned off to juvenile affairs commissions), the share of theft would be no less than in the 1960s. See *Kriminologiia* (M., 1968), p. 427.

63. Goliakov, 'Usilenenie okhrany', loc. cit., p. 4. See also I. T. Goliakov, 'Ob usilenii okhrany gosudarstvennoi, osshchestvennoi i lichnoi sobstvennosti', *SGiP* (1947, No. 7), pp. 1–9.

64. Interviews. Goliakov made public his attitude toward the theft laws for the first time in a 1957 article, where he referred to the raising of theft penalties in 1947 as 'unjustifiably sharp', and 'as placing the court within cruel limits'. See I. T. Goliakov, 'K proektu ugolovnogo kodeksa RSFSR', *SIu* (1957, No. 2), pp. 32–3.

65. I. T. Goliakov, 'Protiv izvrashchenii smysla ukazov ot 4 iunia 1947 g.', *SZ* (1947, No. 11), p. 21.

66. Piontkovskii, op. cit., p. 23.

67. Ibid., p. 28.

68. N. D. Durmanov, 'Nakazuemost khishcheniia gosudarstvennogo i obshchestvennogo imushchestva, krazhi lichnogo imushchestva i razboia po ukazam ot 4 iunia 1947 g.', *SZ* (1947, No. 10), pp. 3–8.

69. Ibid., pp. 3–4.

70. The example is given by I. T. Goliakov. See Goliakov, 'Protiv izvrashchenii', loc. cit., p. 22.

71. Durmanov, loc. cit., p. 5.

72. 'Postanovlenie soveshchaniia Ministra iustitsii SSSR, Generalnogo Prokurora SSSR i Predsedatelia Verkhovnogo Suda SSSR po povodu stati prof. N. Durmanova, "Nakazuemost khishchenii godusarstvennogo i obshchestven-

nogo imushchestva, krazhi lichnogo imushchestva i razboia po ukazam ot 4 iunia 1947g.'', pomeshchannoi v zhurnale, *Sotsialisticheskaia zakonnost* No. 10 za 1947g.', *SZ* (1947, No. 11), p. 19.

73. Goliakov, 'Protiv izvrashchenii', loc. cit., pp. 21–3.

74. 'Rukovodiashchee postanovlenie Plenuma Verkhovnogo Suda No. 6/4/U ot 19 marta 1948 g.', as cited by V. A. Kurinov, *Ugolovnaia otvetstvennost za khishchenie gosudarstvennogo i obshchestvennogo imushchestva* (M., 1954).

75. Zinaida Andreevna Vyshinskaia was the daughter of A. Ia. Vyshinskii, the Procurator-General of the USSR from 1937 to 1940, Deputy Minister of Foreign Affairs from 1940 to 1949, and Minister of Foreign Affairs, 1949 to 1953.

76. Z. A. Vyshinskaia, *Ob ugolovnoi otvetstvennosti za khishchenie gosudarstvennogo i obshchestvennogo imushchestva* (M., 1948), p. 25.

77. 'Rukovodiashchee postanovlenie Plenuma', loc. cit. For further discussion of the interpretation of these edicts by the USSR Supreme Court, see 'Osnovnye voprosy praktiki primeneniia ukaza 4 iiuna 1947 g., "Ob ugolovnoi otvetstvennosti za khishchenii gosudarstvennogo i obshchestvennogo imushchestva"', *SZ* (1951, No. 1), pp. 10–27.

78. Fainsod, op. cit.

79. Skilling, 'Group Conflict in Soviet Politics', *loc. cit.*, p. 401, suggests that there were probably ups and down in the influence of specialists during the Stalin years.

80. Brzezinski and Huntington, op. cit., pp. 191–234.

3. THE POST-STALIN EXPANSION OF PARTICIPATION

1. On the criminal justice reform, see Berman, op. cit., pp. 66–96; and Peter Juviler, 'Criminal Law and Social Control', *Contemporary Soviet Law: Essays in Honor of John N. Hazard* (ed. Donald Barry *et al.*; The Hague, 1974), pp. 17–54.

2. Interviews. The elimination of the Special Board was effected by administrative order and was not made public until 1956.

3. The restoration of the Procuracy's supervisory function was further encouraged by new legislation. See 'Polozhenie o prokurorskom nadzore', utverzhdeno 24 maia, 1955, in *Sbornik zakonov SSSR i Ukazov Prezidiuma Verkhovnogo Soveta SSSR, 1938–1967* (three volumes; M., 1968–1970), II, pp. 573–85.

4. 'Ob amnestii, "Ukaz Prezidiuma Verkhovnogo Soveta ot 27 marta 1953 g."', ibid., pp. 627–8.

5. P. S. Romashkin, 'Osnovnye problemy kodifikatsii sovetskogo ugolovnogo zakonodatelstva', *SGiP* (1957, No. 5), pp. 73–4.

6. In the previous chapter we saw how unpopular some of the more severe Stalinist measures were; for example, the 1947 laws against theft.

7. Ivanov, loc. cit., p. 206; interviews. A. A. Piontkovskii also wrote the keynote article, which started the discussion of the draft code's contents. See A. A. Piontkovskii, 'Osnovnye voprosy proekta ugolovnogo kodeksa SSSR', *SZ* (1954, No. 1), pp. 25–38.

8. V. M. Chikhvadze, 'Nekotorye voprosy sovetskogo ugolovnogo prava v sviazi s razrabotkoi proekta Ugolovnogo Kodeksa SSSR', *SGiP* (1953, No. 4), pp. 59–71; and V. S. Tadevosian, 'K razrabotke proekta Ugolovnogo Kodeksa SSSR', ibid., pp. 72–8.

9. See *SGiP* and *SZ* for summer and fall of 1954.

10. It appeared that the participants in this conference came mainly from Leningrad, as members of the Leningrad University law faculty presented nearly all of the papers. *Teoreticheskaia konferentsiia po voprosam proekta UK SSSR: tezisy dokladov* (L., 1955). My thanks to Mr Morris McCain of Yale University for showing me his notes on this source.

11. D. S. Karev, 'O kodifikatsii i sistematizatsii zakonodatelstva SSSR i soiuznykh respublik', *SZ* (1956, No. 2), p. 7; A. N. Vasilev, 'K proekta UK SSSR', *SGiP* (1954, No. 7), p. 120.

12. 'Za povyshenie roli pravovoi nauki v kodifikatsii sovetskogo zakonodatelstva', *SGiP* (1956, No. 1), pp. 3–13.

13. Ibid., p. 4.

14. Ibid., p. 12.

15. Interviews.

16. The editors' willingness to express their critical views so directly at the end of 1955 (when the editorial was written) suggests that there were hints of a new atmosphere before Khrushchev's speech to the 20th Party Congress. A study of the last months of 1955, also the first months of Khrushchev's rule, would confirm to what extent this was the case.

17. N. S. Khrushchev, 'Secret Speech', loc. cit.

18. Traditionally the Russian word *obshchestvennost* referred not to the public as a whole, but to its more informed and active segments.

19. A. A. Ushakov, 'V. I. Lenin i kodifikatsiia sovetskogo prava', *SGiP* (1956, No. 5), pp. 1–10; O. I. Chistiakov, 'Organizatsiia kodifikatsionnykh rabot v pervye gody sovetskoi vlasti (1917–23)', ibid., pp. 10–22.

20. Chistiakov, loc. cit., p. 22.

21. The reader may recall that under Lenin the criminal codes had been republican rather than all-union in nature; the 1936 Stalin Constitution had shifted the jurisdiction to the all-union level. In returning jurisdiction to the republics, Khrushchev was making a symbolic gesture to some of the national minorities, a gesture easy to make because the practice was 'Leninist' and little political power was involved. For the legal basis of the change, see 'Ob otnesenii k vedeniiu soiuznykh respublik zakonodatelstva ob ustroistve sudov soiuznykh respublik, priniatiia grazhdanskogo, ugolovnogo i protsessualnykh kodeksov', Zakon priniatii Verkhovnym Sovetom SSSR 11 febrala 1957 g., *Vedomosti Verkhovnogo Soveta SSSR* (1957, No. 4), p. 63.

22. When the draft USSR Criminal and Criminal Procedure codes were set aside in 1956, they had already received preliminary approval from the Praesidium of the Supreme Soviet and passed through editorial revisions at the hands of the Commissions on Legislative Suggestions, Ivanov, *loc. cit.*; M. A. Gedvilas and S. G. Novikov, 'O deiatelnosti komissii zakonodatelnykh predpolozhenii Verkhovnogo Soveta SSSR', *SGiP* (1957, No. 9), p. 17.

23. See Solomon, 'Soviet Criminology', loc. cit., pp. 583–93; B. S. Utevskii, 'Razvitie sovetskoi ispravitelnoi-trudovoi nauki', *Trudy Vysshei Shkoly MOOP*, Vyp. 16 (M., 1967), pp. 114–27.

24. The preparation of the new Fundamental Principles of Criminal Legislation began shortly after the decision to shift jurisdiction for criminal law to the republics. The legislation embodying that decision was prepared simultaneously with the draft Fundamental Principles itself and was promulgated only in February 1957.

Gedvilas and Novikov, loc. cit., pp. 17–18.

25. The abolition of the USSR Ministry of Justice and the dispersal of many of its functions to the republican ministries and others to the Juridical Commission of the USSR Council of Ministers was a characteristic Khrushchevian attempt to improve efficiency through decentralization.

26. Boris Samoilovich Utevskii, a leading penologist in the 1920s, co-author of three textbooks on corrective-labor law with E. G. Shirvindt (1927, 1931, 1957), spent the later Stalin years at the All-Union Institute of Juridical Sciences. In 1956 Utevskii became the head of a new kafedra for corrective labor law at the MVD Higher School. After an illness in 1958 he relinquished the post, but remained a member of the kafedra despite his seventy years. Through his eighty-third birthday in 1970 Utevskii remained an active and independent-minded scholar. Interviews.

27. Interviews.

28. Interviews.

29. See 'V Institute Prava AN SSSR', *SGiP* (1957, No. 3), pp. 123–30; 'Vo Vsesoiuznom Institute Iuridicheskikh Nauk', *SGiP* (1957, No. 6), pp. 125–30; 'Rabotu po kodifikatsii sovetskogo zakonodatelstva – na uroven novykh zadach', *SZ* (1957, No. 5), pp. 1–5.

30. 'Rabotu po kodifikatsii', loc. cit.

31. Ibid., p. 5.

32. Ibid.

33. 'Vazhnyi shag v dalneishem razvitii sovetskoi demokratii', *SGiP* (1957, No. 7), p. 9; interviews.

34. Interviews. Gedvilas and Novikov wrote that the Commissions on Legislative Suggestions did work on the preparation of this legislation during the summer of 1957, but this was only formally so. The Commissions had in fact delegated the job of collecting and processing the comments from the legal community to the original drafting commission. Gedvilas and Novikov, loc. cit., p. 122.

35. Ibid., pp. 18–24.

36. 'Osnovnye nachala ugolovnogo zakonodatelstva Soiuza SSR i soiuznykh republik (proekt)', *SGiP* (1958, No. 6), pp. 3–12; and in *SZ* (1958, No. 6), pp. 7–16; and in *Sovety deputatov trudiashchikhsia* (1958, No. 6), pp. 19–27.

37. See *SGiP* and *SZ* for 1956, Nos. 7–12. Soviet criminal law scholars also wrote two articles about the draft Fundamental Principles of Criminal Legislation in the popular political journal *Sovety deputatov trudiashchikhsia*, which appeared in issues 8 and 9 of 1958; but these articles explained the new legislation more than they contributed to the debate over its contents.

38. 'Vazhnyi shag v dalneishem razvitii sovetskoi demokratii', loc. cit., pp. 1–9.

39. 'V Komissiakh Zakonodatelnykh Predpolozhenii Soveta Soiuza i Soveta Nationalnostei Verkhovnogo Soveta SSSR', *SGiP* (1958, No. 6), p. 1, and in *SZ* (1958, No. 6), p. 7.

40. Interviews.

41. Brzezinski and Huntington, op. cit., pp. 212–15; Barry, 'The Specialist in Soviet Policy-making', loc. cit.

42. Among the other signs of criminal law scholars' involvement with the new legislation which were readily apparent was their part in the ceremonial functions relating to its promulgation. These included attendance by a delegation of criminal law scholars, headed by Prof. S. A. Golunskii, who addressed the Supreme Soviet; and the holding of celebratory meetings to welcome the legislation after it had been

passed into law. *Zasedaniia Verkhovnogo Soveta SSSR 5ogo sozyva, 2aia sessiia (22-25 dekabria 1958 g.)*, *Stenograficheskii otchet* (M., 1959), pp. 528-34; V. K. 'Obsuzhdenie novogo vsesoiuznogo zakonodatelstva v institute prava A. N. SSSR', *SGiP* (1959, No. 4), pp. 114-17; G. M. Sh. 'Nauchnaia sessiia vsesiouznogo instituta iurdicheskikh nauk, posviashchennaia novym ugolovnogo zakonodatelstva i sudoproizvodstva', ibid., pp. 117-20.

43. 'O vvedenii uslovno-dosrochnogo osvobozhdeniia iz mest zakliucheniia', ukaz Prezidiuma Verkhovnogo Soveta SSSR ot 14 iiuniia 1954 g., *Sbornik zakonov SSSR i ukazov Prozidiuma Verkhovnogo Soveta SSSR* (M., 1959), pp. 548-9.

44. A. Liubavin and A. L. Remenson, 'Dosrochnoe osvobozhdenie v poriadke zacheta rabochikh dnei', *SZ* (1957, No. 6), pp. 14-19.

45. Ibid.

46. B. S. Utevskii, 'Voprosy nakazaniia v ugolovnom zakonodatelstve', *SZ* (1957, No. 7), pp. 8-9; interviews.

47. A number of other scholars also supported the idea of a differentiated system of parole eligibility. See P. G. Volodarskii, 'Institut dosrochnogo osvobozhdeniia v sovetskom ugolovnom prave i praktika ego primeneniia', *SGiP* (1957, No. 7), p. 47; N. D. Durmanov, *Osvobozhdenie ot nakazaniia po sovetskomu pravu* (M., 1957), p. 47; I. D. Perlov, 'Protsessualnye voprosy dosrochnogo i uslovno-dosrochnogo osvobozhdeniia', *SZ* (1955, No. 2), p. 18; and A. S. Shliapochnikov, 'Nekotorye voprosy borby s prestupnostiu', *SIu* (1957, No. 3), p. 42.

48. See Article 39 of 'Osnovnye Nachala Ugolovnogo Zakonodatelstva Soiuza SSSR i Soiuzaykh Respublik, Proekt', loc. cit., p. 11.

49. Interviews. To compare the original with the amended version of the parole article, see ibid., and Article 44 of 'Osnovy Ugolovnogo Zakonodatelstva Soiuza SSR i Soiuzaykh Respublik', *Spravochnik partiinogo rabotnika*, II (1959), pp. 616-17.

50. Liubavin and Remenson, loc. cit., p. 19; M. A. Efimov, 'Nekotorye voprosy uslovno-dosrochnogo i dosrochnogo osvobozhdeniia', *Pravovedenie* (1958, No. 1), p. 93.

51. See notes 59 and 60 below.

52. Utevskii, loc. cit.; Efimov, loc. cit., p. 91.; 'Obzor statei i pisem, postupivshikh v redaktsii v sviazi s obsuzhdeniem ugolovnogo i ugolovnogo-protsessualnogo zakonodatelstva', *SGiP* (1958, No. 12), p. 113.

53. Efimov, loc. cit.; M. A. Efimov, 'O dosrochnom i uslovno-dosrochnom osvobozhdenii', *SGiP* (1958, No. 11), pp. 108-11; M. A. Efimov, 'Uslovno-dosrochnoe osvobozhdenie ne dolzhno byt bezuslovnym', *SIu* (1959), No. 5), p. 51.

54. 'Osnovnye Nachala Ugolovnogo Zakonodatelstva', *Spravochnik partiinogo rabotnika*, loc. cit.

55. See the speech by the Procurator-General of the USSR, R. D. Rudenko, at the Supreme Soviet meeting which approved the Fundamental Principles of Criminal Legislation. *Zasedaniia Verkhovnogo Soveta SSSR, 5ogo sozyva*, loc. cit.

56. Iu. M. Tkachevskii, 'Uslovno-dosrochnoe osvobozhdenie', *SZ* (1959, No. 11), pp. 31-7; interviews.

57. The research section for corrective-labor institutions in the MVD RSFSR operated from late 1955 until 1958, during which time it published a periodical for internal use only entitled *Ispravitelnye-trudovye uchrezhdeniia*. When the section was closed in 1958, most of its functions were assumed by the corrective-labor law sector at Vysshaia shkola MOOP. Interviews. From 1959 on the ministry published a

new periodical on penology, *K novoi zhizne*.

58. A. M. Iakovlev, 'Sovokupnost prestuplenii, povtornost i retsidiv po sovetskomu ugolovnomu pravu', *SGiP* (1956, No. 10), pp. 48–54; interviews.

59. B. S. Nikiforov, 'O retsidive i sudimosti', *SGiP* (1957, No. 5), pp. 100–5.

60. Shliapochnikov, 'Nekotorye voprosy', loc. cit., pp. 40–3.

61. N. A. Struchkov, 'Problemy nakazaniia v proektakh obshchesoiuznogo i respublikanskogo ugolovnogo zakonodatelstve', *SGiP* (1958, No. 7), p. 104.

62. See articles 23 and 44 of 'Osnovnye Nachala Ugolvonogo Zakonodatelstva', *Spravochnik partiinogo rabotnika*, loc. cit.

63. Interviews.

64. A. M. Iakovlev, 'Naznachenie i ispolnenie nakazaniia retsidivistam', *SGiP* (1959, No. 9), pp. 89–94.

65. Iakovlev's work on recidivism led to his doctoral dissertation and to a book, *Borba s retsidivnoi prestupnostiu* (M., 1964).

66. Iakovlev, 'Sovokupnost prestuplenii', loc. cit.

67. Iakovlev, 'Naznachenie i ispolnenie', loc. cit.

68. *Ugolovnyi kodeks RSFSR* (M., 1962), Article 24, Note 1.

69. S. Stepichev, 'Opredelenie osobo opasnogo retsidivista dolzhno byt edinym', *SZ* (1962, No. 1), pp. 27–30.

70. Interviews.

71. Ibid. Criminal law scholars also prepared drafts of sections of the Fundamental Principles of Criminal Legislation and of the RSFSR Criminal Code which did not raise or reflect policy issues; but this activity had little significance for our assessment of the scholars' participation *in policy-making*. Where the policy-making process was not initiated, the scholars' contribution to the writing of the legislation could only be technical in nature.

72. Note that during the late 1950s Soviet criminal law scholars seemed to have participated in much the same way in decisions relating to criminal procedure as they did in decisions relating to criminal law. See John Gorgone, 'Soviet Jurists in the Legislative Arena,' *Soviet Union*, III, No. 1 (1976), pp. 1–36.

73. Brzezinski and Huntington, op. cit.

74. Barry, loc. cit.; Barry and Berman, loc. cit.

4. THE INSTITUTIONALIZATION OF PARTICIPATION

1. See Chapters 5 through 7.

2. For a detailed account of Soviet criminology's demise in the early Stalin years, see Solomon, 'Soviet Criminology', loc. cit. See also Iu. P. Kasatkin, 'Ocherk istorii izuchenii prestupnosti v SSSR', *Problemy iskoreneniia prestupnosii* (ed. V. N. Kudriavtsev; M., 1965, pp. 187–225.

3. For example, see M. D. Shargorodskii and N. S. Alekseev, 'Aktualnye problemy ugolovnogo prava', *Uchenye zapiski Leningradskogo gosudarstvennogo universiteta*, No. 18 (Seriia iuridicheskikh nauk, no. 5), pp. 154–296; and 'O sostoianii i zadachakh nauki sovetskogo ugolovnogo prava', *SGiP* (1955, No. 2), pp. 1–10. Interviews.

4. In the late 1920s the noted penologist E. G. Shirvindt had served simul-

taneously as the chief of the prison administration (GUMZ) under the NKVD RSFSR and as the director of the State Institute for the Study of Crime and the Criminal. He lost both positions in 1931 and found work first in the USSR Commissariat of Water Transport and then in 1933 at the USSR Procuracy as senior assistant for the supervision of places of confinement. However, Shirvindt was denounced in 1934 as a 'right opportunist' for having believed in the possibility of 'correcting all men' (see *Ot tiurem k vospitatelym uchrezhdeniiam*, ed. A. Ia. Vyshinskii; M., 1934, p. 43), and in 1936 he was arrested, to remain in the camps until his release in 1955. See B. S. Utevskii, 'Vidnyi deiatel ispravitelno-truodovoi sistemi', *K novoi zhizne* (1966, No. 5); 'Evsei Gustavovich Shirvindt', *SGiP* (1958, No. 12), p. 130.

5. The career of Aleksei Adolfovich Gertsenzon had three phases. A promising young criminologist in the 1920s, by the end of that decade Gertsenzon was the author of two books, including a study of alcoholism and crime in the RSFSR. When the Moscow Criminological Center closed in 1931, Gertsenzon moved to the Institute of Criminal Policy (the reorganized State Institute for the Study of Crime and the Criminal), where the second phase of his career began. At the new post Gertsenzon served as criminal statistics specialist; between 1933 and 1947 he wrote four textbooks on the subject. Always anticipating the revival of criminology, Gertsenzon included sections on crime study in each of these texts; and, as we have seen above, took part in the 1944–5 attempt to revive the field. In addition, Gertsenzon contributed to the history of criminal law with a study of the 'revolutionary democrat' Jean Paul Marat. After 1956 Gertsenzon's career entered its final stage, as Aleksei Adolfovich returned again to criminology. As head of the leading criminology research sector from 1957 until his death in 1970 (after 1963 located within the All-Union Institute for the Study and Prevention of Crime), Gertsenzon gave both moral and intellectual encouragement to aspiring young criminologists. He was the leading methodologist of Soviet crime study and the teacher of a new generation of criminologists. During these years Gertsenzon served as the chairman of two legislative commissions – one which prepared the RSFSR criminal code in 1959 and one which drafted a major statute on alcoholism prevention in 1965. See 'Shestdesiatletie A. A. Gertsenzona', *Pravovedenie* (1962, No. 2), p. 170; A. S. Shliapochnikov, 'Pamiati vydaiushchego sovetskogo kriminologà, *Voprosy borby s prestupnostiu*, Vyp. 13 (1971), pp. 178–88. Interview.

6. During these years criminological research was initiated at universities in Moscow, Leningrad, Riga, and Voronezh and at the Kharkov Juridical Institute. Penological research was conducted by the corrective-labor law kafedra of MOOP Higher School. The kafedra became the main center for such research between 1958, when the MVD research section was closed, and 1965, when the MOOP institute was founded. Utevskii, 'Razvitie sovetskoi ispravitelno-trudovoi nauki', loc. cit.

7. On the revival of sociology in the USSR, see Fischer, op. cit.; Katz, loc. cit.; and Elizabeth Weinberg, op. cit.

8. V. N. Kudriavtsev, 'Ukrepliat sviaz nauki i praktiki', *Biulleten Verkhovnogo Suda SSSR* (1963, No. 6).

9. Solomon, 'Soviet Criminology', loc. cit., pp. 572–9; also 'Disput k vosprosu ob izuchenii prestupnosti v SSSR', *Revoliustsiia prava* (1929, No. 3), pp. 47–78.

10. See Hermann Mannheim, *Comparative Criminology* (two volumes; London, 1965).

11. See Solomon, 'Bibliography', loc. cit., items C25, C31, C34, and B. S. Utevskii, 'Sotsiologicheskie issledovaniia i kriminologiia', *Voprosy filosofii* (1964, No. 2), pp. 46-51.

12. Ibid.

13. A. A. Gertsenzon, *Vvedenie v sovetskuiu kriminologiiu* (M., 1965), pp. 35-41. For a portrait of the disagreement in retrospect, see *Kriminologiia*, op. cit., pp. 7-25.

14. On the criminologists' efforts to demonstrate the ideological acceptability of their field, see Solomon, 'Soviet Criminology', loc. cit., pp. 586-7.

15. A. A. Gertsenzon, *Predmet, metod, i sistema sovetskoi kriminologii* (M., 1962), p. 10.

16. For example, see the full report of the Perm *oblast* study, *Gosudarstvennye i obshchestvennye mery preduprezhdeniia prestupnosti* (M., 1963). See also Solomon, 'Bibliography', items E21, E22, E23, E27.

17. N. R. Mironov, 'O nekotorykh voprosakh preduprezhdeniia prestupnosti i drugikh anitobshchestvennykh iavlenii i borby s nimi v sovremennykh usloviiakh', *SGiP* (1961, No. 5), p. 9.

18. See *Science and Ideology in The Soviet Union*, op. cit.

19. L. I. Ilichev, 'Nauchnaia osnova rukovodstva razvitiem obshchestva, Nekotorye problemy razitiia obshchestvennykh nauk', *Stroitelstvo kommunizma i obshchestvennye nauki. Materially sessii obshchego sobraniia Akademii Nauk SSSR, 19-20* oktiabriia, 1962 (M., 1962). For the official 'conclusions' of the conference, see 'Postanovlenie obshchego sobraniia akademii nauk SSSR', *Vestnik Akademii Nauk* (1962, No. 12).

20. *Stroitelstvo kommunizma*, op. cit., p. 120. As of 1961 P. N. Fedoseev was the director of the Institute of Philosophy of the Academy of Sciences and the Academic Secretary of the Academy's section for Economic, Philosophical, and Legal Sciences. In 1962, he became a Vice-president of the Academy and shortly thereafter a full member of the party's Central Committee. For further biographical details see *Deputaty verkhovnogo soveta SSSR Sedmoi sozyv* (M., 1966), p. 458.

21. 'Iuridicheskaia nauka v usloviiakh kommunisticheskogo stroitelstva', *Kommunist* (1963, No. 16), p. 33.

22. Ibid., p. 27.

23. Ibid., p. 34.

24. Ibid.

25. See Loren R. Graham, 'Reorganization of the USSR Academy of Sciences', *Soviet Policy-Making*, op. cit.

26. A number of judicial agencies were overburdened, after the abolition in 1963 of the RSFSR Ministry of Justice with its 800 employees. Particularly needful of assistance were the apparat of the USSR and RSFSR Supreme Courts, which had taken over administration of the court system, and the Juridical Commissions of the USSR and RSFSR Councils of Ministers, which had gained responsibility for supervising the *advokatura* and the *notariat* and for providing legal assistance to various government ministries. 'Ob uprazdnenii Ministerstva Iustitsii RSFSR i obrazovanie iuridicheskoi komissii Soveta Ministrov RSFSR', *SIu* (1963, No. 10), p. 4.

27. Kudriavtsev, 'Ukrepliat sviaz', loc. cit.; interviews.

28. See 'O zadachakh Instituta sovetskogo zakonodatelstva', *Uchenye zapiski VNIISZ*, II (1964); and S. Borodin, 'Vsesoiuznyi nauchno-issledovatelskii institut okhrany obshchestvennogo proiadka', *SZ* (1965, No. 2).

29. The full Russian name of the Institute was *Vsesoiuznyi institut poziucheniiu prichin i razrabotke mer preduprezhdenii prestupnosti* (All-Union Institute for the Study of the Causes of Crime and the Elaboration of Methods of Crime Prevention). Soviet criminologists themselves usually referred to the Institute as 'Institut Prokuratury' (Procuracy Institute); indeed, this was the name written on the sign attached to the institute's front door. The Institute's ties with the Procuracy were so close that some of its employees, only partly in jest, referred to it as 'nauchnyi otdel Prokuratury' (the Procuracy's scientific department).

30. 'Polozhenie o Vsesoiuznom institute po izucheniiu prichin i razrabotke mer preduprezhdenii prestupnosti', utverzhdeno Gen. Prok. SSSR i Pred. Verkhovnogo Suda SSSR, 15 iunia 1963, in *Sbornik deistvuiushchikh prikazov i instruktsii generalnogo prokurora SSSR* (M., 1966).

31. Of the Institute's ten sectors (as of 1969), four studied crime, its causes, and crime prevention (general criminology, juvenile delinquency, property offenses, crimes against the person); four others focused upon the operations of the administration of justice (criminal law, courts, procuracy supervision, preliminary investigation); and the remaining two sectors studied police science and forensic psychology. All of these sectors were established at the time of the Institute's founding in 1963 except forensic psychology, which was added in 1965. The size of the sectors varied from ten to twenty persons, including a sector head, senior and junior research workers. Graduate students (*aspiranty*) attached to the sectors augmented their research forces. Kudriavtsev, 'Ukrepliat sviaz', loc. cit.; 'Otchet Vsesoiuznogo institut po izucheniiu prichin i razrabotke mer preduprezhdenii prestupnosti o vypolnenii nuachnykh issledovanii za 1965 god', *Informatsionnoe pismo* [Instituta], No. 4 (M., 1966), section two.

32. 'O nomenklaturakh dolzhnostnei rukovodiashchikh rabotnikov organov prokuratury, naznachaemykh i osvobozhdaemykh generalnym prokurorom SSSR', Prikaz Generalnogo Prokurora SSSR ot 31 iiulia, 1965, No. 66, *Sbornik deistvuiushchikh prikazov*, loc. cit. Before the file of a person recommended for one of these positions reached the Procurator-general it had to include the approval of a party organ (the level would depend upon the position and upon the man chosen). Moreover, these appointments were supposed to be discussed at the USSR Procuracy Collegium meeting. 'O poriadke predstavlenii rabotnikov k naznacheniem na dolzhnosti i osvodozhdenii ot dolzhnosti vkhodiashchiakh v nomenklatury generalnogo prokurora SSSR', Instruktsiia ot iuliia 1965, loc. cit.

33. In accordance with the rules on the role of party organizations in research institutes (see 'Partorganizatsiia NII', *Partiinaia zhizn* (1963, No. 16)), the party organization at the Procuracy Institute worked at improving the level of political consciousness and the quality of social relations among research staff. According to a recent party secretary there (interview), the party group mediated conflicts between researchers and administration and between individual researchers; it tried to maintain a sense of group commitment to the work and an awareness of the relationship between the Institute's work and societal goals; and it watched that promotions, hiring and firing were fair.

The trade union organization administered the social welfare program, including vacations, and occasionally served as a forum for disciplining a non-party researcher.

34. Kudriavtsev, loc. cit.

35. The annual reports of the Institute covered the following topics: the research

themes performed by the Institute and by each sector, with indication of all reports and publications which issued from them; the activities of the Academic Council; conferences in which Institute workers took part; legislative projects which the Institute helped prepare; measures taken to raise the qualifications of practical workers; efforts to coordinate research and ties with other scientific institutions; the teaching record of the Institute; international ties, including visits paid abroad and foreign guests of the Institute; and a short self-critical list of shortcomings in the Institute's work. See 'Otchet . . . za 1965', loc. cit., and 'Otchet Vsesoiuznogo instituta po izucheniiu prichin i razrabotke mer preduprezhdenii prestupnosti o vypolnenii nauchnykh issledovanii za 1966 god', *Informatsionnoe pismo*, No. 9 (1967).

36. See, for example, the dust-jacket of I. I. Karpets, *Problema prestupnosti* (M., 1969).

37. The most creative of the Institute's administrators, V. N. Kudriavtsev, authored an original study of crime causation, *Prichinnost v kriminologii* (M., 1968). In 1972 Kudriavtsev left the Procuracy Institute to become director of the Institute of State and Law of the Academy of Sciences, the most prestigious of Soviet legal research institutes at the time. In the fall of 1974 he was elected a corresponding member of the Academy of Sciences. 'Vybory v Akademii nauk SSSR', *SGiP* (1975, No. 2), p. 138.

38. See 'Grigorii Ivanovich Kocharov', *SZ* (1969, No. 10), p. 90.

39. In addition to the representatives of the judicial agencies here named, the membership of the 1966 Academic Council of the Procuracy Institute included S. N. Bratus, director of the Institute of Soviet Legislation (VNIISZ); A. N. Vasiliev, head of the police science kafedra, Moscow University; D. S. Karev, Prof. of criminal procedure, Moscow University; A. G. Lekar, deputy chief MOOP Higher School; S. P. Mitrichev, head, police science kafedra, Judicial Correspondence Institute; M. F. Pankratov, Editor, *Sotsialisticheskaia zakonnost*; Iu. V. Solopanov, director of the MOOP Institute (VNIIOOP); and the full directorate of the Institute – its director, two assistant directors, sector heads, party and trade union chiefs. 'Sostav uchenogo soveta instituta', *Informatsionnoe pismo*, No. 4 (1966), pp. 38–9.

40. 'Otchet . . . za 1965', loc. cit.; 'Otchet . . . za 1966', loc. cit.; 'Puti i perspektivy razvitiia sovetskoi kriminologii', *Informatsionnoe pismo*, No. 12 (M., 1967); 'Sotsialnaia obuslovennost prestupnogo povedeniia i rol biologicheskikh faktorov', *Nauchnaia informatsiia po voprosam borby s prestupnostiu (Informatsionnoe pismo, No. 13)* (M., 1968).

41. This description of the planning process is based upon interview material.

42. An exchange described to me as 'typical' of the final scrutiny of the plan by the Academic Council reached the level of banality. An 'outside' member of the Council questioned the need for a study of rape, 'when murder was the more serious problem'. Institute representatives had to point out that there were across the USSR five concurrent studies of murder, but none of rape. Interview.

43. The principal bone of contention between the criminologists and the judicial agencies was the penchant of judicial officials for adding supplementary assignments to the Institute during the course of the plan year. Criminologists objected to these additional assignments and blamed on them the failure of the Institute to complete all of its planned items. This complaint was mentioned in both the 1965 and 1966 annual reports. 'Otchet . . . za 1965', loc. cit.; 'Otchet . . .

za 1966', loc. cit.

44. Examples of this sequence are found in Chapter 3. Closed publications consisted of special printings, which would bear the words 'for internal use [dlia sluzhebnogo polzovania]' and be readily available only to judicial officials and to legal scholars. They would not be sold publicly, but instead distributed privately to a list of persons and institutions. Most libraries did not allow readers to view closed publications, without special permission.

The closed publication format was used not only when topics were sensitive, but also when quick circulation of information was required. The Procuracy Institute had the right to issue closed publications through its own editorial section.

45. Some research projects were reported only to their sponsors, without any publication of the results even in internal publications. One example was a major statistical study of crime in the USSR, 1917–67, which the Institute prepared in conjunction with officials at the request of the Supreme Court. The result was a monograph-size volume, with many tables and graphs.

Another example was a study of the application and effectiveness of the death penalty, commissioned by the Praesidium of the Supreme Soviet. Criminologists studied a sample of cases where the death penalty was applied for intentional murder between 1961 and 1965, and all cases where the death penalty was applied for other crimes during that period. With the help of officials from the Procuracy and the Supreme Court, the scholars prepared a *dokladnaia zapiska*, which included a history of Soviet legislation on the death penalty, analysis of court practice, and suggestions for changes in legislation and continued study of the problem. They also prepared *spravki* on the application of the death penalty in pre-revolutionary Russia, on the death penalty in Western legislation and its application in the West, on the history of Soviet legislation on the death penalty; and on the use of the death penalty in the USSR, 1920–7. 'Otchet . . . za 1965', loc. cit.

46. For example, when V. G. Tanasevich and colleagues uncovered a series of technical problems which seemed to account for the high rate of theft in the construction industry (lack of controls in dispensing materials, shortcomings in accounting procedures, inadequate norms governing material responsibility for losses, ineffective system of guarding warehouses and construction sites, hiring persons previously convicted of abusing their responsibility, a formal relationship of employers to the fulfilment of orders by employees, the absence of material interest in doing the job properly), they prepared a *predstavlenie* (representation), which the Procuracy Institute sent via the USSR Procuracy to Gostroi SSSR and its republican affiliates. It was alleged that the reforms instituted as a result of Tanasevich's recommendations substantially reduced the ministry's losses. In one trust within Gosstroi, Glavsreduralstroi, the losses fell from 141,000 rubles in 1964 to 21,000 rubles in 1965. 'Koordinatsiia nauchnykh issledovanii po problemam borby s kiishcheniem sotsialisticheskogo imushchestva, dolzhnostnymi i khozaistvennymi prestupleniiami', *Informatsionnoe pismo*, No. 10 (M. 1967).

47. Actual criminal statistics were excluded from closed as well as from open publications; in both cases statistical relationships were usually given in percentage form.

At the time of its founding the Procuracy Institute obtained the right to use statistical and case material, both current and archival, from all legal agencies. This meant that Institute's own security section (*pervyi otdel*) had the task of 'clearing' each member of the Institute's staff who might be called to use this 'secret material'. Criminologists working at universities had to arrange their own access data each time they needed to use it.

48. For example, *Rabota raionogo prokurora po borbe s prestupnostiu* (ed. A. S. Pankratov; M., 1965), and two *posobie* 'procuracy supervision in juvenile cases' and 'investigating and preventing child murders'. 'Otchet . . . za 1965', loc. cit.

49. See Solomon, 'Bibliography', F29, F33, F34.

50. *Metodicheskoe pismo o polozhitelnom opyte raboty Prokuratury goroda Leningrada po borbe s prestupnostiu nesovershennoletnikh* (M., 1966). Procuracy Institute scholars also prepared methodological letters on theft in the dairy industry (1965) and on fighting petty theft (1966). 'Otchet . . . za 1965', loc. cit.; 'Otchet . . . za 1966', loc. cit.

51. B. S. Vorontsov, 'Opyt konkretnogo sotsiologicheskogo issledovaniia po voprosu preduprezhdeniia prestupnosti nesovershennoletnikh v usloviiakh **pro**-myshlennogo goroda', *Nauchnaia informatsiia po voprosam borby s prestupnostiiu Informatsionnoe pismo No. 14* (M., 1968). Interview.

52. 'Otchet . . . za 1966', loc. cit.

53. Conferences for 1965 included: the first seminar for teachers of the course, 'Fundamentals of Soviet Criminology'; a conference organized by the Central Committee of the Lithuanian republican party on crime prevention; a conference organized by MOOP UkSSR; a conference in Kishinev on methods in legal research; conferences on juvenile delinquency, in Leningrad and in the Estonian republic; a conference on recidivist crime in Latvia, and others. This is only a partial list from 'Otchet . . . za 1965', loc. cit.

54. As of January 1967 the Institute had thirty-seven aspirants (twenty full-time and seventeen part-time) and one hundred and eighty correspondence students (*soistateli*). Of the latter, one hundred and ten worked in the procuracy or in investigatory organs, thirty in the courts, fifteen in MOOP, and twenty-five in other organizations. 'Otchet . . . za 1966', loc. cit.

55. Kh. Sheinin, 'Nauchno-konsultativnye sovety pri sudakh', *SZ* (1968, No. 2); *Organizatsiia suda i prokuratury v SSSR* (ed. B. A. Galkin; M., 1967), pp. 164–5.

56. As of the beginning of 1968, the USSR Supreme Court Advisory Council included from the Procuracy Institute the following scholars: Gertsenzon (criminology sector head); Karpets (the director); Kudriavtsev (the assistant director); Minkovskii (Juvenile delinquency sector head); Perlov (courts and criminal procedure sector head); Sakharov (member of *aktiv*, who taught at Lumumba University). Other members of the Council included Durmanov, Karev, and Menshagin from Moscow University, Kurliandskii from the KGB Higher School, Piontkovskii from the Institute of State and Law, and Pankratov, editor of *Sotsialisticheskaia zakonnost*. 'O sostave nauchno-konsultativnogo soveta pri Verkhovnom Sude SSSR', Postanovlenie verkhovnogo suda SSSR ot 12 dekabriia, 1967, *Biulleten verkhovnogo suda SSSR* (1968, No. 1).

The RSFSR Supreme Court also had an advisory council, which included from the Procuracy Institute: Gertsenzon, Gukovskaia (juvenile delinquency sector), Perlov, Sakharov, and Shliapochnikov (criminology sector). Other members included Karev and Kriger from Moscow University, Struchkov from MOOP Higher School, and Natashev from the MOOP Institute. 'Ob utverzhdenii sostava nauchno-konsultativnogo soveta pri verkhovnomu sude RSFSR', Postanovlenie No. 39 Plenuma verkhovnogo suda RSFSR ot 24 oktiabriia, 1967, *Biulleten verkhovnogo suda RSFSR* (1967, No. 12).

57. According to the Institute's reports its staff participated in the preparation of more than a dozen different Supreme Court edicts in 1965 and in 1966. For example, in 1965, Minkovskii's sector prepared suggestions for a Supreme Court edict 'On intensifying the fight with narcotics among juveniles', 'Otchet . . . za 1965', loc. cit., and 'Otchet . . . za 1966', loc. cit.

58. Sheinin, loc. cit., and reports on Supreme Court plenums and Collegium meetings in *Biulletin verkhovnogo suda SSSR, passim,* and in *SZ, passim.*

59. 'O metodicheskom sovete', Prikaz Generalnogo prokurora SSSR, ot 27 iiuliia 1960, No. 59, in *Sbornik deistvuiushchikh prikazov,* loc. cit.; and interviews. For 'orders' (*prikazy*) in whose preparation Institute scholars participated, see 'Otchet . . . za 1965', loc. cit., and 'Otchet . . . za 1966', loc. cit. The RSFSR Procuracy and some *oblast* level procuracies also had methodological councils.

60. 'Otchet . . . za 1965', loc. cit., and 'Otchet . . . za 1966', loc. cit.

61. Ibid.

62. The 1961 Program of the CPSU science declared that in the USSR science was 'in the process of becoming a productive force', thus moving from the superstructure to the base in Marxist categories. As the decade progressed, philosophers in the USSR became less tentative about science's status as a productive force; and even referred science as 'the most important productive force'. Also in the later half of the decade it became fashionable to treat the 'scientific-technological revolution' as the prime force in contemporary social development for both the capitalist and the socialist worlds. The eventual victory of socialist over capitalism, some commentators averred, would issue from socialism's superior capacity to utilize science and technology. See the '1961 Programme of the Communist Party of the Soviet Union', *Soviet Communism Programs and Rules* (ed. Jan Triska; San Francisco, 1962), pp. 23–129; Rachkov, op. cit.; Markov, op. cit.; *Sovremennaia nauchno-tekhnicheskaia revoliutsiia, Istoricheskoe issledovanie* (M., 1967) and in an expanded edition (M., 1970).

63. In the USSR of the 1920s politicians from Lenin down showed an interest in the 'scientific organization of labor' (*NOT*) ideas which were current in America and Europe; and there was considerable research and experimentation on the use of Taylor's ideas in Soviet industry. Strong interest in Taylorism had revived by 1963–4, but this interest became translated into a movement only after the September 1965 Plenum of the CPSU Central Committee supported *NOT*'s revival. During the later 1960s wide variety of Soviet factories, trusts, and even ministries began introducing *NOT* methods, which resulted in an onslaught of books and pamphlets explaining how these methods might be applied in various settings. For an overview of the history of *NOT* in the USSR, see Samuel Lieberstein, 'Technology, Work, and Sociology in the USSR: the *NOT* Movement', *Technology and Culture,* xvi, No. 1 (January 1975), pp. 48–66.

64. With the economic reform of 1965 the leadership of the CPSu lent its support to the revival of management science studies in the USSR. In 1966 the first All-Union Scientific Technical Conference on improving the Management of Industrial Production was convened, and for the occasion a comprehensive bibliography on the management of industry was prepared, including works written from 1917 to 1966. But the real expansion of studies relating to management of industry came in the years 1967–9. A bibliography of Soviet writings on the subject during these three years contained as many items as the bibliography for the fifty years preceding. See *Organizatsiia upravleniia promyshlennosti. Bibliograficheskii spravochnik,*

1917–1967. (Sost. M. M. Dizhur and T. N. Krivoruchko; M., 1967); and M. M. Dizhur and R. A. Kruglova, *Organizatsiia upravleniia promyshlennosti.* Bibliograficheskii ukazatel 1967–1969 (two volumes, M., 1970).

The study of the management or administration of other social and governmental institutions also expanded during this same period. See for example the series *Nauchnoe upravlenie obshchestvom* (beginning in 1968) for examples of this writing.

65. During the middle and late 1960s industrial sociology flourished in the USSR, as a number of large factories themselves hired staff sociologists to study their problems with work discipline, incentives, labor protection, or efficiency. Sometimes, these studies led to the compilation of 'plans of social development' for the factories, which were designed to parallel the economic plans. But the amount of resources devoted to social development was obviously small compared with those assigned to the plants' main functions. For a thorough discussion of social planning on the enterprise level, see *Planirovanie sotsialnykh protsessov na predpriiatii* (L., 1969). See also the series *Chelovek i obshchestvo*, issued by the Institute for Complex Social Research of Leningrad University, especially No. 7 (1970).

66. See in particular the work of V. G. Afanasev and his kafedra at the Party's Academy of Social Science, which kafedra was founded in 1966. Afanasev's own monograph *Nauchnoe upravlenie obshchestvom* (M., 1968) became well known in Soviet scholarly and administrative circles; but the kafedra also published a series of collections of articles about the rationalization of administration and decision-making, which bore the same title. On the use of expertise and information in decision-making, see particularly A. V. Kireev, 'Nauchnyi kharakter politiki KPSS', *Nauchnoe upravlenie obshestvom*, II (1968), pp. 3–50. For a close analysis of the writings of Afanasev see three articles by Donald V. Schwartz: 'Recent Soviet Adaptations of System Theory to Administrative Theory', *Journal of Comparative Administration*, v, No. 2 (August 1973), pp. 233–64; 'Information and Administration in the Soviet Union: Some Theoretical Considerations', *Canadian Journal of Political Science*, VII, No. 2 (June 1974), pp. 3–50; and 'Decision-making, Administrative Decentralization and Feedback Mechanisms: Comparisons of Soviet and Western Models', *Studies in Comparative Communism*, VII, Nos. 1–2 (spring/summer 1974), pp. 146–83.

67. See Chapter 9, notes 48 and 49.

68. V. K. Zvirbul, *Deiatelnost prokuratury po preduprezhdeniiu prestupnosti (Nauchnye osnovy)* (M., 1971); *Sovershenstvovanie prokurorskogo nadzora a SSSR (Sbornik statei)* (M., 1973); A. Safonov, 'Opyt vnedreniia nauchnykh rekomendatsii v praktiku', *SZ* (1973, No. 5); N. Kosoplechev *et al.*, 'Nauchnye rekomendatsii po kriminologii raionnym i gorodskim prokuroram', *SZ* (1973, No. 11).

69. R. Nishanov, 'O proektakh zakonov', *Izvestiia* (12 July 1969), p. 1.

CRIMINOLOGISTS' PARTICIPATION IN THE 1960s

1. Issues in criminal procedure, such as the presence and role of the defense counsel at preliminary investigation or preventive detention, were subjects of decisions taken in 1969, but they attracted the involvement not of criminologists but of a different set of criminal law scholars. On the efforts of some scholars to gain greater rights for defense counsel, see John Hazard, 'Social Control Through Law', *Politics in the USSR: Seven Cases* (ed. Alexander Dallin and Alan Westin; N.Y., etc.,

1966), pp. 207–41; and *Soviet Law and Government*, Vol. IX, No. 4 (spring 1971).

2. Most changes in the substantive criminal law of the RSFSR in the middle 1960s were small ones requiring merely editorial rewriting or changes reflecting the state's need to keep its code contemporary. More than half of these were introduced by an edict of the Praesidium of the RSFSR Soviet of 3 July 1965. These affected or added articles 156, 210, 212', 213', 225, 245, 255, and 257. Some examples of their effects include: adding the use of narcotics and excessive use of alcohol to the list of activities in which an adult could not legally encourage a minor to indulge; adding two new plants to the list of narcotic plants not to be grown in the USSR; adding provisions against 'borrowing' automobiles and stopping trains. Four other articles in 1966 and 1967 accounted for changes in articles 142, 190, 197, and 218. These dealt with political questions outside of criminal policy proper, such as the relations between church and state, violations by foreigners of the rules of movement on Soviet territory, theft of weapons or explosives, and slandering the Soviet government or defiling its flag. For the exact changes in the code see *Ugolovnyi kodeks RSFSR* (M., 1968); and for discussion of changes relating to political offenses, see Harold Berman, 'Introduction and Analysis', *Soviet Criminal Law and Procedure* (ed. Berman and Spindler; second ed., Cambridge, Mass., 1972), pp. 81–91.

3. Although it would have been desirable to study administrative as well as legislative decisions, I could not gather enough data about any particular administrative decision to warrant extended discussion.

4. On juvenile delinquency: 'Polozhenie o komissiakh po delam nesovershennoletnikh', utverzhdeno Ukazom Prezidiuma Verkhovnogo Soveta RSFSR ot 3 iiunia 1967 f. (M., 1968); 'Polozhenie ob obshchestvennykh vospitateliakh nersovershennoletnikh', utverzhdeno Ukazom Prezidiuma Verkhovnogo Soveta RSFSR ot 13 dekabriia 1967 g. (M., 1968). On alcoholism and crime: 'Ob usilenii otvetstvennost za khuliganstvo', Ukaz Prezidiuma Verkhovnogo Soveta SSSR ot 26 iiulia 1966, *Biulleten Verkhovnogo Suda SSSR* (1966, No. 4), pp. 7–11; 'O prinuditelnom lechenii i trudovom perevospitanii zlostnykh pianits (alkogolikov)' Ukaz Prezidiuma Verkhovnogo Soveta RSFSR No. 333 ot 8 aprelia 1967, *Vedomosti Verkhovnogo Soveta RSFSR* (1967, No. 15), pp. 333–4. On parole and recidivism: 'Ob administrativnom nadzore organov militsii za litsami, osvobozhdennymi iz mest lisheniia svobody', Ukaz Prezidiuma Verkhovnogo Soveta SSSR ot 26 iuliia 1966, *Vedomosti Verkhovnogo Soveta SSSR* (1966, No. 30); 'O vnesenii izmenenii i dopolnenii v Osnovakh ugolovnogo zakonodatelstva Soiuza SSR i soiuznykh respublik', *Izvestiia* (12 July 1969), pp. 4–5. On the penal system: 'Polozhenie o nabliudatelnykh komissiakh pri ispolkomakh raionnykh i gorodskikh sovetov deputatov trudiashchikhsia RSFSR', utverzhdeno Ukazom Prezidiuma Verkhovnogo Soveta RSFSR ot 30 sentiabria 1965, *Vedomosti Verkhovnogo Soveta RSFSR* (1965, No. 40), pp. 803–7; 'Polozhenie o trudovykh koloniiakh dlia nesovershennoletnikh Ministerstva Okhrany Obshchestvennogo Poriadka SSSR', *Sbornik Zakonov SSSR i Ukazov Prezidiuma Verkhovnogo Soveta SSSR Tom 3: 1968–1970* (M., 1971), pp. 395–414; 'Osnovy ispravitelno-trudovogo zakonodatelstva Soiuza SSR i soiuznykh respublikh', loc. cit., pp. 365–90.

5. The reforms in the penal system were developed mainly by officials and scholars at MOOP and its research institute, where security measures were tighter than in other judicial agencies and institutes. For detailed comment on the penal system after these reforms, see Walter D. Connor, *Deviance in Soviet Society* (N.Y. and London, 1972), ch. 9.

One other legislative act omitted from study here established administrative supervision for certain categories of returning offenders. It too was prepared primarily by MOOP personnel. Interview.

6. The decisions in Soviet criminal policy during this period were ordinary or incremental in nature rather than strategic or fundamental. Individually they contributed to the development of policy along general lines already set; cumulatively they served as a vehicle for the emergence of new emphases in policy. But none of the decisions markedly alter existing patterns of policy, as would a strategic or fundamental one. A useful discussion of different kinds of decisions is in Etzioni, op. cit., pp. 288–90.

7. From an analysis of the role of educational specialists in Soviet decision-making, Schwartz and Keech derived the hypothesis that 'the more and greater the disputes on the top policy-making level, the more likely it is that policy groups will be involved and listened to.' However, in a study of the role of American scientists in decision-making, Schooler wrote 'scientists cannot exert influence in an executive environment fraught with political conflict (not conflict over scientific matters). . . . Fundamental and persistent conflicts . . . would be the most hostile environment for scientists' influence and participation.' See Schwartz and Keech, 'Public Influence and Educational Policy in the Soviet Union', loc. cit., p. 177; and Dean Schooler, Jr., *Science, Scientists and Public Policy* (N.Y., 1971), pp. 43–4.

8. By a 'political conflict' we mean any dispute or disagreement about a policy matter which includes party or ministerial leaders on at least one side of the dispute. Disagreements which are found only among specialists or officials are not 'political' conflicts.

9. Berman, op. cit., pp. 84–8; Berman, 'Introduction and Analysis', loc. cit., pp. 71–81; Peter Juviler, 'Criminal Law and Social Control', loc. cit., pp. 36–8; I. M. Galperin, 'Ob ugolovnoi otvetsvennosti retsidivistov v svete nekotorykh kriminologicheskikh pokazatelei effecktivnosti borby s residivnoi prestupnostiu', *Effecktivnost ugolovnopravovykh mer borby s prestupnostiu* (ed. B. S. Nikiforov; M., 1968), pp. 233–5.

10. In 1957 the MVD chiefs had urged the commission which prepared the draft Fundamental Principles of Criminal Legislation to grant corrective-labor officials the authority to extend the sentences of inmates who committed crimes while in confinement (such as attempted escape), a request which the commission flatly denied. The 1962 law authorizing the *courts* to extend sentences of such offenders through the application of the legal stigma of 'specially dangerous recidivist' was a response to renewed MVD efforts to deal with this problem. Interviews.

11. Interviews.

12. Barry and Berman, loc. cit., pp. 326–8; Marianne Armstrong, 'The Campaign Against Parasites', *Soviet Policy-making*, op. cit., pp. 163–82.

5. DELINQUENCY PREVENTION

1. Commissions on juvenile affairs were established not only on the city and regional levels, but also for whole provinces and republics, although these higher commissions were engaged mainly in supervising the work of the lower ones. At all levels, the commissions were formally attached to the executive committees of the corresponding soviets; usually the head of the commission was one of the deputy

chairmen of the soviet to which it was attached. On the legal structure of the commissions, see E. V. Boldyrev, *Mery preduprezhdeniia pravonarushenii nesovershennoletnikh v SSSR* (M., 1964), pp. 104-9.

2. The immediate predecessors of the juvenile affairs commissions were the commissions for the placement of children and adolescents, established in 1958. From 1918 to 1935 there had existed juvenile affairs commissions not unlike the ones established in 1961; but from 1935 until after Stalin's death there were no commissions dealing especially with young troublemakers. On the history of Soviet institutions for handling juvenile offenders see ibid., pp. 12-44; and Peter H. Juviler, 'Revolutionary Law and Order: Delinquency, Crime and Soviet Policy', unpublished book manuscript (N.Y., 1975), chs. 4, 5, 7 and 11.

3. In 1959-60, after the Fundamental Principles of Criminal Legislation hsd raised the age of criminal responsibility to sixteen for most offenses and to fourteen for the most serious ones, a variety of administrative agencies shared the duty of processing cases where under-aged persons committed what would have been classed as criminal offenses had they reached the age of responsibility. The establishment of the juvenile affairs commissions provided a much-needed single agency where authority for disposing of such cases could be concentrated. As it happened, the commissions came also to hear some cases where minors old enough to bear criminal responsibility were at fault; for the courts often exercised their right to refer such cases to the commissions 'for consideration of the question of applying compulsory measures of an educational character'. *Ugolovnyi kodeks RSFSR* (M. 1968), Article 10. Interviews.

4. Boldyrev, op. cit., pp. 104-9.

5. V. S. Pronina, 'Nekotorye voprosy organizatsii i deiatelnosti komissii po delam nesovershennoletnikh', *Preduprezhdenie prestupnosti nesovershennoletnikh*, (M., 1965), pp. 125-7.

6. The model statute for the juvenile affairs commissions was published in 1959 as part of the same draft edict as the model statutes for the public patrols and for the comrades courts. See 'Proekt Zakona o povyshenii roli obshchestvennosti v borbe s narusheniiami sovetskoi zakonnosti i pravil sotsialisticheskogo obshchezhitiia', mentioned in V. S. Tadevosian, 'O komissiiakh po delam nesovershennoletnikh', *SGiP* (1959, No. 11), p. 124.

7. Tadevosian, loc. cit., V. S. Pronina, 'Rol sovetskoi obshchestvennosti v borbe s pravonarusheniiami nesovershennoletnikh', *SGiP* (1959, No. 10), pp. 89-92.

8. Tadevosian, loc. cit., pp. 126-7.

9. Interview.

10. See V. G. Tadevosian, 'V. I. Lenin o detiakh i borba s prestupnostiu nesovershennoletnikh', *SZ* (1958, No. 4), pp. 13-17.

11. Boldyrev, op. cit., pp. 127-8.

12. When the study began in 1962, Boldyrev was a member of Gertsenzon's sector at the Institute of State and Law. In 1963, Boldyrev moved with the sector to the Procuracy Institute where he completed the study.

13. Ibid., pp. 115-58.

14. Apparently, no commentaries or aids for commission members had yet been issued. The first one which I encountered was published in 1964. See P. G. Volodarskii, *Prakticheskoe posobie dlia komissii po delam nesovershennoletnikh* (M., 1964).

15. Ibid., pp. 158-72.

16. A comparison of court records on juvenile crime in 1963 with the records from

1945 indicated an apparent decline in juvenile crime rates. As Soviet scholars realized, these figures did not tell the whole story. To begin with, the use of 1945 as a base year was misleading because the juvenile crime rates were artificially inflated by the resurgence of homeless children after the war. The levelling off of juvenile crime during the 1950s was probably due to the disappearance of the homeless children and to the lower birthrates during the late 1930s and the war. Naturally, as the first post-war babies came of age in 1960, juvenile crime rates started to rise again; in fact, between 1961 and 1963 juvenile crime rose from 2.9 per cent to 9.1 per cent of all criminal offenses recorded in the USSR. When between 1963 and 1965 court records registered another drop in juvenile crime, it was due mainly to the increased proportion of juvenile cases handled outside of the courts by the juvenile affairs commissions. For example, in Latvia, the number of cases heard by the commissions doubled between 1961 and 1965. Commissions usually kept no records, and their cases were not included in the crime statistics kept by the courts.

Sources for this data include the following: G. M. Minkovskii, 'Ob issledovanii prestupnosti nesovershennoletnikh', *Problemy nauchnogo kommunizma*, vol. 1 (M., 1968), pp. 246–69; A. B. Sakhorov, *Pravonarushenie podrostka i zakon* (M., 1967); I. D. Perlov, 'Nekotorye voprosy dalneishego sovershenstvovaniia zakonodatelstva i praktiki ego primeneniia v oblasti borby s prestupleniiami nesovershennoletnikh', *Borba s prestupnostiiu nesovershennoletnikh* (M., 1965); L. A. Kliuchinskaia, *Nesovershennoletnie i ugolovnyi zakon* (Riga, 1967), p. 57; and lectures by G. M. Minkovskii and N. F. Kuznetsova at the law faculty of Moscow University.

17. 'O merakh po iskoreneniiu beznadzornosti i prestupnosti sredi nesovershennoletnikh', Postanovlenie TsK KPSS ot 15 oktiabria 1963, mentioned by I. D. Perlov in 'Nekotorye voprosy dalneishego sovershenstvovaniia zakonodatelstva i praktiki ego primeneniia v oblasti bobry s prestupleniiami nesovershennoletnikh', *Borba s prestupnostiu nesovershennoletnikh. Sbornik statei po materialam teoreticheskoi konferentsii, Noiabr 1964.* (M., 1965).

18. *Metodicheskoe pismo o polozhitelnom opyte raboty Prokuratury goroda Leningrada*, op. cit.; B. S. Vorontsov, loc. cit.; L. A. Kliuchinskaia, op. cit. See also Peter Solomon, 'A New Soviet Administrative Ethos—Examples from Crime Prevention', unpublished paper presented at Northeastern Slavic Conference of the AAASS, Montreal, Quebec, May 5–8, 1971.

19. Larger units (four to six persons) were usually called 'sections', while smaller ones (one to three persons) constituted 'groups'. Interviews.

20. Besides the new statutes on juvenile affairs commissions and on public guardians studied here, these initiatives also resulted in legislation to improve the conditions of working youth, an especially crime-prone group; and in new statutes for juvenile corrective-labor colonies. For the texts of these laws and commentary, see 'O meropriatiiakh po rasshireniiu obucheniia i ustroistva na rabotu v narodnoe khzaistvo molodezhi, okanchivaiushchei obshcheobrazovatelnyi shkoly v 1966 godu', Postanovlenie TsK KPSS i Soveta Ministrov SSSR ot 2 febraliia 1966, No. 83, slightly abridged text in *Spravochnik profsoiuznogo rabotnika 1967*(M., 1967), pp. 240–4; and A. F. Troshin, 'Trudoustroistvo i trudovoe vospitani–vazhnoe sredstvo preduprezhdeniia beznadzornosti i prestunpnosti sredi nesovershennoletnikh', *Preduprezhdenie prestupnosti nesovershennoletnikh* (M., 1965), pp. 158–80. 'Polozhenie o trudovykh koloniiakh dlia nesovershennoletnikh', loc. cit.; and N. Guskov, 'Novoe polozhenie o trudovykh koloniiakh dlia nesovershennoletnikh',

SZ, (1968, No. 9).

21. F. I. Kalinychev, *Prezidium verkhovnogo soveta SSSR* (M., 1969), p. 60; interviews.

22. Interviews.

23. Minkovskii's sector on the study and prevention of juvenile crime had a strong interdisciplinary base. Besides criminal law scholars it included V. S. Pronina from administrative law and A. F. Troshin, a specialist in labor law.

24. 'Otchet . . . za 1965', loc. cit.; interviews.

25. Interviews. For an exposition of Minkovskii and Pronina's proposals, see Pronina, 'Nekotorye voprosy organizatgii', loc. cit., pp. 116–37.

26. Ibid., p. 125.

27. Interviews.

28. Under Brezhnev references in the press to the replacement of governmental organs by public organizations, as a preparation for the approach of communism, virtually disappeared.

29. Pronina, 'Nekotorye voprosy organizatsii', loc. cit., p. 126.

30. Ibid., p. 116.

31. E. V. Melnikova, 'Koordinatsiia nauchnykh rabot po problemam borby s prestupnostiu nesovershennoletnikh', *Informatsionnoe pismo* [*instituta*], No. 2, (M., 1965).

32. L. M. Kliuchinskaia was the leading specialist on juvenile crime in the Latvian SSR during the 1960s. While working in the research sector on crime of Latvian State University, Kliuchinskaia was also a member of the republic commission on juvenile affairs and a close advisor to the republican procuracy. Her practical activity included organizing educational programs for officials, organizing conferences. Interview.

33. Interview. For exposition of Minkovskii's proposals see G. Minkovskii and E. V. Melnikova, 'Sheftstvo nad trudnymi podrostkami – put k preduprezhdeniiu prestupnosti nesovershennoletnikh', *SZ* (1966, No. 1), pp. 25–9.

34. Ibid.

35. See G. M. Minkovskii, 'Ob isslevodanii', loc. cit., p. 264.

36. Melnikova, loc. cit. Professor Miasishchev from the Bekhterev psychiatric institute in Leningrad and F. R. Filippov, prorector of the Nizhne-Tagilskii pedagogical institute also spoke in favor of public guardians.

37. Interviews.

38. G. Minkovskii and V. Pronina, 'Sudba podrostka', *Izvestiia* (19 August 1965), p. 3.

39. Interviews; 'Otchet . . . za 1965', loc. cit.

40. Minkovskii and Melnikova, loc. cit.

41. Minkovskii, 'Ob issledovanii', loc. cit.

42. For discussion of the party-state edict on criminal policy, see chapter nine. 'O borbe s prestupnostiu', Postanovlenie TsK KPSS i Soveta Ministrov ot 23 iiulia 1966 (no open source). Much of the contents of this edict were reported in the introductory material published before all editions of the hooliganism law in the public press and in scholarly journals. See 'V TsK KPSS, Prezidiume verkhovnogo soveta SSSR i soveta ministrov SSSR', *Izvestiia* (27 July 1966), p. 2, and *Pravda* (27 July 1966), p. 2.

43. As we saw in Chapter 3, variations in republican definitions of 'specially dangerous recidivist' caused difficulties for judges who had to apply the concept.

44. The differences between the Latvian republic statute on juvenile affairs commissions and the RSFSR statute were as follows: the Latvian statute excluded all phrases referring to autonomous republics and districts and also provision for commissions in sparsely populated areas; the Latvian statute contained references to articles in the Latvian criminal code; article 25 of the Latvian code on categories of children excluded from special educational institutions (reform schools) listed only deaf, dumb, blind, mentally ill, and retarded; and omitted children with physical defects, who were included in this category in the RSFSR. See 'Polozhenie o komissiakh po delam nesovershennoletnikh', loc. cit., and L. A. Kliuchinaskaia, *Komissi po delam nesovershennoletnikh Nauchno-prakticheskii kommentari k polozheniiu o komissiakh po delam nosovershennoletnikh i po ikh rabotu* (Riga, 1970).

45. 'Polozhenie i komissiakh po delam nesovershennoletnikh', loc. cit.

46. 'Polozhenie ob obshchestvennykh vospitateliakh nesovershennoletnikh', loc. cit.

47. V. S. Pronina, *Kommentarii k polozheniiam o komissiakh po delam nesovershennoletnikh* (M., 1968); Kliuchinskaia, op. cit.

48. A Deputy Procurator-General reported in May 1968 that 'checks' (*proverki*) had shown that many 'public guardians' had been appointed – in Gorki *oblast* 200, in Moscow oblast 348, in Perm oblast 332, and in the Latvian republic 1,282. See 'Informatsionnoe pismo No. 21/31 Zam. Prok. Soiuza SSR o rabote instituta obshchestvennykh vospitatelei nesovershennoletnikh', (16 May 1968), *Biulleten po obmenu opytom raboty po delam nesovershennoletnikh*, No. 7 (Riga; July 1968), p. 45.

6. ALCOHOLISM AND HOOLIGANISM

1. The Russian temperance movement may have contributed to the Tsarist government's decision to institute prohibition, but the immediate cause was the regime's fear in the early months of the First World War for the success of the mobilization and for the performance of supporting enterprises. The results of the enforced sobriety were meagre; for it led to a dramatic increase in homebrewing and in the use of 'surrogates with alcoholic content'. *Alkogolizm – put k prestupleniiu* (ed. A. A. Gertsenzon; M., 1966), p. 122.

2. Berman, 'Introduction and Analysis', loc. cit., p. 28. The 1961 RSFSR Criminal Code defined hooliganism as 'intentional actions violating the public order in a coarse manner and expressing a clear disrespect for society'. In practice, the grounds for a hooliganism arrest varied from disciplinary breaches like swearing in public to more serious acts like fighting publicly, even destroying property and inflicting physical injury in the process. The limiting condition was that all of these actions had to occur in a public place; thus, according to the law, 'scandals' at home or in a communal apartment were not hooliganism. See *Ugolovnyi kodeks RSFSR*, Article 206, and for English translation *Soviet Criminal Law*, op. cit., p. 233. For a dicussion of the problem of abusive and destructive behavior in private, see N. Alekseev, 'Khotite, zhaluites', *Izvestiia* (24 April 1966), p. 6.

3. One study of alcoholism and crime in the 1920s was written by A. A. Gertsenzon; see his *Prestupnost i alkogolizm v RSFSR* (M., 1930). Alcoholism prevention work was coordinated by medical authorities who worked in the 'Society for the Fight with Alcoholism', which lasted until 1930. *Alkogolizm*, op. cit., pp. 58–9.

4. Berman, 'Introduction and Analysis', loc. cit., p. 30 and p. 36.

5. While before 1956 the minimum sentence for hooliganism convictions had been one year's deprivation of liberty, the new regulations established that those convicted of petty hooliganism would be punishable by detention from three to fifteen days.

The RSFSR Criminal Code of 1961 carried the reform further by providing that unless committed repeatedly petty hooliganism no longer was a crime, but an administrative offense. In addition, the code established a wide choice of sanctions for those guilty of (ordinary) hooliganism – deprivation of liberty for terms not exceeding a year (no minimum), correctional tasks for the same period, or social censure. Ibid., p. 38, pp. 45–7.

6. The measures included new laws against *samogonstvo* (homebrewing) which was still widespread in all but the most urban areas; against public drinking (restaurants were to serve no more than one hundred grams of vodka per person and most bars were closed); and against the sale of alcoholic beverages to minors or to the general public before 10 a.m. For details see 'Ob usilenii borby s pianstvom i o vedenii poriadka v torgovle krepkimi spirtymi napitkami', Postanovlenie TsK KPSS i Soveta Ministrov ot 15 dekabriia 1968, *Spravochnik partiinogo rabotnika*, No. 2 (M., 1959), p. 404.

7. Neither the campaign against homebrewing nor the legislation against public drinking reduced liquor consumption, but it did produce dramatic increases in the sale of state-produced liquor in the stores. Between 1952 and 1962 vodka sales for the USSR as a whole doubled, and the sale of wine trebled. According to one study, the average person in Dmitrovskii *raion* in Moscow spent eighty-three rubles a year on drink (about 10 per cent of his salary). Residents of the city of Perm testified that they spent four and a half times as much annually on alcohol as on all forms of cultural life combined (books, movies, etc.). Still, incidents of homebrewing were frequent. In one case a homebrewer was discovered when a vigilant grocery clerk asked a shabbily dressed customer why he was purchasing one hundred and fifty-nine kilograms of sugar! *Alkogolizm*, op. cit., pp. 85–93.

Closing bars in cities had little impact, because lovers of drink invented a system for evasion, the well-known practice of drinking 'in threes' or 'in twos' (*na troe, na dvoe*). This meant finding another person or two, usually strangers, who were willing to share the purchase and immediate consumption of a three-quarter liter bottle of vodka. For further discussion of Soviet drinking habits and of the evasion of anti-alcoholic measures, see Connor, op. cit., pp. 35–79.

8. Depending upon the locale, hooliganism represented between 25 and 40 per cent of all crime in Soviet cities. *Sovetskaia kriminologiia* (M., 1966), p. 257. Hooligans were nearly always drunk at the time of their offense. A number of early criminological studies indicated rates of over 90 per cent (see Solomon, 'Bibliography', E21, E27, K15) and Procuracy Institute staff reported that in some provinces drunkenness among apprehended hooligans stood at 100 per cent. *Alkogolizm*, op. cit., p. 14.

9. For mention of the letters, see for example *Literaturnaia Gazeta* (12 June 1965), p. 2; *Izvestiia*(23 June 1965), p. 3; *Literaturnaia Gazeta* (3 February 1966), p. 2; N. V. Zhogin, *Borba s khuliganstvom – delo veskh i kazhdogo* (M., 1967), pp. 8–10; 'V TsK KPSS', loc. cit.

10. *Alkogolizm*, op. cit., pp. 4–10; *Kriminologiia*, op. cit., p. 331; Gertsenzon, *Vvedenie v sovetskuiu kriminologiiu*, op. cit., p. 166. The most careful treatment of the

relationship between alcoholism and murder is V. P. Vlasov and G. I. Kocharov, *Opyt kontrolnogo kriminologicheskogo izucheniia umyshlennykh ubiistv* (M., 1966).

11. *Problemy sudebnoi psikhiatrii*, vyp. 9 (1961), p. 372, cited in *Alkogolizm*, p. 6. The same figure is mentioned in *Kriminologiia*, op. cit., p. 331.

12. One fifth of offenders drunk at the time of their first crime became recidivists, compared with one tenth of the total criminal population. Among recidivists, two-thirds were alcoholics. Among more serious recidivists, those who had committed their first crime before the age of fifteen (19 per cent, 95 per cent were alcoholics. *Alkogolizm*, pp. 11–14.

13. 'Effektivnost borby s khuliganstvom i dinamika nekotorykh tiazhkikh prestuplenii', *VNIIOOP Informatsionnye soobshcheniia*, Vypusk 6 (M., 1966).

14. Interviews.

15. *Ugolovnyi kodeks RSFSR*, Article 62.

16. E. V. Boldyrev and E. V. Kuznetsova, 'V sektore po izucheniiu i preduprezhdeniiu prestupnosti', *SGiP* (1961, No. 11). There had also been an attempt in 1927 to apply compulsory treatment to 'alcoholics who represented a social danger'. An instruction was issued by Narkomiust, but it was poorly implemented, 'because officials completely disregarded the social danger of alcoholics . . .and this because medical rather than judicial organs were then fully responsible for establishing the treatment for alcoholics. . . .' *Alkogolizm*, op. cit., p. 52.

17. As of 1965 ten republics had established legal instruments for the commitment of chronic alcoholics for compulsory treatment. The criteria for a compulsory treatment order varied from republic to republic. One criterion, evidence of 'public nuisance or an anti-social parasitic way of life', suggested that some republics introduced the commitment procedure in the wake of the anti-parasitism campaign of 1961–2. Five republics required a court order for committal; four others authorized executive committees of local soviets to make the decisions. *Alkogolizm*, pp. 53–5.

18. G. V. Anashkin, 'Diagnoz prostupka', *Izvestiia* (4 March 1965), p. 3.

19. Kalinychev, op. cit.

20. Interviews. See Gertsenzon, *Prestupnost i alkogolizm v RSFSR*, op. cit.

21. These themes included: the influence of alcohol upon crime in the USSR: alcoholism and crime in pre-revolutionary Russia and in capitalist countries; Soviet legislation against homebrewing; limiting alcoholic consumption in the USSR; the use of legal, administrative, and medical measures against alcoholism in the USSR. Ibid.; 'Otchet . . . za 1965', loc. cit.

22. The *Izvestiia* alcoholism discussion appeared in the following issues:

17 June, p. 3 'Moi papa pet' (letter)

20 June, p. 6 'Delo vovse ne semeinoe' (letters/discussion)

22 June, p. 3 'Khavit slov' (letter)

23 June, p. 4 'Obshchestvennoe obvinenie' (three letters)

25 June, p. 4 'Muzhskoi razgovor' (letter from a correspondent)

27 June, p. 6 Round-table discussion – first part under the heading 'Alkogolizmu besposhchadnaia voina'; appearances by Gertsenzon and Kosogovskii.

3 July, p. 4 Round table continues — second part under the heading 'Pokonchit so zlom'; appearances by B. Uralnis, V. Rozhov, G. Rozantsev, G. Minkovskii, V. Volodin, S. Borodin.

7 July, p. 4 'Imenem odnoselcham – selskii skhod obsuzhdaet vopros borby s

pianstvom' (how a rural meeting dealt with alcoholism).

14 July, p. 4 A. Kholiavchenko, 'Vot s chego eto nachinaetsia' (comment on round-table discussions)

21 August, p. 4 N. Troyan, 'Vrednye poblazhki' (continuation of the discussion)

27 August, p. 4 V. Rozhkov, 'V rabochii krug', (what one motor factory did about drunkenness)

23. The disagreement between Kosogovskii and the others suggested conflicts which had already arisen in practice. In Belorussia, where compulsory treatment of alcoholics had been in operation since 1963, medical and custodial staff had disputed the priority of treatment and of punitive goals. The question was who was in charge – the doctors or the officials. The doctors might order a regime of rest and full diets, while officials insisted upon heavy work schedules and prison rations. Protesting to the Belorussian procuracy, the doctors claimed that the custodian staff ran the prophylactories like prisons and made fulfilment of production quotas their first priority. See V. Kupal, 'Borba s pianstvom – borba s prestupnostiu', *K novoi zhizne* (1966, No. 12), pp. 25–6; and further discussions in the same journal (1967, No. 7), pp. 41–3. *K novoi zhizne* was a monthly journal of MOOP written for the staff of prisons and corrective-labor institutions. The journal, which began in 1962, was semi-popular in nature, mixing short serious articles by scholars and officials with short stories and lighter entertainment material.

24. According to official statistics, vodka and hard liquor sales accounted for 11.1%, wine and fruit liqueurs for 3.9%, and beer for 1.6% of the total turnover (*tovarooborot*). Together alcoholic beverages accounted for more than one quarter of the income derived from sale of grocery products. See *Statisticheskii biulleten* (1961, No. 4), pp. 87–9, as cited in *Alkogolizm*, loc. cit., p. 88.

Recently an American economist has calculated the costs to the Soviet government of possible restrictions on alcoholic beverage production and of changes in its structure. See Vladimir G. Treml, 'Production and Consumption of Alcoholic Beverages in the USSR: A Statistical Study', *Journal of Studies on Alcohol*, xxxvi, No. 3 (March 1975), pp. 285–320.

25. Gertsenzon proposed reviving the Society for the Struggle against Alcoholism which had existed in the 1920s. See *Alkogolizm*, op. cit., p. 59, p. 151.

26. Ibid., p. 151; interviews.

27. 'Otchet . . . za 1965', loc. cit.

28. Interviews with the late Professor A. A. Gertsenzon; *Alkogolizm*, op. cit., pp. 151–4.

29. Nikolai Atarov, 'Nuzhen zakon protiv alkogolizma', *Literaturnaia Gazeta*, 11 January 1966, p. 2.

30. M. Merman, 'Poka pritsel netochen', *Literaturnaia Gazeta*, 3 February 1966, p. 2.

31. L. Kashin and G. I. Rozantsev, 'Pravila i iskliucheniia', loc. cit.

32. Loc. cit.

33. Gertsenzon, 'Takoi zakon nuzhen', *Izvestiia* (6 February 1966), p. 3.

34. *Izvestiia*, 7 February–19 April 1966.

35. V. Tikunov, 'Sniskhozhdeniia khuligam ne budet', *Izvestiia* (21 April 1966), p. 3.

36. 'O sudebnoi praktike po delam o khuliganstve', Postanovlenie Plenuma ot 22 dekabria 1964, No. 17, *Sbornik Postanovlenii Plenuma Verkhovnogo Suda SSSR 1924–1970* (M., 1970), pp. 486–90.

37. G. Z. Anashkin, 'Lichnost, obstoiatelstvo i otvetstvennost', *Izvestiia* (12 June 1965), p. 2.

38. Tikunov, loc. cit. Another explanation is that Soviet policemen did not regard drunken rowdy behavior as criminal. Among Russian workers and peasants drinking excessively was more a form of recreation than of deviance. Since many policemen were themselves recent migrants from the villages, they may well have shared these attitudes.

39. We did not have access to any collections of MOOP *prikazy*.

40. 'Effektivnost borby s khuliganstvom', loc. cit.

41. The account of this research was published in an information letter of the MOOP institute, but there were no indications who the authors were.

42. 'Effektivnost borby s khuliganstvom', loc. cit.

43. In selecting Lukianov to direct the experiment, Tikunov had chosen a worthy partner. Lukianov had already advocated stepping up the repression of hooliganism during the fall of 1965. See his 'Surovo karat khuliganov', *Izvestiia* (23 October 1965), p. 3. There was only one other article on hooliganism in the government newspaper during the second half of 1965.

44. 'Effektivnost borby s khuliganstvom', loc. cit.

45. Some Soviet criminologists interpreted the data this way. See 'Effektivnost borby s khuliganstvom', loc. cit. Interviews.

46. For an earlier indication of Tikunov's penal philosophy, see V. S. Tikunov, 'Obshchestvo i pravoporiadok', *Trud* (9 January 1965).

47. G. Grebennikov and K. Rasparin, 'Sotsialisticheskaia ditsiplina nezyblema', *Pravda* (25 April 1966).

48. Tikunov, 'Sniskhozhdeniia khuliganam ne budet', loc. cit. Note that Lukianov, the Leningrad police chief, did refer to some data from the study in 'Ne davat spiski khuliganam', *Leningradskaia Pravda* (29 May 1966).

49. Grebennikov and Rasparin, loc. cit.; 'Khuligan – chelovek vne obshchestva', *Komsomolskaia Pravda* (27 April 1966), p. 4; 'Sniskhozhdeniia khuliganam budet', loc. cit.

50. Ibid.

51. *Izvestiia* (21 April 1966), p. 3.

52. Alekseev, loc. cit.

53. For example, see letters and commentaries – Zhbanov, 'I dukh i bukva', *Izvestiia* (24 May 1966), p. 3; 'Pisma dlia razmyshlenii', *Izvestiia* (9 June 1966), p. 6; 'Protest Galiny Shalakovoi', *Izvestiia* (28 June 1966), p. 3. See also a statement by an RSFSR Supreme Court member on keeping hooligans in jail before trial – N. Prusakov, 'Opasnaia sniskhoditelnost', *Izvestiia* (31 May 1966), p. 5.

54. Interviews.

55. I raised the question of the hooliganism commission with a number of Procuracy Institute scholars but found that they were all reluctant to discuss it, even though they did not object to my questions about other *ad hoc* commissions. None of these scholars admitted having served on the commission which revised the hooliganism law, although some ventured names of colleagues 'who might have'. However, the annual report of the Procuracy Institute for 1966 indicated that some Institute scholars did participate in the preparation of the hooliganism law. See 'Otchet . . . za 1966', loc. cit.

Criminologists' distaste for the hooliganism law seemed to stem partly from disapproval of the very concept of 'hooliganism' (it was too vaguely defined to satisfy some lawyers) and partly from irritation that Tikunov's 'law and order' approach had been substituted for more carefully devised prophylactic measures.

56. Compulsory treatment of alcoholics in the RSFSR was approved by political leaders July 1966. See 'V TsK KPSS', loc. cit. When in April 1967 the Praesidium of the RSFSR Supreme Soviet issued legislation establishing compulsory treatment, it introduced one novelty. In the RSFSR, unlike in the other republics, alcoholics would have to pay for their own room and board in the *profilaktori* out of their earnings. See 'O prinuditelnom lechenii i trudovom perevospitanii zlostnykh pianits (alkogolikov)', loc. cit., pp. 333–4; and *Alkogolizm*, op. cit.

57. See Anashkin, 'Diagnoz prostupka', loc. cit. To some observers the decisions of 1966/67 might appear entirely repressive in character. One's evaluation would depend upon one's appraisal of compulsory treatment of alcoholics. Taken in the context of anti-alcoholism measures compulsory treatment might be regarded as punitive (see Connor, op. cit., pp. 65–8), but if compulsory treatment of alcoholics is viewed as an alternative to the imprisonment of hooligans, the measure appears more 'educational'.

58. 'Ob usilenii otvetstvennost za khuliganstvo', loc. cit., sections 4 and 10.

59. The new penalties for petty hooliganism included detention (*arrest*) for ten to fifteen days, rather than the previous three to five days, during which the costs of food and lodging would have to be borne by the prisoner, i.e. in the form of a supplementary fine. The alternatives to a prison term of this sort were one to two months' corrective work and a fine of ten to thirty rubles, both of which represented considerable increases over the previous norms. To compare with the old rules, see *Soviet Criminal Law*, op. cit., p. 37.

For the more serious grades of hooliganism, the new minimum terms were as follows: for hooliganism six months' deprivation of freedom or six months' corrective work or thirty rubles fine; for malicious hooliganism a prison term of not less than one year. See 'Ob usilenii otvetstvennosti za khuliganstvo', sections 9 and 10.

60. Ibid., section 13. Note that the stipulation that drunkenness at the time of a criminal act may be a 'circumstance aggravating responsibility', was later added to the Fundamental Principles of Criminal Legislation of the USSR and the Union Republics. See 'O vnesenii izmenenii i dopolnenii', loc. cit., pp. 4–5.

61. N. V. Zhogin, *Borba s khuliganstvom – delo vsekh i kazhdogo* (M., 1967), pp. 7–9.

62. 'V TsK KPSS', loc. cit.

63. 'Delo vsekh i kazhdogo', *Pravda* (28 July 1966), p. 1; 'Delo vsekh i kazhdogo', *Pravda* (2 August 1966); 'Po vole narodov', *Izvestiia* (29 July 1966), p. 1; 'Podmetat', *Izvestiia* (7 August 1966).

64. 'O borbe s prestupnostiu', loc. cit.

65. 'Press-konferentsiia tsentralnogo televedeniia Prokuratury SSSR i Verkhovnogo Suda SSSR', *SZ* (1966, No. 11). The participants included first deputy Procurator-General M. Maliarov, member of the Collegium of the USSR Procuracy P. Kudriavstev, Chairman of the Criminal Section of the USSR Supreme Court G. Anashkin, and 'aide' (*pomoshchnik*) to the Procurator-General B. Shagurin, the procurator of Moscow M. Malkov, correspondents for *Pravda, Izvestiia, Trud, Sovetskaia Rossiia, Krokodil*, and *Smena*, and representatives of central radio and television. Using a question and answer format, the participants attempted to explain the provisions of the new law to the public.

66. *Informatsionnoe pismo* (instituta), No. 7 (M., 1967).
67. *O merakh po usilenii borby s narusheniiami obshestvennogo poriadka* (M., 1967). See also E. V. Boldyrev, V. I. Ivanov and P. F. Pashkevich, 'Voprosy ugolovnogo prava i ugolovnogo protsessa v novom zakonodatelstve ob otvetstvennosti za khuliganstvo', *Uchenye zapiski VNIISZ*, Vyp. 12 (M., 1968).
68. 'Novoe ugolovnoe zakonodatelstvo ob usilenii borby s khuliganstvom', *Pravovedenie* (1967, No. 2), pp. 111–15.
69. 'O praktike primenenii Ukaza Prezidiuma Verkhovnogo Soveta SSSR ot 26 iiulia 1966 g. "Ob usilenii otvetstvennosti za khuliganstvo"', Postanovlenie Prezidiuma Verkhovnogo Soveta SSSR ot 13 oktiabria 1967, No. 577, *Vedomosti Verkhovnogo Soveta SSSR*, (1967, No. 43), pp. 666–8.
70. Connor, op. cit., p. 67.
71. Ibid., p. 78; *ABSEES*, III, No. 2 (36) (October 1972), pp. 65–8.
72. 'O merakh po usileniiu borby s pianstvom i alkogolizmom', *Pravda*, (16 June 1972), p. 1.
73. Shliapochnikov, 'Pamiati vydaiushchego sovetskogo kriminologa', loc. cit., p. 178.
74. For those interested in reading further on the Soviet struggle against alcoholism, see Connor, op. cit., pp. 35–79; and David E. Powell, 'Alcoholism in the USSR', *Survey*, XVI, No. 1 (winter 1971), pp. 123–37.

7. PAROLE AND RECIDIVISM REFORMS

1. 'Osnovnye Nachala Ugolovnogo Zakonodatelstva', loc. cit., Article 44.
2. 'Ob usilenii borby s osobo opasnymi prestupleniami', Ukaz Prezidiuma Verkhovnogo soveta SSSR ot 5 maia 1964, *Vedomosti Verkhovnogo Soveta SSSR* (1961, No. 19), pp. 475–6; 'O vnesenii izmenenii i dopolnenii v stati 22 i 44 Osnov ugolovnogo zakonodatelstva', Ukaz Prezidiuma Verkhovnogo Soveta SSSR ot 4 apreliia 1962, loc. cit., pp. 408–9.
3. *Ugolovnyi Kodeks RSFSR* (M., 1962), Article 53.
4. Vyshinskaia and Shlykov, loc. cit., pp. 193 ff.; 'O sudebnoi praktike po uslovno-dosrochnomu osvobozhdeniiu osuzhdennykh ot nakazaniia', Postanovlenie Plenuma Verkhovnogo Suda ot 4 marta 1961, *Sbornik postanovlenii plenuma, loc. cit.*, pp. 362–76.
5. Ibid., 'O nekotorykh voprosakh, voznikshikh v sudebnoi praktike po primeneniiu zakonodatelstva ob uslovno-dosrochnogo osvobozhdeniia ot nakazaniia i zamene nakazaniia bolee miagkim', Postanovlenie Plenuma verkhovnogo suda ot 13 dekabria 1963 No. 19 loc. cit., pp. 372–6; 'O vypolnenii sudami postanovlenii Plenuma Verkhovnogo Suda ot 4 marta 1961 g. i ot 18 dekabria 1963 g. o praktike uzlovno-dosrochnogo ozvobozhdeniia osuzhdennykh ot nakazaniia', Postanovlenie Plenuma Verkhovnogo Suda ot 11 oktobriia 1965 No. 7, loc. cit., pp. 376–9.
6. A Mishutin, 'Ne dopuskat narushenii zakona o dosrochnom i uslovno-dosrochnom osvobozhdenii', *SZ* (1964, No. 2), pp. 16–21.
7. See 'Osnovnye Nachala Ugolovnogo Zakonodatelstva', loc. cit., Articles 23 and 44; and *Ugolovnyi kodeks RSFSR* (M., 1962), Article 24.
8. Interview.
9. See Zakon Verkhovnogo Soveta RSFSR ot 25 iiuniia 1962 g. in *Vedomosti Verkhovnogo Soveta RSFSR* (1962, No. 29), p. 449.

10. See Stepichev, loc. cit.; 'Otkliki chitatelei: Opredelenie osobo opasnogo retsidiva dolzhno byt edingm', *SZ* (1962, No. 12), pp. 48–50.

11. Ibid.

12. Interviews.

13. 'Otchet... za 1965', loc. cit.

14. Interviews.

15. 'Otchet... za 1965', loc. cit.

16. V. Chvanov and E. Bogat, 'Vinovnost i nakazanie', *Literaturnaia Gazeta* (13 May 1965), p. 2; A. Usov, 'Chelovek ne bylinka', loc. cit. (27 May 1965), p. 2.

17. N. Chetunov, 'Kat pobedit zlo', loc. cit. (20 May 1965), p. 2; G. Zlobin, 'Opponent ne prav', loc. cit. (10 June 1965), p. 2.

18. G. V. Anashkin, 'Lichnost, obstoiatelstva i otvetstvennost', loc. cit.

19. 'Ob effektivnost ugolovnogo nakazaniia (za kruglym stolom)', *SZ* (1965, No. 8), pp. 2–6.

20. See Vyshinskaia and Shlykov, loc. cit.

21. 'V Verkhovnom Sude SSSR', *SZ* (1965, No. 12), pp. 31–5. This plenum also adopted the third of the decrees on parole, mentioned in note 5.

22. Ibid.

23. V. Andreev, 'Kak ispolnen prigovor', *Izvestiia* (16 November 1965), p. 5.

24. V. N. Kudriavtsev, 'Zakon i sotsiologiia', *Izvestiia* (25 November 1965), p. 2.

25. Interviews; Vyshinskaia and Shlykov, loc. cit., p. 174.

26. Ibid., p. 175.

27. Ibid., pp. 164–80.

28. Ibid., p. 188.

29. Some courts heard fifty to sixty petitions a session, and one court had achieved the record of one hundred and forty parole petitions in one sitting. Ibid., p. 200.

30. Ibid., p. 203.

31. Ibid., p. 179.

32. Ibid., p. 202.

33. Ibid., pp. 211–13.

34. Ibid., pp. 208–11. Note that this same idea was advocated by two penologists at about the same time. See A. I. Remenson, 'Teoreticheskie voprosy ispolneniia lishenii svobody i perevospitaniia zakliuchennykh', Avtoreferat doktorskoi dissertatsii (Tomsk, 1965), p. 25; N. A. Efimov, 'Problemy lisheniia svobody kak vida nakazaniia v zakonodatelstve, sudebnoi i ispravitelno-trudovoi praktike', Avtoreferat doktorskoi dissertatsii (Leningrad, 1966), pp. 16–17.

35. *Ugolovnyi kodeks RSFSR*, Article 24, note 1.

36. Iakovlev, op. cit., p. 120.

37. Interviews. Galperin, loc. cit., pp. 235–8.

38. Ibid., p. 238.

39. Ibid., pp. 233–5. A few years earlier the legal scholar P. Grishanin of MOOP Higher School had suggested that such factors as the number of previous convictions be considered when an offender was to be designated as a 'specially dangerous recidivist'. But Grishanin addressed his remarks to judges making these discretionary decisions rather than to legislators setting the rules within which judges had to operate. Galperin went beyond Grishanin in proposing that conditions be built into the legislation governing the designation of offenders as 'specially dangerous recidivists' on the basis of crimes committed in confinement. See P. F. Grishanin, 'Praktika priznaniia zakliuchennykh, sovershivshikh pre-

stupleniia, osobo opasnymi retsidivistami', *Slu* (1964, No. 20), pp. 11–12.

40. See Berman, 'Introduction and Analysis', loc. cit., p. 6; Connor, op. cit., pp. 200–6; A. S. Mikhlin *et al.*, 'Effektivnost ispravitelnykh rabot kak mery nakazaniia', *Effektivnost ugolovnopravovykh mer*, loc. cit., pp. 93–106.

41. Ibid., p. 142; T. I. Sergeeva, L. F. Pomchalov, 'Effektivnost kratkosrochnogo lisheniia svobody', loc. cit., pp. 28–9. Note that studies from Eastern Europe and from other parts of the USSR confirmed Mikhlin's findings. See M. A. Efimov, op. cit., and V. N. Kudriavstev, 'Problemy nakazaniia, ne sviazannogo s lisheniem svobody', *Slu* (1968, No. 1).

42. Mikhlin, loc. cit., p. 147.

43. Ibid., pp. 98–101.

44. Sergeeva and Pomchalov, loc. cit.

45. Ibid., p. 38.

46. Ibid., p. 79, pp. 85 ff.

47. 'Otchet... za 1965', *loc. cit.*; 'Otchet... za 1966', *loc. cit.* Interviews.

48. *Informatsionnoe pismo* (Instituta), No. 6 (1966). 'A. S. Mikhlin *et al.*, 'Ob effektivnosti ispravitelnykh rabot kak mery ugolovnogo nakazaniia', *SZ* (1966, No. 1); I. I. Karpets, 'Ob effektivnosti ugolovnogo nakazaniia', *SZ* (1966, No. 5); *Effektivnost ugolovnopravovykh mer*, op. cit.

49. 'Dopolneniia k zakony', *Izvestiia* (5 June 1966); Interviews.

50. 'V TsK KPSS', loc. cit.

51. 'Nauchno-metodicheskaia konferentsiia v Verkhovnom Sude SSSR', *SZ* (1966, No. 9), pp. 11–20.

52. Persons attending the conference included members and peoples' assessors of the Supreme Court, members of the advisory councils of the USSR and RSFSR Supreme Courts, chairmen of the republican supreme courts, and of a number of oblast courts, some ordinary judges, representatives of the Central Committee *apparat*, the Praesidium of the Supreme Soviet, and scholars from universities and institutes in Moscow, Leningrad, Sverdlovsk, Kazan, Irkutsk and others. Ibid., p. 11.

53. Karpets, loc. cit.; 'Ob effektivnosti ugolovnogo nakazaniia' (K nauchno-metodichekoi konferentsii), *SZ* (1966, No. 5).

54. 'Nauchno-metodicheskaia konferentsiia', loc. cit., pp. 16–18.

55. Suggestions were sent to the Supreme Court on 'shortcomings in the assignment of this sanction by the courts', to the Procurator-General, 'to increase procuracy supervision of this measure', and to MOOP, 'to eliminate shortcomings in its application'. See 'Otchet... za 1966 god', op. cit.

56. Interview with a commission member.

57. Interview.

58. The text of the new parole legislation was 'O vnesenii izmenenii i dopolnenii v Osnovakh ugolovnogo zakonodatelstva Soiuza SSR i soiuznykh respublik', op. cit., article 2. For the revised text of the Fundamental Principles of Criminal Legislation, including the parole regulations which took effect in the fall of 1969, see 'Osnovy ugolovnogo zakonodatelstva Soiuza SSR i soiuznykh respublik', *Sbornik zakonov SSSR Tom 3, 1968-1970*, loc. cit., pp. 330–53.

59. The changes in the groups of crimes used for determining liability for the stigma of 'specially dangerous recidivist' may be summarized as follows: the first list of serious offenses for which two occurences warranted the designation 'specially dangerous recidivist' remained the same; but theft, robbery, swindling, and

speculation – except in aggravated forms – were dropped from the second list of crimes for which four occurrences (or two plus one from the first list) were required. Another condition added in 1969 was that the actual crime which earned the offender his stigma (the last one in the series) had to have drawn at least a five-year sentence, if on the first list, or a three-year sentence, if on the second list. This meant that if the last crime had mitigating circumstances which reduced its sentence below the usual level of severity for that offense, it could not serve as part of the grounds for awarding the stigma. See 'O vnesenii izmenenii i doopolnenii v Osnovakh', loc. cit., Article 1.

60. Any of these persons who were previous parole failures remained ineligible for further parole.

61. 'O vnesenii izmenenii i dopolnenii v Osnovakh', loc. cit.

62. I. Galperin, 'Priznanie osobo opasnym retsidivistom po st. 23 Osnov ugolovnogo zakonodatelstva soiuza SSR i soiuznykh respublik', *SIu* (1969, No. 11), pp. 16–17; Iu. M. Tkachevskii, 'Uslovno-dosrochnoe osvobozhdenie ot nakazaniia (Dopolneniia i izmeneniia k st. 44 Osnov ugolovnogo zakonodatelstva)', *SZ* (1969, No. 11), pp. 56–8.

63. *Deputaty verkhovnogo soveta SSSR*, loc. cit., p. 321.

64. There was a discrepancy between *Izvestiia*'s announcement of the formation of the commission on changes in the Fundamental Principles of Criminal Legislation, June 1966, and Nishanov's indication that the commission had arranged the research, which, according to the Procuracy Institute reports, had been carried out during 1965. We assumed that it was Nishanov who was mistaken, not *Izvestiia*. The Praesidium of the Supreme Soviet ordered the research from B. S. Nikoforov and the Procuracy Institute in 1965; *after* receiving the results it established the commission of which Nikiforov was a prominent member. R. Nishanov, 'O proektakh zakonov', *Izvestiia* (12 July 1969), p. 1. 'Otchet... za 1965', loc. cit. Interview.

8. THE NATURE OF PARTICIPATION

1. Interviews.

2. 'O borbe s prestupnostiu', loc. cit. For discussion of this edict, see Chapter 9.

3. See Chapter 4.

4. In this chapter we will have many occasions to refer to the three sets of decisions in criminal policy which earlier were presented. Rather than repeat the same cross-references, we give them once here. For the juvenile delinquency reforms, see Chapter 5; for the alcoholism and hooliganism measures, see Chapter 6; for the parole and recidivism regulations, see Chapter 7.

5. Interviews.

6. Not only did we learn from interviews that such informal discussions did take place, but we also observed some of them at meetings of the Academic Council devoted to dissertation defenses.

7. There were also generalists at other levels of the political structure; for example, the 'line' party officials, like *obkom* first secretaries. On the distinction between generalists and specialists in Soviet political careers, see George Fischer, *Soviet Executives and Modern Society* (N.Y., 1968).

8. The Department of Administrative Organs was responsible for supervising

operations and cadres in the army, the security police, and the law enforcement agencies. Its head was a politician of high stature who reported directly to a Secretary of the Central Committee; although he supervised the work of the leading law enforcement officials, he was not necessarily superior to them, especially when, as in the case of Procurator-General R. A. Rudenko, they were members of the Central Committee. The Department Head was assisted by one or two deputy chiefs in managing the work of the Department's sections, including a legal affairs section responsible for the courts, Procuracy, and MOOP. It appeared that the head of this section was of somewhat lower status than a deputy minister in one of those agencies. For two recent heads of this section were later transferred to positions of deputy minister – Nikitin became deputy minister for the Defense of the Social Order in 1966, and Sukharev, his successor as section head, became deputy minister of justice in 1970.

9. *Vysshie predstavitelnye organy vlasti v SSSR* (M., 1969), p. 115.

10. It is probable that the legal affairs section of the Department of Administrative Organs played a larger part in the preparation of the party edict of July 1966 on intensifying the fight against crime.

11. Interviews. More likely than not these materials were also used by the Party Politburo in any deliberations which it might have held on these matters.

12. Between 1964 and 1968, when the decisions studied here were taken, there was no head of the Department of Administrative Organs. After the death of the previous occupant, N. R. Mironov, in a plane crash in 1964, a Secretary of the CPSU, A. N. Shelepin, performed the duties of that post in addition to his other work (see Barghoorn, *Politics in the USSR* (1966 edition), op. cit., p. 349). Later, in 1966, M. A. Suslov began to oversee the Department's work.

13. Brzezinski and Huntington wrote, 'the initiative in formulating most important policy measures probably rests with the Central Committee Secretaries and the department of the central apparat'. Brzezinski and Huntington, op. cit., p. 204. Abdurakhman Avtorkhanov claimed that 'the Central Committee departments are the main channel for the preparation of decisions'. See his *The Communist Party Apparatus* (Chicago, 1966), p. 217.

14. One reason suggested was that the Department's staff was too small. The legal affairs section had five or six members, including one instructor to supervise the court system. The Supreme Court, Procuracy, and Ministry of Internal Affairs were far better equipped to perform the paperwork of compiling memoranda to support their policy proposals. Interview.

15. Interviews. A *proverka* might be described as a spot check of a particular institution, organized by another one operating in a supervisory capacity. Besides the party's Central Committee, the USSR Council of Ministers, the Praesidium of the Supreme Soviet, republican and local soviets and their commissions, ministries, the Procuracy, the audit commission and other agencies carried out *proverki*. Often, these spot checks were followed by administrative orders.

16. On the *ad hoc* commissions, see a later section of this chapter.

17. Kalinychev, op. cit., pp. 26–9.

18. Nor do we know whether or not the documentation prepared by criminologists for the *apparat* of the Praesidium of the Supreme Soviet ever reached members of the Politburo other than the two Praesidium members. For the party-state edict, see 'V TsK KPSS', loc. cit.

19. See Chapter 4.

20. Brzezinski and Huntington, op. cit., p. 216.

21. Minkovskii and Pronina, loc. cit.; Minkovskii and Melnikova, loc. cit.; for references to the *Izvestiia* alcoholism debate, see Chapter 6, note 22.

22. Among contemporary political scientists Charles Lindblom has placed special emphasis upon the process of reaching decisions. See Lindblom, *The Policy-making Process*, op. cit.

23. Brzezinski and Huntington, op. cit., pp. 211–16.

24. See Chapter 4, notes 45 and 46.

25. One piece of follow-up research on hooliganism enforcement was reported in an anonymous article in *Pravovedenie*. See 'Novove ugolovnoe zakonodatelstvo ob usilenii borby s khuliganstvom', loc. cit. See also, *Informatsionnoe pismo* [instituta], no.7, loc. cit.

26. Membership in the advisory council of the Supreme Court and the methodological council of the Procuracy was restricted to scholars who resided in Moscow. Likewise, only Moscow research institutes had central ministerial leaders on their academic councils. Thus, a criminologist in Leningrad had far less opportunity for oral communication with ministerial leaders than did his Moscow colleague at the Procuracy Institute.

27. There were probably additional settings where Moscow criminologists and Procuracy or Supreme Court chiefs could meet. For example, the academic council of other research institutes probably included the directors of the Procuracy Institute and representatives of the legal agencies.

28. During the 1960s frequent members of the *ad hoc* commissions for questions of criminal policy were L. I. Smirnov, Chairman of the RSFSR Supreme Court, and V. I. Terebilov, Deputy Chairman of the USSR Supreme Court. (In 1970 Terebilov became USSR Minister of Justice.) Interviews.

29. See the regular reports of the Supreme Court plenums in *Izvestiia* or the more detailed versions in *Sotsialisticheskaia zakonnost*.

30. See Chapter 3, note 199.

31. Such friendships might have been anticipated, for John Armstrong's study showed that in the USSR, more often than in Western Europe, informal relationships were based upon career contacts. See his 'Sources of Administrative Behavior: Some Soviet and West European Comparisons', *Communist Studies and Social Sciences*, loc. cit., p. 366.

32. Interviews. For example, see V. N. Kudriavtsev and N. V. Zhogin, 'Pravo i moral v nashem obshchestve', *Pravda* (21 September 1966), pp. 2–3.

33. See the unusually warm obituary, 'Grigorii Ivanovich Kocharov', loc. cit.

34. In the spring of 1969 Karpets became the head of the department of criminal investigation in the MVD SSSR.

35. Shliapochnikov, 'Pamiati vydaiushchego sovetskogo kriminologa', loc. cit.

36. Interviews.

37. Barry and Berman, loc. cit., pp. 317–19.

38. One Soviet scholar complained about the lack of regulations governing the composition, organization, and work methods of the various commissions. See A. S. Pigolkin, *Podgotovka proektov normativnykh aktov* (M., 1968), p. 41.

39. Other functions of the USSR Ministry of Justice, such as the supervision of the college of advocates and of the *notariat* and forensic medical bodies, were transferred to the republican ministries of justice; and the administration of the court system was entrusted to the apparat of the USSR Supreme Court. When in

1963 the republican ministries of justice were also abolished, new Juridical Commissions were established under the Councils of Ministers of the Republics to handle both legislative and administrative duties. See V. N. Ershov, 'Iuridicheskaia komissiia', *Entsiklopedicheskii slovar pravovykh zananii Sovetskoe pravo* (ed. S. N. Bratus *et al.*; M., 1965), p. 509. Also, Pigolkin, op. cit., p. 66.

40. Interviews. The research institute working under the Juridical Commission of the USSR Council of Ministers, the All-Union Insitute of Soviet Legislation, was engaged during the 1960s in the collection and publication of a systematic edition of the laws of the USSR, which included criminal laws.

41. *Vysshie predstavitelnye organy*, op. cit., pp. 125–62. This section was written by the Secretary of the Praesidium of the Supreme Soviet, S. G. Novikov. Interviews. See also D. Richard Little, 'Soviet Parliamentary Committees after Khrushchev: Obstacles and Opportunities', *Soviet Studies*, XXIV, No. 1 (July 1972), pp. 41–60.

42. *Vysshie predstavitelnye organi*, op.cit., p. 115; Pigolkin, op. cit., pp. 33, 36–9.

43. The juridical section, headed until 1917 by F. M. Kalinychev (a former official in the Central Committee apparat) was one of six sections in the apparat of the Praesidium of the Supreme Soviet. The responsibilities of the other sections included: the work of the soviets, prizes, international relations, servicing the standing commissions, and financial questions. Kalinychev, *Prezidium verkhovnogo soveta SSSR* (M. 1969), pp. 60–1.

44. In interviews Soviet criminologists regularly distinguished between 'working' and 'editorial' commissions. Pigolkin, op. cit., p. 38, also made this distinction.

45. *Vysshie predstavitelnye organi*, op. cit., pp. 115, 118.

46. Kalinychev, op. cit., p. 60, gave a list of nine out of the approximately twenty special temporary commissions which were formed during the period from 1953 to 1968, and all of these nine concerned legal questions.

47. Individual ministries, or agencies like Gosplan, were often responsible for the preparation of legislative drafts. See Pigolkin, op. cit., p. 32, and interviews.

48. Ibid., pp. 72–3; *Vysshie predstavitelnye organi*, op. cit., pp. 123–4.

49. Brzezinski and Huntington, op. cit., pp. 209–16.

50. Jerry Hough has shown how the content of books on a given subject may vary, depending upon the audience at which they are directed. Using data collected by Franklyn Griffiths, Hough compared the images of the American political system found in Soviet books of the late 1960s with the size of the printed editions and found a direct correlation between the nature of the image and the size of editition. (The size of edition may be taken as an indicator of the intended audience, as editions with printings under 5000 copies are usually directed at scholarly or professional audiences, whereas those over 10,000 are usually intended for broader consumption). See Fainsod and Hough, op. cit., chapt. 8.

51 Boldyrev, op. cit.; Stepichev, loc. cit.; Iakovlev, op. cit.

52. *Alkogolizm*, op. cit.; Pronina, 'Nekotorye voprosy organizatsii', loc. cit.; Minkovskii and Melnikova, loc. cit.; *Effektivnost ugolovnopravovykh mer*, op. cit.

53. Pronina, op. cit.; Kliuchinskaia, op. cit.; *O merakh po usileniiu borby*, op. cit.; Boldryev, *et al.*, loc. cit.; Galperin, 'Priznanie osobo opasnym retsidivistom', loc. cit.; Tkachevskii, loc. cit.

54. Another way of explaining this point is to use the distinction between manifest and latent functions. The manifest, principal and intended functions of criminologists' professional writing were communication and advocacy; but the latent

function, secondary and unintended, could sometimes be the mobilization of professional support for the decisions. On the two kinds of functions see Robert K. Merton, 'Manifest and Latent Functions', *Social Theory and Social Structure* (enlarged edition, N.Y., 1968), pp. 73–138.

55. K. I. Nikitin, 'Dalneishee sovershenstvovanie form i metodov borby s prestupnostiu i inymi narusheniiami obshchestvennogo poriadka', *SGiP* (1966, No. 11), pp. 1–11.

56. Interviews.

57. Not only was the articulation of policy positions the characteristic function of legal scholars' appearances in the press during the mid and late 1960s, but scholars generally wrote a large percentage of the full expositions of policy proposals which appeared in the press. Hough found for his 1971 sample that scholars accounted for almost half of the full-length assertions of policy positions or proposals. See Hough, 'Communication and Persuasion,' loc. cit., p. 193.

58. Minkovskii and Pronina, loc. cit.

59. Kudriavtsev, loc. cit.

60. See Chapter 6, note 22.

61. Gertsenzon, 'Takoi zakon nuzhen', loc.cit. As we saw, there was also a discussion of the need for an anti-alcoholism law in *Liternaturnaia gazeta* during January 1966; but its participations did not include criminologists.

62. Savitskii, loc. cit.

63. Barry and Berman, loc. cit., pp. 317, correctly noted that among the responsibilities of the All-Union Institute of Soviet Legislation there was the collection of suggestions for legislative changes made in the press. However, this indirect mechanism for relaying proposals from the newspapers to decision-makers turned out to be ineffective, because 'the card file of the institute was far from complete, and the practical organs and other research institutes knew little about it and therefore for all practical purposes did not use it.' Pigolkin, op. cit., p. 30.

9. THE EFFECTS OF PARTICIPATION

1. See, for example, Dahl, *Who Governs?*, op. cit.

2. In using a Western definition of influence we do not accept an assumption made by many of its proponents that influence on decisions is tantamount to possession of political power. We shall discuss the relationship between influencing decisions and possessing power in the next chapter.

3. Robert Agger, *et al.*, *The Rulers and the Ruled: Political Power and its Impotence in American Communities* (N.Y., 1964), p. 51; Stewart, loc. cit., pp. 47–8.

4. Wilson, op. cit., p. 316.

5. Ibid., p. 316.

6. Gamson, op. cit., pp. 59–61; Robert Dahl, 'The Concept of Power', *Behavioral Sciences*, II (July 1957), pp. 201–18.

7. Despite the breadth of his definition of influence Robert Dahl did not always use it fully. In his theoretical writings Dahl usually associated influence with conflict situations. However, in at least one place in his research Dahl did consider cooperative as well as conflict decisions. In calculating an index of influence based upon the relative success of different actors in achieving their desired outcomes,

Dahl assumed that the degree of influence was equal whether the actor's proposal was adopted in the face of opposition or in its absence. See Dahl, op. cit., pp. 332-3.

8. Lindblom, op. cit., pp. 30-2.

9. Dahl himself displayed particular interest in comparing the influence of different actors. See 'The Concept of Power', loc. cit., pp. 205ff.

Another reason why so many studies of decision-making have focused upon conflict situations is the assumption that contested decisions are more important than those which we made smoothly. The validity of this assumption depends upon one's criteria of importance. For the analyst concerned with the impact of decisions upon policy, conflict is a poor indicator of importance. For often the most contested decisions will result in compromises which advance the question at hand only in small ways; whereas a series of decisions made cooperatively may introduce a new trend into a policy.

10. See Chapter 6.

11. Dahl, op. cit., p. 332.

12. Ibid.; Gamson, op. cit., pp. 61-70.

13. Dahl, op. cit.

14. According to Yehezkel Dror, four classes of secondary criteria are acceptable for an approximate measurement of a primary variable—independent variables which shape the quality of the evaluated process; dependent variables shaped by the quality of the evaluated process; interdependent variables; and variables non-causally related to the quality of the evaluated process by an interconnecting variable that shapes both the process and the criterion variable. See Dror, op. cit., pp. 26-7.

15. Harold Wilensky, *Organizational Intelligence: Knowledge and Power in Government and Industry* (N.Y. and London, 1967), pp. 45-7.

16. Bruce L. R. Smith, *The RAND Corporation. Case Study of a Non-Profit Advisory Corporation* (Cambridge, 1966), p. 217.

17. Smith, op. cit., pp. 277-81.

18. Although we draw upon a number of different Western social scientists, the principal sources for these correlations are Robert Merton's essay, 'The Role of the Intellectual in Public Bureaucracy', *Social Theory and Social Structure*, loc. cit., pp. 261-78; and Bruce L. R. Smith's monograph, *The RAND Corporation*, op. cit. While Smith's conclusions were based primarily upon research, Merton's were the result of practical experience and observation.

19. Merton, loc. cit., pp. 269-70.

20. Karl Deutsch, *The Nerves of Government* (N.Y., 1966), p. 147.

21. Merton, loc. cit., p. 264.

22. Lazarsfeld and Reitz, loc. cit.

23. In fact, neither criminologists nor MOOP officials furnished 'scientifically based' answers to the problem of alcoholism and crime. By 'scientifically based' we mean recommendations which not only made sense in the light of available data, but which research had shown to have better effects than alternative possibilities.

24. Smith, op. cit., pp. 229-30.

25. Lazarsfeld and Reitz, loc. cit.

26. Merton, loc. cit., p. 265.

27. Smith, op. cit., pp. 278-9.

28. Wilensky, op. cit., p. 66.

29. Merton, loc. cit., p. 271.

30. Lindblom, op. cit., pp. 33–4.

31. Gamson developed this method upon the basis of one of Dahl's research methods. See Gamson, op. cit., pp. 61–5, and Dahl, op. cit., pp. 332–7.

32. Gamson, op. cit., p. 63.

33. The stories of these decisions are found in Part Two.

34. Gamson, op. cit., p. 65.

35. Two decisions studied here illustrate the varied effects which conflict may have upon specialist influence. The hooliganism decision showed how, in Schooler's words, 'scientists cannot exert influence in an . . . environment, fraught with political conflict'; while the parole decision illustrates Schwartz and Keech's image of disputing political leaders appealing to specialists for help. Schooler, op. cit.; Schwartz and Keech, 'Public Influence and Education Policy', loc. cit.

36. This evidence would at the minimum shift the burden of proof to him who would question the influence of criminologists upon these decisions.

37. Interviews.

38. Gertsenzon referred to the 'Leninist principle of the primacy of prevention over repression'. See Gertsenzon, *Ugolovnoe pravo i sotsiologiia (problemy ugolovnogo prava i ugolovnoi politiki)* (M., 1970), p. 182.

The phrase 'crime prevention' is sufficiently ambiguous that it may be used as a stated aim of almost any criminal policy. It is possible, for example, to justify in the name of crime prevention both educational (or prophylactic) measures and repression. Therefore, it is necessary to look behind the rhetoric associated with a given criminal policy to assess its actual content. Before we count crime prevention as an element of criminal policy, we require concrete evidence that prevention is an end in itself and not simply a smokescreen for repression or other ends.

39. 'Polozhenie o nabliudatenlnykh komissiakh', loc. cit. 'Ob administrativnom nadzore', loc. cit.

40. See Chapter 2.

41. 'Ob ustranenii nedostatkov v rabote organov prokuratury po preduprezhdeniiu prestupnosti i narushenii zakonnosti', Ukazanie Zam. Gen. Prok. SSSR ot 31 maia 1965 g., No. 3/N-76, *Sbornik deistvuiushchikh prikazov*, loc. cit.

42. 'V TsK KPSS', loc. cit.

43. See *Rabota raionnogo (gorodskogo) prokurora po preduprezhdeniiu pravonarushenii (nauchno-prakticheskaia konferentsiia kursov prokuratury SSSR)* (Kharkov, 1968). Also interviews. Note also that the fullest explanation of the utility of crime study for procurators appeared in a treatise on the procuracy's role in crime prevention. See Zvirbul, op. cit., pp. 58–112.

44. For example, see '1961 Programme of the Communist Party of the Soviet Union', loc. cit., and N. R. Mironov, *Ukreplenie zakonnosti i pravoporiadka v obshchenarodnom gosudarstve – programnaia zadacha partii* (second edition; M., 1969), pp. 27–30.

46. N. V. Zhogin, 'Zakon i pravovaia nauka', *Izvestiia* (17 June 1968), p. 3.

47. Anashkin, 'Diagnoz prostupka', loc. cit.

48. N. A. Shchelokov, 'Pomogat cheloveku stat luchshe', *Pravda* (31 July 1967), p. 3; Shchelokov, 'Problemy borby s prestupnostiu nesovershennoletnikh i zadachi organov okhrany obshchestvennogo poriadka, SSSR', *Problemy borby s prestupnostiu nesovershennoletnikh i zadachi organov okhrany obshchestvennogo poriadka SSSR (Materialy nauchno-prakticheskoi konferentsii)* (M., 1967), pp. 1–21. Also, N. A.

Shchelokov, 'Glavnoe – preduprezhdenie pravonarushenii', *SZ* (1967, No. 8).

49. Shchelokov, 'Problemy borby s prestupnostiu', loc. cit.

50. 'V Verkhovnom sude SSSR', *SZ* (1965, No. 12), pp. 31–5.

51. Since from 1964 all graduates of law faculties and institutes had some training in criminology, the generation entering high law enforcement posts in the 1980s might be more favorably disposed to criminological ideas than the previous one, which encountered it for the first time while already embarked upon their professional careers.

52. It was even possible to justify repression as serving the goal of prevention, because the principle of deterrence had not been seriously challenged by the supporters of educational and prophylactic measures.

53. See the published summary of this edict, 'V TsK KPSS', loc. cit.

54. Gertsenzon, *Ugolovnoe pravo i sotsiologiia*, op. cit., p. 191.

55. Professor Gertsenzon also regarded the 1966 party-state edict as a mixture of prophylactic and repressive measures. Ibid.

The mixed nature of Soviet criminal policy between 1964 and 1970 contrasts with the predominantly repressive trend in Soviet policy toward political dissent during these years. In the USSR, as elsewhere, policies toward crime control and the regulation and political deviance are usually separate from one another.

10. SPECIALIST PARTICIPATION RECONSIDERED

1. See, for example, G. A. Tokaev, *Comrade X* (London, 1956), pp. 321–30; or for a fictionalized account, A. S. Solzhenitsyn, *The First Circle* (N.Y., 1968).

2. Fainsod and Hough, op. cit.; Hough, 'Communication and Persuasion', loc. cit.; Franklyn Griffiths, 'Images, Politics and Learning', loc. cit.

3. For a summary of the conventional view of the participation of specialists under Stalin, see Skilling, 'Group Conflict in Soviet Politics', loc. cit., pp. 399–400.

4. Griffiths, 'Images, Politics and Learning', loc. cit.; Remnek, op. cit.

5. See Stewart, loc. cit.; and *Interest Groups in Soviet Politics*, op. cit.

6. Hough, 'The Soviet System: Petrification or Pluralism?', loc. cit.

7. One example would be science policy specialists. Interviews. Another example would be Indologists. See Remnek, loc. cit.

8. See Chapter 1, note 49.

9. Sidney Ploss argued that in the post-1968 period Brezhnev and colleagues curtailed the *public* dimension of specialist participation in policy-making, by placing sharp limits upon the boundaries of public discourse concerning policy options. Ploss, loc. cit., pp. 28–31. Although Ploss's argument might hold for some policy realms (e.g. economic), there was no evidence that it applied to many. Moreover, there was no sign of any curtailment of specialist participation *behind the scenes* during these years; and in some fields, for example science policy, the scope of specialist participation increased during the early 1970s.

10. To deal with this difficulty one might have compared the influence of Soviet criminologists with that of American and British criminal law scholars, as well as criminologists. But the secondary literature did not include enough material on the

influence of criminal law scholars in those Western countries.

11. See, for example, Paul Tappan, 'Treatment without Trial', *Social Forces*, xxiv (1946), pp. 306–11, cited in Lemert, op. cit., p. 97.

12. Lemert, op. cit., p. 109.

13. Moynihan, op. cit., especially pp. 38–102. Cloward and Ohlin's theory was set out in Richard Cloward and Lloyd Ohlin, *Delinquency and Opportunity: A Theory of Delinquent Gangs* (N.Y., 1960).

14. For example, the National Commission on the Causes and Prevention of Violence, headed by Dr Milton Eisenhower, used two criminologists, James Short Jr. and Marvin Wolfgang, as its research directors, and commissioned another criminologist Jerome Skolnick, to write on the key reports. See Jerome Skolnick, 'The Violence Commission: Internal Politics and Public Policy', *The Use and Abuse of Social Science* (ed. I. L. Horowitz; New Brunswick, N.J., 1971), pp. 234–48.

15. The Presidential Commission on Crime and Criminal Justice did somewhat better than the other commissions of the period in getting its suggestions implemented, especially at the state level. For discussion of the reasons for this commission's relative success, see an article by criminologist Lloyd Ohlin, 'The President's Commission on Law Enforcement and Administration of Justice', *Sociology and Public Policy: The Case of the Presidential Commissions* (ed. Mirra Komarovsky; N.Y., 1975), pp. 93–115.

Two of the best studies of the role of commissions in American politics were Robert B. Reich, 'Solving Social Crises by Commissions', *Yale Review of Law and Social Action*, iii, No. 3 (1973), pp. 234–71, and Ray C. Rist, 'Policy, Politics, and Social Research: A Study in the Relationship of Federal Commissions and Social Science', *Social Problems*, xxi, No. 1 (summer 1973), pp. 113–28.

16. One of the three Associate Reporters, who along with the Chief Reporter, Herbert Wechsler, drafted the Model Penal Code, was the criminologist Paul Tappan. The staff of thirteen consultants who worked directly on the code included two criminologists, Thorstin Sellin and Sanford Bates; While the Criminal Law Advisory Committee which reviewed the various drafts of the Model Penal Code included among its forty-odd members nine criminologists and two criminal lawyers who might be classed as criminologists (Authur Sherry and Sheldon Glueck). Gerhard Mueller, *Crime, Law and the Scholars: A History of Scholarship in American Criminal Law* (Seattle, 1969), pp. 157–64 and p. 258.

On the impact of the Model Penal Code on new state criminal codes, see Authur H. Sherry, 'The Politics of Criminal Law Reform: the United States', *The American Journal of Comparative Law*, xxi (spring 1973), pp. 201–29; and Herbert Wechsler, 'The Model Penal Code and the Codification of American Criminal Law', *Crime, Criminology and Public Policy*, loc. cit., pp. 419–68.

17. Lord Butler, 'The Founding of the Institute of Criminology in Cambridge', ibid., pp. 1–10; T. S. Lodge, 'The Founding of the Home Office Research Unit', ibid., pp. 11–23.

18. In contrast to American 'crisis commissions', whose work rarely led to new legislation, the British commissions were established as a rule when the government contemplated new legislation on a subject and for that reason sought a review of the evidence. On the differences between commissions in the USA and England, see Reich, loc. cit.

19. *Criminal Justice Act 1967* (Elizabeth II 1967, Chapter 80) (London, 1968).

20. On the introduction of suspended sentences, see Roger Hood, 'Criminology

and Penal Change: A Case Study of the Nature and Impact of Some Recent Advice to Governments', *Crime, Criminology and Public Policy*, loc. cit., pp. 391-402. On the fines and parole provisions, see interviews.

21. W. H. Hammond and Edna Chayen, *Persistent Criminals*, Home Office Research Unit Report No. 5 (London, 1963); D. J. West, *The Habitual Prisoner* (London, 1963).

22. *Preventive Detention*, Report of the Advisory Council on the Treatment of Offenders (London, 1963); *The Adult Offender*, White Paper presented to Parliament by the Secretary of State for the Home Department by Command of Her Majesty (December, 1965); interviews.

23. Minutes of Evidence Taken Before the Sub-Committee on Social Affairs of Standing Committee A, Monday, March 20, 1967, Parliamentary Debates House of Commons, Official Report, pp. 239-40; and interviews. Two memoranda submitted by Dr Hammond and his colleagues to the Home Office's Criminal Division were 'The General Relevance of Research Findings to Proposals in the Criminal Justice Bill' (7 pages, no date), and 'Further Note on Criteria of Eligibility for Extended Sentences', (3 pages, no date).

24. See Chapter 7.

25. Hood, loc. cit., pp. 402-17.

26. Moynihan, op. cit.

27. Interviews. Note that the highest-ranked persons in the British and in the Soviet government to concern themselves with criminology on a regular basis were at approximately the same levels – Deputy Under-Secretary of State (Britain) and Deputy Procurator-General (USSR).

28. Moynihan, op. cit., especially pp. 193-194.

29. Hood, loc. cit., p. 417.

30. Recently, Paul Lazarsfeld and Jeffrey Reitz contended that there was almost always a 'gap' between the knowledge of the social scientist and the kind of recommendations which decision-makers required. This gap 'had to be filled by creative thinking which responds with guesses of varying degrees of risk to the inevitable unanswered questions.' The authors went on to identify a number of 'gap situations' and to explore the reasons for them. See Paul Lazarsfeld and Jeffrey Reitz, *An Introduction to Applied Sociology* (N.Y., 1975), ch. 5.

31. Following Terry N. Clark, we use the term 'power' to refer to an actor's *potential* for gaining his values, goals, or preferences. An actor's potential for achieving his ends may be defined as a function of the resources which he possesses. An act of influence denotes the successful use of some of these resources to achieve an end (i.e. the use or exercise of power). See Terry N. Clark, 'Community Power and Decision-Making', *Current Sociology*, xx, No. 2 (1972), pp. 19-35.

32. Of course, political leaders did not operate in a vacuum and were themselves subject to constraints upon the range of options they could choose in dealing with a given problem. To a degree leaders in any political system were constrained by the opinions and attitudes of the public or that portion of the public upon which the legitimacy of their rule was based. Even more important, the leaders had to deal with the *facts* of a situation. Desired or desirable solutions to problems might have to be rejected as impractical or infeasible. Because political leaders were not free agents, subject as they were to the constraints of facts and of public opinion, their capacity to overrule or ignore specialist claims was not absolute.

33. For example, see Primack and von Hippel, op. cit.; *The Use and Abuse of Social*

Science, op. cit.; and Moshe Lewin, *Political Undercurrents in Soviet Economic Thought* (Princeton, New Jersey, 1974).

34. Because of the phenomenon of weaker actors anticipating the preferences of stronger ones, it becomes possible for the latter's power to have an effect even though they do not use it, in the sense of spending any of their resources. Thus, the really powerful political actor may be able to achieve his ends while maintaining the possibility to so doing in future instances. On some theoretical issues related to anticipation, see Robert Dahl, 'Power', *International Encyclopedia of the Social Sciences* (ed. David Sills; N.Y., 1968), XII, pp. 412–13.

35. Within their respective political systems Soviet leaders appeared to have been somewhat more powerful than their American counterparts. As a result it was possible that Soviet specialists were led to anticipate leadership desires more frequently or more extensively than did American specialists. The question was whether the extent of anticipation by weaker parties varied with the size of the power ratio between the strong and the weak. Without controlled experiment it would be hard to know, but it was our assumption that extent of anticipation would vary systematically only when the differences between the power ratios were very large ones. One doubted that the power ratio of leaders to specialists in the USSR exceeded that which obtained in the USA by a sufficient amount.

36. Examples included the Atomic Scientists' Movement, the crusade against the death penalty, and others. See Alice Kimball Smith, *A Peril and A Hope: The Scientists' Movement in America* (Chicago, 1965); Michael Meltsner, *Cruel and Unusual Punishment* (N.Y., 1973); Primack and von Hippel, op. cit.

37. On the limits of policy debate in the USSR, see Fainsod and Hough, op. cit., ch. 8.

38. When some Soviet criminal law scholars attempted to do so in the early 1960s, they became an object of criticism in a legal periodical. 'It is well known', the editorial ran, 'that after the adoption in 1958 of the Fundamental Principles of Criminal Procedure, which rejected the proposals of certain scholars, some scientific workers continued the dispute instead of actively assisting in the implementation of the legislative act.' 'Za vysokuiu ideinost, printsipalnost i deistvennost pravovoi nauki', *SZ* (1963, No. 11), p. 8, cited in Barry and Berman, loc. cit., pp. 328–9.

39. Primack and von Hippel, op.cit., p. 102. The message of this book was that scientists should overcome these obstacles and take their cases to the public when politics behind the scenes failed to produce the desired result.

40. See, for example, Lemert, op. cit.

41. According to philosopher-planner Donald Schon the precondition for policy innovations was 'the emergence of new ideas in good currency'; and those new ideas usually resulted, in Schon's view, from 'a disruptive event or sequence of events'. Donald Schon, *Beyond the Stable State* (N.Y., 1971), p. 123 and p. 128.

In the same vein political scientist James Q. Wilson concluded a major study of political organizations in the USA with the assertion that 'the most important new policies of government are adopted only after there has been a change in opinion or a new perception of old arrangements sufficient to place new options on the public agenda. . . . Such redefinitions of what constitutes legitimate action', Wilson continued, ' . . . are the result of dramatic or critical events (a depression, a war, a national scandal), extraordinary political leadership, the rise of new political elites, and the accumulated impact of ideas via the mass media of communication.'

Wilson, op. cit., p. 330.

42. In Jack Walker's view an American specialist's reputation as a policy expert normally depended upon how colleagues in the policy realm regarded him. The social basis for a specialist's reputation might act as a restraint upon him. Walker observed that when specialists and officials interacted frequently and developed common assumptions about policy, they seemed to form policy communities which imposed social controls upon their members. When individual members challenged the community's core assumptions, other members, especially the leaders, stood ready to defend the assumptions, particularly when there was no demand for innovation. In this way, the community might 'filter out' radical policy suggestions (prevent their reaching the ears of policy-makers) and at the same time to weaken the reputation of those who promoted such suggestions. See Jack Walker, 'The Diffusion of Knowledge and Policy Change: Toward a Theory of Agenda-Setting', unpublished paper delivered at the 1974 meeting of the American Political Science Association.

Soviet criminal policy-making in the 1960s supplied a case in point. During 1959–61 a criminologist named I. S. Noi repeatedly urged that a large number of Soviet offenders be declared non-imputable and placed in mental hospitals rather than in prisons. In proposing this innovation, for which there was no demand, Noi seemed to have challenged two basic assumptions of Soviet criminal policy – both the prevailing concept of criminal responsibility and the premise that crime was socially caused. As a result, Noi's suggestions met severe criticism on the part of his colleagues; and his proposals were never considered by policy-makers. After dropping this particular campaign, Noi regained the respect of his fellow-scholars, but he was not, as far we know, consulted on policy matters in the middle and late 1960s. For more detail on the Noi proposals, see Peter Solomon, 'Specialists in Soviet Policy-making: Criminologists and Criminal Policy in the 1960s', Ph.D. dissertation (Columbia University, 1973), pp. 302–9.

43. To characterize the pressure to be loyal to current policy which impinged upon the bureaucratic intellectual, Merton coined the aphorism: 'He who is heard does not innovate; he who innovates is not heard.' Merton, loc. cit., p. 271.

44. This was true of most criminologists who worked at universities or teaching institutes. But the principal Soviet criminologist who did launch major criticisms against Soviet criminal policy, I. S. Noi, did work at a teaching institute; as did another criminologist who was outspoken about the limitations placed upon the scope of criminological inquiry, the late Prof. M. D. Shargorodskii.

45. See Chapter 4.

46. In Etzioni's terms the Soviet criminologist's role was that of expert rather than of intellectual. Etzioni, op. cit., pp. 182–8.

47. In the United States, where criminologists encountered fewer obstacles to a role of social critic, a sizeable fraction of these scholars adopted such a critical posture. Not surprisingly, those who presented the most radical critiques of their county's policies were generally excluded from the policy-making process. But the very existence of this critique seemed to help more moderate colleagues both to criticize policies and to propose innovations in policies from time to time.

48. Interviews.

49. Theodore J. Lowi, 'American Business, Public Policy, Case Studies and Political Theory', World Politics, xvi, No. 4, (July 1964), pp. 677–715; Zimmerman, loc. cit.; Schooler, op. cit.

50. Ibid., p. 64.

51. Ibid., p. 140.

52. See Chapter 4.

53. Ibid., pp.

54. Griffiths, 'Images, Politics and Learning', loc. cit., and Remnek, op. cit.

55. The participation in the formation of Soviet policies for science and technology by specialists in social studies of science (the economics of science, organization of science, sociology of science, law and science) has not been documented in published sources, but unpublished research by this author supplies ample evidence about the development to these scholars participation in the early and middle 1960s and its institutionalization in the early 1970s. To illustrate the extent of participation, consider the scholars' involvement in the 1973 Statute of Inventions. The key research and ideas for reforms included in this statute came mainly from economists of science – V. S. Sominskii and his laboratory in Leningrad, which was affiliated with the State Committee on Science and Technology (GKNT). Comments and additional suggestions were supplied by specialists in the sociology of science at the Institute for the History of Science and Technology in Moscow, Science Studies Department. And the actual statute was drafted by staff of GKNT and of the All-union Patent Institute, with help from legal scholars at the Institute of State and Law (from its sector 'Law and the Scientific-Technological Revolution'). Interviews conducted during May 1974 with science policy specialists at the Institute for the History of Science and Technology, at the Institute of State and Law and at the U.S.A. Institute. For the text of the new statute, see 'Polozhenie ob otkrytiiakh, izobreteniiakh i ratsional-izatorskikh predlozheniiakh', utverzhdeno postanovleniim Soveta Ministrov SSSR ot 21 avgusta 1973 g. No. 584, *Sobranie Postanovlenii* (1973, No. 19), pp. 408–58.

56. This may be inferred from Judy, loc. cit., and Stewart, loc. cit.

57. A. H. Brown has recently suggested that the participation of specialists in the USSR might vary with the technicality of a policy realm of or an issue within a given policy realm. It would appear that the technicality of policy realm was not a decisive factor, since neither foreign policy nor criminal policy was an especially technical area of policy. On the other hand, it was still possible that the more technical issues within these and other policy areas were most likely to attract specialist involvement. This hypothesis requires further investigation. See A. H. Brown, *Soviet Politics and Political Science* (London, 1974), p. 88.

58. We have seen that this was the case in the USA, where the degree of specialist influence in criminal policy-making seemed to be near the average for the various policy realms. See Schooler, op. cit.

59. By effectiveness of policy we refer to the extent to which the means chosen facilitate the achievement of underlying goals. We do not intend to introduce our own or anyone else's judgment about the merits of the policy goals themselves.

60. Large improvements in policies, which enable the achievement of a particular goal, often introduce means so radical as to constitute new goals in themselves, thus breaking down the goal/means dichotomy. For example, in order to achieve an improvement in technological innovation, Soviet planners might choose to introduce a major change in the pricing of industrial goods. But such a change would lead to enough other consequences that it have to be considered as a goal in itself.

61. See Hough, 'The Soviet system', loc. cit., pp.

62. This is not to say that institutional pluralism is the only model which should be used in the analysis of Soviet politics. Inkeles was right to urge the employment of a number of models depending upon one's purpose, and to reject the search for a single overarching model of Soviet society. Thus, in addition to 'institutional pluralism', the models of 'developing nation', 'industrial state', and even 'totalitarian system' have some utility in the analysis of Soviet politics and society. See Alex Inkeles, 'Models and Issues in the Analysis of Soviet Society', in Alex Inkeles, *Social Change in Soviet Russia* (Cambridge, Mass., 1968), pp. 419–36.

List of Abbreviations

CPSU   Communist Party of the Soviet Union

L.   Leningrad

M.   Moscow

MGU   Moskovskii Gosudarstvennyi Universitet (Moscow State University)

MOOP   Ministerstvo dliia Okhrany Obshchestvennogo Poriadka (Ministry for the Defense of the Social Order) – the policy ministry from 1958 until 1968, when the name was changed to Ministerstvo Vnutrennykh Del (Ministry of Internal Affairs)

MVD   Ministerstvo Vnutrennykh Del (Ministry of Internal Affairs)

Narkomiust   Narodnyi Kommissariat Iustitsii (People's Commissariat of Justice)

NKVD SSSR   Narodnyi Kommissariat Vnutrennykh Del (People's Commissariat of Internal Affairs)

Pravovedenie   *Izvestiia vysshykh uchebnykh zavedenii – pravovdedenie*

Procuracy Institute   All-Union Institute for the Study and Prevention of Crime (Vsesoiuznyi institut po izucheniiu prichin i razrabotke mer preduprezhdeniia prestupnosti), 1963 –

SGiP   *Sovetskoe gosudarstvo i pravo*

SIu   *Sovetskaia iustitsiia*

SZ   *Sotsialisticheskaia zakonnost*

TsK KPSS   Tsentralnyi komitet kommunisticheskoi partii Sovetskogo Soiuza (Central Committee of the Communist Party of the Soviet Union)

VNIISZ   Vsesoiuznyi nauchno-issledovatelskii institut sovetskogo zakonodatelstva (All-Union Institute of Soviet Legislation), 1963 – .

Sources Consulted

INTRODUCTORY NOTE

The sources used in the preparation of this study fall into six categories:

I   Interviews
II   Periodicals
III Legislative and official material
IV Soviet books and articles
V   Western books and articles
VI Unpublished material

During the course of an academic year in Moscow and a later three-week visit to the USSR we held a substantial number of interviews with Soviet criminologists and a smaller number of interviews with Soviet judicial officials of the middle and lower levels. These interviews constituted an important source of information about criminologists' private communications with political and ministerial leaderers and about some details of the various case studies. Naturally, both the quality of the interviews and the reliability of the informants varied; and we took these variations into account in using the information which issued from these sources. In addition, as a general principle, we did not use information acquired from a given interview, *unless it was corroborated by at least one other interview or a printed source*. Since we conducted a fairly large number of interviews over an extended period of time, it was possible to discuss most matters with a number of persons. Although the interviews were open-ended, there was a core of subjects and questions common to most of them.

Because the great majority of my informants are still alive and working at the same posts as they did in 1968–9 or 1973, I have kept their individual contributions anonymous. The footnotes in this study indicate only when interview material was used as a source, not which particular person(s) provided the information (the only exceptions are when the individual concerned has since died). However, I have provided below a full list of the persons with whom I had formal interviews or useful discussions.

In addition, during a three-month stay in England during the spring of 1968 I conducted a series of interviews with British criminologists and law enforcement officials, which supplied a source for the comparative observations made in Chapter 10. In citing these interviews I have followed the same procedure as with the Soviet ones.

In this list of sources we have included only books and articles used in preparing and documenting the study. A more general and annotated selection of the literature of Soviet criminology (through 1968) is found in a published bibliography: Peter H. Solomon, Jr., 'A Selected Bibliography of Soviet Criminology', *The Journal of Criminal Law, Criminology and Police Science*, LXI, No. 3 (1970), pp. 393–432. In the footnotes of this study we occasionally refer to the bibliography, particularly when we are indicating the existence of a body of literature upon whose contents we did not draw in preparing this study.

I INTERVIEWS

M. A. Alemaskin. Dotsent, psychology faculty, Moscow University. 6 April 1969.

M. M. Babaev. Senior research worker, general criminology sector, Procuracy Institute. 18 November 1968.

A. P. Baradanko. Head of the criminal investigation department, Leningrad City Procuracy. 20 February 1969.

A. D. Berenzon. Senior research worker, Procuracy supervision sector. 31 May 1974.

L. A. Bergerc. Junior research worker, legal research sector, Latvian State University. 25 February 1969.

G. B. Bochkareva. Dotsent, psychology faculty, Moscow University. 6 April 1969.

E. V. Boldyrev. Head of the criminal law sector, All-union Institute for Soviet Legislation. 11 December 1968.

N. D. Durmanov. Professor, criminal law kafedra, Moscow University. 31 May 1974.

A. K. Eistrakh. Head of the juvenile affairs department, Latvian Republic Procuracy. 25 February 1969.

I. M. Galperin. Senior research worker, criminal law sector, Procuracy Institute. 20 November 1968.

A. A. Gertsenzon. Head of the General Criminology Sector, Procuracy Institute. 29 November 1968.

N. P. Grabovskaia. Dotsent, criminal law kafedra, Leningrad State University. Member, Leningrad city juvenile affairs commission. 12 February 1969 and 15 February 1969.

A. M. Iakovlev. Head of the sector for foreign legislation, All-union Institute of Soviet Legislation, 1967–70; deputy director of same, 1971–. Formerly, senior research worker in general criminology at the Procuracy Institute. 11 December 1968 and 21 May 1974.

N. N. Ilina. Head of the juvenile affairs department, RSFSR Procuracy.

25 March 1969.

D. S. Karev. Professor, kafedra of criminal procedure, Moscow State University. 28 March 1969.

G. Ia. Kliava. Head of the legal research sector, Latvian State University. 24 February 1969.

L. A. Kliuchinskaia. Senior research worker, legal research sector, Latvian State University. Member, Latvian republican juvenile affairs commission. 24 February 1969 and 25 February 1969

L. G. Krakhmalnikh. Senior research worker, criminal law sector, All-union Institute of Soviet Legislation. 12 December 1968.

V. N. Kudriavtsev. Deputy director of the Procuracy Institute, 1963–73; Director of the Institute of State and Law, 1973–. 18 November 1969, 12 March 1969 and 28 May 1974.

N. F. Kuznetsova. Dotsent, criminal law kafedra, Moscow University. 25 September 1968, 8 December 1968 and frequent conversations.

N. S. Leikina. Dotsent, criminal law kafedra, Leningrad State University. 14 February 1969.

— Mikhlin. Head of the department of criminal investigation, Latvian Republic Procuracy. 25 February 1969.

G. M. Minkovskii. Head of the juvenile crime sector, Procuracy Institute. 26 November 1968 and occasional conversations.

A. S. Nikiforov. Senior research worker, general criminology sector, Procuracy Institute. 18 November 1968.

B. S. Nikiforov. Head of the criminal law sector, Procuracy Institute, 1963–8; head of the law sector, USA Institute, 1968. 27 November 1968 and 27 May 1974.

L. Osennova. Head of the juvenile affairs sector, Leningrad City Procuracy. 19 February 1969.

V. E. Pirozhkov. Dotsent, kafedra of corrective-labor law, MOOP Higher School. March 1969.

F. M. Reshetnikov. Dotsent, kafedra of criminal and civil law, Patrice Lumumba University (Moscow). 20 November 1968.

A. B. Sakharov. Professor, kafedra of criminal and civil law, Patrice Lumumba University (Moscow). 20 November 1968.

I. S. Samoshchenko. Deputy director of the All-union Institute for Soviet Legislation. 25 April 1969.

I. V. Shmarov. Senior research worker, kafedra of corrective-labor law, MOOP Higher School. 4 January 1969.

A. Iu. Shtromas. Senior research worker, sector for foreign legislation, All-union Institute of Soviet Legislation (to 1972). 11 December 1968, 24 April 1969 and 18 May 1974 (in England).

V. P. Shupilov. Junior research worker, Procuracy Institute, 1967–70; Head of the sector on foreign criminology at same, 1971–. 27 April 1969 and 22 May 1974.

K. G. Skvortsov. Head of the Procuracy supervision sector, Procuracy

Institute, 1973–. 31 May 1974.

N. A. Struchkov. Head, kafedra of corrective-labor law, MOOP Higher School. 4 January 1969.

V. S. Tadevosian. Senior research worker, civil law sector, Institute of State and Law. Formerly head of the department of juvenile affairs in the USSR Procuracy (1935–52). 31 May 1974.

V. G. Tanasevich. Head of the sector for theft of socialist property, Procuracy Institute. 19 November 1968.

Iu. M. Tkachevskii. Dotsent, criminal law kafedra, Moscow State University. Occasional conversations.

B. S. Utevskii. Retired professor of corrective-labor law and criminology. Last post in the corrective-law kafedra, MOOP Higher School. 20 December 1968 and 5 February 1969.

V. P. Vlasov. Senior research worker, sector for crimes against the person, Procuracy Institute. 5 May 1969.

G. Zabrianskii. Aspirant in criminology, Procuracy Institute. 27 September 1968.

A. G. Zlobin. Junior research worker, criminal law sector, Procuracy Institute. 20 November 1968.

V. K. Zvirbul. Head of the Procuracy supervision sector, Procuracy Institute (to 1973). 12 May 1969.

Charlotte Banks. Research coordinator for the Home Office. 25 June 1968.

A. J. E. Brennan. Assistant Secretary and Head of a division of the criminal department, Home Office. 2 July 1968.

Captain Carrington. Principal in the criminal department, Home Office. 19 July 1968.

A. Corben. Principal in the criminal department, Home Office, and Secretary to the Advisory Council on the Penal System. 15 July 1968.

Evelyn Gibson. Chief Statistician of the Home Office. 17 July 1968.

F. L. T. Graham-Harrison. Deputy Under-Secretary, Home Office. 19 July 1968.

W. H. Hammond. Deputy director, Home Office Research Unit. 24 June 1968.

A. E. Hewins. Principal in the criminal department, Home Office. 15 July 1968.

Roger Hood. Research Director, Institute of Criminology, Cambridge University. 23 May 1968.

T. S. Lodge. Director, Home Office Research Unit. 24 June 1968.

Derek McClintock. Research Director, Institute of Criminology, Cambridge University. 21 June 1968.

Richard Sparks. Research Director, Institute of Criminology, Cambridge University. 21 June 1968.

II PERIODICALS

Biulleten verkhovnogo suda RSFSR (1963–70).
Biulleten verkhovnogo suda SSSR (1956–70).
Informatsionnoe pismo [Vsesoiuznogo instituta po izucheniiu prichin i razrabotke mer preduprezhdeniia prestupnosti] (1963–9). Beginning with number 13 (1968), the title was changed to *Nauchnaia informatsiia po borbe s prestupnostiu (Informatsionnoe pismo)*.
Informatsionnyi Biulleten VIIuN [Vsesoiuznogo Instituta Iuridicheskikh Nauk] (1937–9).
Izvestiia (1964–70).
Izvestiia vysshikh uchebnykh zavedenii. Pravovedenie (Leningrad, 1960–1970). Abbreviated as *Pravovedenie*.
K novoi zhizne (1962–9).
Kommunist (1953–70).
Literaturnaia gazeta (1964–70).
Pravda (1964–70).
Sobranie postanovlenii i rasporiazhenii Soveta Ministrov Soiuza SSR (1963–70).
Sotsialisticheskaia zakonnost (1934–75). Abbreviated as *SZ*.
Sovetskaia iustitsiia (1935–40; 1957–72).
Sovetskaia kriminalistika (1957–63). The first eight issues (to 1959) were called *Sovetskaia kriminalistika na sluzhbe sledstviia*.
Sovetskoe gosudarstvo i pravo (1932–75). Abbreviated as *SGiP*.
Trudy vysshei shkoly Ministerva dlia okhrany obshchestvennogo poriadka (1958–69). Abbreviated as *Trudy vysshei shkoly MOOP*.
Uchenye zapiski Vsesoiuznogo nauchno-issledovatelskogo instituta sovestskogo zakonodatelstva (1963–73). Abbreviated as *Uchenye zapiski VNIISZ*.
Vedomosti verkhovnogo soveta RSFSR (1956–72).
Vedomosti verkhovnogo soveta SSSR (1956–72).
Vestnik Moskovoskogo Gosudarstvennogo Universiteta. Seriia prava (1959–72). Abbreviated as *Vestnik MGU*.
Voprosy borby s prestupnostiu (1963–70). The first four issues were called *Voprosy preduprezhdeniia prestupnostiu*.

III LEGISLATIVE AND OFFICIAL MATERIAL

Criminal Justice Act 1967. Elizabeth II 1967, chapter 80. London, 1968.
'1961 Programme of the Communist Party of the Soviet Union', *Soviet Communism Programs and Rules*. ed. by Jan Triska. San Francisco, 1962, pp. 23–129.
'O borbe s prestupnostiu.' Postanovlenie TsK KPSS i Soveta Ministrov ot 23 iiuliia 1966. No open source. For description of contents, see 'V TsK KPSS'.
'O meropriatiiakh po rasshireniiu obucheniia i ustroistva na rabotu v

narodnoe khoziaistvo molodezhi, okanchivaiushchei shkoly v 1966 godu.' Postanovlenie TsK KPSS i Soveta Ministrov SSSR ot 2 febraliia, 1966, No. 83. Abridged text. *Spravochnik profoiuznogo rabotnika 1967*. M., 1967, pp. 240–4.

'O metodicheskom sovete', Prikaz Generalnogo prokurora SSSR, ot 27 iiulia 1960, No. 59. *Sbornik deistvuiushchikh prikazov i instruktsii generalnogo prokurora SSSR*. M., 1966.

'O nekotorykh voprosakh, voznikshkikh v sudebnoi proktike po primeneniiu zakonodatelstva ob uslovno-dosrochnogo osvobozhdeniia ot nakazaniia i zamene nakazaniia bolee miagkim.' Postanovlenie Plenuma verkhovnogo suda ot 13 dekabria 1963 g., No. 19. *Sbornik Postanovlenii Plenuma Verkhovnogo Suda SSSR 1924–1970*. M., 1970, pp. 372–6.

'O nomenklaturakh dolzhnostnei rukovodiashchikh rabotnikov organov prokuratury, naznachaemykh i osvobozhdaemykh generalnym prokurorom SSSR.' Prikaz Generalnogo Prokurora SSSR ot 31 iiulia 1965, No. 66. *Sbornik deistvuiushchikh prikazov i instruktsii generalnogo prokurora SSSR*. M., 1966.

'O praktike primenenii Ukaza Prezidiuma Verkhovnogo Soveta SSSR ot 26 iiulia 1966 g. "Ob usilenii otvetstvennosti za khuliganstvo"' Postanovlenie Prezidiuma Verkhovnogo Soveta SSSR ot 13 oktiabria, 1967, No. 577. *Vedomosti Verkhovnogo Soveta SSSR* (1967, No. 43), pp. 666–8.

'O prinuditelnom lechenii i trudovom perevospitanii zlostnykh pianits (alkogolikov).' Ukaz Prezidiuma Verkhovnogo Soveta RSFSR No. 333 ot 8 aprelia 1967. *Vedomosti Verkhovnogo Soveta RSFSR* (1967, No. 15), pp. 333–4.

'O sostave nauchno-konsultativnogo soveta pri Verkhovnom Sude SSSR.' Postanovlenie verkhovnogo suda SSSR ot 12 dekabriia, 1967. *Biulleten verkhovnogo suda* (1968, No. 1).

'O sudebnoi praktike po delam o khuliganstve.' Postanovlenie Plenuma ot 22 dekabriia, 1964, No. 17. *Sbornik Postanovlenii Plenuma Verkhovnogo Suda SSSR 1924–1970*. M., 1970, pp. 486–90.

'O sudebnoi praktike po uslovno-dosrochnomu osvobozhdeniiu osuzhdennykh ot nakazaniia', Postanovlenie Plenuma Verkhovnogo Suda ot 4 marta 1961. *Sbornik Postanovlenii Plenuma Verkhovnogo Suda SSSR 1924–1970*. M., 1970, pp. 362–76.

'O vvedenii uslovno-dosrochnogo osvobozhdeniia iz mest zakliucheniia.' Ukaz Prezidiuma Verkhovnogo Soveta SSSR ot 14 iiuniia 1954 g., *Sbornik zakonov SSSR i ukazov Prezidiuma Verkovnogo Soveta SSSR*. M., 1959, pp. 548–9.

'O vnesenii izmenenii i dopolnenii v Osnovakh ugolovnogo zakonodatelstva Soiuza SSSR i soiuznykh respublik.' *Izvestiia*. 12 July 1969, pp. 4–5.

'O vnesenii izmenenii i dopolnenii v stati 22 i 44 Osnov ugolovnogo zakonodatelstva.' Ukaz Prezidiuma Verkhovnogo Soveta SSSR ot 4 apreliia 1962. *Vedomosti Verkhovnogo Soveta SSSR* (1961, No. 19), pp. 408–9.

'O vypolnenii sudami postanovlenii Plenuma Verkhovnogo Suda ot 4 marta 1961 g. i. ot 18 dekabria 1963, g. o praktike uslovno-dosrochnogo osvobozhdeniia osuzhdennykh ot nakzaniia.' Postanovlenie Plenuma Verkhovnogo Suda ot 11 oktiabriia 1965, No. 7. *Sbornik Postanovlenii Plenuma Verkhovnogo Suda SSSR 1924–1970.* M., 1970, pp. 376–9.

'Ob administrativnom nadzore organov militsii za litsami, osvobozhdennymi iz mest lishenii svobody.' Ukaz Prezidiuma Verkhovnogo Soveta SSSR ot 26 iiulia 1966. *Vedomosti Verkhovnogo Soveta SSSR* (1966, no. 30).

'Ob amnestii.' Ukaz Prezidiuma Verkhovnogo Soveta ot 27 marta 1953 g. *Sbornik zakonov SSSR i Ukazov Prezidiuma Verkhovnogo Soveta SSSR, 1938–1967.* Three volumes. M., 1968–1970. ii (1968), pp. 627–8.

'Ob otnesenii k vedeniiu soiuznykh respublik zakonodatelstva ob ustroistve sudov soiuznykh respublik, priniatiia grazhdanskogo, ugolovnogo i protsessualnykh kodeksov.' Zakon priniatii Verkhovnom Sovetom SSSR 11 fevralia 1957 g. *Vedomosti Verkhovnogo Soveta SSSR* (1957, No. 4), p. 63.

'Ob ugolovnoi otvetsvennosti za khishchenie gosudarstvennogo i obshchestvenogo imushchestva.' Ukaz Prezidiuma Verkhovnogo Soveta SSSR ot 4 iiunia 1947 g. *Sbornik dokumentov po istorii ugolovnogo zakonodatelstva SSSR i RSFSR, 1917–1952 gg.* Edited by I. T. Goliakov. M., 1953, pp. 430–1. Also in *Vedomosti Verkhovnogo Soveta SSSR* (1947, No. 19).

'Ob usilenii borby s osobo opnasnymi prestupleniami.' Ukaz Prezidiuma Verkhovnogo Soveta SSSR ot 5 maia 1964. *Vedomosti Verkhovnogo Soveta SSSR* (1961, No. 19), pp. 475–6.

'Ob usilenii borby s pianstvom i o vedenii poriadka v torgovle krepkimi spirtnymi napitkami.' Postanovlenie TsK KPSS i Soveta Ministrov ot 15 dekabriia, 1968. *Spravochnik partiinogo rabotnika.* No. 2 (M., 1959).

'Ob usilenii okhrany lichnoi sobstvennosti grahdan.' Ukaz Prezidiuma Verkhovnogo Soveta SSSR ot 4 iuniia 1947 g. *Sbornik dokumentov po istorii ugolovnogo zaknodatelstva SSSR i RSFSR, 1917–1952 gg.* Edited by I. T. Goliakov. M., 1953, p. 431. Also in *Vedomosti Verkhovnogo Soveta SSSR* (1947, No. 19).

'Ob usilenii otvetstvennost za khuliganstvo.' Ukaz Prezidiuma Verkhovnogo Soveta SSSR ot 26 iiulia 1966. *Biulleten Verkhovnogo Suda SSSR* (1966, No. 4), pp. 7–11.

'Ob uprazdnenii Ministerstva iustitsii RSFSR i obrazovanie Iuridicheskoi komissii Soveta Ministrov RSFSR.' *Sovetskaia iustitsiia* (1963, No. 10).

'Ob ustranenii nedostatkov v rabote organov prokuratury po preduprezhdeniiu prestupnosti i narushenii zakonnosti.' Ukazanie Zam. Gen. Prok. SSSR ot 31 maia 1965 g., No. 3/N–76, *Sbornik deistvuiushchikh prikazov i instruktsii generalnogo prokurora SSSR.* M., 1966.

'Ob utverzhdenii sostava nauchno-konsultativnogo soveta pri Verkhovnomu Sude RSFSR.' Postanovlenie No. 39 Plenuma verkhovnogo suda RSFSR ot 24 oktiabriia, 1967. *Biulleten Verkhovnogo Suda RSFSR* (1967, No. 12).

'Osnovnye nachala ugolovnogo zakonodatelstva Soiuza SSSR i soiuznykh republik (proekt).' *SGiP* (1958, No. 6), pp. 3−12; *SZ* (1958, No. 6), pp. 7−16; and *Sovety deputatov trudiashchikhsia* (1958, No. 6), pp. 19−27.

'Osnovy ugolovnogo zakonodatelstva Soiuza SSSR i Soiuznykh Respublik.' *Spravochnik partiinogo rabotnika*. II (1959), pp. 600−18.

'Osnovy ispravitelno-trudovogo zakonodatelstva Soiuza SSR i soiuznykh respublik.' *Sbornik zakonov SSSR i Ukazov Prezidiuma Verkhovnogo Soveta SSSR Tom 3: 1968−1970*. M., 1971.

'Osnovy ugolovnogo zakonodatelstva Soiuza SSR i soiuznykh respublik.' *Sbornik zakonov SSSR i ukazov Prezidiuma Verkhovnogo Soveta SSSR 1938−1967*. Two volumes. M., 1968. Volume 2, pp. 428−45.

'Osnovy ugolovnogo zakonodatelstva Soiuza SSR i soiuznykh respublik.' *Sbornik zakonov SSSR i ukazov Prezidiuma Verkhovnogo Soveta SSSR. Tom 3, 1968−1970*. M., 1971, pp. 330−53.

'Polozhenie o komissiakh po delam nesovershennoletnikh.' Utverzhdeno Ukazom Presidiuma Verkhovnogo Soveta RSFSR ot 3 iiunia 1967 g. M., 1968.

'Polozhenie o nabliudatelnykh komissiakh pri ispolkomakh raionnykh i gorodskikh sovetov deputatov trudiashchikhsia RSFSR.' Utverzhdeno Ukazom Prezidiuma Verkhovnogo Soveta RSFSR ot 30 sentiabria 1965. *Vedomosti Verkhovnogo Soveta RSFSR* (1965, No. 40), pp. 803−7.

'Polozhenie o prokurorskom nadzore.' Utverzhdeno 24 maia, 1955. *Sbornik zakonov SSSR i Ukazov Prezidiuma Verkhovnogo Soveta SSSR, 1938−1967*. Three volumes; M., 1968−70. II (1968), pp. 573−85.

'Polozhenie o trudovykh koloniiakh dlia nesoversehnnoletnikh Ministerstva Okhrany Obshchestvennogo Poriadka SSSR.' *Sbornik Zakonov SSSR i Ukazov Prezidiuma Verkhovnogo Soveta SSSR Tom 3: 1968−1969*. M., 1971, pp. 395−414.

'Polozhenie o Vsesoiuznom institute po izucheniiu prichin i razrabotke mer preduprezhdenii prestupnosti.' Utverzhdeno Gen. Prok. SSSR i Pred. Verkhovnogo Suda SSR, 15 iunia 1963. *Sbornik deistvuiushchikh prikazov i instruktsii generalnogo prokurora SSSR*. M., 1966.

'Polozhenie ob obshchestvennykh vospitateliakh nesovershennoletnikh.' Utverzhdeno Ukazom Prezidiuma Verkhovnogo Soveta RSFSR ot 13 dekabriia 1967 g. M., 1968.

'Postanovlenie obshchego sobrannia akademii nauk SSSR.' *Vestnik akademii nauk* (1962, No. 12).

'Postanovlenie soveshchaniia Ministra iustitsii SSSR, Generalnogo Prokurora SSSR i Predsedatelia Verkhovnogo Suda SSSR po povodu stati prof. N. Durmanova, "Nakazuemost khishchenii gosudarstvennogo i obshchestvennogo imushchestva, krazhi lichnogo imushchestva i raz-

boia po ukazam ot 4 iunia 1947 g. "pomeshchannoi v zhurnale, *Sotsialisticheskaia zakonnost* No. 10 za 1947 g.', *SZ* (1947, No. 11), p. 19.
Ugolovnyi kodeks RSFSR. Ofitsialnyi tekst s prilozheniem postateino-sistematizirovannykh materialov. M., 1962; and M., 1968.
Ugolovnyi kodeks SSSR. Proekt. M.: Vsesoiuznyi institut iuridicheskikh nauk, 1939.
'V TsK KPSS, Prezidiume verkhovnogo soveta SSSR i soveta Ministrov SSSR.' *Izvestiia.* 27 July 1966, p. 2.

IV SOVIET BOOKS AND ARTICLES

(Articles which appeared in newspapers or journals cited in section II are listed here only if (1) they are cited more than once in the text; or (2) the authors are important actors in our story.)
Afanasev, V. G. *Nauchnoe upravlenie obshchestvom.* M., 1965.
Alekseev, N. 'Khotite, zhaluites.' *Izvestiia.* 24 April 1966, p. 6.
Alkogolizm-put k prestupleniiu. Edited by A. A. Gertsenzon. M., 1966.
Anashkin, G. Z. 'Diagnoz prostupka.' *Izvestiia.* 4 March 1965, p. 3.
——. 'Lichnost, obstoiatelstvo i otvetstvennost.' *Izvestiia.* 12 June 1965, p. 2.
Boldyrev, E. V. *Mery preduprezhdeniia pravonarushenii nesovershennoletnikh v SSSR.* M., 1964.
——. 'Nekotorye voprosy ugolovnogo ucheta i statisticheskoi otchetnosti.' *Sovetskaia kriminalistika na sluzhbe sledstviia.* No. 9 (1958).
——., Ivanov, V. I., and Pashkevich, P. F. 'Voprosy ugolovnogo prava i ugolovnogo protsessa v novom zakonodatelstve ob otvestvennosti za khuliganstvo.' *Uchenye zapiski VNIISZ.* Vypusk 12 (M., 1968), pp. 36–53.
——., and Kuznetsova, E. V. 'V sektore po izucheniiu i preduprezhdeniiu prestupnosti.' *SGiP* (1961, No. 11), pp. 125–8.
Borodin, S. 'Vsesoiuznyi nauchno-issledovatelskii institut okhrany obshchestvennogo proiadka.' *SZ* (1965, No. 12).
Chistiakov, O. I. 'Organizatsiia kodifikatsionnykh rabot v pervye gody sovetskoi vlasti (1917–23)', *SGiP* (1956, No. 5), pp. 10–22.
Deputaty verkhovnogo soveta SSSR Sedmoi sozyv. M., 1966.
'Disput k voprosu ob izuchenii prestupnosti v SSSR.' *Revoliutsiia prava* (1929, No. 3), pp. 47–78.
Durmanov, N. D. 'Nakazuemost khishcheniia khishcheniia gosudarstven-nogo i obshchestvennogo imushchestva, krazhi lichnogo imushchestva i razboia po ukazam ot 4 iunia 1947 g.' *SZ* (1947, No. 10), pp. 3–8.
——. *Osvobozhdenie ot nakazaniia po sovetskomu pravu.* M., 1957.
'Effektivnost borby s khuliganstvom i dinamika nekotorykh tiazhkikh prestuplenii.' *VNIIOOP Informatsionnye soobshcheniia.* Vypusk 6 (M., 1966).

Effektivnost ugolovnopravovykh mer borby s prestupnostiu. Edited by B. S. Nikiforov. M., 1968.

Efimov, M. A. 'Nekotorye voprosy uslovno-dosrochnogo i dosrochnogo osvobozhdeniia.' *Provovedenie* (1958, No. 1), pp. 84–94.

Entsiklopedicheskii slovar pravovykh znanii. Sovetskoe pravo. Edited by S. N. Bratus *et al.* M., 1965.

'Evsei Gustavovich Shirvindt.' *SGiP* (1958, No. 12), p. 130.

Galperin, I. M. 'Ob ugolovnoi otvetstvennosti retsidivistov v svete nekotorykh kriminologicheskikh pokazatelei effektivnosti borby s retsidivnoi prestupnostiu.' *Effektivnost ugolovnopravovykh mer borby s prestupnostiu.* Edited by B. S. Nikiforov. M., 1968, pp. 214–48.

——. 'Priznanie osobo opasnym retsidivistom po st. 23 Osnov ugolovnogo zakonodatelstva soiuza SSR i soiuznykh respublik.' *SIu* (1969, No. 11), pp. 16–17.

Gedvilas, M. A., and Novikov, S. G. 'O deiatelnosti komissii zakonodatelnykh predpolozhenii Verkhovnogo Soveta SSSR.' *SGiP* (1957, No. 9), pp. 12–24.

Gertsenzon, A. A. 'Osnovnye printsipy i polozheniia proekta ugolovnogo kodeksa SSSR.' *Trudy pervoi nauchnoi sessii Vsesoiuznogo instituta iuridicheskikh nauk, 27 ianvariia-3 fevralia 1939.* Edited by I. T. Goliakov. M., 1940.

——. *Predmet, metod, i sistema sovetksoi kriminologii.* M., 1962.

——. *Prestupnost i alkogolizm v RSFSR.* M., 1930.

——. 'Puti razvitiia sovetskoi nauki ugolovnogo prava.' *SGiP* (1947, No. 11), pp. 73–86.

——. 'Sovremennaia burzhuaznaia kriminologiia.' *SGiP* (1963, No. 2), pp. 115–23.

——. 'Takoi zakon nuzhen.' *Izvestiia.* 6 February 1966, p. 3.

——. *Ugolovnoe pravo i sotsiologiia (Problemy ugolovnogo prava i ugolovnoi politiki).* M., 1970.

——. *Vvedenie s sovetskuiu kriminologiiu.* M., 1965.

Goliakov, I. T. 'K proektu ugolovnogo kodeksa RSFSR.' *SIu* (1957, No. 2), pp. 30–3.

——. 'Ob usilenii okhrany gosudarstvennoi, obshchestvennoi i lichnoi sobstvennosti.' *SGiP* (1947, No. 7), pp. 1–9.

——. 'Osnovnye problemy nauki sovetskogo sotsialisticheskogo prava.' *Trudy pervoi nauchnoi sessii Vsesoiuznogo instituta iuridicheskikh nauk, 27 ianvariia-3 fevralia 1939.* Edited by I. T. Goliakov. M., 1940.

——. 'Protiv izvrashchenii smysla ukazov ot 4 iunia 1947 g.' *SZ* (1947, No. 11), pp. 20–3.

——. 'Usilenie okhrany gosudarstvennoi, obshchestvennoi i lichnoi sobstvennosti.' *SZ* (1947, No. 9), pp. 4–7.

Grebennikov, G., and Rasparin, K. 'Sotsialisticheskaia ditsiplina nezyblema.' *Pravda.* 25 April 1966, p. 4.

Iakovlev, A. M. *Borba s retsidivnoi prestupnostiu.* M., 1964.

——. 'Naznachenie i ispolnenie nakazaniia retsidivistam.' *SGiP* (1959,

No. 9), pp. 89–94.
——. *Prestupnost i sotsialnaia psikhologiia.* M., 1971.
——. 'Sovokupnost prestuplenii, povtornost i retsidiv po sovetskomu ugolovnomy pravu.' *SGiP* (1956, No. 10), pp. 48–54.
Ilichev, L. I. 'Nauchnaia osnova rukovodstva razvitiem obshchestva Nekotorye problemy razvitiia obshchestvennykh nauk.' *Stroitelstvo kommunizma i obshchestvennye nauki. Materialy sessii obshchego sobraniia Akademii Nauk SSSR, 19–20 oktiabriia, 1962.* M., 1962.
'Informatsionnoe pismo No. 21/31 Zam. Prok. Soiuza SSSR o rabote instituta obshchestvennykh vospitatelei nesovershennoletnikh.' 16 May 1968. *Biulleten po obmenu opytom raboty po delam nesovershennoletnikh.* No. 7 (Riga, July 1968), p. 45.
'Iuridicheskaia nauka v usloviiakh kommunisticheskogo stroitelstve.' *Kommunist* (1963, No. 16), pp. 27–35.
Ivanov, V. I. 'Razvitie kodifikatsii ugolovnogo zakonodatelstva.' *Razvitie kodifikatsii sovetskogo zakonodatelstva.* M., 1968, pp. 183–208.
Kalniychev, F. I. *Prezidium verkhovnogo soveta SSSR.* M., 1969.
Karpets, I. I. 'Ob effektivnosti ugolovnogo nakazaniia.' *SZ* (1966, No. 5), pp. 19–23.
——. 'O nekotorykh voprosakh metodologii v ugolovnom prave i kriminologicheskikh issledovanii.' *SGiP* (1964, No. 4), pp. 91–101.
——. *Problema prestupnosti.* M., 1969.
Kasatkin, Iu. P. 'Ocherk istorii izuchenii prestupnosti v SSSR.' *Problemy iskoreneniia prestupnosti.* Edited by V. N. Kudriavtsev. M., 1965, pp. 187–225.
Khrushchev, N. S. 'Secret Speech Concerning the Cult of the Individual.' Delivered at the Twentieth Congress of the CPSU, 25 February 1956. *The Anti-Stalin Campaign and International Communism.* Edited by the Russian Institute of Columbia University. N. Y., 1956, pp. 1–90.
Kliuchinskaia, L. A. *Komissii po delam nesovershennoletnikh Nauchno-prakticheskii kommentarii k polozheniiu o komissiakh po delam nesovershennoletnikh i po ikh rabotu.* Riga, 1970.
——. *Nesovershennoletnie i ugolovnyi zakon.* Riga, 1967.
Kriminologiia. M., 1968.
Kudriavtsev, V. N. 'Osnovnye napravleniia v kriminologicheskikh issledovanii.' *Problemy nauchnogo kommunizma.* Vyp. 2 (M., 1968), pp. 223–35.
——. 'Problemy nakazaniia, ne sviazannogo s lisheniem svobody.' *SIu* (1968, No. 1).
——. *Prichinnost v kriminologii.* M., 1968.
——. 'Razvivat nauku sovetskogo ugolovnogo prava.' *SZ* (1956, No. 1), pp. 26–31.
——. 'Ukrepliat sviaz nauki i praktiki.' *Biulleten verkhovnogo suda SSSR* (1963, No. 6), pp. 43–5.
——. 'Zakon i sotsiologiia.' *Izvestiia.* 25 November 1965, p. 2.
Kurinov, V. A. *Ugolovnaia otvetstvennost za khishchenie gosudarstvennogo i*

obshchestvennogo imushchestva. M., 1954.

Kuznetsova, N. F. *Prestuplenie i prestupnost*. M., 1969.

Liass, N. V. 'Voprosy profilaktiki prestupnosti v SSSR.' *SGiP* (1960, No. 7), pp. 182–6.

Liubavin, A., and Remenson, A. L. 'Dosrochnoe osvobozhdenie v poriadke zacheta rabochikh dnei.' *SZ* (1957, No. 6), pp. 14–19.

Lukianov, Iu. 'Ne davat spiski khuliganam.' *Leningradskaia Pravda*. 29 May 1966.

Markov, N. V. *Nauchno-tekhnicheskaia revoliutsiia: Analiz, perspektivy, posledstviia*. M., 1971.

Melnikova, E. V. 'Koordinatsiia nauchnykh rabot po problemam borby s prestupnostiu nesovershennoletnikh.' *Informatsionnoe pismo* [Instituta]. No. 2 (M., 1965).

Mendelson, G. A., and Tkachevskii, Iu. M. *Alkogolizm i prestupnost*. M., 1959.

Metodicheskoe pismo o polozhitelnom opyte raboty Prokuratury goroda Leningrada po borbe s prestupnostiu nesovershennoletnikh. M., 1966.

Mikhlin A. S., Guskov, V. I., Kirillova, I. A., Melnikova, Iu. B., and Mikhailov, V. T. 'Effektivnost ispravitlenykh rabot kak mery nakazaniia.' *Effektivnost ugolovnopravovykh mer borby s prestupnostiu*. Edited by B. S. Nikiforov. M., 1968, pp. 90–163.

—— et al. 'Ob effektivnosti ispravitlenykh rabot kak mery ugolovnogo nakzaniia.' *SZ* (1966, No. 1).

Minkovskii, G. M. 'Nekotorye voprosy izuchenii prestupnosti nesovershennoletnikh.' *Problemy prestupnosti nesovershennoletnikh*. Edited by V. N. Kudriavtsev. M., 1965, pp. 24–50.

—— 'Ob issledovanii prestupnosti nesovershennoletnikh.' *Problemy nauchnogo kommunizma*. Vyp. 2 (M., 1968), pp. 246–269.

—— and Melnikova, E. V. 'Sheftstvo nad trudnymi podrostkami – put k preduprezhdeniiu prestupnosti nesovershennoletnikh.' *SZ* (1966, No. 1), pp. 25–29.

—— and Pronina, V. 'Sudba podrostka.' *Izvestiia*. August 19, 1965, p. 3.

Mironov, N. R. 'O nekotorykh voprosakh preduprezhdeniia prestupnosti i drugikh antiobshchestvennykh iavlenii i borby s nimi v sovremennykh usloviiakh.' *SGiP* (1961, No. 5), pp. 3–18.

——. *Ukreplenie zakonnosti i pravoporiadka programnaia zadacha partii*. Second edition. M., 1969. Original edition was published in 1964.

Na strazhe sovetskikh zakonov. Edited by R. A. Rudenko. M., 1972.

Nauchnaia konferentsiia 'Problemy sovetskogo ugolovnogo prava v period razvernutogo stroitelstva kommunizma' (14–17 maia 1963 g.). L., 1963.

Nikiforov, B. S. 'O retsidive i sudimosti.' *SGiP* (1957, No. 5), pp. 100–5.

'Novoe ugolovnoe zakonodatelstvo ob usilenii borby s khuliganstvom.' *Pravovedenie* (1967, No. 2), pp. 111–15.

O merakh po usilenii borby s narusheniiami obshchestvennogo poriadka. M., 1967.

'O zadachakh instituta sovetskogo zakonodatelstva.' *Uchenye zapiski*

VNIISZ. Vyp. 2 (1964).

Organizatsiia suda i prokuratury v SSSR. Edited by B. A. Galkin. M., 1967.

Orlov, V. S. *Podrostok i prestuplenie.* M., 1969.

Ostroumov, S. S. 'O sudebnoi statistike.' *SGiP* (1957, No. 1), pp. 60–8.

——. *Prestupnost i ee prichny v dorevoliutsionnoi Rossii.* M., 1960.

'Otchet Vsesoiuznogo instituta po izucheniiu prichin i razrabotke mer preduprezhdenii prestupnosti o vypolnenii nauchnykh issledovanii za 1965 god.' *Informatsionnoe pismo* [Instituta], No. 4 (1966), section two.

'Otchet Vsesoiuznogo instituta po izucheniiu prichin i razrabotke mer preduprezhdenii prestupnosti o vypolnenii nauchnykh issledovanii za 1966 god.' *Informatsionnoe pismo* [Instituta]. No. 9 (1967).

'Partorganizatsiia NII.' *Partiinaia zhizn* (1963, No. 16).

Perlov, I. D. 'Nekotorye voprosy dalneishego sovershenstvovaniia zakonodatelstva i praktiki ego primeneniia v oblasti borby s prestupleniiami nesovershennoletnikh', *Borby s prestupnostiu nesovershennolennikh.* M., 1965.

Pigolkin, A. S. *Podgotovka proektov normativnykh aktov.* M., 1968.

Piontkovskii, A. A. 'Osnovnye voprosy proekta ugolovnogo kodeksa.' *SZ* (1954, No. 1), pp. 25–38.

——. *Stalinskaia konstitutsiia i proekt ugolovnogo kodeksa SSSR.* M., 1947.

Planirovanie sotsialnykh protsessov na predpriiatii. L., 1969.

'Povysit rol obshchestvennykh nauk v stroitelstve kommunizma.' *Kommunist* (1961, No. 10), pp. 31–41.

'Preniia po dokladu A. A. Gertsenzona i sodokladi B. S. Utevskogo i V. S. Trakhtereva.' *Trudy pervoi nauchnoi sessii Vsesoiuznogo instituta iuridicheskokh nauk,* 27 ianvariia-3 fevralia 1939. Edited by I. T. Goliakov. M., 1940, pp. 170–94.

Pronina, V. S. *Kommentarii k polozheniiam o komissiakh po delam nesovershennoletnikh.* M., 1968.

——. 'Nekotorye voprosy organizatsii i deiatelnosti komissii po delam nesovershennoletnikh.' *Preduprezhdenie prestupnosti nesovershennoletnikh.* Edited by V. N. Kudriavtsev. M., 1965, pp. 116–37.

——. 'Rol sovetskoi obshchestvennosti v borbe s pravonarusheniiami nesovershennoletnikh.' *SGiP* (1959, No. 10), pp. 89–97.

Rabota raionnogo (gorodskogo) prokurora po preduprezhdeniiu pravonarushenii (nauchno-prakticheskaia konferentsiia kursov prokuratury SSSR). Kharkov, 1968.

Rabota raionnogo prokurora po borbe s prestupnostiu. Edited by A. S. Pankratov. M., 1965.

'Rabotu po kodifikatsii sovetskogo zakonodatelstva – na uroven novykh zadach.' *SZ* (1957, No. 5), pp. 1–5.

Rachkov, P. A. *Rol nauki v stroitelstve kommunizma.* M., 1969.

Romashkin, P. S. 'Osnovnye problemy kodifikatsii sovetskogo ugolovnogo zakonodatelstva.' *SGiP* (1957, No. 5), pp. 71–84.

Sakharov, A. B. *O lichnosti prestupnika i prichinakh prestupnosti v SSSR.* M., 1961.

——. *Pravonarushenie podrostka i zakon.* M., 1967.

Sergeev, T. I., and Pomchalov, L. F. 'Effektivnost kratkosrochnogo lisheniia svobody.' *Effektivnost ugolovnopravovykh mer borby s prestupnostiu.* Edited by B. S. Nikiforov. M., 1968, pp. 20–89.

Shargorodskii, M. D. 'Analogiia v istorii ugolovnogo prava i v sovetskom ugolovnom prave.' *SZ* (1938, No. 7), pp. 50–80.

——. 'Nekotorye zadachi sovetskoi pravovoi nauki v nastoiashchee vremia.' *Uchenye zapiski LGU.* No. 187 (Seriia iuridicheskikh nauk, vyp. 6; 1955), pp. 3–30.

——., and Alekseev, N. S. 'Aktualnye problemy ugolovnogo prava.' *Uchenye zapiski LGU.* No. 182 (Seriia iuridicheskikh nauk, vyp. 5; 1954), pp. 154–96.

Shchelokov, N. A. 'Glavnoe – preduprezhdenie pravonarushenii.' *SZ* (1967, No. 8), pp. 7–16.

——. 'Pomogat cheloveku stat luchshe.' *Pravda.* 31 July 1967, p. 3.

——. 'Problemy borby s prestupnostiu nesovershennoletnikh i zadachi organov okhrany obshchestvennogo poriadka SSSR.' *Problemy borby s prestupnostiu nesovershennoletnikh i zadachi organov okhrany obshchestvennogo poriadka SSSR (Materialy nauchno-prakticheskoi konferentsii.* M., 1967, pp. 1–21.

Sheinin, Kh. 'Nauchno-konsultativnye sovety pri sudakh.' *SZ* (1968, No. 2), pp. 46–8.

'Shestdesiatletie A. A. Gertsenzona.' *SGiP* (1962, No. 4), p. 170.

Shirvindt, E. G. 'K istorii voprosa ob izuchenii prestupnosti i mer borby s nei.' *SGiP* (1958, No. 5), pp. 137–42.

Shliapochnikov, A. S. *Nekotorye aktualnye problemy sovetskogo ugolovnogo prava i kriminologii (Doklad o opublikovannykh na etu temu rabotakh predstavlennykh na soiskanie uchenoi stepeni doktora iuridicheskikh nauk).* M., 1966.

——. 'Nekotorye voprosy borby s prestupnostiu.' *SIu* (1957, No. 3), pp. 38–43.

——. 'Pamiati vydaiushchego sovetskogo kriminologa.' *Voprosy borby s prestupnostiu.* Vyp. 13 (1971), pp. 178–88.

Sovetskaia kriminologiia. M., 1966.

Sovetskoe ugolovnoe pravo. Bibliografiia 1917–1960. Compiled by F. M. Asknazii and N. V. Marshalova. M., 1961.

*Sovremennaia nauchno-tekhnicheskaia revoliutsiia. Istoricheskoe issledovanie.*M., 1967; and in an expanded edition, M., 1970.

Stepichev, S. 'Opredelenie osobo opasnogo retsidivista dolzhno byt edinym.' *SZ* (1962, No. 1), pp. 27–31.

Tadevosian, V. S. 'O komissiiakh po delam nesovershennoletnikh.' *SGiP* (1959, No. 11), pp. 13–17.

Tadevosian, V. G. 'V. I. Lenin o detiakh i borba s prestupnostiu nesoevershennoletnikh.' *SZ* (1958, No. 4), pp. 13–17.

Tikunov, V. S. 'Obshchestvo i pravoporiadok'. *Trud.* 9 January 1965.

——. 'Snikhozhdeniia khuligam ne budet.' *Izvestiia.* 21 April 1966.

Tkachevskii, Iu. M. 'Uslovno-dosrochnoe osvobozhdenie ot nakazaniia (Dopolneniia i izmeneniia k st. 44 Osnov ugolovnogo zakonodatelstva).' *SZ* (1969, No. 11), pp. 56–8.

Troshin, A. F. 'Trudoustroistvo i trudovoe vospitanie – vazhnoe sredstvo preduprezhdeniia beznadzornosti i prestupnosti sredi nesovershennoletnikh.' *Preduprezhdenie prestupnosti nesovershennoletnikh.* Edited by V. N. Kudriavtsev. M., 1965, pp. 156–180.

Trudy pervoi nauchnoi sessii Vsesoiuznogo instituta iuridicheskikh nauk, 27 ianvariia-3 fevralia 1939. Ed. by I. T. Goliakov. M., 1940.

'Ukreplenie sotsialisticheskoi zakonnosti i iuridicheskoi nauki.' *Kommunist* (1956, No. 11), pp. 12–23.

Utevskii, B. S. 'XX sezd KPSS i zadachi nauki ugolovnogo prava.' *SZ* (1956, No. 9).

——. 'Razvitie sovetskoi ispravitelno-trudovoi nauki.' *Trudy Vysshei Shkoly* [MOOP]. Vyp. 16 (M., 1967), pp. 114–27.

——. 'Sotsiologicheskie issledovaniia i kriminologii.' *Voprosy filosofii* (1964, No. 2), pp. 46–51.

——. 'Vidnyi deiatel ispravitelno-trudovoi sistemi.' *K novoi zhizne* (1966, No. 5).

——. 'Voprosu nakazaniia v ugolovnom zakonodatelstve.' *SZ* (1957, No. 7), pp. 3–9.

——. and Osherovich, B. *Dvadtat let vsesoiuznogo instituta iuridicheskikh nauk.* M., 1946.

'Vazhnyi shag v dalneishem razvitii sovetskoi demokratii.' *SGiP* (1957, No. 7), pp. 1–9.

'Vo Vsesoiuznom institute iuridicheskikh nauk: Rabota Sektsii ugolovnogo prava.' *SIu* (1938, No. 23–4), p. 61.

Vyshinskaia, Z. A. *Ob ugolovnoi otvetstvennosti za khishchenie gosudarstvennogo i obshchestvennogo imushchestva.* M., 1948.

——., and Shlykov, S. A. 'Effektivnost uslovnodosrochnogo osvobozhdeniia ot nakazaniia.' *Effektivnost ugolovnopravovykh mer borby s prestupnostiu.* Edited by B. S. Nikiforov. M., 1968, pp. 164–213.

Vyshinskii, A. Ia. *K polozheniiu na fronte pravovoi teorii.* M., 1937.

Vysshie predstavitelnye organy vlasti v SSSR. M., 1969.

Volkov, Iu. E. *Tak rozhdaetsia kommunisticheskoe samoupravlenie (Opyt konkretno-sotsiologicheskogo issledovaniia).* M., 1965.

'Za povyshenie roli pravovoi nauki v kodifikatsii sovetskogo zakonodatelstva.' *SGiP* (1956, No. 1), pp. 3–13.

Zasedaniia Verkhovnogo Soveta SSSR 5ogo sozyva, 2aia sessiia (22–25 dekabria 1958 g.), Stenograficheskii otchet. M., 1959.

Zhogin, N. V. *Borba s khuliganstvom – delo vsekh i kazhdogo.* M., 1967.

——. 'Zakon i pravovaia nauka.' *Izvestiia.* 17 June 1968, p. 3.

Zvirbul, V. K. *Deiatelnost prokuratury po preduprezhdeniiu prestupnosti (Nauchnye osnovy).* M., 1971.

V WESTERN BOOKS AND ARTICLES

ABSEES (Soviet and East European Abstracts Series). III, No. 2 (36) (October 1972), pp. 65–8.

The Adult Offender. White Paper Presented to Parliament by the Secretary of State for the Home Department by Command of Her Majesty. December 1965.

Agger, Robert, *et al*. *The Rulers and the Ruler: Political Power and its Impotence in American Communities*. N. Y., 1964.

Armstrong, John. 'Sources of Administrative Behavior, Some Soviet and West European Comparisons.' *Communist Studies and the Social Sciences*. Edited by Frederick Fleron. Chicago, 1969, pp. 357–8.

Armstrong, Marianne. 'The Campaign Against Parasites.' *Soviet Policy-making*. Edited by Peter H. Juviler and Henry W. Morton. N.Y., 1967, pp. 163–82.

Avtorkhanov, Abdurakhman. *The Communist Party Apparatus*. Chicago, 1966.

Barghoorn, Frederick C. *Politics in the USSR*. First edition: Boston and Toronto, 1966. Second edition: Boston and Toronto, 1972.

Barry, Donald, and Berman, Harold. 'The Jurists.' *Interest Groups in Soviet Politics*. Edited by H. Gordon Skilling and Franklyn Griffths. Princeton,
——. 'Leaders of the Soviet Legal Profession: An Analysis of Biographical Data and Career Patterns.' *Canadian American Slavic Studies*, VI, No. 1 (spring 1972).
——. 'The Specialist in Soviet Policy-making: The Adoption of a Law.' *Soviet Studies*. XVI (1964), pp. 152–65.

Bauer, Raymond. 'The Study of Policy Formation: An Introduction.' *The Study of Policy Formation*. Edited by Raymond Bauer and Kenneth Gergen. N.Y. and London, 1968, pp. 1–26.

Beerman, R. 'Study of the Soviet Criminal.' *Soviet Studies*. Vol. XIV, No. 1 July 1962), pp. 85–98.

Berman, Harold. 'The Current Movement for Law Reform in the Soviet Union.' *American Slavic and East European Review*. XV (1956), pp. 179–89.
——. 'Introduction and Analysis.' *Soviet Criminal Law and Procedure The RSFSR Codes*. Translated by Harold Berman and James Spindler. Second edition. Cambridge, Mass., 1972.
——. *Justice in the USSR*. Revised edition, enlarged. N.Y., 1963.

Brooks, Harvey. 'The Scientific Advisor.' *Scientists and National Policy-making*. Edited by Robert Gilpin and Christopher Wright. N.Y., 1964, pp. 73–96.

Brown, A. H. *Soviet Politics and Political Science*. London, 1974.

Brzezinski, Zbigniew. *Between Two Ages. America's Role in the Technetronic Era.* N.Y., 1970.
——, and Huntington, Samuel. *Political Power USA/USSR*. N. Y., 1964.

Butler, Lord. 'The Founding of the Institute of Criminology in Camb-
ridge.' *Crime, Criminology and Public Policy: Essays in Honour of Leon
Radzinowicz*. Edited by Roger Hood. London, 1974, pp. 1–10.
Churchward, L. G. 'Policy-making in the U.S.S.R., 1953–1961.' *Policy-
making in the U.S.S.R., 1953–61: Two Views*. Melbourne, 1962,
pp. 32–44.
Clark, Terry N. 'Community Power and Decision-making.' *Current
Sociology*. xx, No. 2 (1972), pp. 19–35.
Connor, Walter D. *Deviance in Soviet Society. Crime, Delinquency, and
Alcoholism*. N. Y. and London, 1972.
Conquest, Robert. *Power and Policy in the USSR. A Study in Soviet Dynastics*.
London, 1961.
Dahl, Robert. 'The Concept of Power.' *Behavioral Sciences*. ii (July 1957),
pp. 201–18.
——. 'Power.' *International Encyclopedia of the Social Sciences*. Seventeen
volumes. Edited by David Sills. N.Y., 1968. xii, pp. 405–15.
——. *Who Governs?* New Haven, 1961.
Deutsch, Karl. *The Nerves of Government*. N. Y., 1966.
Donnison, David. 'Research for Policy.' *Minerva*. x, No. 4 (October 1972),
pp. 519–36.
Dror, Yehezkel. *Public Policy-making Reexamined*. San Francisco, 1968.
Etzioni, Amitai. *The Active Society*. N.Y., 1968.
Fainsod, Merle. *How Russia is Ruled*. First edition. Cambridge, Mass.,
1953. Third edition (with Hough, Jerry F.), forthcoming.
Fischer, George. *Soviet Executives and Modern Society*. N.Y., 1968.
Friedrich, Carl, and Brzezinski, Zbigniew. *Totalitarian Dictatorship and
Autocracy*. Cambridge, 1956. Also second edition, revised by Carl
Friedrich. N.Y. etc., 1965.
Gamson, William. *Power and Discontent*. Homewood, Illinois, 1968.
Gilpin, Robert. *American Scientists and Nuclear Weapons Policy*. Princeton,
N. J., 1962.
Graham, Loren. 'Reorganization of the U.S.S.R. Academy of Sciences.'
Soviet Policy-making. Edited by Peter H. Juviler and Henry W. Morton.
N.Y. etc., 1967, pp. 133–62.
Griffiths, Franklyn. 'A Tendency Analysis of Soviet Policy-making.'
Interest Groups in Soviet Politics. Edited by H. Gordon Skilling and
Franklyn Griffiths. Princeton, N. J., 1971, pp. 335–78.
Hammond, W. H., and Chayen, Edna. *Persistent Criminals*. Home Office
Research Unit Report No. 5. London, 1963.
Hazard, John N. *Law and Social Change in the USSR*. London, 1953.
——. 'Social Control through Law.' *Politics in the USSR: Seven Cases*. Edited
by A. Dallin and A. Westin. N. Y. etc., 1966, pp. 207–41.
Hinde, R.S.E. *The British Penal System, 1797–1950*. London, 1951.
Hood, Roger, 'Criminology and Penal Change: A Case Study in the Nature
and Impact of Some Recent Advice to Governments.' *Crime, Criminology*

and Public Policy: Essays in Honour of Leon Radzinowicz. Edited by Roger Hood. London, 1974.

Hough, Jerry F. 'Communication and Persuasion in The Analysis of Inputs.' Jerry F. Hough, *The Soviet Union and Social Science Theory* (Cambridge, Mass., 1977).

——. 'Political Participation in the USSR', *Soviet Studies*, xxviii, No. 1 (January 1976), pp. 2–20.

——. 'The Soviet System: Petrification or Pluralism.' *Problems of Communism* (March-April 1972), pp. 25–45.

Horowitz, Irving L. 'Social Deviance and Political Marginality.' *Social Problems.* xv, No. 3 (winter 1968) pp. 280–96.

Inkeles, Alex. 'Models and Issues in the Analysis of Soviet Society.' Inkeles, Alex. (ed.), *Social Change in Soviet Russia,* Cambridge, Mass., 1968, pp. 419–36.

Judy, Richard. 'The Economists.' *Interest Groups in Soviet Politics.* Edited by H. Gordon Skilling and Franklyn Griffiths. Princeton, N. J., 1971, pp. 209–52.

Juviler, Peter H. 'Crime and its Study.' *Soviet Politics and Society in the 1970's.* Edited by Henry Morton and Rudolph Tokes. N.Y., 1974, pp. 200–38.

——. 'Criminal Law and Social Control.' *Contemporary Soviet Law: Essays in Honor of John N. Hazard.* Edited by Donald Barry *et al.,* The Hague, 1974, pp. 17–54.

——. 'Family Reforms on the Road to Communism.' *Soviet Policy-making.* Edited by Peter H. Juviler and Henry W. Morton. N.Y. etc., 1967, pp. 29–60.

Katz, Zev. 'Sociology in the Soviet Union.' *Problems of Communism.* xx, No. 3 (May-June 1971), pp. 22–40.

Lane, David. *Politics and Society in the USSR.* N.Y., 1971.

Lazarsfeld, Paul, and Reitz, Jeffrey. *An Introduction to Applied Sociology.* N.Y., 1975.

——. 'Toward a Theory of Applied Sociology (A Progress Report).' N.Y.: Bureau of Applied Social Research of Columbia University, 1970.

Lemert, Edwin. *Social Action and Legal Change: Revolution Within the Juvenile Court.* Chicago, 1970.

Lewin, Moshe. *Political Undercurrents in Soviet Economic Thought.* Princeton, N. J., 1974.

Lindblom, Charles. *The Policy-making Process.* Engelwood Cliffs, N. J., 1968.

Linden, Carl. *Khrushchev and the Soviet Leadership, 1957–1964.* Baltimore, 1968.

Little, D. Richard. 'Soviet Parliamentary Committees after Khrushchev: Obstacles and Opportunities.' *Soviet Studies.* xxiv, No. 1 (July, 1972), pp. 41–60.

Lodge, T. S. 'The Founding of the Home Office Research Unit.' *Crime, Criminology and Public Policy. Essays in Honour of Leon Radzinowicz.* Edited by Roger Hood. London, 1974, pp. 11–23.

Lowi, Theodore. J. 'American Business, Public Policy, Case Studies and Political Theory.' *World Politics*. xvi, No. 4 (July 1964), pp. 677–715.

Lyons, Gene M. *The Uneasy Partnership: Social Science and the Federal Government in the Twentieth Century*. N.Y., 1969.

Mannheim, Hermann. *Comparative Criminology*. Two volumes. London, 1965.

Martin, Ben L. 'Experts in Policy Processes: A Contemporary Perspective.' *Polity*. vi, No. 2. (winter 1973), pp. 149–73.

Merton, Robert K. 'The Role of Applied Social Science in the Formation of Policy: A Research Memorandum.' *Philosophy of Science*. xvi, No. 3 (July 1949), pp. 161–81.

——. 'Manifest and Latent Functions.' *Social Theory and Social Structure*. Enlarged edition. N.Y., 1968, pp. 73–138.

——. 'The Role of the Intellectual in Public Bureaucracy.' *Social Theory and Social Structure*. Enlarged edition, N.Y., 1968, pp. 261–78.

Meyer, Alfred. *The Soviet Political System: An Introduction*. N.Y., 1965.

Morton, Henry W. 'The Structure of Decision-making in the USSR: A Comparative Introduction.' *Soviet Policy-making*. Edited by Peter H. Juviler and Henry W. Morton. N.Y., etc., 1967, pp. 3–25.

Moynihan, Daniel P. *Maximum Feasible Misunderstanding: Community Action in the War on Poverty*. N.Y., 1969.

Mueller, Gerhard. *Crime, Law and the Scholars. A History of Scholarship in American Criminal Law*. Seattle, 1969.

Ohlin, Lloyd. 'The President's Commission on Law Enforcement and Administration of Justice'. *Sociology and Public Policy. The Case of the Presidential Commissions*. Edited by Mirra Komarovsky. N.Y., 1975.

Osborn, Robert. 'Crime and the Environment: the New Soviet Debate.' *Slavic Review*. Vol. xxvii, No. 3 (September 1968), pp. 393–410.

——. *Soviet Social Policies: Welfare, Equality and Community*. Homewood, Illinois, 1970.

Ploss, Sidney. *Conflict and Decision-making in Soviet Russia: A Case Study of Agricultural Policy, 1953–1963*. Princeton, 1965.

——. 'Interest Groups.' *Prospects for Soviet Society*. Edited by Allen Kassof. N.Y., etc., 1968, pp. 76–103.

——. 'New Politics in Russia?' *Survey*. xix, No. 4 (autumn 1973), pp. 23–35.

Powell, David E. 'Alcoholism in the USSR.' *Survey*. xvi, No. 1 (winter 1971), pp. 123–37.

Preventive Detention. Report of the Advisory Council on the Treatment of Offenders. London, 1963.

Radzinowicz, Leon. *Ideology and Crime: A Study of Crime in its Social and Historical Context*. N.Y., 1966.

——. *In Search of Criminology*. Cambridge, Mass., 1962.

Ranney, Austin. 'The Study of Policy Content: A Framework for Choice.'

Political Science and Public Policy. Edited by Austin Ranney. Chicago, 1968.

Reich, Robert B. 'Solving Social Crises by Commissions.' *Yale Review of Law and Social Action*. III, No. 3 (1973), pp. 234–71.

Remnek, Richard B. *Soviet Scholars and Foreign Policy: A Case Study in Soviet Policy toward India*. Durham, N. C., 1975.

Rigby, T. H. 'Policy-making in the U.S.S.R., 1953–61.' *Policy-making in the U.S.S.R.: Two Views*. Melbourne, 1962, pp. 1–26.

Rist, Ray C. 'Policy, Politics, and Social Research: A Study in the Relationship of Federal Commissions and Social Science.' *Social Problems*, XXI, No. 1 (summer 1973), pp. 113–28.

Rothman, David. *The Discovery of the Asylum*. Boston, 1971.

Rusch, Georg, and Kirchheimer, Otto. *Punishment and Social Structure*. N.Y., 1939.

Salisbury, Robert. 'The Analysis of Public Policy: A Search for Theories and Roles.' *Political Science and Public Policy*. Edited by Austin Ranney. Chicago, 1968, pp. 151–78.

Schon, Donald. *Beyond the Stable State*. N.Y., 1971.

Schooler, Dean, Jr. *Science, Scientists and Public Policy*. N.Y., 1971.

Schwartz, D. V. 'Recent Soviet Adaptations of Systems Theory to Administrative Theory.' *Journal of Comparative Administration*. V, No. 2 (August 1973), pp. 233–64.

Schwartz, Joel J., and Keech, William R. 'Public Influence and Educational Policy in the Soviet Union.' *The Behavioral Revolution and Communist Studies*. Edited by Roger Kanet. N. Y., 1971, pp. 151–86.

———. 'Soviet Interest Groups and the Policy Process: The Repeal of Production Education.' *American Political Science Review*. LXII, No. 3 (September 1968), pp. 840–51.

Science and Ideology in the Soviet Union. Edited by George Fischer. N. Y., 1968.

Sharlet, Robert. 'Pashukanis and the Rise of Soviet Marxist Jurisprudence, 1924–1930.' *Soviet Union*. I, No. 2 (1974), pp. 103–21.

Sherry, Arthur H. 'The Politics of Criminal Law Reform: the United States.' *American Journal of Comparative Law*. XXI (spring 1973), pp. 201–29.

Simirenko, Alex. 'An Outline History of Soviet Sociology.' *Soviet Sociology: Historical Antecedents and Current Approaches*. Edited by Alex Simirenko. Chicago, 1966, pp. 13–40.

Skolnick, Jerome. 'The Violence Commission: Internal Politics and Public Policy.' *The Use and Abuse of Social Science*. Edited by I. L. Horowitz. New Brunswick, N. J., 1971, pp. 234–48.

Smith, Bruce L. R. *The RAND Corporation: A Case Study of a Nonprofit Advisory Corporation*. Cambridge, 1966.

Solomon, Peter H., Jr. 'A Selected Bibliography of Soviet Criminology.' *Journal of Criminal Law, Criminology, and Police Science*. LXI, No. 3 (1970), pp. 393–432.

——. 'Soviet Criminology: its Demise and Rebirth, 1928–1963.' *Crime, Criminology and Public Policy: Essays in Honour of Leon Radzinowicz.* London, 1974; and also in *Soviet Union*, I, No. 2 (1974), pp. 122–40.

——. 'Technological Innovation and Soviet Industrialization.' *The Social Consequences of Modernization in Socialist Countries.* Edited by Mark G. Field. Baltimore, 1976.

Solzhenitsyn, A. S. *The First Circle.* N.Y., 1968.

Soviet Law and Government. Volume IX, No. 4 (spring 1971).

Stewart, Philip D. 'Soviet Interest Groups and the Policy Process: The Repeal of Production Education.' *World Politics.* XXII, No. 1 (October 1969), pp. 29–50.

Tatu, Michel. *Power in the Kremlin: From Khrushchev to Kosygin.* N.Y., 1968.

Tokaev, G. A. *Comrade X.* London, 1956.

Treml, Vladimir. 'Production and Consumption of Alcoholic Beverages in the USSR: A Statistical Study.' *Journal of Studies on Alcohol.* XXXVI, No. 3 (March 1975), pp. 285–320.

Wechsler, Herbert. 'The Model Penal Code and the Codification of American Criminal Law.' *Crime, Criminology and Public Policy: Essays in Honour of Leon Radzinowicz.* Edited by Roger Hood. London, 1974, pp. 419–68.

Weinberg, Alvin. 'Science and Transscience.' *Minerva.* X, No. 2 (April 1972), pp. 209–22.

Weinberg, Elizabeth Ann. *The Development of Sociology in the Soviet Union.* London, 1974.

West, Donald J. *The Habitual Prisoner.* London, 1963.

Wienert, Helgard. 'The Organization and Planning of Research in the Academy System.' *Science Policy in the USSR.* Paris: OECD, 1969, pp. 191–292

Wilensky, Harold. *Organizational Intelligence: Knowledge and Policy in Government and Industry.* N.Y., 1967.

Wilson, James Q. 'Crime and the Criminologists.' *Commentary.* LVIII, No. 1 (July 1974), pp. 47–53.

——. *Political Organizations.* N.Y., 1973.

Zimmerman, William. 'Issue Area and Foreign Policy Process.' *American Political Science Review.* LXVII, No. 4 (December 1973), pp. 1204–12

VI UNPUBLISHED MATERIAL

Bell, Daniel. 'The Post-Industrial Society: Technocracy and Politics.' Unpublished paper prepared for the Seventh World Congress of Sociology, Varna, Bulgaria, 1970.

Efimov, N. A. 'Problemy lisheniia svobody kak vida nakazaniia v zakonodatelstve, sudebnoi i ispravitelno-trudovoi praktike.' Avtoreferat doktorskoi dissertatstsii. Leningrad, 1966.

Eran-Feinberg, Oded. 'Soviet Thought on the Role of the Communist Party in the Third World, with Special Reference to the Arab-radical regimes; A Study of Opinion Groups within the Soviet Elite.' Unpublished Ph.D. dissertation, Indiana University, 1970.

Griffiths, Franklyn. 'Images, Politics and Learning in Soviet Behavior toward the United States.' Unpublished Ph.D. dissertation, Columbia University, 1972.

Hough, Jerry F. 'The Mass Media and the Policy-making Process in the Soviet Union and the United States: Implications for Comparative Studies.' Unpublished paper prepared for the 1967 Annual Meeting of the American Political Science Association, Chicago, September 5–9, 1967.

Juviler, Peter. 'Social Disorganization in the Soviet Union: the Debates over Remedies.' Unpublished paper. N.Y., 1966.

——. 'Revolutionary Law and Order: Delinquency, Crime and Soviet Policy.' Unpublished book manuscript. N.Y., 1975.

Kuznetsova, N. F. Lecture course on 'Fundamentals of Soviet Criminology.' Moscow University law faculty, fall semester, 1968. Especially lectures of 2 October 1968 and 20 November 1968.

Lakoff, Sanford. 'The Political Theory of Scientific Society. Paper presented to the Symposium on Science and Democracy at the Annual Meeting of the American Association for the Advancement of Science, Chicago, 27 December 1970. Revised draft, August 1971.

Minkovskii, G. M. Guest lecture in course 'Fundamentals of Soviet Criminology.' Moscow University law faculty, fall semester, 1968. Delivered on 16 October 1968.

Remenson, A. I. 'Teoreticheskie voprosy ispoleneniia lishenii svobody i perevospitaniia zakliuchennykh.' Avtoreferat doktorskoi dissertatatsii. Tomsk, 1965.

Solomon, Peter H., Jr. 'Specialists in Soviet Policy-making: Criminologists and Criminal Policy in the 1960's.' Unpublished Ph.D. dissertation, Columbia University, 1973.

Solomon, Susan Gross. 'Theory and Research in Soviet Social Inquiry.' Unpublished M. A. thesis, Columbia University, 1967.

Turk, Austin T. 'Political Criminality and Political Policing.' Unpublished article. Toronto, 1974.

Walker, Jack. 'The Diffusion of Knowledge and Policy Change: Toward a Theory of Agenda-Setting.' Unpublished paper delivered at the 1974 meeting of the American Political Science Association, Chicago, Illinois.

GLOSSARY OF RUSSIAN WORDS USED IN TEXT

aktiv The members of an organization, who stand ready for special duties without pay; or a list of those persons. (Cf. party *aktiv*; tradeunion *aktiv*.)

apparat The staff of an organization.

apparatchik A full-time paid party official.

dokladnoe pismo Report letter. One of the forms for private communications between scholars and ministerial and political leaders.

dokladnaia zapiska Report note. A shorter version of *dokladnoe pismo*.

druzhiny Volunteer, unpaid defenders of the public order, who perform some police functions.

instruktor The lowest rank of a full-time paid party official. In the Central Committee *apparat*, the rank-and-file *apparatchik*.

kafedra Chair. The basic subdivision on a faculty in Soviet universities.

kommandirovka An official or business trip, sponsored by one's employer.

nomenklatura A list of positions of employment, the filling of which falls under the responsibility of a particular official or institution.

obshchestvennost The public, or any persons who as citizens perform work on a voluntary, unpaid basis. (Cf. *na obshchestvennykh nachalakh*, as a volunteer.)

predstavlenie A representation. A form of official communication between ministries or administrative units.

profilaktori The institutions for the confinement of alcoholics undergoing compulsory treatment.

sektor Sector. The basic organizational unit in a research institute.

shefstvo Wardship. The informal and voluntary system for providing adult support and guidance to juvenile delinquents, which was replaced in 1967 by the public guardians.

spravka Note. The shortest of the forms of private written communication used by scholars for reporting to ministerial and political leaders.

Index

STUDIES OF THE RUSSIAN INSTITUTE

PUBLISHED BY CAMBRIDGE UNIVERSITY PRESS

VERA DUNHAM, *In Stalin's Time: Middleclass Values in Soviet Fiction*
JONATHAN FRANKEL, *Vladimir Akimov on the Dilemmas of Russian Marxism, 1895–1903*
EZRA MENDELSOHN, *Class Struggle in the Pale: The Formative Years of the Jewish Workers' Movement in Tsarist Russia*

PUBLISHED BY COLUMBIA UNIVERSITY PRESS

JOHN A. ARMSTRONG, *Ukrainian Nationalism*
EDWARD J. BROWN, *The Proletarian Episode in Russian Literature*
HARVEY L. DYCK, *Weimar Germany and Soviet Russia, 1926–1933: A Study in Diplomatic Instability*
RALPH TALCOTT FISHER, JR., *Pattern for Soviet Youth: A Study of the Congress of the Komsomol, 1918–1954*
MAURICE FRIEDBERG, *Russian Classics in Soviet Jacket*
ELLIOT R. GOODMAN, *The Soviet Design for a World State*
JOHN N. HAZARD, *Settling Disputes in Soviet Society: The Formative Years of Legal Institutions*
DAVID JORAVSKY, *Soviet Marxism and Natural Science, 1917–1932*
HENRY KRISCH, *German Politics under Soviet Occupation*
DAVID MARSHALL LANG, *The Last Years of the Georgian Monarchy, 1658–1832*
GEORGE S. N. LUCKYJ, *Literary Politics in the Soviet Ukraine, 1917–1934*
HERBERT MARCUSE, *Soviet Marxism: A Critical Analysis*
KERMIT E. MCKENZIE, *Comintern and World Revolution, 1928–1943: The Shaping of Doctrine*
CHARLES B. MCLANE, *Soviet Policy and the Chinese Communists, 1931–1946*
JAMES WILLIAM MORLEY, *The Japanese Thrust into Siberia, 1918*
ALEXANDER G. PARK, *Bolshevism in Turkestan, 1917–1927*
MICHAEL BORO PETROVICH, *The Emergence of Russian Panslavism, 1856–1870*
OLIVER H. RADKEY, *The Agrarian Foes of Bolshevism: Promise and Default of the Russian Socialist Revolutionaries, February to October, 1917*
OLIVER H. RADKEY, *The Sickle Under the Hammer: The Russian Socialist Revolutionaries in the Early Months of Soviet Rule*
ALFRED J. RIEBER, *Stalin and the French Communist Party, 1941–1947*
RICHARD G. ROBBINS, JR., *Famine in Russia 1891–1892*
ERNEST J. SIMMONS, editor, *Through the Glass of Soviet Literature: Views of Russian Society*
THEODORE K. VON LAUE, *Sergei Witte and the Industrialization of Russia*
ALLEN S. WHITING, *Soviet Policies in China, 1917–1924*

PUBLISHED BY THE FREE PRESS

HENRY W. MORTON and RUDOLF L. TÓKÉS (eds.), *Soviet Politics and Society in the 1970s*

PUBLISHED BY GREENWOOD PRESS

THAD PAUL ALTON, *Polish Postwar Economy.*
ABRAM BERGSON, *Soviet National Income and Product in 1937*

ALEXANDER DALLIN, *Soviet Conduct in World Affairs*
DAVID GRANICK, *Management of the Industrial Firm in the USSR: A Study in Soviet Economic Planning*
THOMAS TAYLOR HAMMOND, *Lenin on Trade Unions and Revolution, 1893–1917*
ALFRED ERICH SENN, *The Emergence of Modern Lithuania*

PUBLISHED BY THE UNIVERSITY OF MICHIGAN PRESS

RICHARD T. DE GEORGE, *Soviet Ethics and Morality*

PUBLISHED BY PRINCETON UNIVERSITY PRESS

PAUL AVRICH, *The Russian Anarchists*
PAUL AVRICH, *Kronstadt 1921*
EDWARD J. BROWN, *Mayakovsky: A Poet in the Revolution*
MILTON EHRE, *Oblomov and His Creator: The Life and Art of Ivan Goncharov*
LOREN R. GRAHAM, *The Soviet Academy of Sciences and the Communist Party, 1927–1932*
PATRICIA K. GRIMSTED, *Archives and Manuscript Repositories in the USSR: Moscow and Leningrad*
ROBERT A. MAGUIRE, *Red Virgin Soil: Soviet Literature in the 1920's*
T. H. RIGBY, *Communist Party Membership in the U.S.S.R., 1917–1967*
WILLIAM G. ROSENBERG, *Liberals in the Russian Revolution*
WALTER SABLINSKY, *The Road to Bloody Sunday*
RONALD G. SUNY, *The Baku Commune, 1917–918*
JOHN M. THOMPSON, *Russia, Bolshevism, and the Versailles Peace*

WILLIAM MILLS TODD III, *The Familiar Letter as a Literary Genre in the Age of Pushkin*
WILLIAM ZIMMERMAN, *Soviet Perspectives on International Relations, 1956–1967*

PUBLISHED BY TEACHERS COLLEGE PRESS

HAROLD J. NOAH, *Financing Soviet Schools*

PUBLISHED BY ARDIS PUBLISHERS

ELIZABETH | VALKENIER, | *Russian Realist Art, The State and Society; The Peredvizhniki and Their Tradition*